C++ Black Book

Steven Holzner

President and CEO
Keith Weiskamp

Publisher
Steve Sayre

Acquisitions Editor
Kevin Weeks

Marketing Specialist
Tracy Rooney

Project Editor
Sybil Ihrig
Helios Productions

Technical Reviewer
Michael L. Mullins

Production Coordinator
Kim Eoff

Cover Designer
Jody Winkler

Layout Designer
April Nielsen

CD-ROM Developer
Chris Nusbaum

C++ Black Book

The Coriolis Group, LLC
14455 N. Hayden Road
Suite 220
Scottsdale, Arizona 85260

(480) 483-0192
FAX (480) 483-0193
www.coriolis.com

Library of Congress Cataloging-in-Publication Data
Holzner, Steven.
C++ black book / by Steven Holzner.
p. cm.
Includes index.
ISBN 1-57610-777-9
1. C++ (Computer program language) I. Title.
QA76.73.C153 H645 2000
005.13'3--dc21 00-050860
CIP

Printed in the United States of America
10 9 8 7 6 5 4 3 2 1

The Coriolis Group, LLC • 14455 North Hayden Road, Suite 220 • Scottsdale, Arizona 85260

Dear Reader:

Coriolis Technology Press was founded to create a very elite group of books: the ones you keep closest to your machine. Sure, everyone would like to have the Library of Congress at arm's reach, but in the real world, you have to choose the books you rely on every day *very* carefully.

To win a place for our books on that coveted shelf beside your PC, we guarantee several important qualities in every book we publish. These qualities are:

- *Technical accuracy*—It's no good if it doesn't work. Every Coriolis Technology Press book is reviewed by technical experts in the topic field, and is sent through several editing and proofreading passes in order to create the piece of work you now hold in your hands.
- *Innovative editorial design*—We've put years of research and refinement into the ways we present information in our books. Our books' editorial approach is uniquely designed to reflect the way people learn new technologies and search for solutions to technology problems.
- *Practical focus*—We put only pertinent information into our books and avoid any fluff. Every fact included between these two covers must serve the mission of the book as a whole.
- *Accessibility*—The information in a book is worthless unless you can find it quickly when you need it. We put a lot of effort into our indexes, and heavily cross-reference our chapters, to make it easy for you to move right to the information you need.

Here at The Coriolis Group we have been publishing and packaging books, technical journals, and training materials since 1989. We're programmers and authors ourselves, and we take an ongoing active role in defining what we publish and how we publish it. We have put a lot of thought into our books; please write to us at **ctp@coriolis.com** and let us know what you think. We hope that you're happy with the book in your hands, and that in the future, when you reach for software development and networking information, you'll turn to one of our books first.

Keith Weiskamp
President and CEO

Jeff Duntemann
VP and Editorial Director

Look for these related books from The Coriolis Group:

Software Project Management: From Concept to Deployment
by Kieron Conway

3D Game Programming with C++
by John De Goes

Open Source Development with CVS
by Karl Fogel

Visual C++ 6 Core Language Little Black Book
by Bill McCarty

Also recently published by Coriolis Technology Press:

Data Modeling Essentials, 2nd Edition
by Graeme C. Simsion and Graham C. Witt

Mac OS 9.1 Black Book
by Mark R. Bell and Debrah D. Suggs

Windows Admin Scripting Little Black Book
by Jesse M. Torres

Windows 2000 Active Directory Black Book
by Adam Wood

XML Black Book, 2nd Edition
by Natanya Pitts

To Nancy, of course (how could it ever be otherwise?)

❧

About the Author

Steven Holzner has written 64 books on computing, many of them on C++, including some bestsellers in the field. He's a former contributing editor to *PC Magazine*, teaches programming in special corporate classes around the US, and runs his own Internet programming company. His books have sold well over a million copies and have been translated into 16 languages. Steven did his undergraduate work at MIT, earned his Ph.D. at Cornell, and has served on the faculty of both of those universities. Steve and Nancy divide their time between the Berkshires and a house in the Austrian Alps.

Acknowledgments

A book such as the one you're holding is the work of many people, not just that of the author. I'd particularly like to thank project editor Sybil Ihrig of Helios Productions for doing such outstanding project coordination and page composition and making the production process work so smoothly; copyeditor Gail Taylor for a superb, sensitive, and intelligent edit; technical reviewer Mike Mullins for a much-appreciated and terrific technical edit that sometimes involved finding solutions beyond the normal call of duty; and proofreader Scott Strayer. At Coriolis, I'd like to thank Kevin Weeks and Jeff Duntemann for useful discussions on the content of this book, and I'd also like to express my appreciation to Paula Kmetz and Kim Eoff for coordinating the "big picture" of editorial and production tasks, respectively. Thanks to you all!

Contents at a Glance

Table of Contents

Introduction

Welcome to the *C++ Black Book.* This book is designed to give you everything you need to master ANSI/ISO C++, from the basics to the most advanced topics. (That's the American National Standards Institute and the International Organization for Standardization—more about those organizations in Chapter 1.) Everything's here, ready for you to use. This book covers the ANSI/ISO C++ standard in depth, and it's written to give you as much of the whole C++ story as one book can hold. Not only will we see the full C++ syntax—from the most basic to the newest additions to the language—but we'll also dig into the ways in which C++ is used today.

Learning and developing applications with C++ can be challenging, and this book is here to smooth your path. There are hundreds of C++ topics discussed in depth here, packed into the book in a format that makes it easy to read the book straight through or to use it for quick lookup. C++ is the language of choice for serious programmers today, and the *C++ Black Book* was written to be the only resource you need in order to understand it. And as your C++ skills mature, this is the book designed to be the one next to your computer, ready and accessible for clarifying any C++ mysteries you encounter.

What's in This Book

There are hundreds of real-world topics covered in this book, such as how references work and when to use pointers instead of arrays, how to optimize your code, and how to get the most out of C++. Each of the topics in this book comes with examples showing how it works. That's one important aspect about this book—there's always an example for every topic, ready to be run.

This book is divided into hundreds of separate, easily accessible topics, each of which addresses a separate issue. As much of the C++ story as can fit into one book is packed into this one. Here's an overview of some of the topics we'll cover.

Essential C++

- Getting a copy of the ANSI/ISO C++ standard
- Finding a C++ compiler (including free ones)
- Creating preprocessor macros

Data and C++ Operators

- Declaring variables
- Conversion between data types
- Operator precedence in C++
- Handling higher math

Derived Types: Arrays, Strings Structures, Unions, and Enumerations

- Declaring an array
- Handling C-style strings
- Using structures
- Creating bit fields
- Creating unions
- Using enumerations

Conditional and Loop Statements and Operators

- The **while**, **do-while**, and **for** loops
- Creating and using pointers
- Using **new** and **delete** with arrays

Pointers and Memory Management

- Similarities between pointers and arrays in C++
- Pointer arithmetic
- Using static, dynamic, reinterpret, and **const** casts

Functions, References, Linkage, and Templates

- Passing arguments to functions
- Returning values from functions
- Overloading a function
- Understanding storage classes, scope, and linkage
- Creating variables with global scope
- Using internal and external linkage with multiple files

- Mixed-language linking
- Creating function templates

Classes and Objects

- Creating a class
- Using access specifiers
- Creating constructors
- Creating inline methods
- Creating static data members

Friend Functions, Operator Overloading, and Copy Constructors

- Creating friend functions
- Creating a copy constructor
- Conversions to and from objects
- Conversions, friends, and operator overloading
- Creating friend classes
- Creating nested and local classes

Class Inheritance

- Using inheritance
- Virtual methods and runtime polymorphism
- Creating abstract classes and pure virtual methods
- Using private inheritance
- Using protected inheritance
- Creating class libraries

Multiple Inheritance and Class Templates

- Inheriting multiple base classes
- Using virtual base classes
- Runtime type information
- Defining class templates

- Using non-type arguments in class templates
- Using class templates with multiple types
- Using class templates recursively and as base classes

Runtime Type Information, Namespaces, and Exceptions

- Creating a namespace
- Creating and throwing exceptions
- Throwing exceptions from functions
- Nesting **try** blocks and rethrowing exceptions

I/O Streams and File Handling

- Using manipulators
- Creating a streamable class
- Creating custom manipulators
- Checking stream states
- Creating a file
- Appending to a file
- Checking file stream states
- Working with binary files
- Reading and writing with **fstream**

The Standard Template Library

- Using the Standard Template Library
- Using iterators
- Using STL algorithms
- Using predefined iterators
- Using **istream** and **ostream** iterators
- Using reverse iterators
- Using insertion iterators and inserters
- Using the STL containers: **vector**, **list**, **deque**, **stack**, **queue**, **priority_queue**, **set**, **map**, **multiset**, **multimap**, and **bitset**.
- Function objects (functors)

As you can see, there's a tremendous amount of C++ coming up—and I hope what C++ has to offer will prove as irresistible to you as it has to so many others.

Conventions Used in This Book

There are a few conventions I'll be using in this book that you should be aware of. For example, I'll highlight new code that I add to an existing listing to make it easier to pick out the additions, like this:

```
#include <iostream>
using namespace std;
int main()
{
    int sum;
    int ten = 10;
    float pi = 3.14159;

    sum = static_cast <int> (pi) + ten;

    cout << "The integer sum = " << sum << endl;
}
```

I'll use square brackets, [and], to indicate optional parameters in formal statement definitions like this:

```
type name [= value][, name [= value]...];
```

I'll also add tips and notes to the text like this:

TIP: *This is a tip. Tips give some added information about how to do something, such as where to go on the Internet for certain resources, or how the unexpected behavior of a particular C++ keyword can be used to good advantage.*

NOTE: *This is a note. Notes give additional information, such as why it's not a good idea to use a C++ statement a certain way, or point out where a certain compiler doesn't actually do what you expect it should.*

What You'll Need

To use this book and develop your own C++ programs, you'll need a C++ compiler, the program you use to translate your C++ code into executable files. Compilers are discussed in Chapter 1—see "Finding a C++ Compiler" in that chapter. You might also take a look at Internet sites such as **www.cyberdiem.com/vin/learn.html** that list available C++ compilers (some of them are free) and C++ resources.

There are many C++ compilers available, with varying amounts of ANSI/ISO C++ compliance. Because C++ is standardized by international agreement, it's become easier to handle, and there is less variation between C++ compilers. However, it's important to realize that there *are* still differences. Every code listing in this book was tested on four different compilers on a number of operating systems by both myself and the technical editor, but very few C++ compilers are entirely ANSI/ISO compliant, which means that the way your compiler does things and the way ANSI/ISO C++ does things might differ in some cases. I'll try to alert you to the compiler variations that you might run into—for example, while most compilers use the new C++-style header files, some can use only the old-style headers. But you should know that implementing the C++ standard is a huge task for any compiler, so if your compiler doesn't behave the way you expect, or if it chokes systematically on some of the examples in this book, take a look at its documentation and the discussions in the book to try to resolve what's going on.

There are also plenty of C++ resources available on the Internet—for example, a casual search for "C++ tutorial" turns up no fewer than 5,660 matches. Here's a short starter list of C++ tutorials on the Internet:

- **http://home.onestop.net/cplusclass**
- **http://www.intap.net/~drw/cpp/index.htm**
- **http://www.icce.rug.nl/docs/cplusplus/cplusplus.html**

You can also find tutorials on C, the language that C++ is based on, such as this one:

- **http://www.cm.cf.ac.uk/Dave/C/CE.html**

There are a number of Usenet groups for C++ authors (note that not all of these groups may be available on your Usenet server):

- **alt.comp.lang.learn.c-c++**
- **comp.lang.c++**
- **comp.lang.c++.moderated**
- **comp.std.c++**

Keep in mind that C++ is really a community of thousands of developers, and keep in touch with that community if you can. And please keep in touch with me as well—I want to make sure this stays the best possible C++ book out there. If you come up with any additions, changes, or improvements to the book you'd like to see, please send them in to the publisher (**ctp@coriolis.com**), and I'll add them. And that's all the introduction we need—it's time to get started mastering C++ now in Chapter 1.

Chapter 1

Essential C++

(continued)

In Depth

Welcome to the big book of C++. If you want to get into C++ programming, this is the place. You'll find all that you need in this book. C++ programming is not like ordinary programming—it inspires passion, devotion, even obsession. Everywhere in the C++ world you look, you'll find C++ fanatics—and for good reason. C++ has long been a programmer's language, lean enough and close enough to the machine to satisfy nearly everyone's need for precision and control. It's got a strong, clean feel to it, and enough power to make a little go a long way. It's also powerful enough to become obscure very quickly when you start doing some advanced pointer work, and the result is that you'll find programmers clinging to their own ways of doing things and insisting that they're the *only* way to go. It's my hope that this book will help turn you into a C++ fanatic too.

There's a lot to learn and master here, and we're going to see it all. I'm going to try to lay it out in the best possible way, with plenty of examples, to make our path as smooth as possible. Bjarne Stroustrup, the creator of C++, has advised programmers to "ease yourself into the language," and that's just what we'll do.

In this book, we're going to learn all about C++ in the best way: by seeing it at work. We'll avoid the dry cataloging type of teaching, which piles up layer after layer of formal theory. Instead, we're going to see the language in its own environment, which will give us a working knowledge of just what it can do. Here, the programmer is in charge—the idea behind C++ is to give more power to the programmer, and that's what we'll be doing. We're going to see all that C++ has to offer, from object-oriented programming and memory control to templates and generic programming techniques. It's worthwhile starting with a history of the language to put things in perspective.

The History of C++

As you probably know, the C++ language itself is actually a superset of the C programming language (its first name was C with Classes). The reason the C language is called C is, simply, that it is the successor to the language called B. That language was developed by Ken Thompson in 1970, working on a DEC PDP-7, which is far less powerful than a modern PC. The original UNIX operating system ran on that machine, and that's also where B got its start. (B itself was the successor to a language called BCPL, which was written by Martin Richards.)

However, B was a little restricted. In 1972, Dennis Ritchie and Ken Thompson created the C language to augment B's power. C did not become popular immediately after its creation; in fact, it remained almost an esoteric topic for the next six years. In 1978, however—a historic year for C and C++ programmers—Brian Kernighan and Dennis Ritchie wrote a famous book for Prentice-Hall named *The C Programming Language*. And that simple book changed everything.

Now that word was out, there was an explosion of interest, and C was implemented on 8-bit computers under the CP/M operating system. It wasn't until the introduction of the IBM PC in 1981, however, that C really came into its own. When the PC revolution began, C was in a perfect position to take advantage of it. As the number of PCs shot upwards, so did the number of C users. C broke away from its original UNIX background and became a popular language on microcomputers.

It's worth stressing that it became popular for a very good reason: programmers liked using it. Unlike many other languages, C gave the programmer a great deal of control over the computer. With that control comes responsibility—there are many things you can do in C that will ruin your program or crash your computer. That is, you have the power to do things in C that other languages would never allow you to do. And programmers liked that; they liked finding a language that was a tool, not an obstacle. To programmers, C was much like assembly language without the drawback of having to do everything for yourself—in other words, C seemed much like the perfect combination of control and programming power.

ANSI Standardizes C

All this made for such a popular language that different companies started to bring out their own versions of C, and each one began to go in a different direction. The C revolution was in danger of splintering into many incompatible programming packages. For that reason, the American National Standards Institute (ANSI) created a special subcommittee named X3J11 to create a standard version of C. This was an extremely important development for C and C++ programmers; the language, which had been going off in all directions at the same time, became standardized and coherent once more. For that reason, ANSI C did indeed become standard C.

C++ Appears

As the popularity of C grew, so did the number of applications written in C. In time, C programs grew longer and longer, and some people began to feel that the standard programming constructions just weren't up to the task. One solution was to make the program more modular, more compartmentalized, and you could use functions to do that. However, some functions might end up needing to share data, some needed to coordinate with others, and again, you could end up with dozens of things to keep in mind (and dozens of functions in the program's global scope).

In 1983, Bjarne Stroustrup developed C++, inspired in part by other languages like Simula67. The name C++ itself, as you may know, comes from the C operator ++, which increments its argument—and so C++ is intended to be augmented C. C++ is much like C, but with a number of important extensions. In other words, all that we know about C still applies—but C++ offers us even more power. Primary among the additions C++ brings to C is the idea of an *object*.

An object is really just like a new kind of programming structure, except that it can hold both data and functions—both of which can be private to the object if you want them to be. As mentioned above, the driving force behind objects is modularity. Programmers found that when they were struggling with large programs, the more modular their programs the better (C++ was originally written to be used when programs got very long, over 2,500 lines). That's what C++ does; it helps us wrap up sections of our programs into discrete units, each of which serves some (easily remembered) purpose.

Although C++ was originally developed to introduce large-scale modularity to C, there are other parts of C++ that made it attractive even if your program is short. One such aspect is its legendary flexibility; we can redesign just about all of the C operators in C++ as well as do (previously) unheard-of things with functions. For example, through function overloading, we'll be able to call the same function with parameters of different types (e.g., int, float). C++ will decide which version of the function to use based on the types of the parameters we're passing (in C, naturally, this would be an error).

What originally attracted programmers to C++ was object-oriented programming (OOP), and I remember seeing dozens of programmers in the early days being attracted to the OOP banner, whether they needed it or not. There's also another aspect of C++, more recently introduced and now made standard, that is also as highly regarded: *generic programming*. Generic programming, like OOP, makes code reuse easier, and in fact, that's its speciality. Generic programming lets you think in terms of *algorithms*, which are specific techniques for getting things done, such as a really efficient way you've found to sort numbers. Using generic programming and C++ *templates*, you can implement the algorithm once in your code and use it with many different types of data, even with objects.

ANSI/ISO Standardizes C++

Like C, early C++ was in danger of becoming fragmented. Many different companies offered many different versions of C++, and they started diverging quickly. The original work on C++ was done at Bell Laboratories, and many programmers thought that what came out of Bell Labs was true C++, and they would list their programs as consistent with C++ version 2.0 or 3.0, and so on. Others followed the lead of companies like Microsoft, which introduced many changes to the language.

Fortunately, C++ has now been standardized. This standardization process has taken a long time; in 1990, the American National Standards Institute (ANSI), started a new standardization committee, called X3J16, to standardize C++ around the world. Not long after that, the International Organization for Standardization (ISO) started its own committee (ISO-WG-21) on the same topic. ANSI and ISO joined forces, also in 1990. However, the full committee only met three times a year, so it took until 1995 for them to release a draft, called a committee draft (CD) of standard C++. After much public comment, they released a second CD (called CD2) in December 1996. These committee drafts not only standardized C++, but they also added new features, such as templates, runtime type identification (RTTI), and the Standard Template Library (STL), which I'll have a lot to say about later in the book. (In fact, ANSI C now includes some of the features first added in C++, such as function prototyping and the **const** statement.)

The final draft international standard (FDIS) of C++ was released in November 1997, and after all this, the actual international standard (IS) itself was finally adopted in June, 1998.

All this means that C++ is now a standardized language. This is great from a programmer's point of view, because it means that you can count on certain features being available to you in your programs, no matter which company's C++ you use, as long as it's ANSI/ISO C++ compliant. And that means you can move your program from system to system as you like, and the C++ support in each system should recognize your C++ code without problems (although it's often not quite that easy).

This book is written to be compliant with ANSI/ISO C++ throughout and, if you're familiar with earlier versions of C++, in a few pages, I have some words on how to convert your programs to that standard. ANSI/ISO C++ is now the gold standard, and if you come across a C++ book that is not ANSI/ISO C++ compliant, drop it like a hot potato.

***TIP:** Want your own copy of the ANSI/ISO standard for C++? It's available for a fee; see "Where Can I Get a Copy of the ANSI/ISO C++ Standard?" later in this chapter.*

That's enough for history—now it's time to get to the focus of this book, some actual C++ code.

C++ Programming

C++ is a superset of C, which means it includes all of C. That does not mean we'll be learning C before learning C++, however. C++ has its own way of doing things, its own *idiom*, and we'll be working with pure C++ in this book. That means that although you can still do everything in C++ that you could in C, you usually do things the C++ way instead. Much of C++ programming has to do with learning the C++ way of doing things.

Here's an example; this short program is written in C, and all it does is to display the message "Hello from C.":

```
#include <stdio.h>

/* Print "Hello from C." */

main()
{
    printf("Hello from C.");

    return 0;
}
```

Although you can use this program with a C++ package, this program does things the C way, and a C++ programmer would spot the difference in an instant. For example, this program uses the C routines declared in the *header* file stdio.h and, in particular, uses the routine **printf** to display the text. The **main** part of the code can be declared without a return type in C, but not in C++ (we're about to see what that means). And so on.

Because there's so often a difference between the C way and the C++ way, this book is going to stick to the pure C++ way, which means we'll be using the C++ way of doing things from first to last. The code above will work under standard

C++ (although you might get a warning or two from your implementation of C++). However, here's the same code written in the C++ idiom:

```
#include <iostream>
using namespace std;

// Display a welcoming message.

int main()
{
    cout << "Hello from C++." << endl;

    return 0;
}
```

I'm going to go through the actual mechanics of this program in intimate detail in the Immediate Solutions part of this chapter, but it's worthwhile getting an overview here. The first line looks like this:

```
#include <iostream>
using namespace std;

// Display a welcoming message.

int main()
{
    cout << "Hello from C++." << endl;

    return 0;
}
```

The first thing to note is that everything is in lowercase. That's the way C++ is designed—all C++'s keywords are lowercase, and uppercase won't work for those keywords.

TIP: *You can use uppercase for the names you define in your programs, if you wish—the C++ keywords are all lowercase in part so that when you use any uppercase letters, it's clear that they're your own names you're defining and not part of the language. For a look at all the keywords in C++, see "The Reserved C++ Keywords" later in this chapter.*

In this case, I'm using the **#include** directive to include the header file named iostream in our program. I'm doing this because later in the code, I plan to use the built-in C++ object **cout** to display text from this program, and I have to tell C++ about **cout** before using it. The iostream header file is what tells C++ about **cout**, and when I use the **#include** directive, that entire header file is inserted into our program at that point.

The **#include** directive is an instruction to the C++ *preprocessor*, which is what actually inserts the iostream header file into the code. Like C, C++ has a preprocessor, which prepares the code to be converted to an executable program the computer can run. All preprocessor directives start with #, and the two big preprocessor directives are **#include**, which inserts another file into the current one, and **#define**, which lets you define constant values you can use in your code (although C++ is getting away from **#define** in favor of **const**).

***TIP:** Standard C++ header files like iostream are not supported by every C++ installation; if yours doesn't support standard C++ header files, you should use the older syntax **#include <iostream.h>** instead. See "Basic Skills: Using Header Files" later in this chapter for more information.*

Now we've specified the declarations of routines and objects like **cout** by including the iostream header. This is a modern standard C++ header file, and it's actually a little different from older, non-standard C++ and C header files. The difference is that the routines and objects specified in iostream are part of a special *namespace* named **std** (for standard). What are namespaces all about? When you write your own programs, you will define your own routines and objects, and when you combine your work with code written by other people, the names of those items may conflict with names that have already been taken.

To avoid that, C++, like other languages such as Java and Perl, lets you specify a namespace in which to define the routines and objects of your program. As we'll see in Chapter 12, items in different namespaces can't conflict. For that reason, the ANSI/ISO committee decided to use namespaces for the names it made a standard part of C++, and all items declared in the iostream header file are part of the **std** namespace. To indicate that we want to make that namespace the default namespace, you can add the statement **using namespace std** like this:

```
#include <iostream>
using namespace std;

// Display a welcoming message.

int main()
{
    cout << "Hello from C++." << endl;

    return 0;
}
```

Now the built-in object **cout** is available to our code, and we'll use it to display output from the program.

Next in our code is a C++ *comment*, which is an annotation added to C++ code to make it more readable:

```
#include <iostream>
using namespace std;

// Display a welcoming message.

int main()
{
    cout << "Hello from C++." << endl;

    return 0;
}
```

In this case, the comment explains what this program will do. You use comments to annotate your code for your own purposes or to make it easier for others to understand what's going on. As far as C++ is concerned, everything on a line following // is ignored; it's as if the program looked like this, as far as the compiler is concerned:

```
#include <iostream>
using namespace std;

int main()
{
    cout << "Hello from C++." << endl;

    return 0;
}
```

As we'll see in the Immediate Solutions section of this chapter, there are two types of comments in C++: these new C++ comments that begin with //, and the old, C-style comments, which are surrounded with the characters /* and */ like this:

```
#include <iostream>
using namespace std;

/* Display a welcoming message. */
```

```
int main()
{
    cout << "Hello from C++." << endl;

    return 0;
}
```

You'll often find C++ programmers sticking with the C++-style of comments, even though they are limited to one line and the C-style comments can span multiple lines (see "**// Display a welcoming message.**" later in this chapter), if for no reason other than to stick to the C++ way of doing things.

To actually get our code to run, I include it in a special *function* named **main**:

```
#include <iostream>
using namespace std;

// Display a welcoming message.

int main()
{
    .
    .
    .
}
```

You're probably familiar with the idea of functions; they're the basic building blocks of programming. We'll see more details in the Immediate Solutions section, but we might note here that every C++ program needs a **main** function, because that's where control is first passed to the program by the operating system in which it is running (there are some exceptions to this rule, as mentioned in the section "**int main()**" later in this chapter).

That's how functions work—the code in them is run when the function is *called*. The code in the function is enclosed by the curly braces, { and }, as you see above. The **main** function is a special one, because it's called by the operating system when you run your program. That means that the code you want to execute first when the program starts goes into **main**; **main** is called the program's *entry point*. I'll discuss the **int** keyword in front of the **main** function, which indicates that **main** will return an integer value to the operating system, in the Immediate Solutions section (see "**int main()**").

Now that our code is running, we can display the "Hello from C++." message using the iostream object named **cout**. (We'll see all about objects in Chapter 8; **cout** is already available to us in even the simplest programs, so we don't have to worry about where it comes from until later in the book, in Chapter 13.) This object, **cout**, handles the text-based output you want to display from a program. In C, you could use the **printf** function to display formatted output (and you still can in C++, of course), but **cout** is both smarter and more versatile than **printf**. The **cout** object doesn't need to be told what kind of data, such as numeric or textual, that you're displaying (the way **printf** does), and you can customize the process of working with **cout** to display the data in your C++ objects. Here's how I use **cout** to display the message "Hello from C++.":

```
#include <iostream>
using namespace std;

// Display a welcoming message.

int main()
{
    cout << "Hello from C++." << endl;
        .
        .
        .
}
```

Programmers coming to C++ from C might want a minute or two to get used to using **cout**. As you can see, I'm using the << *operator* here to send the text "Hello from C++." to cout. You're probably familiar with the idea of operators—you use operators to perform work on data values called *operands* (for example, 2 + 3 uses the + operator to add the operands 2 and 3). C programmers know the << operator as the left-shift operator, which lets you multiply values by powers of 2, and may be surprised to see the same operator sending text output to the display. In C++, however, one operator can perform many different tasks. In this case, the left-shift operator is *overloaded* to allow it to send data to **cout** for display.

NOTE: *We'll see how to overload operators ourselves in Chapter 9. For example, if we define a new type of object to hold text strings, we can overload the + operator to specify how that operator can add two strings together.*

Here, I'm using the << operator to send the message "Hello from C++." to **cout**, which in turn displays that text on the screen. Note that I'm also using << a second time in the same line of code, and sending the keyword **endl** to **cout**. The

endl keyword is an iostream *manipulator*, which you can use to control how **cout** acts. In this case, the **endl** manipulator makes the output skip to the next line. This is the same as inserting a *newline* character into the output, which you can do directly by referring to the newline character as '**\n**' like this:

```
#include <iostream>
using namespace std;

// Display a welcoming message.

int main()
{
    cout << "Hello from C++." << '\n';
        .
        .
        .
}
```

See "Basic Skills: Using Character Escape Sequences" later in this chapter for more details on special characters like '**\n**'; I'll also discuss manipulators further in Chapter 13.

C++ Statements

Note that at the end of the selected line of code above, there's a semicolon (;). The semicolon acts as a terminator, much like a period at the end of a sentence, and *simple statements* in C++ end with semicolons. Statements in C++ are much like sentences in text—they usually perform one discrete action. For example, the simple statement we've used in our program sends the text "Hello from C++." to **cout**, followed by a newline character to skip to the next line on the screen:

```
cout << "Hello from C++." << '\n';
```

Besides simple statements, C++ also supports one other type, *compound statements*. A compound statement is made up of one or more simple C++ statements, surrounded by curly braces, { and }, with no semicolon after the final }. In general, where you can use a simple statement, you can also use a compound statement in C++. For example, the **if** statement, which lets you make decisions, and which I'll look at later in this chapter (see the Immediate Solution section "Basic Skills: Making Decisions with the **if** Statement") and in detail in Chapter 4, has this syntax:

```
if (expression) statement;
```

Here, ***expression*** is an expression, which in C++ means it is made up of a single operand, or multiple operands and operators, and ***statement*** is a C++ statement. If the ***expression*** turns out to be true, ***statement*** is executed. For example, say we have this **if** statement:

```
if (5 > 0)
    cout << "Five is greater than zero." << endl;
```

In this case, I'm testing if five is greater than zero with the expression 5 > 0. Five is indeed greater than zero, so the expression is true, which means the associated statement is executed, displaying the message "Five is greater than zero." On the other hand, say you want to execute two statements instead of one if the tested expression is true; in that case, you can use a compound statement like this, surrounding two simple statements with curly braces:

```
if (5 > 0){
    cout << "Five is greater than zero." << endl;
    cout << "Or did you already know that?" << endl;
}
```

In this way, you can use either simple statements or compound statements in C++. We'll see how this works throughout this and the next few chapters.

In our program, the next simple statement is **return 0;**:

```
#include <iostream>
using namespace std;

// Display a welcoming message.

int main()
{
    cout << "Hello from C++." << endl;

    return 0;
}
```

This statement finishes the **main** function and ends our code. You use the **return** statement to send back, or *return*, values from functions, as we'll see in depth in Chapter 6. This statement has a very special purpose in the **main** function: It sends back a value of 0 from the **main** function to the operating system, and that value, which indicates normal program termination (a non-zero value would indicate an error), ends the program.

That completes our first program. There's one last thing to note: the indentation of the lines of code inside the **main** function. I've indented those lines by four spaces to indicate that they're part of the **main** function:

```
#include <iostream>
using namespace std;

// Display a welcoming message.

int main()
{
    cout << "Hello from C++." << endl;

    return 0;
}
```

C++ code can become very dense, and indenting code like this has become standard over the years. As our code becomes more complex, indenting code like this can be invaluable in indicating which code encloses which other code; you don't need to use four spaces (using two spaces is also popular), but I encourage you to indent your code as well.

That's our first program; how do we get it to run and display some output? The first step is to enter it into a C++ source file.

Creating C++ Source Files

To turn your C++ code into an executable program that you can run, you've got to type it into a *source file* ("source" means the C++ "source code" that the program comes from). How you actually do that depends on your C++ installation (see "Writing a C++ Program" later in this chapter); for example, in Microsoft Visual C++, you use that package's built-in editor to create C++ source files. You can also use your favorite text editing program to create C++ source files if your C++ installation can work with them. For example, you might use vi or emacs or even pico in UNIX to enter your code into source files. Or you might use WordPad or Notepad in Microsoft Windows. The most important thing is that your C++ package must be able to read your source file. In particular, that usually means staying away from fancy word processors like Microsoft Word, unless they can store files in plain text format.

How should you name the C++ file? That also depends on your C++ installation; in UNIX, for example, some common file extensions for C++ source files are .C (uppercase C; lowercase c is reserved for C programs), .cc, .cxx, and .cpp. In DOS and Windows, .cpp is the most common, and for that reason, I'll use .cpp as the best overlap between the operating systems. For example, you might type the program we developed above into a file named hello.cpp.

At this point, then, you've got the code of our first program in a C++ source file, hello.cpp—how do you get that code to actually run? The next step is to *compile* it.

Compiling and Running C++ Programs

To convert your C++ source code to an executable program that you can run, you must have a C++ compiler. There are some free ones out there (see "Finding a C++ Compiler" later in this chapter), and UNIX usually comes with a C++ compiler built in. You can also use fancy, expensive compilers, but you do need a compiler.

The job of the compiler is to translate your C++ program from something you understand into something your computer understands. Because how you use the compiler varies a great deal depending on the compiler, I'll cover this process in more detail in "Basic Skills: Compiling a Program." For compilers you invoke on the command line (that is, at the UNIX or DOS prompt), you typically type the name of the program to compile right after the compiler program's name. For example, if the name of your compiler program is cppcompiler (for example, cppcompiler.exe in Windows) and it's meant to be run at the command line, you can compile hello.cpp like this (in this book, I'll use % as the generic command-line prompt to stand for both the UNIX and DOS command-line prompt):

```
%cppcompiler hello.cpp
```

This creates the executable file for you to run; in DOS, for example, that executable file will be named hello.exe. The details vary by compiler and operating system, of course, and you'll have to check out the compiler documentation or ask someone for the details; in UNIX, for example, this file will typically be named a.out.

So how do you get this executable file to run? Typically, you just enter the name of the executable program at the command line prompt, as in this case (see "Basic Skills: Compiling a Program" later in this chapter for more details on running your programs):

```
%hello
```

When you do, the program runs immediately, and you see the result:

```
%hello
Hello from C++.
```

And now we've compiled and run our first C++ program. That's how the process works in outline; for the specific details on your compiler, see its documentation if it's available (too often it's not), or pester someone until they tell you what you want to know.

The Reserved C++ Keywords

As we create our own C++ programs, we'll be creating our own names, and those names should not conflict with terms that C++ has reserved for its own use. You'll find the C++ reserved keywords in Table 1.1—note that not all of those keywords do something yet (for example, **asm**, which some implementations use to include low-level machine-specific assembly language in a program, does not have an official use yet in standard C++), but they're all reserved for C++'s use.

Table 1.1 Reserved C++ keywords.

Keywords			
asm	auto	bad_cast	bad_typeid
bool	break	case	catch
char	class	const	const_cast
continue	default	delete	do
double	dynamic_cast	else	enum
except	explicit	extern	false
finally	float	for	friend
goto	if	inline	int
long	mutable	namespace	new
operator	private	protected	public
register	reinterpret_cast	return	short
signed	sizeof	static	static_cast
struct	switch	template	this
throw	true	try	type_info
typedef	typeid	typename	union
unsigned	using	virtual	void
volatile	while		

Converting to ANSI/ISO Standard C++

Even if you're already a C++ programmer, you may not be familiar with ANSI/ISO standard C++. Here is a short list of items to help you make the conversion—if you're not already a C++ programmer, you might want to refer back to this list throughout the book to make sure what you're doing is standard C++:

- Use **const** instead of **#define** to define constants (see Chapter 2 for more details).
- Use **inline** instead of **#define** for inline functions (see Chapter 7 for more details).
- Use function prototypes; they're optional in C, but not in standard C++ (see Chapter 6 for more details).
- Use the new type cast operators, **dynamic_cast**, **static_cast**, **const_cast**, and **reinterpret_cast** instead of the old way of casting, such as **(double)** (see Chapter 5 for more details).
- Use the new C++-style headers (see "Basic Skills: Using Header Files" for more details).
- Use namespaces (see Chapter 11 for more details).
- Use the **auto_ptr** template, which automates delete operations (see Chapter 15 for more details).
- Use the built-in **string** class (see Chapter 15 for more details).
- Use the Standard Template Library (STL) (see Chapters 15, 16, and 17 for more details).

That's all the preparation we need. It's time to turn to the Immediate Solutions section of the chapter, where I'll cover in greater detail what we've already seen, and I'll add a number of other basic skills, such as reading input from the keyboard, as well as take a preliminary look at the **if** statement and loop statements like the **for** and **while** statements. These basic skills will be covered in more depth throughout the book, but they're also ones we'll need as we go along. To make sure you have a good foundation for the coming chapters, please make sure those skills are firmly under your belt.

Immediate Solutions

Where Can I Get a Copy of the ANSI/ISO C++ Standard?

If you have a C++ question that you just can't get answered anywhere else, you can always turn to the ANSI/ISO C++ standard itself, whose technical name is X3J16-14882.

Where can you get a copy? You can get a hard copy from the National Committee for Information Technology Standards (NCITS) in Washington, D.C. Request document FDC 14882 (it's rather expensive). On the Internet, you can also get a hard copy (also not free): at **www.ansi.org**. (As of this writing, you select Standards Info, then search for "14882-1998," but note that that already has changed between the time I wrote this and when the book went through tech review.) The actual name of the document in this case is "ISO/IEC 14882-1998, Information Technology - Programming Languages - C++." There's one more option—you can download a copy from the Internet as a PDF at **http://webstore.ansi.org/ansidocstore/product.asp?sku=ISO%2FIEC+14882%2D1998**. (At this writing, it's about 2MB and at U.S.$18, the cheapest option.) You'll need the Adobe Acrobat reader to read the document; this reader is free at **www.adobe.com** (as of this writing, you can download it from **www.adobe.com/products/acrobat/readermain.html**). It's a fairly substantial document—775 pages.

NOTE: *The ANSI/ISO C++ standard itself is really targeted for those who want to create C++ compilers, and you might find it hard to wade through.*

Finding a C++ Compiler

If you don't have a C++ compiler, you'll need one to create executable files from your C++ code. Where can you find a C++ compiler? There are plenty around, and you can pay plenty of money if you want to. How you use your compiler depends on the compiler, but at the risk of giving you information that may have been superceded by the time you read this, I'll take a look at things in overview.

Compilers in UNIX

C++ is usually built into UNIX systems, so you won't have to look very far. For example, the C++ compiler on UNIX systems is often named CC (note that it's in capital letters to distinguish it from the C compiler, cc). If your UNIX installation doesn't have CC built in, try looking for g++, the Free Software Foundation's GNU C++ compiler. Both these compilers have UNIX man pages you can consult for the complete details on how to use them (for example, enter the command **man CC** at the command prompt). For some tips on how to use the various compilers, see "Basic Skills: Compiling a Program" later in this chapter.

Compilers in DOS/Windows

There are several high-powered C++ compilers available in Windows, such as Borland C++ and Microsoft Visual C++. Both cost money—but here's a great tip: there's a DOS version of the C++ engine in Borland C++ that's available (as of this writing) for free at **ftp://ftpd.inprise.com/download/bcppbuilder/freecommandlinetools.exe**. If that's blocked or things have changed by the time you read this, take a look at **www.borland.com** for the new details (the current download page is **www.borland.com/bcppbuilder/freecompiler/**). This compiler is ANSI/ISO compliant, very up to date, and it's also free. The actual compiler's name is bcc32.exe, and you can run it from the command line, just as you can CC or g++ in UNIX—highly recommended if you're using DOS/Windows.

There are, of course, plenty of other C++ compilers out there for Windows, and some are even free, such as the one supported by Cygwin, the partial port of GNU UNIX tools to Windows, which you'll find at **http://sources.redhat.com/cygwin/**. For some tips on how to use the various compilers, see "Basic Skills: Compiling a Program" later in this chapter.

Macintosh Compilers

Among the best known C++ compilers for the Macintosh are the Symantec C++ compiler and the Metrowerks Code Warrior compiler. Unfortunately, neither is free, and I haven't been able to find free C++ compilers for the Mac yet (let me know if you know of any—or for that matter, any other free ANSI/ISO compliant compilers—and I'll list them here in the next edition of the book). For some tips on how to use the various compilers, see "Basic Skills: Compiling a Program" later in this chapter.

Writing a C++ Program

As discussed in the introduction to this chapter (see "Creating C++ Source Files"), you need to put your C++ code into a C++ source file before the compiler can work with it. In the fancier compilers like Borland C++ and Microsoft Visual C++, you use an Integrated Development Environment (IDE), which comes with a built-in editor, to create your code. There might even be "wizard" tools to write a great deal of your code for you. (A typical Visual C++ program targeted at Windows has about ten pages of code inserted automatically by Visual C++ before you even start working on it.) If you're using a compiler with an IDE, stick to using the integrated editor for creating your C++ programs. Although it's often possible to write source code files outside the IDE and add them to your C++ projects later, you risk incompatibilities and confusion about source code versions unless you use the IDE tools.

On the other hand, if you're using a command-line compiler like CC or bcc32.exe, you're responsible for creating your C++ source code files yourself. You can use almost any text editor capable of storing plain text files, such as vi or emacs in UNIX or WordPad or Notepad in Windows (avoid the fancy word processors unless they can store your C++ code as plain text files). There are even some terrific programmer's editing tools that will highlight the keywords of your C++ program in different colors and check syntax as you write. All that's really needed, however, is an editing program that can create C++ source files that your compiler can read.

How should you name your C++ source code files? Again, that depends on your compiler; most C++ source files have a name and an extension, such as hello.cpp. In UNIX, typical source file extensions are .C, .cc, cxx, and .cpp. In Windows, you usually use .cpp (sometimes you can use .cp). On the Macintosh, it's usually either .cp or .cpp. In this book, I'll use .cpp as a common denominator. The length of the file name as a whole may be limited by your operating system or compiler. After you've created your source file, you pass it to your compiler, as discussed in "Basic Skills: Compiling a Program" later in this chapter.

Our First C++ Program

We saw this program in overview in the In Depth section of this chapter, but here I'm going to go through it in detail:

```
#include <iostream>
using namespace std;

// Display a welcoming message.
```

```
int main()
{
    cout << "Hello from C++." << endl;

    return 0;
}
```

This program just displays the message "Hello from C++." on the screen, and I'm going to take it apart line by line over the next few sections. Knowing exactly how this code works provides an essential framework for the work we'll do in the following chapters.

#include <iostream>

The first line of our first program is an **#include** preprocessor directive:

```
#include <iostream>
using namespace std;

// Display a welcoming message.

int main()
{
    cout << "Hello from C++." << endl;

    return 0;
}
```

This preprocessor directive inserts the header file iostream into the code at this point, and that header file tells C++ about many functions and objects, including the **cout** object that we're going to use later in the program. As we'll see in Chapter 6 and briefly in "Basic Skills: Using Header Files" later in this chapter, header files are typically used to declare functions and objects to C++ so it knows how to use them; such declarations are not needed in many other languages, but C++ insists on them.

NOTE: *Any code that uses **cout** or **cin** must include the iostream header.*

Preprocessor Directives

Preprocessor directives are handled before the code is passed to the C++ compiler—in fact, the original C++ as written by Bjarne Stroustrup was a package named cfront that worked as a preprocessor, converting the C++ code to C code, which was then passed on to the C compiler. The C++ compiler is different; it includes a preprocessor that handles preprocessor directives before the C++ compilation process starts.

Here are the allowed preprocessing directives in standard C++:

- **#define**—Defines a token
- **#elif**—The else-if directive
- **#else**—The else directive
- **#error**—Current error
- **#if**—The if directive
- **#ifdef**—The if-defined directive
- **#ifndef**—The if-not-defined directive
- **#include**—Includes a file
- **#line**—Current line
- **#pragma**—Special function run before the rest of the code
- **#undef**—Undefine

You can use these preprocessor directives with predefined tokens like **__cplusplus**, which is *defined* if the current program is C++, and *undefined* otherwise. You can check if a token is defined with an **if** directive, which starts with **#if** and ends with **#endif**; in this case our code line is included in our program if the program is written in C++:

```
#ifdef __cplusplus
cout << "This is a C++ program." << endl;
#endif
```

Here are some predefined tokens you can use in your code:

- **__cplusplus**—Defined if the current program is in C++
- **__STDC__**—Defined if the current program is in standard C
- **__LINE__**—Holds the current line number
- **__FILE__**—Holds the current file name
- **__DATE__**—Holds the date of compilation
- **__TIME__**—Holds the time of compilation

The preprocessor also supports *macros*, which are sections of predefined code that are expanded in your program as they're encountered by the preprocessor.

Macros have fallen out of favor, replaced largely by templates, inline functions, and more sophisticated techniques, but there's still at least one that remains very useful—the **assert** macro. You use this macro to insert code into your program that will test an expression (just like the ones you test in an **if** statement), and if that expression is false (see "Basic Skills: True or False Values in C++" later in this chapter), the program is terminated and an error message displayed. Here's how to use **assert** in code:

```
assert(expression);
```

When it encounters an **assert** macro like this, the preprocessor will insert the code to check ***expression*** at runtime and terminate the program if necessary. This macro is great for debugging your programs, because it allows you to check what's happening in your code when your program runs, but take the **assert** macros out for the final version of the program (the information they display will usually be of no use to the user) in favor of exception handling (see Chapter 12).

It's also possible to write your own macros—see "Creating Preprocessor Macros" later in this chapter.

It's worth taking a look at the name of the header file we're including here—iostream. As discussed later in "Basic Skills: Using Header Files," standard C++ header files now have no extension. That's different from the old way of doing things in C and C++, when header files had the extension .h (the ANSI/ISO committee wanted to give C++ standard header files an extension, but they just couldn't agree on what it should be, so they compromised on nothing). And many old C style header files have been adapted into C++ standard header files now—and renamed without an extension and with an additional c in front of their names. Here's a list of the header file types you're likely to encounter:

- *C Old Style header files*—End in .h, like stdio.h (use in C, C++)
- *C++ Old Style header files*—End in .h, like iostream.h (use in C++)
- *C++ New Style header files*—No extension, like iostream, (use in C++ with a namespace like **std**)
- *Converted C header files*—Added prefix of c, no extension, like cctype (use in C++)

The new C++ standard style header files also place all the names they define in a special namespace, **std**, and we'll take a look at that namespace next.

using namespace std;

The next line in our first program is the namespace statement highlighted below:

```
#include <iostream>
using namespace std;

// Display a welcoming message.

int main()
{
    cout << "Hello from C++." << endl;

    return 0;
}
```

I added this line because we're using the new C++-style header file iostream. The names in iostream are part of the namespace **std**, which stands for standard. I discussed namespaces briefly in the In Depth section of this chapter, and we'll see them in detail in Chapter 11. Like other languages such as Java and Perl, C++ now uses namespaces to let you avoid conflicts between the names you use in a program and the names other programmers may have used. Even if you use the same name in two different namespaces, there is no conflict, so, for example, a function written by someone else can't overwrite yours by mistake. The names in standard C++ have been made part of the **std** namespace, so technically, you're supposed to prefix each such name with **std::**, as we'll see in Chapter 11. That would make our program look like this:

```
#include <iostream>

// Display a welcoming message.

int main()
{
    std::cout << "Hello from C++" << std::endl;

    return 0;
}
```

This works as well as the earlier version of this code, but most programmers find it easier to use a **using namespace std** statement to make that the *default namespace*. When you've made **std** the default namespace, you no longer have to prefix everything with **std::**—that prefix is assumed. We'll see a great deal more about namespaces in Chapter 11.

// Display a welcoming message.

The next line of our program is a comment:

```
#include <iostream>
using namespace std;

// Display a welcoming message.

int main()
{
    cout << "Hello from C++." << endl;

    return 0;
}
```

As mentioned in the In Depth part of this chapter, comments are annotations added to a program that let you explain something about the program's purpose, creation, version, or function. They're stripped out by the compiler and ignored—comments are only for your use, not the compiler's.

There are two types of comments in C++: C++-style comments and C-style comments. The comment in the code above is a C++-style comment, which means it's a one-line comment. The C++ compiler ignores everything on the line after the double slash, //. That also means you can use this style of comment to annotate individual lines, like this:

```
#include <iostream>
using namespace std;

int main()
{
    cout << "Hello from C++." << endl; // Display a welcoming message.

    return 0;
}
```

The second type of comment in C++, the C-style comment, starts with the characters /* and ends with the characters */. Because it has definite start and end markers, it's not restricted to a single line like the C++-style comment (which uses the end of the line as the end of the comment). That means you can create multiline comments like this:

```
#include <iostream>
using namespace std;

/* The purpose of this program is
   to display the welcoming message,
   which is "Hello from C++."      */

int main()
{
    cout << "Hello from C++." << endl;

    return 0;
}
```

There are many variations for using the C-style comments; here's another version:

```
#include <iostream>
using namespace std;

/************************************/
/* The purpose of this program is    */
/* to display the welcoming message, */
/* which is "Hello from C++."        */
/************************************/

int main()
{
    cout << "Hello from C++." << endl;

    return 0;
}
```

One thing to note here is that you cannot *nest* C-style comments—that is, you cannot enclose one inside another. The reason for that is that after the comment has started, the C++ compiler looks for the first */ marker to end the comment, and if it finds additional non-C++ text after that point, it'll get confused:

```
#include <iostream>
using namespace std;

/* Comments start with /* and end with */, and
   you cannot nest them, which means this is an
   invalid program, and will not compile.    */
```

```
int main()
{
    cout << "Hello from C++." << endl;

    return 0;
}
```

int main()

The next line in the program starts the **main** function:

```
#include <iostream>
using namespace std;

// Display a welcoming message.

int main()
{
    cout << "Hello from C++." << endl;

    return 0;
}
```

As mentioned in the In Depth section of this chapter, the **main** function is the point where control is passed to your program from the operating system. That is to say, the main function is where you place the code you want executed first, and generally speaking, it's essential to have a **main** function in all C++ programs—with a few exceptions, such as Windows dynamic link libraries (DLLs) or shared code in memory that some compilers support and which can be called by multiple separate processes. Even those exceptions need another program to specifically call their code, however. There's one more exception: programs you develop in packages like Microsoft Visual C++ that are targeted at Windows and that display windows use a special starting function named **WinMain**. (There's no special reason for that name—because it's Microsoft's compiler, they can do what they want.)

We'll see how to create functions in detail in Chapter 6. Functions are the building blocks of C++ programs, and normally, all the code in a C++ program is enclosed in a function. In addition, standard C++ comes with more than 140 predefined functions, ready for you to call, and we'll be investigating those functions throughout the book.

Note the structure of the **main** function; the first line is **int main()**, followed by curly braces enclosing the code that forms the body of the function and that is executed when the function is called. The **int** keyword indicates that this function returns an integer value. (We'll see more on how functions return values and how to make use of those values in Chapter 6.) In this case, the integer value we return is 0 with the **return 0**; statement at the end of **main**.

In C programs, you can omit the return type specifier in front of **main** (that is, **int**), but not in C++ programs. As covered in Chapter 6, besides specifying the return type of a function, you can also specify the type or types of data values, called arguments, *passed* to a function for it to work on. Those data values are listed in the parentheses after the function's name; however, the **main** function does not take any arguments, so I'm leaving the parentheses empty here. In C++, that means there are no arguments passed to a function—but in standard C, it means only that you're not saying anything about the types or number of arguments. Another option in C++ is to place the keyword **void** in the parentheses of a function that takes no arguments—this creates the same result as leaving the parentheses empty:

```
int main(void)
{
    cout << "Hello from C++." << endl;

    return 0;
}
```

cout << "Hello from C++." << endl;

This is the actual line of code that produces the output from our first program:

```
#include <iostream>
using namespace std;

// Display a welcoming message.

int main()
{
    cout << "Hello from C++." << endl;

    return 0;
}
```

We saw this line of code in the In Depth section of this chapter. In C programs, you typically use a built-in function named **printf** to display text output from a program:

```
#include <stdio.h>

/* Print "Hello from C." */
```

```
main()
{
    printf("Hello from C.");

    return 0;
}
```

You use the **printf** function to display formatted text, and you're responsible for formatting the output the way you want it when you use **printf**. On the other hand, **cout** is a special stream object in C++ that handles many of the details for you. You can pass text or numbers to **cout**, and it'll be able to handle both by itself. In our first program, we're passing a text string, "Hello from C++.", and the iostream manipulator **endl** to **cout** using the << operator (for the details on manipulators, see Chapter 13). You can use the << operator in stages, as we have here, to pass multiple items to **cout**. When you run the program, the text we've sent to **cout** appears like this:

```
%hello
Hello from C++.
```

The **endl** manipulator makes the output skip to the next line, and it is not necessary in this case if you're running this program in DOS, because when the program terminates, the output skips to the next line when the command prompt reappears—although that's not the case in UNIX. Another option that works the same way as **endl** is to use the *character escape sequence* **'\n'** to make the output skip to the next line:

```
#include <iostream>
using namespace std;

// Display a welcoming message.

int main()
{
    cout << "Hello from C++." << '\n';

    return 0;
}
```

The backslash, \, in **'\n'** indicates to C++ that the following character is to be interpreted as part of a character escape sequence. In this case, C++ interprets the **'\n'** and sends a newline character to the output. In fact, you can treat the **'\n'** as part of the text string to display like this:

```
cout << "Hello from C++.\n";
```

There are plenty of other character escape sequences that **cout** understands, such as backspaces and tabs; for the details, see "Basic Skills: Using Character Escape Sequences" later in this chapter.

The **cout** object is an important one we'll see throughout the book. Although it may seem that **cout** just takes your data and displays it as it likes, you can customize its behavior in every way. See also "Basic Skills: Formatting Output" later in this chapter for more on using **cout** to produce formatted output. The **cout** object comes with built-in defaults for displaying all types of data, however, and that makes it much easier than using the old C function **printf** (although **printf** is still available to you in C++ programs).

There's also a corresponding object, **cin**, for reading text-based input; see "Basic Skills: Reading Keyboard Input" later in this chapter.

NOTE: *In Windows programming, you no longer write to* ***cout****. Instead, you use the predefined Windows functions like* ***TextOut*** *to write to windows; in general, input and output in a windowing environment are very different from input and output in a standard C++ program.*

---

return 0;

The last statement in the **main** function is typically **return 0;**:

```
#include <iostream>
using namespace std;

// Display a welcoming message.

int main()
{
    cout << "Hello from C++." << endl;

    return 0;
}
```

This specifies the value returned by that function. Usually, when you return a value from a function, that return value is passed back to the part of the C++ program that called the function, but the return value from the **main** function is different, because it's been called by the operating system itself. In this case, a value of 0 is returned to the operating system, indicating normal program termination.

TIP: *If you pass a non-zero value back from the main function, it's considered an error code; you can make use of that return value in both UNIX and DOS (although in DOS, you need to handle the return value in a .bat file).*

You can actually omit the **return 0;** statement at the end of **main**, and C++ will add it to the code. It's the one place where a return value is implied, and C++ will handle the details if you omit it. Although this is part of the C++ standard, I don't advise relying on it—C++ is notorious for requiring everything to be spelled out, and I'm sure some C++ implementations won't supply a **return** statement at the end of **main** for you if you omit it.

Other ways of ending a program include the **exit** and **abort** statements; see "Using the **exit** and **abort** Statements" in Chapter 4.

Related solution:	Found on page:
Using the **exit** and **abort** Statements	195

Basic Skills: Compiling a Program

After your program is ready to go, you've got to compile it to run it. The actual details of compiling your C++ code depend on your compiler, but I'll take a look at the process in outline here.

In the fancy C++ integrated development environments, you usually make your C++ code part of a *project*, and you use menu items like Make or Build or Build All to create an executable file. Typically, such packages can create different types of programs for you, such as might run in DOS, or in a window in Windows, or as a dynamic link library or as a Web application. Here, the details of the compilation process are compiler specific; on the other hand, such C++ packages come with a lot of documentation to help you through the process.

In standard UNIX, the process is easier. Here, the compiler you use is something like CC or g++, and you only need to pass the name of the file or files you want to compile to the compiler on the command line like this:

```
%g++ hello.cpp
```

In some versions, you might have to specify that you want to link in the C++ library explicitly, something like this:

```
%g++ hello.cpp -lg++
```

This compiles your C++ source code into a new file, hello.o, and then *links* it with the C++ standard libraries to add the code needed to support C++. The result is a file named a.out, which is an executable file, and you can run it like this:

```
%a.out
Hello from C++.
```

To find out more, use the **man** command for the compiler you're using, such as **man CC** or **man g++**. If you want to rename a.out, you can use UNIX commands like the **mv** command.

In DOS, the process is similar at the command line. For example, in the free version of Borland C++, the compiler is named bcc32.exe, and it's unpacked into a directory named bin. The files you include in C++ code, like iostream, are put into a directory named include, and the C++ library routines are put into a directory named lib. If you've unpacked everything in a directory named c:\bcc, your command-line might look something like this, where I'm using the **-I** *switch* to indicate where the include files are and the **-L** switch to indicate where the C++ library files are:

```
C:\cpp>c:\bcc\bin\bcc32 -Ic:\bcc\include -Lc:\bcc\lib hello.cpp
Borland C++ 5.5 for Win32 Copyright (c) 1993, 2000 Borland
hello.cpp:
Turbo Incremental Link 5.00 Copyright (c) 1997, 2000 Borland
```

TIP: *You use compiler switches like* **-I** *or* **-L** *on the command line to customize the behavior of your compiler; check your compiler's documentation to see what command-line switches are available (there are usually plenty of them).*

This creates hello.exe, ready to run. You can also compile multiple source code files, such as a.cpp, b.cpp, c.cpp, and so on like this:

```
C:\cpp>c:\bcc\bin\bcc32 -Ic:\bcc\include -Lc:\bcc\lib a.cpp b.cpp c.cpp
```

In this case, a.cpp is usually the source file that contains the **main** function. The resulting .exe file here is called a.exe, named after the first file you compiled.

Basic Skills: Running a Program

How you actually run the compiled and linked program depends on your operating system. In Windows, you enter the name of the executable file, such as hello, on the command line, omitting the .exe extension if there is one, and press Enter to start the program.

In UNIX, the name of the executable file is something like a.out, unless you've taken steps to rename it, and that's the name you should enter at the command line to run the program.

In the IDE-based C++ compilers (such as Microsoft Visual C++), there should be a Run or Execute menu item you use to run your compiled and linked program.

***TIP:** If your program doesn't terminate normally and appears to be stuck, you can usually end it by pressing Ctrl+C if you've started it at the command line, or select the appropriate menu item (such as Stop Running) in the IDE-based C++ implementations.*

***TIP:** Some C++ implementations create programs which, when run, display their results in a window in a flash and close the window immediately, before you can see what happened. If you're having that problem, try putting the statement **cin.get();** at the very end of the **main** function. This statement waits for you to press a key such as Enter; after you press a key, the program will end. For more on **cin.get**, see "Using **cin** to Read Individual Characters and Whole Strings" in Chapter 2.*

Basic Skills: Storing Data

One of the crucial skills we'll use in every chapter from now on is storing data in *variables*. If you've programmed before, you know what variables are; they're named memory locations in which you can store data, and programs wouldn't be much use without data to operate on. (Chapter 2 is all about variables in greater depth.)

As with other languages, you can create variables in C++; unlike with some languages, variables are strongly *typed* in C++. A variable's type indicates what kind of data you can store in it; for example, you can store integers like 0, 215, or –36 in the C++ **int** type, floating point numbers like 3.1415, 2.7128, or 1.5 in the **float** type, and so on. You should always be aware of a variable's type, because C++ won't let you assign data of a specific type to a variable if the variable's type is too different. (See Chapter 2 for more on the types of variables and how you convert between them, and plenty of examples.) This is an issue that C++ programmers become very familiar with very fast.

Here's an example; in this case, I'm creating an integer variable named **number_of_buddhas** with the **int** keyword and storing the number of Buddha figurines in a collection, 729, in it:

```
#include <iostream>
using namespace std;

// Display the number of Buddha figurines.
```

```
int main()
{
    int number_of_buddhas = 729;
    .
    .
    .
```

Here, I've *declared* an integer variable named **number_of_buddhas** in a declaration statement, and *initialized* the value in the variable to 729. The built-in types like **int** and **float** are called *simple* types, and after you declare a variable of a simple type, C++ sets aside space for it in memory and you can use it in your program. By initializing the variable at the same time as I declare it, I start it off holding a specific value, in this case, 729.

Now I can use this new variable, **number_of_buddhas**, in code like this, where I display the number of Buddha figures in the collection simply by passing that variable to **cout**:

```
#include <iostream>
using namespace std;

// Display the number of Buddha figurines.

int main()
{
    int number_of_buddhas = 729;

    cout << "There are " << number_of_buddhas;
    cout << " Buddha figurines in my collection." << endl;

    return 0;
}
```

Here's the result of this code—as you can see, **cout** has displayed the value in the variable **number_of_buddhas**, as it should:

```
%numberbuddhas
There are 729 Buddha figurines in my collection.
```

I didn't have to initialize the **number_of_buddhas** variable to any specific value; I could have simply declared that variable with the declaration statement:

```
int number_of_buddhas;
```

I could then have used the = *assignment operator* to assign a value to that variable. (For an overview of C++ operators, see "Basic Skills: Using C++ Operators" later in this chapter.) This code works just as the previous example did:

```
int main()
{
    int number_of_buddhas;

    number_of_buddhas = 729;

    cout << "There are " << number_of_buddhas;
    cout << " Buddha figurines in my collection." << endl;

    return 0;
}
```

You can also declare a number of variables on the same line if you separate them with commas like this:

```
int main()
{
    int number_of_cats, number_of_dogs;

    number_of_cats = 297;
    number_of_dogs = 319;

    cout << "I have " << number_of_cats << " cats and ";
    cout << number_of_dogs << " dogs." << endl;

    return 0;
}
```

Here's the output of this program:

```
%catsanddogs
I have 297 cats and 319 dogs.
```

For the sake of overview, you can find the standard C++ simple variable types in Table 1.2, and we'll see more about them in Chapter 2. Note that not all compilers might support all types; for example, the **wchar_t** wide character type is typically used for wide character codes like Unicode and most compilers don't support Unicode yet.

Table 1.2 C++ simple variable types.

Type	Contents
bool	Holds true (non-zero) or false (zero) values
char	Contains characters like 'a', 'b', or 'c'
wchar_t	Wide characters, such as Unicode
signed char	**char** type with numeric sign
unsigned char	**char** type with no sign
short	Integer that is larger than or equal to **char**, and shorter than or equal to type **int**
short int	Same as **short**
signed short	Same as **short**
unsigned short	**short** integer without a sign
int	Basic integer type
signed int	Same as **int**
unsigned int	Unsigned integer
long	Long integer
signed long	Same as **long**
unsigned long	Unsigned long integer
float	Floating point number
double	Double precision floating point number, usually has more precision than **float**
long double	Floating point number with even more precision than **double**, although many implementations treat **long double** as the same as **double**
void	Void type

Besides the simple types in Table 1.2, you can also define your own data types with C++ statements such as **typedef**, **struct**, **class**, and so on, and we'll see how that works in detail in Chapters 3 and 8.

There's one more point worth noting here: Places where you can store values, like variables, are given a special name in programming—*lvalue*. This term originally stood for "left value," because when you assign a value to a variable, it's on the left side of the = assignment operator. These days, lvalues are also sometimes called *location values*, because they correspond to specific locations in memory (for example, simple numeric expressions like 5 + 2 cannot be lvalues). You'll often find the term lvalue in C++ documentation as a shorthand referring to memory locations. Expressions that are not lvalues are called *rvalues*, which originally stood for right values, because they can appear on the right side of an assignment operator, but not on the left (in some languages, like Perl, expressions like 5 + 2 actually can be lvalues in some circumstances, but not in C++). These days, rvalues are also sometimes called *read values*.

Basic Skills: True or False Values in C++

In C++, expressions are sometimes evaluated not for numerical results but for *truth* value. This is a particularly important point, because the truth value of an expression is used in control statements like **if** statements and loop statements. The convention in C++ is that when evaluated for their truth value, values that are non-zero are considered true, and values that are zero are considered false. This is a point that will be important throughout the book.

The **bool** data type, first introduced in Table 1.2, is specially designed to hold values of true or false. In fact, you can assign the C++ keywords **true** or **false** to it, as well as the results of expressions. The name **bool** is short for boolean; boolean variables are often called *flags*, and the true/false values they hold can refer to settings in your program, such as whether spellchecking is on or a particular drawing tool is enabled.

NOTE: *When C++ returns a value of true or false from a function or stores a value of true or false in a variable, compilers almost invariably use 0 for false and 1 for true.*

Basic Skills: Reading Keyboard Input

We've used **cout** a good deal already in this chapter to display output, and it's time to introduce the corresponding object to read input: **cin**. Like **cout**, **cin** makes the process of reading from the keyboard much easier than it was in C, where you used a function called **scanf** to read input that you had to specify an exact format for. Like **cout**, **cin** lets you rely on default formatting, handling different types of data smoothly.

Here's an example using **cin** that reads and echoes text from the user. First, I'll need to set aside some space for the text we read from the keyboard, and to do that, I'll use the standard C++ class named **string**. In this case, I'll use the **string** class just like any simple variable type, but as we'll see in Chapter 16, there is a lot of power in the **string** class. Here's how I create a new string variable named **input**:

```
#include <iostream>
#include <string>
using namespace std;

// Read and display data.

int main()
{
    string input;
        .
        .
        .
```

Now we can read from **cin** and send what we've read to the **input** variable; because we're reading from **cin** (as opposed to writing to **cout**), I use the >> operator here, not <<, and ask the user to type a word:

```
#include <iostream>
#include <string>
using namespace std;

// Read and display data.

int main()
{
    string input;

    cout << "Type a word: ";

    cin >> input;
        .
        .
        .
```

The user can enter a word at the keyboard, and after they press the Enter key, that word is stored in the variable named **input**. We can display the value in that variable with **cout** like this:

```
#include <iostream>
#include <string>
using namespace std;

// Read and display data.
```

```
int main()
{
    string input;

    cout << "Type a word: ";

    cin >> input;

    cout << "You typed: " << input << endl;

    return 0;
}
```

That's all there is to it; here's what the program, cin.cpp, looks like at work:

```
%cin
Type a word: Hello
You typed: Hello
```

If the user types in more than one word, each one is assigned to a different variable by **cin**; here's an example where I'm asking the user to enter four words:

```
#include <iostream>
#include <string>
using namespace std;

// Read and display data.

int main()
{
    string input1, input2, input3, input4;

    cout << "Type four words: ";

    cin >> input1 >> input2 >> input3 >> input4;

    cout << "You typed: " << input1 << " " << input2 << " ";
    cout << input3 << " " << input4 << endl;

    return 0;
}
```

Here's what this program, fourwords.cpp, looks like at work:

```
%fourwords
Type four words: This is a test...
You typed: This is a test...
```

You can also use **cin** to read numeric values, as we'll see in Chapter 2. Usually, **cin** does not return any values until the user presses the Enter key at the end of the line. However, we'll see how to read characters one by one using the **cin** object's built-in function **get**, and also how to read a whole multiword line of text at once in Chapter 2 (see "Using **cin** to Read Individual Characters and Whole Strings" in Chapter 2).

Related solution:	Found on page:
Using **cin** to Read Individual Characters and Whole Strings	89

Basic Skills: Using Character Escape Sequences

As you know, you can use the character escape sequence **'\n'** to make the output skip to a new line when using **cout**. Placing a backslash, \, in front of a character makes C++ look for a character escape sequence and treat it in a special way; using a backslash like this is called "escaping" a character or character sequence.

You can find the character escape sequences supported in standard C++ in Table 1.3.

Table 1.3 C++ character escape sequences.

Escape Sequence	Represents
\a	Bell (alert)
\b	Backspace
\f	Formfeed
\n	New line
\r	Carriage return
\t	Horizontal tab
\v	Vertical tab
\'	Single quotation mark
\"	Double quotation mark
****	Backslash
\?	Literal question mark
ooo	Character code in octal notation
\x*hhh*	Character code in hexadecimal notation

Some of the character escape sequences in Table 1.3 are quite useful; here's an example in which I use the backspace character, **\b**. First, I have the program type out a prompt, "Type a word:______", and then I use six backspace characters to position the cursor right after "word:" and on top of the first underscore, like this:

```
#include <iostream>
#include <string>
using namespace std;

// Read and display data.

int main()
{
    string input;

    cout << "Type a word:______\b\b\b\b\b\b";

    cin >> input;

    cout << "You typed: " << input << endl;

    return 0;
}
```

Basic Skills: Formatting Output

The **cout** object contains a number of built-in functions that you can use to format the output it displays; such built-in functions in an object are called *methods*, as we'll see in Chapter 8. One **cout** method is **precision**, which lets you set the numeric precision used to display numbers. To set the numeric precision to 3 digits, you call the precision method like this: **cout.precision(3)** (as we'll see in Chapter 8, you can call a method of an object using the dot operator, .). Here's how I display two values of pi, after storing it as a floating point value and then setting the numeric precision:

```
#include <iostream>
using namespace std;
```

```
int main()
{
    float pi = 3.14159;

    cout << "Pi: " << pi << endl;

    cout.precision(3);

    cout << "Pi with a precision of three digits: " << pi << endl;

    return 0;
}
```

Here's the output of this program, precision.cpp:

```
%precision
Pi: 3.14159
Pi with a precision of three digits: 3.14
```

There's another way to set the precision like this—you can use the **setprecision()** manipulator. As with the **endl** manipulator, you pass the **setprecision()** manipulator to the **cout** object, but this time, you set the numeric precision inside the parentheses of this manipulator like this:

```
#include <iostream>
#include <iomanip>
using namespace std;

int main()
{
    float pi = 3.14159;

    cout << "Pi: " << pi << endl;

    cout << setprecision(3) << "Pi with a precision of three digits: "
        << pi << endl;

    return 0;
}
```

This program yields the same result as the previous one. In fact, there are plenty of other ways to format output, such as using the **setf** method and other manipulators, as we'll see in Chapter 13.

Basic Skills: Making Decisions with the **if** Statement

We're going to look at the **if** statement in Chapter 4 in great depth, but it's an essential building block we'll need before that point, so it's worth taking a look in overview now. Here's what the two forms of the **if** statement look like:

```
if (expression) statement
if (expression) statement else statement
```

The **if** statement lets you execute code depending on whether or not ***expression*** is true or false. If ***expression*** is true, the code in the following ***statement*** (which can be either a simple statement or a compound statement) is executed. There can also be an **else** clause in an **if** statement, and if so, the code in that clause is executed when if ***expression*** is false.

In the next example, I ask the user to enter an integer to be compared against zero, and when they do, use an **if** statement to display the text "That integer is greater than zero." if the integer is greater than zero, and the text "That integer is zero or less than zero." otherwise. How do I compare the integer to zero? I'll use the expression **number > 0**, which uses the > comparison operator (for more on the available operators, see the next section, "Basic Skills: Using C++ Operators"). That expression is true if the value in the variable number is greater than zero, and false otherwise. Here's what the actual **if** statement looks like in code:

```
#include <iostream>
using namespace std;

// Using the if statement.

int main()
{
    int number;

    cout << "Enter an integer to be checked: ";

    cin >> number;

    if (number > 0){
        cout << "That integer is greater than zero." << endl;
    }
    else {
        cout << "That integer is zero or less than zero." << endl;
    }
```

```
    return 0;
}
```

We're going to study the **if** statement in depth in Chapter 4, but it's essential that you have some familarity with it now so we can put it to work in Chapter 2.

Basic Skills: Using C++ Operators

One of the basic skills you should be equipped with is a knowledge of the C++ operators (operators are covered in more depth in Chapters 2 and 4). For example, the + operator lets you add the numbers 23 and 19 like this:

```
#include <iostream>
using namespace std;

//Using the addition operator.

int main()
{
    int sum;

    sum = 23 + 19;

    cout << "23 + 19 = " << sum << endl;

    return 0;
}
```

Here's the result of running this program, addition.cpp:

```
%addition
23 + 19 = 42
```

There are quite a few operators in standard C++, and we'll see them throughout the book, starting in Chapter 2. For the sake of reference, you can find all the C++ operators in Table 1.4, divided into groups by operator precedence (see "Operator Precedence in C++" in Chapter 2). I'll introduce them as needed over the next few chapters.

Table 1.4 C++ operators.

Operator	Name or Meaning
--	
::	Scope resolution
::	Global
--	
.	Member selection (object)
->	Member selection (pointer)
++	Postfix increment
--	Postfix decrement
[ ]	Array subscript
( )	Function call
( )	Conversion
typeid( )	type name
const_cast	Type cast (conversion)
dynamic_cast	Type cast (conversion)
reinterpret_cast	Type cast (conversion)
static_cast	Type cast (conversion)
--	
sizeof	Size of object
sizeof ( )	Size of type
++	Prefix increment
--	Prefix decrement
(*type*)	Type cast (conversion)
new	Allocate object
new[ ]	Allocate array
delete	Deallocate object
delete[ ]	Deallocate array
*	Dereference
&	Address-of
+	Unary plus
-	Arithmetic negation (unary)
!	Logical NOT
~	Bitwise complement
--	

(continued)

Table 1.4 C++ operators *(continued)*.

<table>
<tr><th>Operator</th><th>Name or Meaning</th></tr>
<tr><td>.*</td><td>Apply pointer to class member (objects)</td></tr>
<tr><td>->*</td><td>Dereference pointer to class member</td></tr>
<tr><td>*</td><td>Multiplication</td></tr>
<tr><td>/</td><td>Division</td></tr>
<tr><td>%</td><td>Remainder (modulus)</td></tr>
<tr><td>+</td><td>Addition</td></tr>
<tr><td>-</td><td>Subtraction</td></tr>
<tr><td><<</td><td>Left shift</td></tr>
<tr><td>>></td><td>Right shift</td></tr>
<tr><td><</td><td>Less than</td></tr>
<tr><td>></td><td>Greater than</td></tr>
<tr><td><=</td><td>Less than or equal to</td></tr>
<tr><td>>=</td><td>Greater than or equal to</td></tr>
<tr><td>==</td><td>Equality</td></tr>
<tr><td>!=</td><td>Inequality</td></tr>
<tr><td>&</td><td>Bitwise AND</td></tr>
<tr><td>^</td><td>Bitwise exclusive OR</td></tr>
<tr><td>|</td><td>Bitwise OR</td></tr>
<tr><td>&&</td><td>Logical AND</td></tr>
<tr><td>||</td><td>Logical OR</td></tr>
<tr><td>e1?e2:e3</td><td>Conditional</td></tr>
</table>

(continued)

Table 1.4 C++ operators *(continued)*.

Operator	Name or Meaning
=	Assignment
*=	Multiplication assignment
/=	Division assignment
%=	Modulus assignment
+=	Addition assignment
-=	Subtraction assignment
<<=	Left-shift assignment
>>=	Right-shift assignment
&=	Bitwise AND assignment
|=	Bitwise inclusive OR assignment
^=	Bitwise exclusive OR assignment
--	
throw	Throw an exception
--	
,	Comma
--	

Related solution:	***Found on page:***
Operator Precedence in C++	98

Basic Skills: Working with Loops

A basic skill essential for work in C++ is working with *loops*, such as the **for** and **while** statements. We'll see loops in detail in Chapter 4, but you should be familiar with them before that point.

As you probably know, a loop statement repeatedly executes the code in its body until a termination condition is met. For example, the **for** loop is a good choice when you want to use a numeric index that you automatically increment or decrement each time through the loop. Here's what the **for** loop looks like in general:

```
for (initialization_statement; test_expression; post_expression) statement
```

Note that ***statement*** can be a simple statement, or it can be a compound statement that includes several single statements inside curly braces. This loop executes ***statement*** repeatedly as long as ***test_expression*** is true. You can initialize the loop, usually by creating and initializing a *loop index*—a variable that keeps track of the number of times the loop has iterated— in ***initialization_statement*** (in fact, you can initialize and use multiple loop indices in a **for** loop), provide a ***test_expression*** that will end the loop when that expression becomes false, and provide an expression to be executed each time after ***statement*** is executed—usually to increment a loop index for the next iteration—in ***post_expression***.

Here's an example; in this case, I'm asking the user how many times they want to see a greeting string displayed and looping that many times, displaying the greeting each time:

```
#include <iostream>
using namespace std;

// Test out the for loop.

int main()
{
    int number;

    cout << "How many times do you want to see the greeting? ";

    cin >> number;

    for (int loop_index = 0; loop_index < number; loop_index++){
        cout << "Hello from C++." << endl;
    }

    return 0;
}
```

There are a few points to note here: In this case, I'm declaring and initializing a variable named **loop_index** in the *initialization statement* of the loop, testing to see if it exceeds the number of repetitions the user has asked for with the *test expression* **loop_index < number** (when this expression becomes false, the loop terminates), and incrementing **loop_index** every time after the body of the loop has executed with the *iteration expression* **loop_index++**, which uses the C++ increment operator, ++ (listed in Table 1.4; see Chapter 2 for more about this operator), to add 1 to **loop_index**. Here's what this program, greeter.cpp, looks like in action:

```
%greeter
How many times do you want to see the greeting? 5
Hello from C++.
Hello from C++.
Hello from C++.
Hello from C++.
Hello from C++.
```

Another powerful loop statement is the **while** statement:

```
while (expression) statement
```

This loop executes ***statement*** while ***expression*** remains true. Here's an example; in this case, I keep asking the user to enter a number and, while the number they enter is not equal to zero, keep asking for another number:

```
#include <iostream>
using namespace std;

// Check integers.

int main()
{
    int number;

    cout << "Enter a non-zero integer to be checked: ";

    cin >> number;

    while (number != 0){

        if(number > 0){
            cout << "That integer is greater than zero." << endl;
        }
        else {
            cout << "That integer is less than zero." << endl;
        }

        cout << "Enter a non-zero integer to be checked: ";
```

```
        cin >> number;
    }

    cout << "You entered zero." << endl;

    return 0;
}
```

Here's what this example, comparer.cpp, looks like in action:

```
%comparer
Enter a non-zero integer to be checked: 1
That integer is greater than zero.
Enter a non-zero integer to be checked: 2
That integer is greater than zero.
Enter a non-zero integer to be checked: -1
That integer is less than zero.
Enter a non-zero integer to be checked: 0
You entered zero.
```

Basic Skills: Using Header Files

Throughout this chapter, we've used the **#include** preprocessor directive to include header files, as in this case, where I'm including the iostream header file:

```
#include <iostream>
using namespace std;

// Display a welcoming message.

int main()
{
    cout << "Hello from C++." << endl;

    return 0;
}
```

Header files usually contain declarations, definitions, and preprocessor directives like **#include** to include other header files, and storing such items in header files helps make your code cleaner. You can create your own header files, and we'll see the value of doing so throughout the book.

Here's a quick example, useheader.cpp, that uses a header file. In this case, I'll modify the code that we first saw in "Basic Skills: Formatting Output" in this chapter:

```
int main()
{
    float pi = 3.14159;

    cout << "Pi: " << pi << endl;

    cout << setprecision(3) << "Pi with a precision of three digits: "
        << pi << endl;

    return 0;
}
```

This code needs the iostream and iomanip header files to work, which means it needs these statements:

```
#include <iostream>
#include <iomanip>
```

In this case, however, I'll put these statements in a new header file, named useheader. Now I can use the **#include** preprocessor directive to include that header file in useheader.cpp like this (note that in cases like this, you enclose the name of the file in double quotes, not angle brackets):

```
#include "useheader"
using namespace std;

int main()
{
    float pi = 3.14159;

    cout << "Pi: " << pi << endl;

    cout << setprecision(3) << "Pi with a precision of three digits: "
        << pi << endl;

    return 0;
}
```

In this case, I'm giving the header file no extension, following the standard C++ usage. However, you will also encounter header files with the extension .h and on some systems even .hxx. What types of headers use what extensions? Here's the list, repeated here for convenience:

- *C Old Style header files*—End in .h, like stdio.h (use in C, C++)
- *C++ Old Style header files*—End in .h, like iostream.h (use in C++)
- *C++ New Style header files*—No extension, like iostream, (use in C++ with a namespace like **std**)
- *Converted C header files*—Added prefix of c, no extension, like cctype (use in C++)

Note in particular the converted C header files in this list—many of the old C-style headers were converted to the new C++ style and use the namespace **std**, so they have no extension. To indicate that they are converted C style headers, their names are prefixed with a c, like cmath or cctype.

The C++ Standard Library now provides 32 C++ header files: <algorithm>, <iomanip>, <list>, <ostream>, <streambuf>, <bitset>, <ios>, <locale>, <queue>, <string>, <complex>, <iosfwd>, <map>, <set>, <typeinfo>, <deque>, <iostream>, <memory>, <sstream>, <utility>, <exception>, <istream>, <new>, <stack>, <valarray>, <fstream>, <iterator>, <numeric>, <stdexcept>, <vector>, <functional>, and <limits>.

The resources of the Standard C Library are provided in 18 additional header files: <cassert>, <ciso646>, <csetjmp>, <cstdio>, <ctime>, <cctype>, <climits>, <csignal>, <cstdlib>, <cwchar>, <cerrno>, <clocale>, <cstdarg>, <cstring>, <cwctype>, <cfloat>, <cmath>, and <cstddef>.

Throughout the book, I'll be sure to indicate which C++ header files to use as they are needed. Note that if your C++ compiler doesn't support the new way of doing things—that is, using standard C++ header files without extensions that use the **std** namespace—you should switch back to the old C++ style, where header files use the extension .h, and remove this namespace statement from the examples in this book:

```
using namespace std;
```

Here's one more point to bear in mind when you're creating your own header files: If you have multiple files, you may find yourself including the same header file more than once, and that can be a problem. Say you've declared a variable in a header file, and you try to include that header file a second time because another part of the program also includes the same file—in that case, the C++ compiler will object that the variable has already been declared. If you run up against this problem, there's a simple solution—you can define a symbol, usually corresponding to the header file name, with the **#define** preprocessor directive. And you use preprocessor directives like **#ifndef** (which means "if not defined") to surround the code in a header file, checking if that symbol has already been defined:

```
#ifndef __HEADER_NAME
#define __HEADER_NAME
//Header file contents go here.
#endif
```

Now the contents of the header file are included only if they have not *already* been included in the program.

Creating Preprocessor Macros

You can create your own preprocessor macros simply by using **#define** to write code that will be inserted wherever you use the macro in your code. Although macros have largely been superceded by inline functions, which are safer to use, it's still worth seeing an example. You can refer to the data that a macro is to operate on with the letters **a**, **b**, and so on. Here's an example that uses the ?: operator (which we'll see discussed in "The If-Then-Else Operator: ?:" in Chapter 2); in this case, I'm creating a macro named maximum that finds the maximum of two numbers:

```
#include <iostream>
using namespace std;

#define maximum(a, b) (a < b) ? b : a

int main()
{
    int max = maximum(5, 3);

    cout << "The maximum of 5 and 3 = " << max << endl;

    return 0;
}
```

Here's what this program, macro.cpp, looks like when it's running:

```
%macro
The maximum of 5 and 3 = 5
```

Related solution:	Found on page:
The If-Then-Else Operator: ?:	108

Microsoft's C#

Microsoft is introducing a customized version of C++ that's been modified and trimmed down, named, at this writing, C#. In many ways, the idea appears simply to make C++ like Java, removing the parts that Microsoft considers inconvenient or possibly insecure. Here's a description of C# from the August 2000 Visual Basic Programmer's Journal (at this writing, this article is at **http://www.devx.com/upload/free/features/vbpj/2000/08aug00/ts0008/tsvc0008/tsvc0008.asp**):

> C# enables you to develop components and applications rapidly with robust code. Microsoft designed C# as a pure object-oriented language, and the company wanted to eliminate those parts of the C++ language that allowed developers to introduce bugs. To make C# more productive and simple, Microsoft removed a lot of constructs from C++ to eliminate redundant ways to accomplish the same thing, making it easier to write and understand the code. The product designers stripped out things such as macros, templates, #include syntax, and the multiple syntax ways of accessing objects. Instead of having to figure out when to use the dot (.), dereference (->), or scope (::) operators, you always use dot notation.
>
> To prevent buggy code, C# handles memory management and eliminates pointers—the root of all evil. Through the Common Language Runtime, the system garbage collects your objects for you at the appropriate times, so you don't have to worry about dangling pointers, reference counting, or memory leaks. The language doesn't allow globals, eliminating global concurrency issues. Finally, C# doesn't allow multiple implementation inheritance. You can inherit from multiple interfaces, but interfaces by definition have no implementation, so the ambiguities that make multiple inheritance messy are no longer a concern.

Whether or not this version of C++ takes off or not is still at issue. Although C# might be more secure for programs targeted at the Web and other specialized uses, it's still in question whether C++ programmers will want to give up all that power.

That completes the foundation we'll need for the coming chapters—all the basic skills we need are in place. With these skills under our belts, it's time to turn to Chapter 2.

Chapter 2

Working with Data and C++ Operators

(continued)

In Depth

No C++ program beyond the most trivial is going to get very far without data to work on. In fact, that's one of the main emphases beyond object-oriented programming, because classes and objects are intended to be data-centric. C++ comes with many built-in ways to store and organize your data—with the simple types and the derived types. The simple types include the data types we've already seen briefly in the previous chapter—**char**, **int**, **float**, **long double**, and so on. The derived types include structures, enumerations, arrays, and others. We'll work with the simple data types in this chapter, and the derived types in the next chapter, Chapter 3.

We've already seen the most popular simple data type—the **int**, or integer, type—at work in the previous chapter. In this example, I stored the number of cats on hand in an integer variable named **number_of_cats**, and the number of dogs in a **int** variable named **number_of_dogs**:

```
int main()
{
    int number_of_cats, number_of_dogs;

    number_of_cats = 297;
    number_of_dogs = 319;

    cout << "I have " << number_of_cats << " cats and ";
    cout << number_of_dogs << " dogs." << endl;

    return 0;
}
```

What kinds of numbers can you store in simple **int** variables? Unfortunately, that's not a simple question to answer, as we'll see in the Immediate Solutions section, because C++ implementations can differ on this point. The C++ standard does not specify the actual amount of memory storage space that each type has, although it does specify the minimum storage space for each type—for example, an **int** data type must be stored with at least 16 bits (although most implementations use at least 32 today).

***NOTE:** I'll be referring to bits, bytes, and words in this chapter. As you probably know, the actual data in a computer is stored in* binary *format, which means that it's stored as bits, which are set to either 0 or 1. A bit can be considered a single digit in a binary (base two) number, and eight of them together form a* byte*. Although a bit can hold only the value 0 or 1, a byte, which is an eight-digit binary number, can hold numbers from 0 up to $2^8 - 1$, or 255 (in binary, 255 is 11111111, which means all binary digits in it are set to 1, the maximum value each digit can have; 256 is 100000000 in binary, nine digits, which is one more binary place than a byte can hold). A* word *in computer storage terms is 16 bits, which means it can hold values from 0 to $2^{16} - 1$, or 65535. (Someone once had a fit of cuteness and called four-digit binary numbers nibbles, or, believe it or not, nybbles. I won't be using that term here.)*

Creating Variables Using the C++ Simple Data Types

As you know, variables come in different types and serve as placeholders in memory for data. The different types have to do with the format the data is stored in, and how much memory is set aside to hold that data. For example, the integer variable type, the **int** type, is usually made up of four bytes, or 32 bits. We'll see how to determine what size **int** variables are in your C++ implementation in "What Is the Storage Capacity of the Integer Types?" and "What Is the Storage Capacity of the Floating Point Types?" later in this chapter. A 32-bit number by itself can hold numbers from 0 to 4,294,967,295. However, the **int** type can also store negative numbers, so if an **int** is 32 bits in your C++ implementation, its range is divided into a range of possible values from -2,147,483,648 to 2,147,483,647 (see "Signed and Unsigned Data" later in this chapter).

Before you use a variable in C++, you must declare it, specifying its data type. Here's how you declare variables in C++ (in this book, I'll use square brackets, [and], to indicate optional parameters in formal statement definitions like this):

```
type name [= value][, name [= value]...];
```

Here, ***type*** is the type of the variable you're declaring, ***name*** is the name you want to give it, and ***value*** is its initial value. Although we've seen the process briefly in the previous chapter, I'll take a more detailed look at declaring variables now. In this case, I'll just declare a variable of the **int** type; this variable is named **days**, like this:

```
#include <iostream>
using namespace std;

int main()
```

```
{
    int days;
        .
        .
        .
}
```

Assuming that the **int** type is 32 bits, this code allocates 32 bits of storage in memory and labels the location of that storage, as far as the C++ compiler is concerned, as **days**, which means you can now refer to that name in code. Here's how I store a numeric value of 365 in **days**, using the C++ assignment operator, =:

```
#include <iostream>
using namespace std;

int main()
{
    int days;

    days = 365;
        .
        .
        .
}
```

Here, the value 365 is an integer *literal*, which means a literal value that you place directly in your code; I'll take a look at what kinds of literals C++ allows in this chapter (literal numbers like this are stored as **int** values unless there's some reason to use a different type). To verify that **days** now holds 365, I can print it out this way:

```
#include <iostream>
using namespace std;

int main()
{
    int days;

    days = 365;

    cout << "Number of days = " << days << endl;

    return 0;
}
```

Here's the result of this code, days.cpp:

```
%days
Number of days = 365
```

As you can see, we've created a variable, stored data in it, and fetched that data back to print it on the screen. There's also a convenient shortcut that lets you initialize a variable when you declare it. Here, I'm declaring **days** and initializing it to 365 in one step:

```
#include <iostream>
using namespace std;

int main()
{
    int days = 365;

    cout << "Number of days = " << days << endl;

    return 0;
}
```

Unlike in C, you can declare a variable wherever you can use a normal statement in C++, which is very convenient, because you can then declare a variable close to where you actually use it (in C, declarations are collected together at the top of the code, which might be a thousand lines of code away from where you use it). Here's an example:

```
#include <iostream>
using namespace std;

int main()
{
    int days = 365;

    cout << "Number of days = " << days << endl;

    int months = 12;

    cout << "Number of months = " << months << endl;

    return 0;
}
```

In fact, some statements, like the **if** statement and **for** statements, actually allow you to declare variables inside the statement itself. We saw the **for** loop in the last chapter—note that the first term in parentheses is the initialization *statement*, not an initialization *expression*:

```
for (initialization_statement; test_expression; iteration_expression)
statement
```


It's legal to declare variables like loop indices in this statement, as we saw in this example from the previous chapter:

```
#include <iostream>
using namespace std;

// Test out the for loop.

int main()
{
    int number;

    cout << "How many times do you want to see the greeting? ";

    cin >> number;

    for (int loop_index = 0; loop_index < number; loop_index++){
        cout << "Hello from C++." << endl;
    }

    return 0;
}
```

Data Typing

C++ puts considerable emphasis on its data types. It's a strongly typed language, which means that it insists that the variables you declare and the data you assign to those variables must have the same or compatible types.

Every simple variable must have a type (and in fact, every C++ expression has a type as well). And C++ is very particular about maintaining the integrity of those types, especially if you try to assign a value of one type to a variable of another type. You can convert between certain data types in C++, such as between the integer types, and I'll take a look at that in this chapter (see "Conversion between Data Types" later in this chapter).

***NOTE:** When working with variables, you might find the C++ compiler issuing a lot of errors and warnings about data types, which can take some getting used to; bear in mind that the inspiration for making C++ very particular about adhering to data types and not mixing them easily was to prevent errors in your code.*

The **int** type is only one kind of simple variable that you can use; I'll take a look at the possibilities in overview here, and in greater depth in the Immediate Solutions section.

- The **bool** type is designed to hold only two types of values: true and false. You use it to keep track of data values that can hold yes or no answers to questions.
- The **char** type can hold the numeric codes for characters such as **'a'**, **'b'**, and so on; this type is usually one byte long (but it's a word long in some C++ implementations). There are also the **wchar_t** (wide characters, for storing Unicode) **signed char**, and **unsigned char** types.
- The integer types are **short** (which is larger than **char**, but shorter or equal to **int**), **unsigned short**, **signed short**, **int**, **signed int**, **unsigned int**, **long** (a long integer, longer than **int**), **signed long**, and **unsigned long**. Note that types like **int** and **signed int** are the same, because **int** variables can store signs by default. You use this type to store integer values, which can include negative values if you use a signed type. Examples include 4, 319, and –244.
- The float types are **float**, **double** (double precision floating point), and **long double** (supposedly a longer version of **double**, but often the same as **double**). You use this type to store numeric values with decimal parts, like 3.14159, 2.7128, or even 1.0000.

Type Conversions

Because C++ is so strongly typed, you can run into problems when you mix data types, as when you assign data of one type to a variable of another. C++ handles such type mixing with *type conversions*. There are two types of conversions: *implicit* and *explicit*. Implicit conversions are handled by the compiler, and you handle explicit conversions yourself. For example, look at this code; here, I'm adding the values in two different types of variables—short and long:

```
#include <iostream>
using namespace std;

int main()
{
    short big = 48272;
    long bigger = 138281285;
```

```
    cout << "The sum of big and bigger = " << bigger + big << endl;

    return 0;
}
```

Although I'm adding a **short** to a **long**, there's no problem; the compiler simply elevates the **short** value to a **long** value to add it to the other **long**. Because there is no possibility of losing any precision here, the compiler handles the conversion itself, that is, implicitly. Here's the result when I run this program, types.cpp:

```
%types
The sum of big and bigger = 138264021
```

On the other hand, take a look at this example; here, I'm adding a floating point number with decimal digits to an integer, and storing the result in an integer:

```
#include <iostream>
using namespace std;
int main()
{
    int sum;
    int ten = 10;
    float pi = 3.14159;

    sum = pi + ten;

    cout << "The integer sum = " << sum << endl;

    return 0;
}
```

In this case, you definitely do lose precision, because C++ chops off the decimal part of the floating point value, 3.14159, and simply adds 3 + 10 and puts the result in the variable **sum**. In cases like this, the compiler should warn you about what's going on, as in this example, when you compile the code with g++:

```
%g++ conversion.cpp
conversion.cpp: In function `int main()':
conversion.cpp:9: warning: assignment to `int' from `float'
```

However, not all compilers will issue a warning (I just tested this code on one that did not, in fact). To indicate to C++ that you know what you're doing in a case like this, and that the loss of precision is acceptable, you can *cast* the floating point number to an integer temporarily. As we'll see in "Conversion between Data Types" later in this chapter, you can do that like this, where I'm casting the floating point variable **pi** to an integer:

```
#include <iostream>
using namespace std;
int main()
{
    int sum;
    int ten = 10;
    float pi = 3.14159;

    sum = static_cast <int> (pi) + ten;

    cout << "The integer sum = " << sum << endl;

    return 0;
}
```

Now the compiler won't complain, and here's the result when you run the program, conversion.cpp:

```
%conversion
The integer sum = 13
```

So how do you actually work with the data in simple variables? With C++ operators.

C++ Operators

We'll take a look at the C++ operators in this chapter, like +, ++, *, and so on. We already saw some C++ operators at work in the previous chapter, as in this example, where I use the addition operator, +, to add 23 and 19:

```
#include <iostream>
using namespace std;

//Using the addition operator.

int main()
{
    int sum;

    sum = 23 + 19;
```

```
    cout << "23 + 19 = " << sum << endl;

    return 0;
}
```

Here's the result of running this program, addition.cpp:

```
%addition
23 + 19 = 42
```

We'll see many of the C++ operators in this chapter, but not all of them, because some are reserved for more advanced use, such as with classes and objects, or pointers, or dynamic memory management, and I'll introduce those operators in the appropriate chapters throughout the book.

Besides working with the C++ simple data types and the C++ operators, I'll also take an introductory look at the C++ **string** class, which is now part of standard C++. Although this class is not a simple data type, you can use it as you would a simple type to store text strings. The **string** class is one of the great things about C++ compared to C, and it at least deserves mention in this chapter on storing data in variables, because it can work just like any other variable type. We'll see a lot more about the **string** class in Chapter 15.

At the end of this chapter, I'll also take a look at some of the C++ utility functions that are available, such as **rand** to generate random numbers, **cos** to find cosines, and **log** to find natural logarithms. I'll start now in the Immediate Solutions section by taking a look at what simple types are available.

Immediate Solutions

What Simple Data Types Are Available?

You can find the simple data types available in standard C++ in Table 2.1. We'll take a look at these types in detail over the next few sections.

Table 2.1 C++ simple variable types.

Type	Contents
bool	Holds true (non-zero) or false (zero) values
char	Contains characters like 'a', 'b', or 'c'
wchar_t	Wide characters, such as Unicode
signed char	**char** type with numeric sign
unsigned char	**char** type with no sign
short	Integer that is larger than or equal to **char**, and shorter than or equal to type **int**
short int	Same as **short**
signed short	Same as **short**
unsigned short	**short** integer without a sign
int	Basic integer type
signed int	Same as **int**
unsigned int	Unsigned integer
long	Long integer
signed long	Same as **long**
unsigned long	Unsigned long integer
float	Floating point number
double	Double precision floating point number, usually has more precision than **float**
long double	Floating point number with even more precision than **double**, although many implementations treat **long double** as the same as **double**
void	Void type

Declaring Variables

As discussed in the In Depth section of this chapter, you must declare all variables before using them in C++. Here's how the declaration statement works:

```
type name [= value][, name [= value]...];
```

Here, ***type*** is the type of the variable you're declaring, ***name*** is the name you want to give it, and ***value*** is its initial value. We've already seen variable declaration at work, as in this example:

```
#include <iostream>
using namespace std;
int main()
{
    int sum;
    int ten = 10;
    float pi = 3.14159;

    sum = static_cast <int> (pi) + ten;

    cout << "The integer sum = " << sum << endl;

    return 0;
}
```

You can also group declarations of the same type on one line, separating the variable names and initial values (if the corresponding variable has one) with a comma, like this:

```
#include <iostream>
using namespace std;
int main()
{
    int sum = 0, ten = 10;
    float pi = 3.14159;

    sum = static_cast <int> (pi) + ten;

    cout << "The integer sum = " << sum << endl;

    return 0;
}
```

And as we've seen, you can also add declarations throughout your code, like this line:

```
#include <iostream>
using namespace std;

int main()
{
    int days = 365;

    cout << "Number of days = " << days << endl;

    int months = 12;

    cout << "Number of months = " << months << endl;

    return 0;
}
```

In fact, as mentioned in the In Depth section of this chapter, some statements, like the **if** statement and **for** statements, allow you to declare variables inside the statement. We took a look at the **for** loop in the In Depth section of this chapter—note again that the first term in parentheses is the initialization *statement*, not an initialization *expression*:

```
for (initialization_statement; test_expression; iteration_expression)
statement
```

In C++, you can declare variables like loop indices in this statement, as we saw in this example:

```
#include <iostream>
using namespace std;

// Test out the for loop.

int main()
{
    int number;

    cout << "How many times do you want to see the greeting? ";

    cin >> number;
```

```
    for (int loop_index = 0; loop_index < number; loop_index++){
        cout << "Hello from C++." << endl;
    }

    return 0;
}
```


Naming Variables

C++ has rules for the names of variables that you declare, and here they are:

- The only characters you can use in variable names are alphabetic characters, numbers, and the underscore character, _.
- The first character cannot be a digit (because C++ will think you're referring to a number).
- Variable names are case sensitive; that is, uppercase is different from lowercase. For example, **number_of_elephants** is different from **number_of_Elephants**. Variables are usually mostly lowercase, and all uppercase is usually reserved for constants, not variables.
- Don't use any reserved C++ keywords as variable names (see Table 1.1 for a list of these keywords).
- There are no limits on the length of a name in standard C++; however, practically speaking, many compilers do have limits, such as 255 (or, in one case I know of, 254) characters.
- Variable names that start with an underscore (_) or two underscores are reserved for use by your C++ implementation.
- If your variable names are made up of multiple words, it's conventional to use underscores or capital letters to separate the words. For example, **bird_whistles_total** or **birdWhistlesTotal**.

You might notice the last point above, which is not a rule so much as a convention; if your variable names are made up of multiple words, it's conventional either to use underscores between the words like **inner_loop_index** or to capitalize the first letter of the second and following words, like **innerLoopIndex**. Which way you do it often depends on your programming heritage: If you come from C programming, underscores may be your choice; if you come from Java, it might be initial capital letters. Although my own preference is for initial capital letters (even though I use C++ more than Java these days), the actual ANSI/ISO C++ standard is written using underscores in variable names (although there is no mention of that fact in the document), so I'll use that convention here.

Working with **char** Data Types

The smallest simple data type is **char**, which, as you can guess from its name, represents the character data type. It's usually one byte long (to check how long it is on your system, see "What Is the Storage Capacity of the Integer Types?" later in this chapter). You can use this type to store individual alphanumeric characters, such as **'a'**, **'T'**, or **'7'**. Here's an example program, char.cpp, that uses this type and asks the user to enter a single character:

```
#include <iostream>
using namespace std;

int main( )
{
    char character;

    cout << "Type one character: ";

    cin >> character;

    cout << "You typed " << character << endl;

    return 0;
}
```

Here's what this program looks like when running:

```
%char
Type one character: A
You typed A
```

Actually, what's stored in **character** is not the letter A, but the numeric code that stands for that character. When you pass a **char** to **cout**, **cout** will convert that character code back to the character itself and display that, because **cout** knows that the **char** type is intended to hold characters. Many C++ implementations still use the American Standard Code for Information Interchange (ASCII) character codes, and the ASCII code for **'A'** is 65. If we were to treat the character code in

character as an integer and not a **char** and displayed it that way, we'd see 65. Here's the new code:

```
#include <iostream>
using namespace std;

int main( )
{
    char character;
    int character_code;

    cout << "Type one character: ";

    cin >> character;

    cout << "You typed " << character << endl;

    character_code = character;

    cout << "That character's code is " << character_code << endl;

    return 0;
}
```

Here's the result of this code:

```
%char
Type one character: A
You typed A
That character's code is 65
```

***TIP:** To convert between characters and numbers, see the **atoi**, **atof**, and **itoa** functions in "The C++ Utility Functions: Math, Time, Trig, Random Numbers, and More" later in this chapter.*

What Type of Character Is It?

You can also use the functions declared in the cctype header file to determine what type of character you're dealing with. For example, I can use the **isalpha**, **isdigit**, **isspace**, and **ispunct** functions to test if a character is aphanumeric, a digit, a space, or a punctuation character, like this:

```
#include <iostream>
#include <cctype>
using namespace std;
```

```
int main()
{
    cout << "Please type a character: ";
    char character;

    cin >> character;

    if(isalpha(character))
        cout << "That character is alphanumeric." << endl;
    else if(isdigit(character))
        cout << "That character is a digit." << endl;
    else if(isspace(character))
        cout << "That character is a space." << endl;
    else if(ispunct(character))
        cout << "That character is a punctuation character." << endl;

    return 0;
}
```

Here's what this program, cctypes.cpp, looks like at work:

```
%cctypes
Please type a character: 7
That character is a digit.
```

Wide Characters

As mentioned, many compilers use the ASCII character code set. ASCII codes extend from 0 to 255; for example, the ASCII code for A is 65, the ASCII code for B is 66, and so on.

On the other hand, the World Wide Web is just that today—world wide. And there are plenty of scripts that are not handled by ASCII, such as Bengali, Armenian, Hebrew, Thai, Tibetan, Japanese Katakana, Arabic, Cyrillic, and others. For that reason, many compiler manufacturers are starting to support Unicode, and C++ has introduced a new wide character type, **wchar_t** (they're called wide characters because they're usually stored as two bytes, not one like **char**). Most compilers don't support wide characters yet.

Because Unicode codes are made up of two bytes, not one, they extend from 0 to 65,535, not just 0 to 255. (However, to make things easier, the Unicode codes 0 to 255 do indeed correspond to the ASCII 0 to 255 codes.) Unicode can therefore include many of the symbols commonly used in world-wide character and ideograph sets today. Only about 40,000 Unicode codes are reserved at this point (of which about 20,000 codes are used for Han ideographs—although in fact, there are over 80,000 such ideographs defined—and 11,000 for Korean Hangul syllables). You can learn more about Unicode at **www.unicode.org**.

***NOTE:** Actually, not even Unicode has enough space for all symbols in common use, so a new specification, the Universal Character System (UCS, also called ISO 10646) uses four bytes per symbol, which gives it a range of two billion symbols—far more than needed. Another way of referring to pure Unicode encoding is by using the UCS-2 encoding (also called ISO-10646-UCS-2), which is compressed, two-byte UCS. You can also use UTF-16, which is a special encoding that represents UCS symbols using two bytes so that the result corresponds to UCS-2. Straight UCS encoding is referred to as UCS-4 (also called ISO-10646-UCS-4).*

Some compilers use **wcin** and **wcout** as the input and output objects for Unicode instead of **cin** and **cout**. Note also that you can designate that a character literal is in Unicode by putting an L in front of it like this: **L'A'**, as well as string literals like this: **L"Hello"**.

The **char** type can also be declared as **signed char** or **unsigned char** if you want to use it as a numeric value. Because the **char** type is usually implemented as a byte, the **signed char** type can hold values from -128 to 127, and the **unsigned char** type can hold values from 0 to 255. How did the range for signed **char** variables end up as -128 to 127 and not, say, -127 to 128? See the next topic for the details.

Signed and Unsigned Data

Because a byte is made up of only ones and zeros, how do you store a negative number in it? There's no special bit for the sign. To store negative numbers, C++ compilers use what's called *two's complement* math. For example, if you store a 1 in a byte, its two's complement, which is 11111111, stands for -1.

Why should 11111111 stand for -1? The reason is simple—look what happens to this number when you add one—you get 100000000, which is nine binary digits, too large to hold in one byte. The upshot is that the leading 1 gets lost, and the byte is left holding 0; in other words, -1 + 1 = 0.

To form a number's two's complement, take its binary representation, and make all 1s 0s and all 0s 1s, then add 1 to the result. Now you know how it works. And it should prepare you for another C++ fact—if you use a signed data type, like **int**, and try to store a number that's so large that the left-most bit is 1, that number is treated as *negative*, not positive. Here's an example where I'm adding two large positive numbers, and because of the way C++ stores negative integers (with the left-most bit set to 1), the erroneous result is *negative*:

```
#include <iostream>
using namespace std;

int main()
{
    int int1 = 28848484802;
    int int2 = 20939393971;

    cout << "The sum = " << int1 + int2 << endl;

    return 0;
}
```

Here's what this program looks when running—clearly, this result is incorrect, and it's time to switch to a longer integer type, or floating point variables:

```
%neg
The sum = -1751728779
```

(Note that this example may not work with your compiler, which may use a different number of bytes for the **int** type.)

Working with **char** Literals

A literal is a constant value that you embed right in your code, as in this case, where I'm assigning the letter **'a'** to a **char** variable:

```
int main()
{
    char character;

    character = 'a';

    cout << "The character = " << character << endl;

    return 0;
}
```

The thing to note here is that character literals like **'a'**, **'b'**, or **'7'** are enclosed in *single quotes*. If you use double quotes, C++ will think you're using a string, not a single character. Wide character literals start with a capital L, like **L'z'**. You can also use character escape sequences as character literals, and you'll find those sequences in Table 2.2.

Note in particular the *xhhh* form in Table 2.1; this allows you to enter the character code for a character directly, using hexadecimal, or base 16. For example, the ASCII code for **'A'** is 65, which is 41 in hexadecimal, so you can refer to **'A'** as **'\x41'**.

---

*TIP: To convert between characters and numbers, see the **atoi**, **atof**, **itoa**, and **ftoa** functions in "The C++ Utility Functions: Math, Time, Trig, Random Numbers, and More" later in this chapter.*

Table 2.2 C++ character escape sequences.

Escape Sequence	Represents
\a	Bell (alert)
\b	Backspace
\f	Formfeed
\n	New line
\r	Carriage return
\t	Horizontal tab
\v	Vertical tab
\'	Single quotation mark
\"	Double quotation mark
****	Backslash
\?	Literal question mark
ooo	Character code in octal notation
\x*hhh*	Character code in hexadecimal notation

Working with Integer Data Types

Integer data types store numbers that have no fractional parts, like 1, 0, 319, 438328291, and so on. There are three different base types for integers: **short**, **int**, and **long**. These types can also be declared as **signed** or **unsigned** (if you don't specify **signed** or **unsigned**, most compilers default to **signed**), which means the corresponding values can hold negative, zero, and positive values, or just zero and positive values. Here are the possibe types you can use:

- **short**—Integer that is larger than or equal to **char**, and shorter than or equal to type **int**
- **short int**—Same as **short**
- **signed short**—Same as **short**
- **unsigned short**—Short integer without a sign
- **int**—Basic integer type
- **signed int**—Same as **int**
- **unsigned int**—Unsigned integer
- **long**—Long integer
- **signed long**—Same as **long**
- **unsigned long**—Unsigned long integer

Here's an example that uses all three basic integer types:

```
#include <iostream>
using namespace std;

int main()
{
    short short_integer;
    int integer;
    long long_integer;

    short_integer = 1;
    integer = 2;
    long_integer = 3;

    cout << "The short integer holds " << short_integer << endl;
    cout << "The integer holds " << integer << endl;
    cout << "The long integer holds " << long_integer << endl;

    return 0;
}
```

Here's the result of this code, int.cpp:

```
%int
The short integer holds 1
The integer holds 2
The long integer holds 3
```

So what is the storage capacity of these integer types? See the next section.

What Is the Storage Capacity of the Integer Types?

Unfortunately, the storage capacity of the integer types varies by C++ compiler. The C++ standard does specify these *minimum* capacities:

- A **short** is at least 16 bits long.
- An **int** at least as long as a **short**.
- A **long** is at least 32 bits, and at least as long as an **int**.

Typically, an **int** variable is 32 bits long, which means a **signed int** can hold values from -2147483648 to 2147483647. How can you find the storage capacities of the integer types for your C++ compiler? You can use the **sizeof** operator, as well as the constants defined in the climits header file. The **sizeof** operator reports the size, in bytes, of an object in memory or of raw type like **int**, and the climits header file defines constants like **MIN_INT** and **MAX_INT** to give you the minimum and maximim values that can be stored in the **int** type. Here's a program, intlimits.cpp, that puts all this to work, displaying the size of the **char**, **short**, **int**, and **long** types, as well as the maximum and minimum values you can store in those types and in those types when they're treated as **unsigned** (the default is **signed**):

```
#include <iostream>
#include <climits>
using namespace std;

int main()
{
    cout << "The char type is " << sizeof (char) << " byte long" << endl;
    cout << "The short type is " << sizeof (short) << " bytes long" << endl;
    cout << "The int type is " << sizeof (int) << " bytes long" << endl;
    cout << "The long type is " << sizeof (long) << " bytes long" << endl;
    cout << endl;
```

```
    cout << "Minimum char value: " << CHAR_MIN << endl;
    cout << "Maximum char value: " << CHAR_MAX << endl;
    cout << "Minimum unsigned char value: 0" << endl;
    cout << "Maximum unsigned char value: " << UCHAR_MAX << endl;
    cout << endl;

    cout << "Minimum short value: " << SHRT_MIN << endl;
    cout << "Maximum short value: " << SHRT_MAX << endl;
    cout << "Minimum unsigned short value: 0" << endl;
    cout << "Maximum unsigned short value: " << USHRT_MAX << endl;
    cout << endl;

    cout << "Minimum int value: " << INT_MIN << endl;
    cout << "Maximum int value: " << INT_MAX << endl;
    cout << "Minimum unsigned int value: 0" << endl;
    cout << "Maximum unsigned int value: " << UINT_MAX << endl;
    cout << endl;

    cout << "Minimum long value: " << LONG_MIN << endl;
    cout << "Maximum long value: " << LONG_MAX << endl;
    cout << "Minimum unsigned long value: 0" << endl;
    cout << "Maximum unsigned long value: " << ULONG_MAX << endl;
    cout << endl;

    return 0;
}
```

Here's the result for a typical compiler—note that **int** is the same as **long**, which is not unusual:

```
The char type is 1 byte long
The short type is 2 bytes long
The int type is 4 bytes long
The long type is 4 bytes long

Minimum char value: -128
Maximum char value: 127
Minimum unsigned char value: 0
Maximum unsigned char value: 255

Minimum short value: -32768
Maximum short value: 32767
Minimum unsigned short value: 0
Maximum unsigned short value: 65535
```

```
Minimum int value: -2147483648
Maximum int value: 2147483647
Minimum unsigned int value: 0
Maximum unsigned int value: 4294967295

Minimum long value: -2147483648
Maximum long value: 2147483647
Minimum unsigned long value: 0
Maximum unsigned long value: 4294967295
```


***NOTE:** Some compilers have additional, non-standard integer types that store even higher precision integer values. Those types are usually named _I64 or _int64, and they store integer values in 64 bits.*

Working with Integer Literals

Integer literals are simple integer numbers in your code; we saw an example with integer literals at the beginning of the In Depth section of this chapter:

```
int main()
{
    int number_of_cats, number_of_dogs;

    number_of_cats = 297;
    number_of_dogs = 319;

    cout << "I have " << number_of_cats << " cats and ";
    cout << number_of_dogs << " dogs." << endl;

    return 0;
}
```

C++ stores integer literals using the **int** type by default unless there's some reason not to (such as the literal is too large for the **int** type). You can also indicate the type of an integer literal with these suffixes:

- l or L stands for a long integer literal, such as 54321L.
- u or U stands for an unsigned int literal, such as 345U.
- ul (in any combination of order and case, such as LU or uL) stands for an unsigned long literal, such as 314159UL.

You can also specify that a literal is in hexadecimal, base 16, by prefixing it with "0x", such as 0x10 (which is 16 in decimal) or that it's in octal by prefixing with a zero, "0", such as 015 (which is 13 in decimal).

NOTE: *Because octal literals start with a zero, you should never preface decimal literals with a zero.*

Working with **bool** Data Types

There's also a C++ type named **bool** that holds only two values, true or false. This type, called the boolean type, was named after George Bool, who worked with mathematical representations of logic. You can use the **bool** type with the C++ keywords **true** and **false**. Because many statements, like the **if** statement, evaluate the truth value of an expression before executing code, boolean variables are often used with such statements. Here's an example:

```
#include <iostream>
using namespace std;

int main()
{
    bool display_the_text;

    display_the_text = true;

    if(display_the_text) {
        cout << "Have you renewed your insurance?" << endl;
    }

    return 0;
}
```

Here's what this example, bool.cpp, looks like at work:

```
%bool
Have you renewed your insurance?
```

Working with **bool** Literals

You can assign the C++ keywords the C++ keywords **true** or **false** like this:

```
bool start_the_process = true;
```

In fact, you can assign any non-zero value to a **bool** variable, and because non-zero values are treated as true in a true/false context (see "Basic Skills: True or False Values in C++" in Chapter 1), the variable ends up holding **true**. Assigning a zero value means that the variable will hold a value of **false**:

```
bool start = -3224; // start holds "true"
bool start = 0;     // start holds "false"
```

Working with Floating Point Data Types

Floating point numbers have fractional (that is, decimal) parts, like 3.14159 (although it's possible that the fractional part is zero, as with 6.0000). You can also store numbers in the format 3.14159E+08, where E stands for "exponent," so this value stands for 3.14159 x 10^8, or 1.2345e-9 (e or E both stand for "exponent" for nearly all compilers), which stands for 1.2345 x 10^{-9}.

There are three floating point types in standard C++: **float**, **double**, and **long double** (all these formats can store signs as well, so there are no corresponding unsigned versions, as there are for integer types). Although the actual capacity of these types depends on your compiler, the C++ standard does make some minimum requirements:

- A **float** must be at least 32 bits.
- A **double** must be at least 48 bits long (and is typically 64).
- A **long double** must at least as large as **double** (and is typically 96 or 128 bits long; in many compilers, **double** and **long double** are the same).

So what is the storage capacity of these types for your compiler? See the next section.

What Is the Storage Capacity of the Floating Point Types?

As with integer types, the precision of floating point values depends on your C++ compiler. However, as with integer types, you can use the **sizeof** operator to determine the size of floating point variables for your compiler in bytes. You can also use the constants defined in the header file cfloat to determine the precision of floating point numbers for your compiler. Here's an example, floatlimits.cpp, that does that. Note that floating point numbers are divided into two parts, the *mantissa* and the *exponent*, and the number of mantissa digits given below are the number of *binary*, not decimal, digits in the mantissa:

```
#include <iostream>
#include <cfloat>
using namespace std;

int main()
{
    cout << "The float type is " << sizeof (float) << " bytes long" << endl;
    cout << "The double type is " << sizeof (double) << " bytes long" <<
        endl;
    cout << "The long double type is " << sizeof (long double)
        << " bytes long" << endl;
    cout << endl;

    cout << "Minimum float value: " << FLT_MIN << endl;
    cout << "Maximum float value: " << FLT_MAX << endl;
    cout << "Number of binary mantissa digits: " << FLT_MANT_DIG << endl;
    cout << "Maximum exponent for decimal numbers: " << FLT_MAX_10_EXP <<
        endl;
    cout << "Minimum exponent for decimal numbers: " << FLT_MIN_10_EXP <<
        endl;
    cout << endl;

    cout << "Minimum double value: " << DBL_MIN << endl;
    cout << "Maximum double value: " << DBL_MAX << endl;
    cout << "Number of binary mantissa digits: " << DBL_MANT_DIG << endl;
    cout << "Maximum exponent for decimal numbers: " << DBL_MAX_10_EXP <<
        endl;
    cout << "Minimum exponent for decimal numbers: " << DBL_MIN_10_EXP <<
        endl;
    cout << endl;

    cout << "Minimum long double value: " << LDBL_MIN << endl;
    cout << "Maximum long double value: " << LDBL_MAX << endl;
    cout << "Number of binary mantissa digits: " << LDBL_MANT_DIG << endl;
    cout << "Maximum exponent for decimal numbers: " <<
        LDBL_MAX_10_EXP << endl;
```

```
    cout << "Minimum exponent for decimal numbers: " <<
        LDBL_MIN_10_EXP << endl;
    cout << endl;

    return 0;
}
```

Here's the result of this program, floatlimits.cpp, in a typical compiler:

```
%floatlimits
The float type is 4 bytes long
The double type is 8 bytes long
The long double type is 10 bytes long

Minimum float value: 1.17549e-38
Maximum float value: 3.40282e+38
Number of binary mantissa digits: 24
Maximum exponent for decimal numbers: 38
Minimum exponent for decimal numbers: -37

Minimum double value: 2.22507e-308
Maximum double value: 1.79769e+308
Number of binary mantissa digits: 53
Maximum exponent for decimal numbers: 308
Minimum exponent for decimal numbers: -307

Minimum long double value: 3.3621e-4932
Maximum long double value: 1.18973e+4932
Number of binary mantissa digits: 64
Maximum exponent for decimal numbers: 4932
Minimum exponent for decimal numbers: -4931
```

NOTE: *How does* ***cout*** *display floating point numbers? By default, standard C++ displays six digits total, switching to e or E notation after a million. Standard C++* ***cout*** *now supresses trailing zeros too (older versions of C++ did not).*

NOTE: *Remember that the precision of floating point numbers is not unlimited—adding .0000000000000000000000000000001 to a floating point number may not actually change it at all.*

Working with Floating Point Literals

There are several ways to indicate that a literal value is a floating point literal. The easiest is simply to place a decimal place in a numeric literal, like this: 1.23. You can also use e or E (you can use either letter) notation to specify a base 10 exponent, such as 1.23e+10, which equals 1.23 x 10^{10} (the + is optional before the exponent, because it's assumed unless you use a - sign), or 1.23E-5, which equals 1.23 x 10^{-5}.

By default, floating point literals are stored as using the **double** type by compilers unless there's some reason not to. If you want to make a floating point literal explicitly a **float**, you can use the suffix f or F, as in 3.14159f or 3.14159F. If you want to make a literal a **long double**, use the suffix l or L, as in 3.14159l or 3.14159L. Here are some examples:

- **2.222f** or **2.222F**—A float literal
- **2.222**—A double literal
- **2.222l** or **2.222L**—A long double literal

Introducing the C++ string Class

We've seen the simple data types in this chapter already, but there's one more type that bears mention, even though it's a C++ class, not a simple data type—the C++ **string** class (technically speaking, it's the C++ **string** template class, based on the Standard Template Library **basic_string** template). We'll see this class in depth in Chapter 15, and we'll get an introduction to it here. This class lets you store text strings almost as though they were simple data types—even though we haven't worked with classes and objects yet, there's no problem here. Here's an example; in this case, I'm creating a string named **string1**, and initializing it to the text "**No**" by placing that text in parentheses after the name of the string, **string1** (as we'll see, this passes the text to the **string** class's *constructor*, initializing the **string** object); in most compilers (but not all), you have to include the string header file as well:

```
#include <iostream>
#include <string>
using namespace std;
```

```
int main()
{
    string string1("No ");
    .
    .
    .
```

You can also create a string as you would a simple variable and assign text to it with the = operator:

```
#include <iostream>
#include <string>
using namespace std;

int main()
{
    string string1("No ");
    string string2;

    string2 = "problems";
    .
    .
    .
```

Now you can add, or concatenate, the two strings with the + operator, and even use the += operator like this:

```
#include <iostream>
#include <string>
using namespace std;

int main()
{
    string string1("No ");
    string string2;

    string2 = "problems";

    string string3 = string1 + string2;

    cout << string3 << endl;
```

```
    string3 += " at all.";

    cout << string3 << endl;

    return 0;
}
```


Here's the result of this code, string1.cpp:

```
%string1
No problems
No problems at all.
```

The **string** objects also come with plenty of built-in methods. As mentioned in Chapter 1, a method is a function that is built into a class or object, and you can access those methods with the dot operator, **.** (see Chapter 8 for more details). Here's an example showing how to find the length of a string with the **length** method, find a substring with the **find** method, find the last occurrence of a character with the **find_last_of** method, and even replace text with new text using the **replace** method:

```
#include <iostream>
#include <string>
using namespace std;

int main()
{
    string string1("No problems.");

    cout << "String length: " << string1.length() << endl;

    cout << "Location of \"problems\" " << string1.find("problems") << endl;

    cout << "Location of last \'o\': " << string1.find_last_of('o') << endl;

    cout << string1.replace(string1.length() - 1, 1, " at all.") << endl;

    return 0;
}
```

Here's the result of this program, stringmethods.cpp (note that the numeric positions displayed here are 0-based; that is, the first character in the string is character 0):

```
%stringmethods
String length: 12
Location of "problem" 3
Location of last 'o': 5
No problems at all
```

For more on the standard C++ **string** class, take a look at the next section.

Using **cin** to Read Individual Characters and Whole Strings

As we saw in the previous chapter, you can use **cin** to read a word at a time from the keyboard, but that's not convenient sometimes when you're working with strings. For example, you may want to read a whole multiword line of text from the keyboard, or just one key at a time. Here's an example; in this case, I'll use the function **getline** (this function is built into C++ as part of the standard template library, of which the **string** class is a part) to read a whole line at once by passing that function the **cin** object itself and the variable we want to place the text in, **string1**. I'll also use the **cin** object's **get** method to read just one key:

```
#include <iostream>
#include <string>
using namespace std;

int main()
{
    string string1;

    cout << "Type a few words: ";

    getline(cin, string1);

    cout << "You typed: " << string1 << endl;

    cout << "Type a word: ";
```

```
    string1 = cin.get();
    cout << "The first character was: " << string1 << endl;

    return 0;
}
```


Here's what this program, stringinput.cpp, looks like in action:

```
%stringinput
Type a few words: Now is the time
You typed: Now is the time
Type a word: Hello
The first character was: H
```


Related solution:	Found on page:
Reading C-Style Strings With **cin** Methods	140

Declaring Constants with **const**

You can use the **const** modifier to declare constants in C++. A constant is a typed value that can't be changed; in C, you often used the preprocessor directive to create constants, like this:

```
#include <iostream>
using namespace std;

#define MAX_DAYS 31;

int main()
{
    int days = MAX_DAYS;

    cout << "There are " << days << " in this month." << endl;

    return 0;
}
```

This works, but C++ actually has a better way—the **const** modifier (although you can still use **#define** in C++, and should do so to define tokens the preprocessor will use—see "Basic Skills: Using Header Files" in Chapter 1). This keyword modifies the declaration of a data item, making it into a constant that can't be modified (a constant is not an lvalue, and the compiler will complain that you need an lvalue to store a new value). Here's how the code listed above looks when **const** is used:

```
#include <iostream>
using namespace std;

int main()
{
    const int MAX_DAYS = 31;

    int days = MAX_DAYS;

    cout << "There are " << days << " in this month." << endl;

    return 0;
}
```

Why is this better? It's better because you can specify a constant's type with **const**, which enables type checking. And you can use **const** with arrays and structures in C++, which you can't do with **#define**. We'll see **const** a lot in this book, because using **const** indicates to the compiler that you're not going to change an item's value, which is useful when you work with pointers.

***NOTE:** When you define a constant, the C++ convention is to use capital letters for the name (like **MAX_DAYS**), or at least to use leading capital letters. Doing so makes it clear that the name corresponds to a constant, not an lvalue.*

Related solution:	Found on page:
Basic Skills: Using Header Files	51

What Type Is a Given Variable?

You can use runtime type information (RTTI) to determine the type of simple variables when a program is running. I'll take a look at RTTI in Chapter 12, but here's a sneak preview. To determine the type of a variable, you can use the **typeid** operator, like this, where I'm displaying the name of an integer variable's type:

```
#include <iostream>
#include <typeid>
using namespace std;
```

```
int main()
{
    int integer1 = 200;

    cout << "The type of integer1 is: " << typeid(integer1).name() << endl;

    return 0;
}
```


Here's the result of this program, typeid.cpp, where we learn that **integer1**'s type is **int**:

```
%typeid
The type of integer1 is: int
```

Conversion between Data Types

As discussed in the In Depth section of this chapter, because C++ variables are strongly typed, you have to be careful when mixing types. Such mixing can occur:

- In expressions of mixed data types
- In assignments
- When passing an argument to a function where the type does not match argument list
- When returning an expression from a function where the type does not match declared return type

As mentioned in the In Depth section of this chapter, there are two kinds of type conversions—*implicit* and *explicit*. What's the difference? Implicit conversions are handled by the compiler, and you handle explicit conversions yourself.

Implicit Type Conversions

As an example, look at this code, which we saw earlier in the In Depth section; here, I'm adding the values in two different types of variables—**short** and **long**:

```
#include <iostream>
using namespace std;

int main()
{
    short big = 48272;
```

```
    long bigger = 138281285;

    cout << "The sum of big and bigger = " << bigger + big << endl;

    return 0;
}
```


Even though I'm adding a **short** to a **long**, there's no problem; the compiler converts the **short** value to a **long** value implicitly to add it to the other **long**.

Here are the rules for conversion in expressions:

- If one operand is **long double**, the other operand is made a **long double**.
- Otherwise, if one operand is **double**, the other operand is made a **double**.
- Otherwise, if one operand is **float**, the other operand is made a **float**.
- Otherwise, if either operand is **unsigned long**, the other operand is made an **unsigned long**.
- Otherwise, if one operand is a **long** and the other is an **unsigned int**, then if the **long** type is a superset of the **unsigned int**, the **unsigned int** is converted to **long**.
- Otherwise, if one operand is a **long**, the other is made a **long**.
- Otherwise, if one operand is an **unsigned int**, the other is made an **unsigned int**.
- Otherwise, both operands are made into **int** types.

The rule is always to promote smaller type to larger type to avoid loss of precision. Everything smaller than an **int** is converted to an **int** when there is any question of loss of precision.

Explicit Type Conversions

There are times when you know what you're doing when mixing data types, and you need to tell the compiler that things are okay. We saw this example in the In Depth section of this chapter:

```
#include <iostream>
using namespace std;
int main()
{
    int sum;
    int ten = 10;
    float pi = 3.14159;
```

```
    sum = pi + ten;

    cout << "The integer sum = " << sum << endl;

    return 0;
}
```


Here, I'm adding 3.14159 to 10 and storing the result in an integer, which means the integer will be left holding 13, because C++ will truncate 3.14159 to 3. If that's okay with you, and you want that to happen, then you should tell C++ that things are fine, and you can do that by casting the floating point variable **pi** to an integer temporarily (the actual value in **pi** is not affected after the statement with the cast is executed). Here are the ways you can perform type casts in C++:

- **(*type*)**—Old style cast.
- **const_cast <*type*> (*expression*)**—This type of cast casts away "const"-ness.
- **dynamic_cast <*type*> (*expression*)**—This type of cast supports runtime identification of class objects addressed by pointer or reference.
- **reinterpret_cast <*type*> (*expression*)**—This type of cast supports low-level reinterpretation of the bit pattern of the expression.
- **static_cast <*type*> (*expression*)**—This type of cast simply makes explicit casts, without runtime type checking, and turns off warning messages.

In the old days, you would simply cast a **float** into an **int** by placing the keyword **int** in parentheses in front of the **float**:

```
#include <iostream>
using namespace std;
int main()
{
    int sum;
    int ten = 10;
    float pi = 3.14159;

    sum = (int) pi + ten;

    cout << "The integer sum = " << sum << endl;

    return 0;
}
```

However, the ANSI/ISO committee was concerned that many programmers used this technique simply to effectively turn off type checking. Now there are four cast operators, **const_cast**, **dynamic_cast**, **reinterpret_cast**, and **static_cast**, to handle the different situations where you need casts. We'll see more about how to use each type of cast throughout the book, as the need for each cast comes up, but the one that's simplest to use here is the **static_cast**, which is the most like the old-style casts. To use this operator, you supply the new type you want the expression you're casting to be, like this:


```
#include <iostream>
using namespace std;
int main()
{
    int sum;
    int ten = 10;
    float pi = 3.14159;

    sum = static_cast <int> (pi) + ten;

    cout << "The integer sum = " << sum << endl;

    return 0;
}
```

And now the compiler will accept the statement with mixed types without problem.

Related solution:	Found on page:
Converting between C-Style Strings and Numbers	137

What C++ Operators Are Available?

This chapter begins our coverage of the C++ operators. Here, we'll take a look at the basic operators like +, -, *, /, %, **sizeof**, ?:, the comma operator (,) and more. We'll see the other operators in the chapters where they make sense to use. For example, you use operators like -> with pointers, so we'll see it in Chapter 5 because it wouldn't make much sense to use it before introducing pointers; the **typeid** operator works with runtime type identification so we'll see it in Chapter 11; operators like || and && are used to connect logical clauses together in conditional and loop statements, so we'll see them in Chapter 4, and so on.

For reference, you'll find the C++ operators in Table 2.3, divided into precedence groups (see the next section for the details on operator precedence). What does the term "Associativity" in that table mean? See the next section also. I'll take a look at most of these operators in the rest of the chapter, in order of their precedence.

Table 2.3 C++ operators.

Operator	Name or Meaning	Associativity
::	Scope resolution	None
::	Global	None
.	Member selection (object)	Left to right
->	Member selection (pointer)	Left to right
++	Postfix increment	None
--	Postfix decrement	None
[ ]	Array subscript	Left to right
( )	Function call	Left to right
( )	Conversion	None
typeid( )	type name	None
const_cast	Type cast (conversion)	None
dynamic_cast	Type cast (conversion)	None
reinterpret_cast	Type cast (conversion)	None
static_cast	Type cast (conversion)	None
sizeof	Size of object	None
sizeof ( )	Size of type	None
++	Prefix increment	None
--	Prefix decrement	None
(*type*)	Type cast (conversion)	Right to left
new	Allocate object	None
new[ ]	Allocate array	None
delete	Deallocate object	None
delete[ ]	Deallocate array	None
*	Dereference	None

(continued)

Table 2.3 C++ operators *(continued)*.

Operator	Name or Meaning	Associativity
&	Address-of	None
+	Unary plus	None
-	Arithmetic negation (unary)	None
!	Logical NOT	None
~	Bitwise complement	None
.*	Apply pointer to class member (objects)	Left to right
->*	Dereference pointer to class member	Left to right
*	Multiplication	Left to right
/	Division	Left to right
%	Remainder (modulus)	Left to right
+	Addition	Left to right
-	Subtraction	Left to right
<<	Left shift	Left to right
>>	Right shift	Left to right
<	Less than	Left to right
>	Greater than	Left to right
<=	Less than or equal to	Left to right
>=	Greater than or equal to	Left to right
==	Equality	Left to right
!=	Inequality	Left to right
&	Bitwise AND	Left to right
^	Bitwise exclusive OR	Left to right
|	Bitwise OR	Left to right

(continued)

Table 2.3 C++ operators *(continued)*.

<table>
<tr><th>Operator</th><th>Name or Meaning</th><th>Associativity</th></tr>
<tr><td>&&</td><td>Logical AND</td><td>Left to right</td></tr>
<tr><td>||</td><td>Logical OR</td><td>Left to right</td></tr>
<tr><td>e1?e2:e3</td><td>Conditional</td><td>Right to left</td></tr>
<tr><td>=</td><td>Assignment</td><td>Right to left</td></tr>
<tr><td>*=</td><td>Multiplication assignment</td><td>Right to left</td></tr>
<tr><td>/=</td><td>Division assignment</td><td>Right to left</td></tr>
<tr><td>%=</td><td>Modulus assignment</td><td>Right to left</td></tr>
<tr><td>+=</td><td>Addition assignment</td><td>Right to left</td></tr>
<tr><td>-=</td><td>Subtraction assignment</td><td>Right to left</td></tr>
<tr><td><<=</td><td>Left-shift assignment</td><td>Right to left</td></tr>
<tr><td>>>=</td><td>Right-shift assignment</td><td>Right to left</td></tr>
<tr><td>&=</td><td>Bitwise AND assignment</td><td>Right to left</td></tr>
<tr><td>|=</td><td>Bitwise inclusive OR assignment</td><td>Right to left</td></tr>
<tr><td>^=</td><td>Bitwise exclusive OR assignment</td><td>Right to left</td></tr>
<tr><td>throw</td><td>Throw an exception</td><td>None</td></tr>
<tr><td>,</td><td>Comma</td><td>Left to Right</td></tr>
</table>

Operator Precedence in C++

Take a look at this code, which tries to add 12 and 24 and then divide the sum by 6 to get 36 / 6 = 6:

```
#include <iostream>
using namespace std;
int main()
{
```

```
    double value;

    value = 12 + 24 / 6;

    cout << "The value = " << value << endl;

    return 0;
}
```

Here's the actual result of this code:

```
%precedence
The value = 16
```


Clearly, there's something going on that's different from what's expected. In fact, C++ sets up a very clear precedence of operators, which means that if it finds two operators at the same level in a statement (that is, not enclosed in parentheses or braces), it'll execute the operator with the higher precedence first. As it happens, the / operator has higher precedence than the + operator, so in the expression above, 24 is first divided by 6 and the result is added to 12, which gives 16.

To specify to C++ exactly the order in which you want operators to be evaluated, you can use parentheses to group those operations you want performed first. Here's how that looks in this case, where the parentheses around 12 + 24 make sure that operation is performed first:

```
#include <iostream>
using namespace std;
int main()
{
    double value;

    value = (12 + 24) / 6;

    cout << "The value = " << value << endl;

    return 0;
}
```

And here's the result of this code:

```
%precdence
The value = 6
```

You'll find the C++ operator precedence spelled out in Table 2.3, in groups from highest to lowest (the operators in each group have the same precedence). When two operators have the same precedence, C++ checks to see if they have right-to-left or left-to-right *associativity*. Operators associate with either the expression on their left or the expression on their right, and in C++ this is called associativity. For example, because multiplication and division associate left to right, in the expression 12 / 6 * 4, you first divide 12 by 6 to get 2, and then multiply by 4 to get 8. How does associativity influence precedence? If there are two left-to-right operators working on the same operand, C++ will apply the left-hand operator first. If there are two right-to-left operators working on the same operand, C++ will apply the right-hand operator first.

Incrementing and Decrementing: ++ and --

The ++ operator increments its operand by one, and the -- operator decrements its operand by one. For example, if **value** holds 0, then after you execute **value++**, **value** will hold 1. These operators were introduced in C to make incrementing and decrementing values, which are very common operations, easier (and they're so popular that they gave their name to C++, as an incremented version of C).

Here's an important point: ++ and -- can be either *postfix* operators (used like this: **value++**) or *prefix* operators (used like this: **++value**). When used as postfix operators, they are executed *after* the rest of the statement, and when used as prefix operators, *before* the rest of the statement. This is something you have to watch out for, because if you have code like this:

```
value2 = value1++;
```

then when the statement is completed, **value2** will actually be left with the *original* value in **value1**, and the value in **value1** will be incremented. Here's an example showing how that works:

```
#include <iostream>
using namespace std;
int main()
{
    int value1 = 0, value2 = 0;

    cout << "value1 = " << value1 << endl;
    cout << "value2 = " << value2 << endl;
```

```
    value2 = value1++;

    cout << "After value2 = value1++..." << endl;
    cout << "value1 = " << value1 << endl;
    cout << "value2 = " << value2 << endl;

    int value3 = 0, value4 = 0;

    cout << endl;
    cout << "value3 = " << value3 << endl;
    cout << "value4 = " << value4 << endl;

    value4 = ++value3;

    cout << "After value4 = ++value3..." << endl;
    cout << "value3 = " << value3 << endl;
    cout << "value4 = " << value4 << endl;

    return 0;
}
```


And here's the result of this code:

```
%increment
value1 = 0
value2 = 0
After value2 = value1++...
value1 = 1
value2 = 0

value3 = 0
value4 = 0
After value4 = ++value3...
value3 = 1
value4 = 1
```

Unary Not: ~ and !

The ~ operator is the bitwise unary Not operator, and ! is the logical unary Not operator. The ~ operator flips all the bits of numeric arguments, and the ! operator flips true values to false and false values to true.

Here's an example; in this case, I'll flip all the bits of the most positive short value, 32767, to find the most negative short value, and I'll flip a boolean value from true to false:

```
#include <iostream>
using namespace std;
int main()
{
    short short1 = 32767;
    bool boolean1 = true;

    cout << "Most negative short = " << ~short1 << endl;
    cout << "!true = " << !boolean1 << endl;

    return 0;
}
```

Here's the result of this code, flip.cpp (some compilers, like Microsoft's Visual C++, may display 0 instead of false):

```
%flip
Most negative short = -32768
!true = false
```

If I had set an integer to 0 and then flipped its bits with the ~ operator to 1111111111111111 in binary, C++ would have displayed the resulting value as -1, because C++ uses two's-complement notation for negative numbers, which means the leading bit is 1 for negative numbers and 0 for 0 and positive numbers (see "Signed and Unsigned Data" earlier in this chapter).

The **sizeof** Operator

You can use the **sizeof** operator to determine the number of bytes used by an object in memory. You can also use this operator on raw types as we did earlier in "What Is the Storage Capacity of the Integer Types?" earlier in this chapter.

Here's an example that displays the size of an integer variable and the integer types:

```
#include <iostream>
using namespace std;
```

```
int main()
{
    int integer = 4;

    cout << "The variable named integer is " << sizeof (integer) <<
        " bytes long" << endl;

    cout << endl;
    cout << "The char type is " << sizeof (char) << " byte long" << endl;
    cout << "The short type is " << sizeof (short) << " bytes long" << endl;
    cout << "The int type is " << sizeof (int) << " bytes long" << endl;
    cout << "The long type is " << sizeof (long) << " bytes long" << endl;
    cout << endl;

    return 0;
}
```

Here's what this code, sizeof.cpp, looks like in action:

```
%sizeof
The variable named integer is 4 bytes long

The char type is 1 byte long
The short type is 2 bytes long
The int type is 4 bytes long
The long type is 4 bytes long
```

Multiplication and Division: * and /

You use * to multiply values and / to divide values in C++. Here's an example in which I use * and / on double values and then do the same thing on integer values. I perform multiplication and division on integer values to show that the fractional part of math results are truncated when you use integers, so if you want to divide and make sure you retain precision, you probably shouldn't be using integers. Here's the code:

```
#include <iostream>
using namespace std;
int main()
```

```
{
    double double1 = 4, double2 = 6, double3 = 5, doubleResult;

    doubleResult = double1 * double2 / double3;

    cout << "4 * 6 / 5 = " << doubleResult << endl;

    int int1 = 4, int2 = 6, int3 = 5, intResult;

    intResult = int1 * int2 / int3;

    cout << "With integer math, 4 * 6 / 5 = " << intResult << endl;

    return 0;
}
```

Here's result of this code, multdiv.cpp (you may get a warning from your compiler when compiling this example):

```
%multdiv
4 * 6 / 5 = 4.8
With integer math, 4 * 6 / 5 = 4
```

Modulus: %

You use the modulus operator, %, to return the remainder of a division operation. For example, 10 / 3 = 3 with a remainder of 1, so 10 % 3 equals 1. Note that the modulus operator is especially useful when you convert between bases, because you can use it to successively strip digits off a number by using the modulus operator with the base you're converting to. Here's a slightly advanced example that does just that, mod.cpp, which converts a number from base 10 to base 16. In this case, I'm using a C++ stack template, which is a construct we'll get to in Chapter 16, to reverse the order of the digits as they are stripped off the number to convert, and the >> operator to shift the number to convert right by four binary places to simulate integer division by 16 (see "Shift Operators: >> and <<" later in this chapter):

```
#include <iostream>
#include <stack>
using namespace std;
```

```
int main()
{
    int value = 32, temp = value;
    stack<int> st;

    while (temp > 0) {
        st.push(temp % 16);
        temp >>= 4;
    }

    cout << "Converting " << value << " yields 0x";

    while(!st.empty()) {
        cout << st.top();
        st.pop();
    }

    return 0;
}
```

Here's the result of this code, mod.cpp:

```
%mod
Converting 32 yields 0x20
```

Addition and Subtraction: + and -

The old standby numeric operators are + and -, which you use for addition and subtraction, respectively. Here's an example:

```
#include <iostream>
using namespace std;
int main()
{
    int operand1 = 5, operand2 = 4, sum, diff;

    sum = operand1 + operand2;
    diff = operand1 - operand2;

    cout << operand1 << " + " << operand2 << " = " << sum << endl;
    cout << operand1 << " - " << operand2 << " = " << diff << endl;
```

```
    return 0;
}
```

Here's the result of this code, addsub.cpp:

```
%addsub
5 + 4 = 9
5 - 4 = 1
```

Shift Operators: >> and <<

You use the shift operators to shift all the bits of a number left or right a specified number of binary places. There are two shift operators: right shift, >>, and left shift, <<. Here's how you use these operators:

```
new_value = value << number_places;
new_value = value >> number_places;
```

For example, 16 >> 2 shifts the number 16 right by two binary places, which is the same as dividing it by 4, so 16 >> 2 equals 4. You commonly use the shift operators when packing binary values into an **int** or **long** as fields, because you can add a number to the **int** or **long**, and then shift it left to make room for the next field of data.

Here's one thing to know: The >> operator respects the sign of its operand, and because a negative value means that the left-most bit is 1, shifting a negative number right introduces a new 1 at the left, so shifting 1111111111111100, which is -4 as a **short**, turns it into 1111111111111110, which is -2. And shifting -1, which is 1111111111111111, gives you 1111111111111111, which is still -1. (For this reason, the Java language introduced a >>> operator, which lets you work with the actual bits in a number when you shift them right and not have a 1 added to the left when shifting negative numbers.)

Here' an example that puts the shift operators to work:

```
#include <iostream>
using namespace std;

int main()
{
    int value = 16, negValue = -1;
```

```
    cout << value << " << 2 = " << (value << 2) << endl;
    cout << value << " >> 2 = " << (value >> 2) << endl;
    cout << negValue << " >> 2 = " << (negValue >> 2) << endl;

    return 0;
}
```

And here's the result of this code, lrshift.cpp:

```
%lrshift
16 << 2 = 64
16 >> 2 = 4
-1 >> 2 = -1
```


Bitwise Operators And, Xor, and Or: &, ^, and |

The bitwise operators let you examine the individual bits of values—that is, they treat their operands as binary numbers, and each bit corresponds to a binary digit. For example, when you use the & bitwise operator with two operands, each bit in one operand is logically *Anded* with the corresponding bit in the other operand, and if both bits are 1, a 1 appears in that place in the result; otherwise a zero will appear in that place. For example, that means that I can test if bit 3 (counted from the right, where the rightmost bit is bit 0) of a value is set to 1 by Anding the value with a number where I know only one bit—the third bit—is set to 1. If the result of the And operation is *not* zero, the third bit of the original value was set. Here's how that looks in code:

```
#include <iostream>
using namespace std;
int main()
{
    int value = 12;
    int bit3setting = value & 1 << 3;

    if (bit3setting != 0) {
        cout << "Bit 3 is set." << endl;
    }
    else {
        cout << "Bit 3 is not set." << endl;
    }
```

```
    return 0;
}
```

And here's the result of this code, setbit.cpp:


```
%setbit
Bit 3 is set.
```

You can find the bitwise operators in Table 2.4. In overview, here's how they work: The Or operator, |, returns 0 when both bits are 0, and returns 1 otherwise. The And operator, &, returns 1 when both bits are 1, and returns 0 otherwise. And the Xor ("exclusive or") operator, ^, returns 1 when one bit is 0 and the other is 1, and returns 0 otherwise.

Table 2.4 The bitwise operators.

x	y	x | y (Or)	x & y (And)	x ^ y (Xor)
0	0	0	0	0
1	0	1	0	1
0	1	1	0	1
1	1	1	1	0

The If-Then-Else Operator: ?:

There's a C++ operator that acts much like an if-else statement, and it's the ?: ternary operator. This operator is called a ternary operator because it takes three operands, a condition and two values:

```
value = condition ? value1 : value2;
```

If ***condition*** is true, the ?: operator returns ***value1***, and it returns ***value2*** otherwise. In this way, the statement above works like this **if** statement:

```
if (condition) {
    value = value1;
}
else {
    value = value2;
}
```

Here's an example where I find the absolute value of a number:

```
#include <iostream>
using namespace std;

int main()
{
    int absval, value = -5;

    absval = value > 0 ? value : -value;

    cout << "The absolute value of " << value << " is " << absval << endl;

    return 0;
}
```

And here's the result of this code, abs.cpp:

```
%abs
The absolute value of -5 is 5
```

Assignment Operators: = and *operator=*

The most basic operators are the assignment operators, and I've been using these operators throughout the book already. You use the = operator to assign a variable a literal value or the value in another variable, like this:

```
#include <iostream>
using namespace std;
int main()
{
    int value = 12;

    cout << "The value = " << value << endl;

    return 0;
}
```

Here's the result:

```
%assign
The value = 12
```

As in C++, you can perform multiple assignments in the same statement (this works because the assignment operator itself returns the assigned value):

```
#include <iostream>
using namespace std;
int main()
{
    int value1, value2, value3;

    value1 = value2 = value3 = 12;

    cout << "value1 = " << value1 << endl;
    cout << "value2 = " << value2 << endl;
    cout << "value3 = " << value3 << endl;

    return 0;
}
```

Here's the result:

```
%multassign
value1 = 12
value2 = 12
value3 = 12
```

Because the result of an assignment is the value assigned, you sometimes see code like this in C++ (for more on the **while** loop, see "The **while** Loop" in Chapter 4, and for more on **cin.get**, see "Using **cin** to Read Individual Characters and Whole Strings" earlier in this chapter), which combines an assignment and a conditional test:

```
#include <iostream>
using namespace std;

int main()
{
    char character;

    while((character = cin.get()) != 'q'){
        cout << character;
    }

    return 0;
}
```

You can also combine many operators with the assignment operator, =. For example, += is the addition assignment operator, which means value += 2 is a shortcut for value = value + 2. Here's an example putting the multiplication assignment operator to work:

```
#include <iostream>
using namespace std;
int main()
{
    int value = 10;

    value *= 2;

    cout << "value * 2 = " << value << endl;

    return 0;
}
```

And here's the result:

```
%app
value * 2 = 20
```

There are quite a few combination assignment operators, and here they are:

- **%=**—Modulus assignment
- **&=**—Bitwise And assignment
- ***=**—Multiplication assignment
- **/=**—Division assignment
- **^=**—Bitwise Xor assignment
- **|=**—Bitwise Or assignment
- **+=**—Addition assignment
- **<<=**—Shift left assignment
- **<=**—Less than or equal to
- **-=**—Subtraction assignment
- **>>=**—Shift right assignment

The Comma Operator

In C++, a comma is also an operator, and you can use it to effectively execute multiple statements in one. Here's an example:

```
int1 = 10, int2 = 20;
```

Here, the expressions separated by the comma are executed left to right; **int1** is left holding 10 and **int2** is left holding 20. The return value of a number of expressions separated by commas is the value of the right-most expression. For another example of the comma operator at work, see "The **for** Loop" in Chapter 4.

Related solution:	*Found on page:*
The **for** Loop	186

The C++ Utility Functions: Math, Time, Trig, Random Numbers, and More

Besides the math operators we've seen in this chapter, C++ also includes a number of utility functions like **cos** for cosine and **sin** for sine. Here's a partial list to get you acquainted with the possibilities—for many of these functions, you'll have to include the cmath header file:

- **abs**—Absolute value
- **acos**—Arccosine
- **asin**—Arcsine
- **atan**—Arctangent
- **atan2**—Two-argument arctangent
- **atof**—C-style character string to float
- **atoi**—C-style character string to integer
- **atol**—C-style character string to long
- **ceil**—Ceiling of a value
- **cos**—Cosine
- **cosh**—Hyperbolic cosine

- **exp**—Raise to the power of e
- **fabs**—Floating point absolute value
- **floor**—Floor of a value
- **itoa**—Integer to C-style character string
- **log**—Get natural logarithm
- **log10**—Get base 10 logarithm
- **ltoa**—Long to C-style character string
- **localtime**—Get local time structure
- **modf**—Floating point modulus
- **pow**—Raise to the power of
- **rand**—Creating random numbers
- **sin**—Sine
- **sinh**—Hyperbolic sine
- **sort**—Sort list
- **sprintf**—Format string
- **sqrt**—Square root
- **srand**—Set random number seed
- **tan**—Tangent
- **tanh**—Hyperbolic tangent
- **time**—Return time in seconds

Here's an example that displays a random number using the **rand** function. To use that function, you should first *seed* the random number generator by passing the **srand** function a seed value; it's easy to use the **time** function (passing it a value of 0 to get the current time in seconds) to return a value you can use as the random number seed.

After you've used the **srand** function, the random number returned by **rand** is an integer in the range 0 to **RAND_MAX** (**RAND_MAX** is a value that is implementation specific). To get a random number between 0 and *n*, you can divide the value returned by **rand** by **RAND_MAX**, then multiply by **n**; to get a random number between **m** and **m + n**, just do the same and add **m** to the result. For example, in this code, I ask the user to enter the maximum random number they want and use **rand** to generate it (some Unix compilers will require the -lm switch to link in the math library—note also that some compilers do not support RAND_MAX):

```
#include <iostream>
#include <cmath>
#include <ctime>
using namespace std;

int main()
{
    double max;

    srand(time(0));

    cout << "Enter maximum random number you want: ";

    cin >> max;

    double random = (static_cast<double> (rand())) / RAND_MAX * max;

    cout << "Here's a random number between 0 and " << max <<
        ": " << random << endl;

    return 0;
}
```

Here's what this program, rand.cpp, looks like at work:

```
%rand
Enter maximum random number you want: 12
Here's a random number between 0 and 12: 10.3121
```

***NOTE:** For another example of **rand** at work, this time creating random integers between 1 and 10, see "The **do-while** Loop" in Chapter 4.*

We might note that calling **time(0)** returns the current time in seconds, which is a value like 969193206; to get the current time in hours, minutes, and seconds, you can use code like this (this code uses pointers and structures, concepts we'll see in Chapters 3 and 5):

```
time_t t = time(0);
int seconds = localtime(&t)->tm_sec;
int minutes = localtime(&t)->tm_min;
```

```
int hours = localtime(&t)->tm_hour;
int day_of_month = localtime(&t)->tm_mday;
int month = localtime(&t)->tm_mon;  //Month (0-11)
int year = localtime(&t)->tm_year;  //Years since 1900
int weekday = localtime(&t)->tm_wday; //Weekday (0-6)
int day_of_year = localtime(&t)->tm_yday; //Day of the year
int isdst = localtime(&t)->tm_isdst;   //Non-zero for daylight savings time
```


For some examples of converting between numbers and strings with the **itoa** and **atoi** functions in the above list, see "Converting between C-Style Strings and Numbers" in the next chapter.

Related solution:	Found on page:
Converting between C-Style Strings and Numbers	137

Handling Higher Math

How do you calculate a hyperbolic cosecant anyway? Can standard C++ do it? Yes, although not directly. Table 2.5 shows you how to calculate other results using the built-in standard C++ functions in the cmath header file.

Table 2.5 Calculated math functions.

Function	Calculate This Way
Secant	sec(x) = 1 / cos(x)
Cosecant	cosec(x) = 1 / sin(x)
Cotangent	cotan(x) = 1 / tan(x)
Inverse Sine	arcsin(x) = atan(x / sqrt(-x * x + 1))
Inverse Cosine	arccos(x) = atan(-x / sqrt(-x * x + 1)) + 2 * atan(1)
Inverse Secant	arcsec(x) = atan(x / sqrt(x * x – 1)) + sign((x) – 1) * (2 * atan(1))
Inverse Cosecant	arccosec(x) = atan(x / sqr(x * x - 1)) + (sign(x) – 1) * (2 * atn(1))
Inverse Cotangent	arccotan(x) = atan(x) + 2 * atn(1)
Hyperbolic Sine	sinh(x) = (exp(x) – exp(-x)) / 2
Hyperbolic Cosine	cosh(x) = (exp(x) + exp(-x)) / 2
Hyperbolic Tangent	tanh(x) = (exp(x) – exp(-x)) / (exp(x) + exp(-x))
Hyperbolic Secant	sech(x) = 2 / (exp(x) + exp(-x))
Hyperbolic Cosecant	cosech(x) = 2 / (exp(x) – exp(-x))

(continued)

Table 2.5 Calculated math functions *(continued)*.

Function	Calculate This Way
Hyperbolic Cotangent	cotanh(x) = (exp(x) + exp(-x)) / (exp(x) – exp(-x))
Inverse Hyperbolic Sine	arcsinh(x) = log(x + sqrt(x * x + 1))
Inverse Hyperbolic Cosine	arccosh(x) = log(x + sqrt(x * x – 1))
Inverse Hyperbolic Tangent	arctanh(x) = log((1 + x) / (1 – x)) / 2
Inverse Hyperbolic Secant	arcsech(x) = log((sqrt(-x * x + 1) + 1) / x)
Inverse Hyperbolic Cosecant	arccosech(x) = log((sign(x) * sqrt(x * x + 1) + 1) / x)
Inverse Hyperbolic Cotangent	arccotanh(x) = log((x + 1) / (x – 1)) / 2
Logarithm to base N	logN(x) = log(x) / log(N)

Chapter 3

Derived Types: Arrays, Strings, Structures, Unions, and Enumerations

In Depth

This chapter is all about C++ derived types—arrays, C-style strings, structures, unions, and enumerations. These types are called derived types, because you build them yourself from simpler building blocks. For example, say you're teaching a class on C++ to four students. It's no problem to keep track of the scores of those students in your automated tracking system (written in C++, of course). However, the word soon gets around about your dynamic teaching style and unsurpassed C++ insight, and the class soon swells to four hundred students. Now what do you do? Put four hundred variables into your program to track student grades? What if you need to track more than one grade per student?

It's time to advance to the next level of data handling. C++ supports several different constructs that let you build more powerful data structures, and those include the constructs we'll take a look at in this chapter—arrays, C-style strings, structures, unions, and enumerations.

Arrays

As you probably know, *arrays* are programming constructs that let you associate data items of the same type together in a way that can be indexed numerically. For example, say you want to keep track of the test scores of five students; in that case, you can create an array named **scores** with five **int** elements in it:

```
#include <iostream>
using namespace std;

int main()
{
    int scores[5];
        .
        .
        .
```

That's one way to declare a one-dimensional array, by specifying a type and a name and enclosing the number of elements you want in square brackets, [and] (array declarations are explained formally in "Declaring Arrays" later in this chapter). After you've declared this array, you can refer to the five elements in the array with a numeric index, also specified in square brackets like this: **scores[2]**. The first element in the array has index 0, the next index 1, and so on (unlike in other languages like BASIC, all arrays begin with element 0 in C++). Using an index value, you can address each element in the array separately. For example, here's how I place values in the array and display one of them:

```
#include <iostream>
using namespace std;

int main()
{
    int scores[5];

    scores[0] = 91;
    scores[1] = 21;
    scores[2] = 41;
    scores[3] = 81;
    scores[4] = 91;

    cout << "The score of the third person is " << scores[2] << endl;

    return 0;
}
```

There's a shortcut way of initializing the data in an array (see "Initializing Arrays" later in this chapter)—you can list the values you want each element to have in curly braces in the array declaration like this:

```
#include <iostream>
using namespace std;

int main()
{
    int scores[5] = {91, 21, 41, 81, 91};

    cout << "The score of the third person is " << scores[2] << endl;

    return 0;
}
```

This works just as before. The importance of arrays is that they let you associate a set of items of the same type and access those elements with a numeric index. This is particularly useful, because computers excel at working with numeric indices, letting you increment or decrement such an index under programmatic control (such as in a loop—see "Using Arrays" in this chapter) and so successively accessing all the elements of the array from code. Besides one-dimensional arrays, as shown in this example, you can also create and work with multi-dimensional arrays (also demonstrated in "Using Arrays" later in this chapter).

NOTE: *You can also mix pointers and arrays in many ways, as we'll see in Chapter 5.*

C-Style Strings

In the previous chapter, I took a look at the C++ **string** class (see "Introducing the C++ **string** Class" in Chapter 2), which makes handling text strings easy in C++. The C way of handling strings, however, was to store individual characters in an array of type **char** (and getting away from that usage was one of the major achievements of C++). There is nothing special about a C-style string of text—it's just an array of type **char**—except for one thing: the last character is a zero. That last character marks the end of the string. However, there are still some things that you drop back to the C-style string usage for, such as converting numbers to strings (for example, converting the floating point number 3.14159 to the text string "3.14159"), and I'll take a look at C-style strings in this chapter.

To create a C-style string, you create an array of type **char** and assign each character in the string to an element in the array, and then add a zero byte, which you can represent as **'\0'** as the string terminator to mark the end of the string (see "Working with **char** Literals" in Chapter 2). Here's one way of doing that, where I'm storing the word "Hello" in a C-style string named **word**:

```
char word[6];
word[0] = 'H';
word[1] = 'e';
word[2] = 'l';
word[3] = 'l';
word[4] = 'o';
word[5] = '\0';
```

As you can imagine, creating strings like this can get a little tedious, so there are one or two shortcuts. For example, you can use the initialization shortcut for arrays we just saw in the previous section (where you list the values for the array in curly braces). In fact, C and C++ allow you to initialize an array of type **char** to a quoted string, like this:

```
#include <iostream>
using namespace std;
```

```
int main()
{
    char word[] = {'H', 'e', 'l', 'l', 'o', '\0'};
    char other_word[] = "Hello";
    .
    .
    .
```

Note also that you don't have to specify the size of the array in the square brackets when initializing it this way, because C++ will know how many elements to create based on the size of the string you're storing (see "Initializing Arrays" later in this chapter).

The C++ **cout** object knows about C-style strings, so you can display such strings like this:

```
#include <iostream>
using namespace std;

int main()
{
    char word[] = {'H', 'e', 'l', 'l', 'o', '\0'};
    char other_word[] = "Hello";

    cout << other_word << endl;

    return 0;
}
```

The C way of handling strings has been around a long time, and there are plenty of utility functions in the standard C library to work with them. We'll take a look at some of them in this chapter, such as **strstr** for searching strings or **strcmp** for comparing them (the C++ **string** class has plenty of utility methods too; see Chapter 16 for more details).

TIP: *You can convert a C++* ***string*** *object to a C-style string with its* ***c_str*** *method, and pass a C-style string to a C++* ***string*** *object's constructor (i.e., pass it in parentheses when creating the* ***string*** *object) to convert a C-style string to a C++* ***string*** *object. You can also assign a C-style string to a C++* ***string*** *object directly.*

Structures

Both arrays and C-style strings are made up of elements of the same basic type, but sometimes you need more heterogeneous data constructs. For example, say you want to store not only a person's first and last name as strings, but also their age as an integer. C++ supports *structures* for this kind of problem. You use structures to create your own data structures, which create a new data type that you can declare variables with.

For example, here's how you'd create a structure named **person** that is built from two C++ strings, **first_name** and **second_name**, and an integer named **age**:

```
struct person {
    string first_name;
    string second_name;
    int age;
};
```

Now you can declare variables of the new **person** type like this:

```
#include <iostream>
#include <string>
using namespace std;

int main()
{
    struct person {
        string first_name;
        string second_name;
        int age;
    };

    person ralph;
    person alice;
        .
        .
        .
```

And you can access the *members* of a structure using the dot (.) notation like this, where I'm storing data in the data structure and then displaying that data:

```
#include <iostream>
#include <string>
using namespace std;

int main()
{
    struct person {
        string first_name;
        string second_name;
```

```
        int age;
    };

    person ralph;
    person alice;

    ralph.first_name = "Ralph";
    ralph.second_name = "Kramden";
    ralph.age = 39;

    cout << "The first person is " << ralph.first_name << " ";
    cout << ralph.second_name << ", age " << ralph.age << endl;

    return 0;
}
```

Here's the result of this code:

```
%struct
The first person is Ralph Kramden, age 39
```

You can also store structures in arrays—see "Creating and Using Arrays of Structures" later in this chapter. Using this construct, you can create your own advanced data structures and treat them almost as you would a simple type.

Unions

Unions are specialized data structures in which all members share the same data. This allows you, among other things, to refer to the same data with different names. Here's an example where I use the **union** keyword to create a union named **one_union** with two double variables, **double_variable** and **double_variable2**:

```
union one_union
{
    double double_variable;
    double double_variable2;
};
```

Now I can create a variable of the **one_union** type named **union1** and place a value in the **double_variable** member like this:

```
#include <iostream>
using namespace std;
```

```
int main()
{
    union one_union
    {
        double double_variable;
        double double_variable2;
    };

    one_union union1;

    union1.double_variable = 3.14159;
    .
    .
    .
```

Because this is a union type of structure, both **union.double_variable** and **union.double_variable2** point to the same data in memory, so displaying both of them displays the same value:

```
#include <iostream>
using namespace std;

int main()
{
    union one_union
    {
        double double_variable;
        double double_variable2;
    };

    one_union union1;

    union1.double_variable = 3.14159;

    cout << "union1.double_variable = " << union1.double_variable << endl;
    cout << "union1.double_variable2 = " << union1.double_variable2 << endl;

    return 0;
}
```

Here's what this program looks like when it's running:

```
%union
union1.double_variable = 3.14159
union1.double_variable2 = 3.14159
```

Because all members of a union point to the same data in memory, you'll run into problems if you mix types, because, for example, **double** variables are stored in a completely different format than integers are. See "Creating Unions" later in this chapter for more information.

Enumerations

Another way to effectively create your own simple type is to create an *enumeration*. An enumeration lets you name the values that a variable of that type can take. For example, say you want to work with the days of the week, Sunday, Monday, Tuesday, and so on, and you don't want to refer to them with integers such as 0, 1, 2, but would rather give them real names. You can do that with an enumeration named **day** like this, which lists a set of symbolic names:


```
enum day
{
    Sunday,
    Monday,
    Tuesday,
    Wednesday,
    Thursday,
    Friday,
    Saturday
};
```

Now when you create a variable of the **day** type, you can assign it values from the list of possible values you've specified, as in this case, where I create a variable named **today** of this type:

```
#include <iostream>
using namespace std;

int main()
{
    enum day
    {
        Sunday,
        Monday,
        Tuesday,
        Wednesday,
        Thursday,
        Friday,
        Saturday
    };
```

```
    enum day today = Friday;
    .
    .
    .
```

Now you can work with the **today** variable as you would any other variable, with the understanding that it holds values from the enumeration instead of, say, double or floating point numbers:


```
#include <iostream>
using namespace std;

int main()
{
    enum day
    {
        Sunday,
        Monday,
        Tuesday,
        Wednesday,
        Thursday,
        Friday,
        Saturday
    };

    enum day today = Friday;

    if(today == Friday){
        cout << "Today is Friday." << endl;
    }

    return 0;
}
```

This is great if you get tired of dealing with numbers in your code and want to use symbolic names for values instead. By the way, behind the scenes, C++ actually does use numbers for the values in an enumeration—Sunday is given the integer value 0, Monday the integer 1, and so on. For more details, see "Using Enumerations" later in this chapter.

And that's all the introduction to this topic we need—it's time to get to the Immediate Solutions.

Immediate Solutions

Declaring Arrays

As discussed in the In Depth section of this chapter, you use an array to associate data items of the same type into a set easily addressed with a numeric index. Here's how you declare an array formally:

```
type name [constant_expression] [[constant_expression] ... ]
```

***NOTE:** In this declaration, the square brackets immediately around the **constant_expression** parameters are part of the declaration and do not indicate optional parameters.*

The ***type*** parameter indicates the type of each element in the array, ***name*** is the name of the array, and the ***constant_expression*** parameters specify the number of elements in each dimension of the array. Here's an example where I'm declaring an integer array named **scores** with five elements:

```
int scores[5];
```

You can add additional dimensions to an array by specifying the number of elements in those dimensions in additional square brackets, as in this case, where I'm declaring a 3×5 integer array:

```
int scores[3][5];
```

With this declaration, every element in **scores** is now indexed with two numeric indices, not just one, such as **scores[0][1]** or **scores [2][3]**. This means you can store, for example, three test scores for each of five students—the test score of the first student on test 1 could be **scores[0][0]**, the same student's score on test 2 could be in **scores[1][0]**, and so on. For more on how to use multi-dimensional arrays, see "Using Arrays" later in this chapter.

There's another way to declare an array where you don't have to specify its size in square brackets—you can declare an array and initialize it at the same time, and C++ will use the initialization part of the declaration to dimension the array for you. To see how this works, see "Initializing Arrays," coming up next.

*NOTE: Some languages let your "grow" or shrink arrays at runtime (as in BASIC with the **ReDim** statement). If you want your arrays to grow or shrink at runtime in C++, you should probably be using pointers and the **new** and **delete** operators to allocate and release memory instead, as covered in Chapter 5.*

Initializing Arrays

You can initialize an array when you declare it, by specifying the initialization values in a comma-separated list in curly braces like this:

```
int array1[4] = {0, 1, 2, 3};
```

This sets element 0 of this array to 0, element 1 to 1, and so on. You can also list fewer items than there is space for in the array, and C++ will set the values of all the unspecified elements to 0:

```
int array2[4] = {0, 1, 2};
```

This array will hold the values 0, 1, 2, and 0. (Note that if you do not initialize elements in an array, C++ makes no guarantee that those elements will hold 0.) Because C++ sets the elements following those in the initialization list to 0, here's an easy way to declare an array of 1,000 elements, setting them all to 0 with one quick initialization:

```
int array3[1000] = {0};
```

There's also a shortcut when you initialize arrays—if you don't give the dimensions of an array, but do provide an initialization list, C++ will dimension the array by itself, because it knows the size of the array from the number of items in the initialization list. This example creates an array with four elements:

```
int array4[] = {0, 1, 2, 3};
```

You can also initialize **char** arrays with a string of text this way:

```
char word[] = "Hello";
```

This also adds a final zero byte at the end of this **char** array, **'\0'**, to form a C-style string (see "Creating C-Style Strings" later in this chapter for more details).

Here's an example showing how to initialize a two-dimensional array. Such arrays may be thought of in terms of rows and columns—for example a 3×5 array of integers has three rows and five columns. Here's how you can initialize such an array, giving the initialization values in three rows, each with five columns:

```
int scores[3][5] = {
    { 92 , 73 , 57 , 98 , 89 },
    { 88 , 76 , 23 , 95 , 72 },
    { 94 , 82 , 63 , 99 , 94 }
};
```

With most compilers, you can skip size of the array in the *first* array dimension (that's 3 here) when initializing multi-dimensioned arrays, because the compiler can figure that size itself from the number of elements you use to initialize the array. That means this is an equivalent declaration:

```
int scores[][5] = {
    { 92 , 73 , 57 , 98 , 89 },
    { 88 , 76 , 23 , 95 , 72 },
    { 94 , 82 , 63 , 99 , 94 }
};
```


Using Arrays

You access the elements in an array by numeric index. That index starts at zero, so the first element in a one-dimensional array is element 0, the next is element 1, and so on. For a two-dimensional array named **prices**, the first element is **prices[0][0]**, the element in the third row and fourth column of the array is **prices[2][3]**, and so on.

Here's an example, scores.cpp. In this case, I'm creating an array named **scores**, filling it with data, and displaying one of the elements:

```
#include <iostream>
using namespace std;

int main()
{
    int scores[5];
```

```
    scores[0] = 91;
    scores[1] = 21;
    scores[2] = 41;
    scores[3] = 81;
    scores[4] = 91;

    cout << "The score of the third person is " << scores[2] << endl;

    return 0;
}
```


Here's what this program looks like when running:

```
%scores
The score of the third person is 41
```

Being able to access the elements of an array by index is very useful when you want to loop over all the elements of an array in a loop. Here's an example; in this case, I'll loop over a two-dimensional array that stores three test scores for five students, displaying the average score for each test:

```
#include <iostream>
using namespace std;

int main()
{
    int test_index, student_index, scores[3][5] = {
        { 92 , 73 , 57 , 98 , 89 },
        { 88 , 76 , 23 , 95 , 72 },
        { 94 , 82 , 63 , 99 , 94 }
    };
    float sum;

    for (test_index = 0; test_index < 3; test_index++){
        for (student_index = 0, sum = 0; student_index < 5; student_index++)
            sum = sum + scores[test_index][student_index];
        cout << "Average for test " << test_index + 1 << " is " << sum / 5
            << endl;
    }

    return 0;
}
```

Here's the result of this program, array.cpp:

```
%array
Average for test 1 is 81.8
Average for test 2 is 70.8
Average for test 3 is 86.4
```

***NOTE:** As we'll see in Chapter 5, pointers can mimic many of the traditional operations you can perform with arrays.*

You might note that in this case, I used the number of test scores, 5, directly in the code when dividing to find the average score. However, if you have an arbitrary array, you might not know its size ahead of time. It turns out that there is an easy way to determine the size of an array—see the next section for the details.

Determining the Size of an Array

You can use the **sizeof** operator to find the size of a one-dimensional array, because **sizeof** will tell you both the total size of the array in bytes and the size of each element in the array, and all you have to do is to divide one by the other. Here's an example, arraysize.cpp, showing how this works; in this example, I find the size of the array named **scores** both in bytes and in elements:

```
#include <iostream>
using namespace std;

int main()
{
    int scores[5] = {92 , 73 , 57 , 98 , 89 };

    cout << "The array is " << sizeof(scores) << " bytes long." << endl;

    cout << "The array has " << sizeof(scores) / sizeof(int) << " elements."
        << endl;

    return 0;
}
```

Here's the result of this code:

```
%arraysize
The array is 20 bytes long.
The array has 5 elements.
```

Note that this doesn't work quite so well with multi-dimensional arrays: Because you'll just get the size of the whole array and the size of one element with **sizeof**, you'll need the number of elements in all but one dimension (such as how many rows, or how many columns, there are in a two-dimensional array) before you can determine the number of elements in the remaining dimension.

NOTE: *When we create arrays from templates in Chapter 16, we'll see that there are easier ways to find an array's length.*

Related solution:	Found on page:
The **sizeof** Operator	102

Creating C-Style Strings

Arrays of type **char** that end with a zero byte were treated as text strings in C (see the discussion in "C-Style Strings" earlier in this chapter). We saw there are two ways to declare and initialize such strings—assign each character individually in the character array and add a zero byte, **'\0'**, at the end for the string terminator, or let C++ handle some of the details by initializing the character array to a double-quoted string like this, in the example program cstring.cpp:

```
#include <iostream>
using namespace std;

int main()
{
    char word[] = {'H', 'e', 'l', 'l', 'o', '\0'};
    char string1[] = "Hello";

    cout << string1 << endl;

    return 0;
}
```

The **cout** object knows all about C-style strings, so you can display them using that object, as shown in this code (in C, you used the C library function **printf** to display C-style strings).

TIP: Because a C-style string is a true ***char*** *array, you can access each character in it with an array index, like this:* ***string1[3] = 'x'.***

As you may recall from the previous chapter, C++ has a **string** class, based on the **basic_string** template, and that class is generally far superior to C-style strings. I recommend you stick with the **string** class when you can, and use C-style strings only when necessary. I'll take a look at the C library functions designed to be used with C-style strings in the next few sections.

TIP: You can convert a C++ ***string*** *object to a C-style string with its* ***c_str*** *method, and pass a C-style string to a C++* ***string*** *object's constructor (i.e., pass it in parentheses when creating the* ***string*** *object) to convert a C-style string to a C++* ***string*** *object. You can also assign a C-style string to a C++* ***string*** *object directly.*

Related solution:	Found on page:
Introducing the C++ **string** Class	86

Finding a C-Style String's Length

The standard C library function **strlen** returns the number of characters in a C-style string (not including the terminating zero byte). Here's an example, strlen.cpp, that finds the length of a C-style string:

```
#include <iostream>

using namespace std;
int main()
{
    char string1[] = "Hello";

    cout << "The length of string1 is " << strlen(string1) << " characters."
        << endl;

    return 0;
}
```

Here's the result of this program, strlen.cpp:

```
%strlen
The length of string1 is 5 characters.
```

Comparing C-Style Strings

You can use the **strcmp** standard C library function to compare C-style strings. This function will return an integer greater than, equal to, or less than 0, depending on whether the first string is lexicographically greater than, equal to, or less than the second string. Here's an example, strcmp.cpp, that compares two C-style strings and displays the results:

```
#include <iostream>

using namespace std;
int main()
{
    char string1[] = "bat";
    char string2[] = "cat";

    int result = strcmp(string1, string2);

    if (result > 0){
        cout << "string1 is lexicographically greater than string2" << endl;
    } else if (result == 0) {
        cout << "string1 is lexicographically equal to string2" << endl;
    } else if (result < 0) {
        cout << "string1 is lexicographically less than string2" << endl;
    }

    return 0;
}
```

Here's the result of running this program, showing that "bat" comes before "cat" alphabetically:

```
%strcmp
string1 is lexicographically less than string2
```

Searching C-Style Strings

You can use the **strstr** function to search for the first occurrence of a C-style substring in a C-style string. This function returns a *pointer* to the found substring in the string (if the substring is not found, **strstr** returns 0). We'll see pointers in Chapter 5, but it's still worth taking a look at **strstr** now. For this example, all you need to know about pointers is that they "point" to a location in memory, and we can treat the resulting pointer to the substring as a string itself. Here's an example, strstr.cpp; in this case, I search for the substring "ing" in the string "We are building a house." The **strstr** function returns a pointer to the location of the start of the substring, and if I pass that pointer to **cout** as the beginning of a C-style string, it will display all the text including and following "ing":

```
#include <iostream>

using namespace std;
int main()
{
    char string1[] = "We are building a house.";
    char string2[] = "ing";
    char* string3;

    string3 = strstr(string1, string2);

    cout << string3 << endl;

    return 0;
}
```

Here's the result of this program:

```
%strstr
ing a house.
```

Concatenating C-Style Strings

You can use the standard C library function **strcat** to append one string to another; this function returns a pointer to the resulting string. We will cover pointers in Chapter 5; for a brief discussion, see "Searching C-Style Strings" earlier in this chapter. Here's an example showing how to use **strcat**; in this case, I'm concatenating the strings "Hello" and "there" and displaying the result:

```
#include <iostream>

using namespace std;
int main()
{
    char string1[] = "Hello";
    char string2[] = " there";
    char* string3;

    string3 = strcat(string1, string2);

    cout << string3 << endl;

    return 0;
}
```

Here's the result of this program, strcat.cpp:

```
%strcat
Hello there
```

This function, **strcat**, actually appends **string2** to **string1**. Some compilers will encounter a problem if the source and destination strings end up overlapping, while other compilers will reallocate new space for **string1** automatically. If you're having problems, or just want to be safe, you should make **string1** big enough to hold both strings, something like this:

```
char string1[40] = "Hello";
```

Copying C-Style Strings

You can use the standard C library function **strcpy** to copy a C-style string into another one. Here's an example; in this case, I'm copying **string2** into **string1**:

```
#include <iostream>

using namespace std;
int main()
```

```
{
    char string1[] = "bat";
    char string2[] = "cat";

    strcpy(string1, string2);

    cout << string1 << endl;

    return 0;
}
```

Here's what this program, strcpy.cpp, looks like at work; as you can see, the contents of **string1** have been replaced with the contents of **string2**:

```
%strcpy
cat
```


Converting between C-Style Strings and Numbers

If you have a floating point number that you want to make part of a string, things can be a little awkward, because you can't use a cast here. Instead, you can use the C library functions like **itoa** to convert from an integer to a C-style string, or the function **atoi** to convert from a C-style string to an integer. Here's an example, stringconvert.cpp, that uses the **itoa** function to convert from an integer to a string, **atoi** to convert back to a string, and **atof** to convert a C-style string to a **float**:

```
#include <iostream>
#include <string>
using namespace std;

int main()
{
    char new_text[8];
    int new_integer, integer = 255;
    float new_float;
    string new_string, string_object("3.14159");

    itoa(integer, new_text, 10);
    cout << "Converting the integer to a character string yields: "
        << new_text << endl;
```

```
    new_string = new_text;
    cout << "Converting the character string to a string object yields: "
        << new_string << endl;

    new_integer = atoi(new_text);
    cout << "Converting the text back to an integer yields: "
        << new_integer << endl;

    new_float = atof(string_object.c_str());
    cout << "Converting the string object into a float yields: "
        << new_float << endl;

    return 0;
}
```

Here's the result of this program, stringconvert.cpp:

```
%stringconvert
Converting the integer to a character string yields: 255
Converting the character string to a string object yields: 255
Converting the text back to an integer yields: 255
Converting the string object into a float yields: 3.14159
```

You can also use the standard C library **sprintf** function (named for "formatted string print") to format a number into a string. Here's how you use this function in general:

```
sprintf (string, format, list)
```

Here, ***string*** is the string you want the result to appear in, ***format*** is a conversion string that specifies how you want the result formatted, specifying one conversion for each element in ***list***. You can use these conversions in ***format***:

- **%%**—A percent sign
- **%c**—A character with the given number
- **%d**—A signed integer, in decimal
- **%e**—A floating-point number, in scientific notation
- **%E**—Like **%e**, but using an uppercase E
- **%f**—A floating-point number, in fixed decimal notation
- **%g**—a floating-point number, in **%e** or **%f** notation

- **%G**—Like **%g**, but with an uppercase G
- **%n**—Stores the number of characters output in the next variable
- **%o**—An unsigned integer, in octal
- **%p**—A pointer (the value's address in hexadecimal)
- **%s**—A string
- **%u**—An unsigned integer, in decimal
- **%x**—An unsigned integer, in hexadecimal
- **%X**—Like **%x**, but with uppercase letters
- **%D**—Same as **%ld**
- **%F**—Same as **%f**
- **%i**—Same as **%d**
- **%O**—Same as **%lo**
- **%U**—Same as **%lu**
- **-** —Left-justify within the field
- **#**—Prefix non-zero octal with 0, non-zero hex with 0x
- ***.number***—"Precision": number of digits after the decimal point for floating point values, the maximum length for strings, or the minimum length for integers
- **+**—Prefix positive number with a plus sign
- **0**—Use zeros, not spaces, to right-justify
- **h**—Interpret integer as a **short**
- **l**—Interpret integer as a **long**
- ***number***—Minimum field width
- **space character**—Prefix positive number with a space

Here's an example, sprintf.cpp, where I'm converting the number 1234.56789 to a string, keeping only four decimal places—note that many compilers will require you to include cstdio to use **sprintf**:

```
#include <iostream>
#include <cstdio>
using namespace std;
```

```
int main()
{
    char formatted_string[20];

    float number = 1234.56789;
    sprintf (formatted_string, "%.4f\n", number);
    cout << formatted_string << endl;

    return 0;
}
```


Here's the result of this program (note that **stprintf** rounds the number to 1234.5679):

```
%sprintf
1234.5679
```


Related solution:	*Found on page:*
The C++ Utility Functions: Math, Time, Trig, Random Numbers, and More	112

Reading C-Style Strings with **cin** Methods

You can use several methods of the **cin** object to read keyboard input and store the result in a C-style string: **cin.getline** and **cin.get** (to see how to read individual characters and store text in C++ **string** objects, see "Using **cin** to Read Individual Characters and Whole Strings" in Chapter 2).

Using **cin.getline**

Here's an example, getline.cpp, that reads from the keyboard and stores the resulting string in a C-style string, **string1**:

```
#include <iostream>
using namespace std;

int main()
{
    const int total = 50;
    char string1[total];

    cout << "Type some words: ";
```

```
    cin.getline(string1, total);

    cout << "You typed: " << string1 << endl;

    return 0;
}
```

Note that you must pass the C-style string you want the text stored in and the number of characters to read to **cin.getline**. This method will read that number of characters minus 1, because it has to allow space for the **'\0'** at the end of the string.

Besides **cin.getline**, you can also use **cin.get**.

Using **cin.get**

You can use the **cin.get** method to read individual characters (see "Using **cin** to Read Individual Characters and Whole Strings" in Chapter 2), and there's also a form of **cin.get** with which you can read a whole line of text at once. To use this form, you pass the C-style string to store the text in and the maximum number of characters to read to **cin.get** (**cin.get** will read input until the maximum number of characters minus 1 has been reached, or the user presses Enter).

Here's one thing to note: **cin.get** reads all the way up to the terminating **'\n'** if there is one, but does *not* read that **'\n'**. To clear the **'\n'** character from the input buffer, you can use the method **cin.clear**, or you can call **cin.get** a second time. Here's an example, get.cpp, using **cin.get**, which stores text in a C-style string; in this case, I'm *chaining* the use of **cin.get** to first read the text and then calling that method again to read the final **'\n'**. Here's the code:

```
#include <iostream>
using namespace std;

int main()
{
    const int total = 50;
    char string1[total];

    cout << "Type some words: ";

    cin.get(string1, total).get();

    cout << "You typed: " << string1 << endl;

    return 0;
}
```

Here's what this program looks like in action:

```
%get
Type some words: Now is the time.
You typed: Now is the time.
```


Related solution:	Found on page:
Using **cin** to Read Individual Characters and Whole Strings	89

Declaring Structures

As discussed in the In Depth section of this chapter, you can use structures to create your own data types, which can be composites of various other heterogeneous data types. Here's how you declare a structure in general, using the **struct** keyword in both C and C++:

```
struct [name] {[member-list]}
```

In this case, ***name*** is the name for the structure, and ***member-list*** is the comma-separated list of members you want in the new structure type.

NOTE: *C++ structures are considerably more powerful than C structures, because C++ structures are actually classes and so can have methods. More on methods in Chapter 8.*

Here's an example; in this case, I'm declaring a structure named **person** with two strings in it, **first_name** and **second_name** (note that you terminate the structure declaration with a semicolon):

```
#include <iostream>
#include <string>
using namespace std;

int main()
{
    struct person {
        string first_name;
        string second_name;
    };
    .
    .
    .
```

Now I can declare variables of this structure type and access the data members of each variable with the dot (.) operator:

```
#include <iostream>
#include <string>
using namespace std;

int main()
{
    struct person {
        string first_name;
        string second_name;
    };

    person ralph;
    person alice;

    ralph.first_name = "Ralph";
    ralph.second_name = "Kramden";

    cout << "The first person is " << ralph.first_name << " ";
    cout << ralph.second_name << endl;

    return 0;
}
```

***NOTE:** In C, when you declare variables of a structure's type, you need to precede the declaration with the word **struct** (as in **struct person ralph;**), but not in C++.*

Here's the result of this code:

```
%struct
The first person is Ralph Kramden
```

Declaring a data structure in a function like **main** restricts the use of the structure to the same function; you can also declare a data structure outside any function, which will make it available to all the code in the file:

```
#include <iostream>
#include <string>
using namespace std;

struct person {
    string first_name;
```

```
    string second_name;
};

int main()
{
    person ralph;
    person alice;

    ralph.first_name = "Ralph";
    ralph.second_name = "Kramden";

    cout << "The first person is " << ralph.first_name << " ";
    cout << ralph.second_name << endl;

    return 0;
}
```

Note that you can also declare variables of the structure's type immediately after the structure declaration (but before the terminating semicolon), as in this case:

```
#include <iostream>
#include <string>
using namespace std;

int main()
{
    struct person {
        string first_name;
        string second_name;
    }ralph, alice;

    ralph.first_name = "Ralph";
    ralph.second_name = "Kramden";

    cout << "The first person is " << ralph.first_name << " ";
    cout << ralph.second_name << endl;

    return 0;
}
```

In fact, you can declare structures without a name, as anonymous structures, as in this case (some compilers, like Visual C++, seem to have a problem using the C++ **string** class inside an anonymous structure, but not simple types like **int** or **float**):

```
#include <iostream>
#include <string>
using namespace std;

int main()
{
    struct {
        string first_name;
        string second_name;
    }ralph, alice;

    ralph.first_name = "Ralph";
    ralph.second_name = "Kramden";

    cout << "The first person is " << ralph.first_name << " ";
    cout << ralph.second_name << endl;

    return 0;
}
```

You can also initialize the data in a data structure when you declare it; see the next section for the details.

Initializing Structures

C++ allows you to initialize the data in structures when you declare them, using the same kind of syntax you use to initialize arrays. Here's an example:

```
#include <iostream>
#include <string>
using namespace std;

int main()
{
    struct person {
        string first_name;
        string second_name;
    };

    person ralph = {"Ralph", "Kramden"};
    person alice = {"Alice", "Kramden"};
```

```
    cout << "The first person is " << ralph.first_name << " ";
    cout << ralph.second_name << endl;

    return 0;
}
```

Unfortunately, I've found that not all compilers let you use this syntax. Here's another way of initializing structures, which works when you declare them—and again, this technique will not work with all compilers, unfortunately:


```
#include <iostream>
#include <string>
using namespace std;

int main()
{
    struct person {
        string first_name;
        string second_name;
    } ralph = {"Ralph", "Kramden"}, alice = {"Alice", "Kramden"};

    cout << "The first person is " << ralph.first_name << " ";
    cout << ralph.second_name << endl;

    return 0;
}
```

Using Structures

It's easy to use structures; as we've seen in the In Depth section of this chapter, after you've declared your structure type and created variables of that type, you can access the members of a structure individually using the dot operator (.), like this:

```
#include <iostream>
#include <string>
using namespace std;
```

```
int main()
{
    struct person {
        string first_name;
        string second_name;
    };

    person ralph;
    person also_ralph;

    ralph.first_name = "Ralph";
    ralph.second_name = "Kramden";
    .
    .
    .
}
```

That's all it takes. You can access all of the simple data members you store inside a structure with the dot operator, and that's all you need. In fact, you can also put more complex types such as arrays inside structures, as in this code:

```
#include <iostream>
#include <string>
using namespace std;

int main()
{
    struct person {
        string names[2];
    };

    person ralph;
    person also_ralph;

    ralph.names[0] = "Ralph";
    ralph.names[1] = "Kramden";
    .
    .
    .
}
```

And in fact, many compilers (but not all compilers) support storing structures inside other structures.

Assigning Structures to Other Structures

Here's another convenient operation you can perform with structures—you can assign one to another. Here's an example showing how that works:

```
#include <iostream>
#include <string>
using namespace std;

int main()
{
    struct person {
        string first_name;
        string second_name;
    };

    person ralph;
    person also_ralph;

    ralph.first_name = "Ralph";
    ralph.second_name = "Kramden";

    also_ralph = ralph;

    cout << "The first person is " << also_ralph.first_name;
    cout << " " << also_ralph.second_name << endl;

    return 0;
}
```

The assignment operation copies over a structure member by member. Here's what this program, structassign.cpp, looks like in action:

```
%structassign
The first person is Ralph Kramden
```

Creating and Using Arrays of Structures

You can also create and use arrays of structures, and they work as you'd expect. Here's an example, structarray.cpp, in which I'm creating an array of structures, placing data in it, and displaying that data:

```
#include <iostream>
#include <string>
using namespace std;
```

```
int main()
{
    struct person {
        string first_name;
        string second_name;
    };

    person people[2];

    people[0].first_name = "Ralph";
    people[0].second_name = "Kramden";

    cout << "The first person is " << people[0].first_name;
    cout << " " << people[0].second_name << endl;

    return 0;
}
```


Here's what this program, structarray.cpp, looks like in action:

```
%structarray
The first person is Ralph Kramden
```

Some compilers, but not all, allow you to initialize an array of structures in the way you'd expect, by specifying the initializing values for each structure element in the array this way:

```
#include <iostream>
#include <string>
using namespace std;

int main()
{
    struct person {
        string first_name;
        string second_name;
    };

    person people[2] =
    {
        {"Ralph", "Kramden"},
        {"Alice", "Kramden"}
    };
```

```
        cout << "The first person is " << people[0].first_name;
        cout << " " << people[0].second_name << endl;

        return 0;
    }
```


Creating Bit Fields

One use for structures in both C and C++ is to configure data in a way that makes it easy to access the individual bits. Here's an example, bitfield.cpp; in this case, I'm creating a structure named **flags** that will be created of individual bits that can be set to 0 or 1 and so indicate the state of some condition that can be toggled on or off (variables that keep track of such on-off states are often called flags).

In this case, I'll set up some flags for a hypothetical drawing program that needs to keep track of what drawing tool the user is currently using with four flags: **line_flag**, **brush_flag**, **ellipse_flag**, and **rectangle_flag**, each made up of a single bit. I'll also keep track of the current drawing color with 4 bits, which allows 16 different colors. To specify the width of bit fields, you use a colon and a positive integer like this:

```
struct flags
{
    int color : 4;
    bool line_flag : 1;
    bool brush_flag : 1;
    bool ellipse_flag : 1;
    bool rectangle_flag : 1;
}
```

Now I can use this structure in the program, create a variable named **current_flags** of this structure type, and access the items in it just as I would any other structure (being careful not to exceed the storage capacity of such items). In this case, I'll set the rectangle drawing tool's flag to true, and then test it:

```
#include <iostream>
using namespace std;

int main()
{
    struct flags
    {
```

```
        int color : 4;
        bool line_flag : 1;
        bool brush_flag : 1;
        bool ellipse_flag : 1;
        bool rectangle_flag : 1;
    };

    flags current_flags;
    current_flags.rectangle_flag = 1;

    if(current_flags.rectangle_flag){
        cout << "You're drawing rectangles." << endl;
    } else {
        cout << "You're not drawing rectangles." << endl;
    }

    return 0;
}
```

Here's the result of this program, bitfield.cpp:

```
%bitfield
You're drawing rectangles.
```


Creating Unions

As discussed in the In Depth section of this chapter, a union is a type of structure in which the members *overlap*, sharing the same memory location. Here's what the formal declaration of a union looks like:

```
union [name] {[member-list]}
```

In this case, ***name*** is the name for the union, and ***member-list*** is the comma-separated list of members you want in the new union type. Here's an example named **one_union**:

```
union one_union
{
    int int_variable;
    long long_variable;
    double double_variable;
    double double_variable2;
};
```

In this case, I'm placing variables that have different internal storage formats (**int**, **long**, and **double**) in the union, which is dangerous, because they all share the same memory location. That means that if I place data in **double** format in this union and try to read the **int** variable, the result will be meaningless.

Here's an example, union.cpp, in which I'm putting this union to work, first placing a value in the **int** member, then in the first **double** member, **double_variable** (which overwrites the integer value) and then displaying the data accessing those two members. As you'd expect, the displayed **int** data is meaningless. I'll also display the value in the second **double** variable, **double_variable2**, which naturally holds the same data as **double_variable**, and so demonstrates one use for unions—to let you access the same data with different names:

```
#include <iostream>
using namespace std;

int main()
{
    union one_union
    {
        int int_variable;
        long long_variable;
        double double_variable;
        double double_variable2;
    };

    one_union p;

    p.int_variable = 1;
    p.double_variable = 3.14159;

    cout << p.int_variable << endl;
    cout << p.double_variable << endl;
    cout << p.double_variable2 << endl;

    return 0;
}
```

Here's what union.cpp looks like when running:

```
%union
-266631570
3.14159
3.14159
```

As with structures, you can also make unions anonymous by not giving them a name.

If you declare an anonymous union inside a structure, you can refer to any of the members of the union as members of the structure, but of course all the members of the same union will refer to the same data in memory.

Declaring Enumerations

As discussed in the In Depth section of this chapter, you can declare your own symbolic constants using the **enum** statement. Here's what such a declaration looks like:

```
enum [name] {enumerator-list}
```

In this case, ***name*** is the name for the enumeration, and ***enumerator-list*** is the comma-separated list of members you want in the new enumeration type. Variables of the **enum** type can be assigned values as given in ***enumerator-list*** (as well as others from the range that the list defines—see "Using Other Values in Enumeration Ranges" later in this chapter).

Using **enum** provides an alternative to using **#define** or **const** to define a set of constants in a program, and it has the advantage that the actual numerical values are generated for you by the compiler, and that—unlike **#define**—the enumeration obeys scoping rules (see Chapter 6 for more on scope). Here's an example we saw in the In Depth section of the chapter, in which I create an enumeration named **day** and put it to work:

```
#include <iostream>
using namespace std;

int main()
{
    enum day
    {
        Sunday,
        Monday,
        Tuesday,
        Wednesday,
        Thursday,
        Friday,
        Saturday,
    };
```

```
    enum day today = Friday;

    if(today == Friday){
        cout << "Today is Friday." << endl;
    }

    return 0;
}
```

NOTE: *The comma after the last constant in the enumeration is optional; many programmers use a comma there in case they add new values to the enumeration and forget to add a comma before the new value.*

As with structures, you can declare variables of the enumeration type right after the enumeration declaration like this:

```
#include <iostream>
using namespace std;

int main()
{
    enum day
    {
        Sunday,
        Monday,
        Tuesday,
        Wednesday,
        Thursday,
        Friday,
        Saturday,
    } today;

    today = Friday;

    if(today == Friday){
        cout << "Today is Friday." << endl;
    }

    return 0;
}
```

Behind the scenes, the members of an enumeration are given integer values by the compiler (the default is to give the first item in the enumeration the value 0). However, you can specify values for the members of an enumeration yourself, as in this case:

```
enum day
{
    Sunday,
    Monday,
    Tuesday = 5,
    Wednesday,
    Thursday,
    Friday,
    Saturday,
};
```


With a typical compiler, Sunday will end up holding 0, Monday will hold 1, Tuesday will hold 5, Wednesday will hold 2, Thursday will hold 3, Friday will hold 4, and Saturday will hold 5. Enumerations can contain duplicate constant values—the only important point to remember is that the names of the constants you declare in an enumeration must not conflict with any other names visible in the part of the program where you use them. In fact, you can define *all* the values used in an enumeration, like this:

```
enum numbers
{
    one = 1,
    three = 3,
    five = 5,
    seven = 7,
};
```

You can also declare unnamed enumeration data types. Here's an example; note that I'm declaring the variable of this type in the same declaration as the enumeration itself, because you can't refer to the nameless enumeration as a type in code:

```
#include <iostream>
using namespace std;

int main()
{
    enum
    {
        Sunday,
        Monday,
        Tuesday,
        Wednesday,
        Thursday,
```

```
        Friday,
        Saturday,
    } today;

    today = Friday;

    if(today == Friday){
        cout << "Today is Friday." << endl;
    }

    return 0;
}
```


Using Enumerations

Using enumerations is easy. As discussed in the In Depth section of this chapter, you use enumerations to list symbolic constants that variables of the enumeration type may be assigned. Here's an example that we saw in the In Depth section, enum.cpp; first I declare the enumeration, named **day** in this case, which can take the possible values Sunday, Monday, Tuesday, Wednesday, Thursday, Friday, or Saturday:

```
#include <iostream>
using namespace std;

int main()
{
    enum day
    {
        Sunday,
        Monday,
        Tuesday,
        Wednesday,
        Thursday,
        Friday,
        Saturday,
    };
    .
    .
    .
```

Now I'm free to use variables of the **day** type and assign them values from the enumeration:

```
#include <iostream>
using namespace std;

int main()
{
    enum day
    {
        Sunday,
        Monday,
        Tuesday,
        Wednesday,
        Thursday,
        Friday,
        Saturday,
    };

    enum day today = Friday;

    if(today == Friday){
        cout << "Today is Friday." << endl;
    }

    return 0;
}
```

In the code, I assign a variable of this type the value Friday and then compare it to that value. Here's the result of this program, enum.cpp:

```
%enum
Today is Friday.
```

In some C++ implementations, such as Microsoft Visual C++, you can explicitly assign a new integer value to a variable of an enumerated data type, using a type cast:

```
day today;
today = static_cast<enum day> (10);
```

However, most of the C++ authorities I've seen recommend strongly against changing the value of enumeration variables, which really should be treated as constants.

You might think that variables of an enumeration type can take only values as defined in the enumeration, but that's not completely true. You can actually assign such variables other values from the range defined by the enumeration as well—see the next section for the details.

Using Other Values in Enumeration Ranges

Variables of an enumeration type are not necessarily restricted to the values explicitly specified in the enumeration. For example, say that I have an enumeration named **day** with constants defined to hold the values 1, 4, and 5:

```
#include <iostream>
using namespace std;

int main()
{
    enum day
    {
        Sunday = 1,
        Monday = 4,
        Tuesday = 5,
    };
        .
        .
        .
```

Normally, you'd just use the defined values. You can, however, assign a variable of this enumeration type other integer values in the range defined by the enumeration (which is 1 to 5 here). For example, if I create a variable of the **day** type named **today**, I can assign it a value of 3—which does *not* correspond to one of the defined enumeration constants—with this syntax:

```
#include <iostream>
using namespace std;

int main()
{
    enum day
    {
        Sunday = 1,
        Monday = 4,
```

```
        Tuesday = 5,
    };

    enum day today;

    today = day(3);
    .
    .
    .
```

And I can display that value like this:

```
#include <iostream>
using namespace std;

int main()
{
    enum day
    {
        Sunday = 1,
        Monday = 4,
        Tuesday = 5,
    };

    enum day today;

    today = day(3);

    cout << "The actual value in the variable today is " << today << endl;

    return 0;
}
```

Here's what this program, erange.cpp, looks like when running:

```
%erange
The actual value in the variable today is 3
```

Being able to use values not explicitly defined in the enumeration in this way gives the enumeration a little more flexibility than most programmers expect.

Using typedef

You can use **typedef** statements to provide an alias for a built-in or user-defined type, which can help make your code much more readable. Here's an example, where I'm making the word **salary** an alias for the type **double**:

```
typedef double salary;
salary dough = 45000.00;
```

Using **typedef** often makes what particular types are used for more clear, as in this case, where I'm aliasing the name **device_ready_flag** to the type **bool**:

```
typedef bool device_ready_flag;
```

Chapter 4

Conditional and Loop Statements and Operators

In Depth

The next step up from using simple operators in your code is to use *conditional statements*, also called *branching statements*, or *selection statements* (which is what the official ANSI/ISO C++ specification calls them). You use conditional statements to make decisions based on the value of your data and to make the flow of the program go in different directions accordingly, and we'll take a look at them in this chapter.

Closely allied with conditional statements are *loop statements*, also called *iteration statements* (as in the official ANSI/ISO C++ specification). These statements let you execute code repeatedly under programmatic control. We've seen conditional statements and loop statements in this book already, and they were introduced in Chapter 1, but this is the chapter where we nail down all the facts on these statements.

We'll also take a look at the kinds of operators you use with these statements—relational and logical operators—as well as other program flow statements like **break**, **continue**, **exit**, and **abort**.

Conditional Statements

As mentioned, conditional statements let you make decisions in code. Say for example that you want to report on the weather, and if it's below 80 degrees Fahrenheit, you want to print out a message that reads "It's not too hot." You can do that by checking the current temperature with an **if** statement like this, which compares the value in the variable **temperature** to 80, and if that value is less than 80, prints out that message:

```
#include <iostream>
using namespace std;

int main()
{
    int temperature = 73;

    if (temperature < 80) {
        cout << "It\'s not too hot." << endl;
    }

    return 0;
}
```

The **if** statement tests its *condition*, the part that appears in the parentheses, which in this case is **temperature < 80**. The C++ < (less than) relational operator is used to test if the value in **temperature** is less than 80. Because I've set that value to 73, the **if** statement's condition is true, which means the code in the body of the **if** statement will be executed. Here's the result of this code, temperature.cpp:

```
%temperature
It's not too hot.
```

You can make **if** statements more complex, adding **else** clauses, which must follow an **if** statement and which are executed in case the **if** statement's condition turns out to be false. Here's an example:

```
#include <iostream>
using namespace std;

int main()
{
    int temperature = 73;

    if (temperature < 80) {
        cout << "It\'s not too hot." << endl;
    }
    else {
        cout << "It\'s too hot!" << endl;
    }

    return 0;
}
```

As we'll see, there are other conditional statements as well, and I'll put them to work in this chapter, giving the C++ syntax a thorough workout.

Loop Statements

Loops are fundamental programming constructs that let you handle tasks by executing specific code repeatedly. For example, you might want to handle the items in a set of data by working with each item in succession or to keep performing a task until a particular condition becomes true. The basic loop statement is the **for** statement, which lets you execute a block of code using a loop index. Each time through the loop, the loop index will have a different value, and you can use the loop index to specify a different data item in your data set, like when you use the loop index as an index into an array.

Here's how you use a **for** loop in general; note that ***statement*** can be a simple statement, or it can be a compound statement that includes several simple statements inside curly braces:

```
for (initialization_statement; test_expression; post_expression) statement
```

This loop executes ***statement*** repeatedly as long as ***test_expression*** is true. You can initialize the loop, usually by creating and initializing a loop index, in ***initialization_statement*** (in fact, you can initialize and use multiple loop indexes in a **for** loop). You can then provide a ***test_expression*** that will end the loop when that expression becomes false, and provide an expression to be executed each time after ***statement*** is executed—usually to increment a loop index for the next iteration—in ***post_expression***.

Here's an example to make this clear; in this case, I'll use a **for** loop to sum up the grades of six students in an array and compute the average grade. Here's how that looks in code—note that I am actually declaring and initializing the loop index to 0 in the initialization expression of the **for** loop, which C++ allows you to do:

```
#include <iostream>
using namespace std;

int main()
{
    double grades[] = {88, 99, 73, 56, 87, 64};
    double sum, average;

    sum = 0;

    for (int loop_index = 0; loop_index < sizeof(grades) / sizeof (double);
        loop_index++) {
        sum += grades[loop_index];
    }

    average = sum / (sizeof(grades) / sizeof (double));

    cout << "Average grade = " << average << endl;

    return 0;
}
```

This code loops over all items in the **grades** array and adds them, leaving the result in the variable named **sum**, which I then divide by the total number of entries in the array to find the average value. I loop over all elements using a loop index that starts at 0 and is steadily incremented each time through the loop, up to the last item in the array. Here's the result of this code, average.cpp:

```
%average
Average grade = 77.8333
```

As you can see, the **for** loop is a powerful one; in fact, it's just one of the many topics coming up here, so it's time to start using operators, conditional statements, and loops, and I'll do that now in the Immediate Solutions.

Immediate Solutions

The if Statement

When you want to test conditions and execute code accordingly, it's time to use the conditional statements in C++, such as the **if** statement. Here's what the two forms of the **if** statement look like:

```
if (expression) statement
if (expression) statement else statement
```

The **if** statement lets you execute code depending on whether or not ***expression*** is true or false. If ***expression*** is true, the code in the following ***statement*** (which can be either a simple statement or a compound statement) is executed. There can also be an **else** clause in an **if** statement, and if so, the code in that clause is executed when if ***expression*** is false. Note that ***statement*** can be either a simple statement or a compound statement that can be made up of a number of statements enclosed in curly braces.

For example, one way to get an absolute value of a number is to start by checking if the number is greater than 0, and if so, just print out the number itself. Here's how I make that test with an **if** statement:

```
#include <iostream>
using namespace std;

int main()
{
   int value = 10;

    if(value > 0)
        cout << "Abs(" << value << ") = " << value << endl;

    return 0;
}
```

And here's the result of this code, absval.cpp:

```
%absval
Abs(10) = 10
```

Note that in this case, the statement that's executed if the condition of the **if** statement is true is a single statement, but you can also execute multiple statements if you make them part of a compound statement in a code block, like this:

```
#include <iostream>
using namespace std;

int main()
{
    int value = 10;

    if(value > 0) {
        cout << "The number was positive." << endl;
        cout << "Abs(" << value << ") = " << value << endl;
    }

    return 0;
}
```

Here's the result of this code:

```
%absval
The number was positive.
Abs(10) = 10
```

The **else** Statement

Note that the **if** statement in the absolute value example so far only displays an absolute value if the value itself is greater than 0. However, I can expand that **if** statement by adding an **else** clause, which is executed if the **if** statement's condition is false. Here's how that looks, with the code enabled to handle negative numbers as well as positive ones:

```
#include <iostream>
using namespace std;
```

```
int main()
{
    int value = -10;

    if(value > 0) {
        cout << "Abs(" << value << ") = " << value << endl;
    }
    else {
        cout << "Abs(" << value << ") = " << -value << endl;
    }

    return 0;
}
```


Here's the result of this code:

```
%app
Abs(-10) = 10
```

Nested if Statements

You can also nest **if** statements inside others; here's an example showing how that works:

```
#include <iostream>
using namespace std;

int main()
{
    double value = 2;

    if (value != 0) {
        if (value > 0)
           cout << "The result = " << (1 / value) << endl;
        else
           cout << "The result = " << (-1 / value) << endl;
    }

    return 0;
}
```

And here's the result of this code, nestedif.cpp:

```
%nestedif
The result = 0.5
```

if-else Ladders

In fact, it's possible to create an entire sequence of **if-else** statements, called an **if-else** *ladder*. Here's an example showing how that works; in this case, I test the value in a string successively until I find a match to the current day of the week like this:

```
#include <iostream>
#include <string>
using namespace std;

int main()
{
    string day = "Wednesday";

    if(day == "Monday")
        cout << "It\'s Monday." << endl;
    else if (day == "Tuesday")
        cout << "It\'s Tuesday." << endl;
    else if (day == "Wednesday")
        cout << "It\'s Wednesday." << endl;
    else if (day == "Thursday")
        cout << "It\'s Thursday." << endl;
    else if (day == "Friday")
        cout << "It\'s Friday." << endl;
    else if (day == "Saturday")
        cout << "It\'s Saturday." << endl;
    else if (day == "Sunday")
        cout << "It\'s Sunday." << endl;
}
```

Here's the result of this code, ifladder.cpp:

```
%ifladder
It's Wednesday.
```

Although it's possible to create **if-else** ladders this way, C++ actually includes a statement expressly for situations like this—the **switch** statement, which I'll take a look at in the next section.

The **switch** Statement

The **switch** statement is C++'s multiway branch statement, and it provides the same kind of functionality as an if-else ladder (see "The **if** Statement" earlier in this chapter), but in a much easier form. Here's what the **switch** statement looks like in general:

```
switch (expression) {
    case value1:
        statement1;
        [break;]
    case value2:
        statement2;
        [break;]
    case value3:
        statement3;
        [break;]
            .
            .
            .
    [default:
        default_statement;]
}
```

Here, the value of the ***expression***, which must be of type **byte**, **char**, **short**, or **int**, or any other type that can easily be made into an **int** by the compiler (most compilers won't let you use **float** values, for example), is compared against the various test values in the **case** statements, ***value1***, ***value2***, and so on. If the value of ***expression*** matches one of the values in a **case** statement, the code associated with that **case** statement is executed. If execution reaches a **break** statement, the **switch** statement ends. If there is a **default** statement (it's optional), and ***expression*** doesn't match the value in any **case** statement, the code in the **default** statement is executed.

Here's an example where I display the day of the week based on a numeric value, using a **switch** statement:

```
#include <iostream>
using namespace std;

int main()
{
    int today = 3;
```

```
    switch(today) {
        case 0:
            cout << "It\'s Monday." << endl;
            break;
        case 1:
            cout << "It\'s Monday." << endl;
            break;
        case 2:
            cout << "It\'s Tuesday." << endl;
            break;
        case 3:
            cout << "It\'s Wednesday." << endl;
            break;
        case 4:
            cout << "It\'s Thursday." << endl;
            break;
        case 5:
            cout << "It\'s Friday." << endl;
            break;
        default:
            cout << "It must be Saturday." << endl;
    }

    return 0;
}
```


Here's the result of this code, daystest.cpp:

```
%daystest
It's Wednesday.
```

If you don't like using numbers in **switch** statements, you can always use an enumeration like this:

```
#include <iostream>
using namespace std;

int main()
{
    enum day {Sunday, Monday, Tuesday, Wednesday,
        Thursday, Friday, Saturday};

    day today = Wednesday;
```

```
    switch(today) {
        case Sunday:
            cout << "It\'s Monday." << endl;
            break;
        case Monday:
            cout << "It\'s Monday." << endl;
            break;
        case Tuesday:
            cout << "It\'s Tuesday." << endl;
            break;
        case Wednesday:
            cout << "It\'s Wednesday." << endl;
            break;
        case Thursday:
            cout << "It\'s Thursday." << endl;
            break;
        case Friday:
            cout << "It\'s Friday." << endl;
            break;
        default:
            cout << "It must be Saturday." << endl;
    }

    return 0;
}
```


You can even nest **switch** statements. In such cases, **case** or **default** labels associate with the most deeply nested **switch** statements that enclose them. For example:

```
switch(day)
{
case Saturday:
    switch(temperature)
    {
    case 68:
        cout << "Perfect weather." << endl;
        break;
    case 80:
        cout << "A little warm." << endl;
        break;
        .
        .
        .
    }
```

```
case Sunday:
    .
    .
    .
```

Note that if you don't specify a **break** statement at the end of a **case** statement, execution will continue with the code in the next **case** statement. Sometimes that's useful, as when you want to execute the same code for multiple **case** test values, like this:

```
#include <iostream>
using namespace std;

int main()
{
   int temperature = 68;

    switch(temperature) {
        case 60:
        case 61:
        case 62:
        case 63:
        case 64:
            cout << "Too cold." << endl;
            break;
        case 65:
        case 66:
        case 67:
        case 68:
        case 69:
            cout << "Cool." << endl;
            break;
        case 70:
        case 71:
        case 72:
        case 73:
        case 74:
        case 75:
            cout << "Warm." << endl;
            break;
        default:
            cout << "Probably too hot." << endl;
    }

    return 0;
}
```

Here's the result of this code, nobreak.cpp:

```
%nobreak
Cool.
```

Relational Operators: >, >=, <, <=, ==, and !=

You use relational operators to create expressions that evaluate to true or false, and you can use those expressions in conditional statements like the **if** statement or as the test expressions in loop statements. For example, here's how I check to make sure the budget is greater than 0, using a C++ **if** statement:


```
#include <iostream>
using namespace std;

int main()
{
    int budget = 1;

    if (budget < 0) {
        cout << "Uh oh." << endl;
    }
    else {
        cout << "Still solvent." << endl;
    }
}
```

Here's the result of this code, budget.cpp:

```
%budget
Still solvent.
```

Here are the relational operators; these operators will return true if their operands match their descriptions here:

- **>** —Greater than (For example, **operand1 > operand2** returns true if **operand1** is greater than **operand2**)
- **>=** —Greater than or equal to
- **<** —Less than
- **<=** —Less than or equal to

- **==** —Equal to
- **!=** —Not equal to

Here's something important: Although you can use these operators with C++ string objects, you should use the **strcmp** standard C library function to compare C-style strings. This function will return an integer greater than, equal to, or less than 0, depending on whether the first string is lexicographically greater than, equal to, or less than the second string. Here's an example, strcmp.cpp, which we saw in Chapter 3, that compares two C-style strings and displays the results:

```
#include <iostream>

using namespace std;
int main()
{
    char string1[] = "bat";
    char string2[] = "cat";

    int result = strcmp(string1, string2);

    if (result > 0){
        cout << "string1 is lexicographically greater than string2" << endl;
    } else if (result == 0) {
        cout << "string1 is lexicographically equal to string2" << endl;
    } else if (result < 0) {
        cout << "string1 is lexicographically less than string2" << endl;
    }

    return 0;
}
```

Here's the result of running this program, showing that "bat" comes before "cat" alphabetically:

```
%strcmp
string1 is lexicographically less than string2
```

You can also combine the expressions you create with the relational operator with the logical operators—see the next section for the details.

***TIP:** Here's a C++ pitfall to avoid—when you're comparing two values, bear in mind that you probably want to use == instead of =. For example, the expression **budget == 0** is true if the value in **budget** is 0, but the expression **budget = 0** assigns a value of 0 to **budget**, and the result of that expression is 0, which is always false. Be careful, because using = instead of == in logical conditions is a very common mistake.*

Related solution:	Found on page:
Comparing C-Style Strings	134

Logical Operators: && and ||

You can use the C++ logical operators to tie together logical expressions. The two logical operators you usually use in logical expressions are the logical And, &&, and logical Or, ||, operators. These operators work with operands, as you see in Table 4.1.

Here's how the logical operators work: The Or operator || returns false when both its operands are false, and true otherwise; the And operator && returns true when both its operands are true, and false otherwise. You use these operators to tie logical expressions together in a way that matches their names—use And when you want both logical clauses to be true and Or when you require only one of two clauses to be true.

Here's an example in which I'll use &&; in this case, the value in **temperature** must be *both* less than 90 and greater than 60 for the condition within the **if** statement's parentheses to be true:

```
#include <iostream>
using namespace std;

int main()
{
    int temperature = 70;

    if (temperature < 90 && temperature > 60) {
        cout << "Time for a picnic." << endl;
    }

    return 0;
}
```

Table 4.1 The logical operators.

x	y	x || y (Or)	x && y (And)
false	false	false	false
true	false	true	false
false	true	true	false
true	true	true	true

Here's the result of this code, picnic.cpp:

```
%picnic
Time for a picnic.
```

You can use the || operator with two expressions to return an overall value of true if *either* expression is true. Here's an example that shows how this works:

```
#include <iostream>
using namespace std;

int main()
{
    int temperature = 70;

    if (temperature > 90 || temperature < 60) {
        cout << "Bad weather, no picnic today." << endl;
    } else {
        cout << "Time for a picnic." << endl;
    }

    return 0;
}
```

The result of this program is the same as in the previous example:

```
%picnic2
Time for a picnic.
```

The && and || operators also have an interesting property—they are *short circuit* operators, which means that if they can determine all they need to know by evaluating the left operand, they won't evaluate the right operand. That's very useful in cases like the following, where I'm testing both whether a value holds 0 and its reciprocal; if the value is indeed 0, the second part of the expression, where its reciprocal is calculated, is not executed, so there's no divide-by-zero overflow error in this code:

```
#include <iostream>
using namespace std;

int main()
{
    double value = 0;
```

```
    if (value != 0 && 1 / value < 1000) {
        cout << "The value is not too small." << endl;
    }
    else {
        cout << "The value is too small." << endl;
    }

    return 0;
}
```

Here's the result of this code, divide.cpp:

```
%divide
The value is too small.
```


Precedence of Logical Operators

It's worth noting that the logical operators have lower precedence than the relational operators. For example,

```
temperature > 68 && temperature < 72
```

is the same as this expression:

```
(temperature > 68) && (temperature < 72)
```

In addition, && has higher precedence than ||, so

```
temperature > 68 && temperature < 72 || temperature > 100
```

is the same as

```
(temperature > 68 && temperature < 72) || temperature > 100
```

When in doubt, use parentheses to specify the order in which you want expressions using relational and logical operators. Here's another point while discussing parentheses: The not operator, !, has higher precedence than both the relational and logical operators, so you probably want to use expressions like **!(temperature**

> 68), not **!temperature > 68** (you might think that the expression **!temperature > 68** is fine if you specifically want to flip the logical value of temperature before performing the comparison, but the ! operator returns only two values, 0 and 1, so this expression is *always* false).

One last reminder: The && and || operators are also called short circuit operators, which means that if they can determine all they need to know by evaluating the left operand, they won't evaluate the right operand. See the previous section, "Logical Operators: && and ||," for more details.

The **while** Loop

A **while** loops keeps executing the statement in its body (which may be a compound statement, with a number of single statements inside curly braces) while a particular logical condition evaluates to true. Here's what a **while** loop looks like in general:

```
while(condition) statement
```

While ***condition*** is true, the **while** loop executes ***statement*** over and over; here, ***statement*** can be a simple statement or a compound statement. Note that if the ***condition*** is not true, the body of the loop is not executed even once.

Here's a simple example of putting the **while** loop to work; in this case, I display a value, successively subtracting 1 from that value and displaying the result, as long as the result is positive. When the value becomes 0, the **while** loop stops, because the condition I've used, **value > 0**, has become false:

```
#include <iostream>
using namespace std;

int main()
{
    int value = 10;

    while (value > 0) {
        cout << "Current value = " << value-- << endl;
    }

    return 0;
}
```

Here's what this **while** loop program, simplewhile.cpp, gives us:

```
%simplewhile
Current value = 10
Current value = 9
Current value = 8
Current value = 7
Current value = 6
Current value = 5
Current value = 4
Current value = 3
Current value = 2
Current value = 1
```

Here's another **while** loop example; in this case, I'm writing a program that will calculate factorials (for example, 6 factorial, written as 6!, is equal to 6 * 5 * 4 * 3 * 2 * 1 = 720):

```
#include <iostream>
using namespace std;

int main()
{
    int value = 6, factorial = 1, temp;

    temp = value;   //make a destructive copy of the data.

    while (temp > 0) {
        factorial *= temp--;
    }

    cout << value << "! = " << factorial << endl;

    return 0;
}
```

Here's how this program, whilefactorial.cpp, calculates the factorial of 6:

```
%whilefactorial
6! = 720
```

Although I've used the conditional expression **temp > 0** in this **while** loop, note that you can also use **temp** alone in the conditional expression, because when

temp becomes zero, it's treated as a value of false, which terminates the loop (you often see this kind of shortcut in C++ code):

```
#include <iostream>
using namespace std;

int main()
{
    int value = 6, factorial = 1, temp;

    temp = value;   //make a destructive copy of the data.

    while (temp) {
        factorial *= temp--;
    }

    cout << value << "! = " << factorial << endl;

    return 0;
}
```

Here's a slightly advanced example, which converts a number from base 10 to base 16 using a **while** loop. In this case, I'm using a stack object created with the standard stack template (a construct we'll get to in Chapter 14) to reverse the order of the digits as they are stripped off the number to convert, and the >> operator to shift the number to convert right by 4 binary places to simulate integer division by 16:

```
#include <iostream>
#include <stack>
using namespace std;

int main()
{
    int value = 32, temp = value;
    char characters[] = {'0', '1', '2', '3', '4', '5', '6',
        '7', '8', '9', 'A', 'B', 'C', 'D', 'E', 'F'};
    stack<int> st;

    while (temp > 0) {
        st.push(temp % 16);
        temp >>= 4;
    }
```

```
    cout << "Converting " << value << " yields 0x";

    while(!st.empty()) {
        cout << characters[st.top()];
        st.pop();
    }
}
```

Here's the result of this code, mod.cpp:

```
%mod
Converting 32 yields 0x20
```


Here's a fact that can come in handy: Because null (i.e., empty) statements are valid in C++, a **while** loop doesn't have to have a body at all. Here's an example showing a crude way of calculating an integer square root—note that all the work here takes place in the condition part of the loop:

```
#include <iostream>
using namespace std;

int main()
{
    int target = 144, sqrt = 1;

    while (++sqrt * sqrt != target) ;

    cout << "sqrt(" << target << ") = " << sqrt << endl;

    return 0;
}
```

And here's the result of this code, sqrt.cpp:

```
%sqrt
sqrt(144) = 12
```

Here's another **while** loop example, which combines an assignment and the use of a relational operator in its conditional expression; this example reads and displays the characters in a line of text until it reaches the character '**q**':

```
#include <iostream>
using namespace std;
```

```
int main()
{
    char character;

    while((character = cin.get()) != 'q'){
        cout << character;
    }

    return 0;
}
```

And here's one last example; this one reads integers until the user enters non-integer text (such as a word), in which case **cin >> number** returns a value of false (because I'm trying to store non-integer data in an integer), terminating the loop:


```
#include <iostream>
using namespace std;

int main()
{
    int number;

    cout << "Enter some integers..." << endl;

    while(cin >> number){
        cout << "You entered: " << number << endl;
    }

    cout << "Your entry was not an integer, so quitting." << endl;

    return 0;
}
```

There's another type of **while** loop—the **do-while** loop, and I'll take a look at that in the next section.

Related solution:	*Found on page:*
Using **cin** to Read Individual Characters and Whole Strings	89

The **do-while** Loop

The **do-while** loop is just like a **while** loop, except that the test condition is evaluated at the end of the loop, not at the beginning. Here's what the **do-while** loop looks like; bear in mind that the statement can be a compound statement with a number of single statements inside curly braces:

```
do
    statement
while(condition);
```

Perhaps the most important use for a **do-while** loop instead of a **while** loop is when you need the body of the loop to be run at least once. For example, here's a case where the value I'm testing is not even available for testing until the end of the loop:

```
#include <iostream>
using namespace std;

int main()
{
    int values[] = {1, 2, 3, 0, 5}, test, index = 0;

    do {
        test = 5 * values[index++];
    } while (test < 15);

    return 0;
}
```

On the other hand, there are times when you should use a **while** loop instead of a **do-while** loop—times when the body of the loop shouldn't run even once if the condition is not true. For example, take a look at this code, in which a **do-while** loop evaluates the reciprocal of a value, but it can only test if the value is nonzero at the end of the loop:

```
#include <iostream>
using namespace std;

int main()
{
    double value;
```

```
    do {
        cout << "Enter a value: ";
        cin >> value;
        cout << "The reciprocal is " << 1 / value << endl;
    } while (value != 0);

    return 0;
}
```

This code lets the user divide by zero, which is a problem. Far better in this case is to use a **while** loop to test for 0 first:

```
#include <iostream>
using namespace std;

int main()
{
    double value;

    cout << "Enter a value: ";
    cin >> value;

    while (value != 0) {
        cout << "The reciprocal is " << 1 / value << endl;
        cout << "Enter a value: ";
        cin >> value;
    };

    return 0;
}
```

Here's another **do-while** example; in this program, dowhile.cpp, I create a random integer value between 1 and 10, asking the user to guess the number, and keep looping until they do (some Unix compilers will require the **-lm** switch to link in the math library—note also that some compilers do not support RAND_MAX):

```
#include <iostream>
#include <cmath>
#include <ctime>
using namespace std;
```

```
int main()
{
    int my_number, user_guess;

    srand(time(0));

    my_number = static_cast <double> (rand()) / RAND_MAX * 10 + 1;

    cout << "I've got a number from 1 to 10, can you guess it?" << endl;

    do{
        cout << "Your guess: ";
        cin >> user_guess;
    } while(user_guess != my_number);

    cout << "You got it." << endl;

    return 0;
}
```


Here's what this program, dowhile.cpp, might look like in action:

```
%dowhile
I've got a number from 1 to 10, can you guess it?
Your guess: 1
Your guess: 2
Your guess: 3
Your guess: 4
You got it.
```


Related solution:	Found on page:
The C++ Utility Functions: Math, Time, Trig, Random Numbers, and More	112

The for Loop

The C++ **for** loop is a good choice when you want to use a numeric index that you automatically increment or decrement each time through the loop, as when you're working with an array. Here's what the **for** loop looks like in general; note that ***statement*** can be a simple statement, or it can be a compound statement that includes several simple statements inside curly braces:

```
for (initialization_statement; test_expression; post_expression) statement
```

This loop executes ***statement*** repeatedly as long as ***test_expression*** is true. You can initialize the loop, usually by creating and initializing a loop index, in ***initialization_statement*** (in fact, you can initialize and use multiple loop indices in a **for** loop). You can then provide a ***test_expression*** that will end the loop when that expression becomes false, and provide an expression to be executed each time after ***statement*** is executed—usually to increment a loop index for the next iteration—in ***post_expression***.

Here's an example, firstfor.cpp, showing how to put the **for** loop to work. Note that I start a loop index at 1—a variable that keeps track of how many times the loop has iterated—and end it when the loop index exceeds 10, which means that the loop body will execute exactly 10 times:

```
#include <iostream>
using namespace std;

int main()
{
    int loop_index;

    for (loop_index = 1; loop_index <= 10; loop_index++) {
        cout << "This is iteration number "
            << loop_index << endl;
    }

    return 0;
}

%firstfor
This is iteration number 1
This is iteration number 2
This is iteration number 3
This is iteration number 4
This is iteration number 5
This is iteration number 6
This is iteration number 7
This is iteration number 8
This is iteration number 9
This is iteration number 10
```

Here's an example that we saw at the beginning of the chapter; this example finds the average student score by looping over all scores and summing them—note that I am declaring and initializing the loop index to 0 in the initialization statement of this program, for.cpp:

```
#include <iostream>
using namespace std;

int main()
{
    double grades[] = {88, 99, 73, 56, 87, 64};
    double sum, average;

    sum = 0;

    for (int loop_index = 0; loop_index < sizeof(grades) / sizeof (double);
        loop_index++) {
        sum += grades[loop_index];
    }

    average = sum / (sizeof(grades) / sizeof (double));

    cout << "Average grade = " << average << endl;

    return 0;
}
```

Here's the result of this code:

```
%average
Average grade = 77.8333
```

When you declare a loop variable like **loop_index** in this example, the *scope* of that variable is limited to the **for** loop (the scope of a variable is the part of the program that you can access it in, as we'll see in Chapter 6). That means you can't access **loop_index** outside the **for** loop.

Note that you can have very general expressions in the expressions in a **for** loop. C++ lets you separate expressions in a **for** loop with a comma, like this, where I'm using two loop indices:

```
#include <iostream>
using namespace std;

int main()
{
```

```
    for (int loop_index = 0, doubled = 0; loop_index <= 10;
        loop_index++, doubled = 2 * loop_index) {
        cout << "Loop index " << loop_index <<
             " doubled equals " << doubled << endl;
    }

    return 0;
}
```

Here's the result of this code, doubled.cpp:

```
%doubled
Loop index 0 doubled equals 0
Loop index 1 doubled equals 2
Loop index 2 doubled equals 4
Loop index 3 doubled equals 6
Loop index 4 doubled equals 8
Loop index 5 doubled equals 10
Loop index 6 doubled equals 12
Loop index 7 doubled equals 14
Loop index 8 doubled equals 16
Loop index 9 doubled equals 18
Loop index 10 doubled equals 20
```


You don't have to give a **for** loop any body at all, in fact—you can use a null (i.e., empty) statement as the loop's body. Here's an example in which I'm summing all the elements of an array in a **for** loop without any code in the loop's body:

```
#include <iostream>
using namespace std;

int main()
{
    int array[] = {1, 2, 3, 4, 5}, sum = 0;

    for (int loop_index = 0;
        loop_index < sizeof(array) / sizeof(int);
        sum += array[loop_index++]) ;

    cout << "The sum = " << sum << endl;

    return 0;
}
```

Here's the result of this code, summer.cpp:

```
%summer
The sum = 15
```

You don't even need a loop index of any kind, as in this example that reads text from the user until they type "quit":

```
#include <iostream>
#include <string>
using namespace std;

int main()
{
    string input;

    cout << "Enter some text (\"quit\" to quit)..." << endl;

    for(cin >> input; input != "quit"; cin >> input){
        cout << "You typed: " << input << endl;
        cout << "Enter some text (\"quit\" to quit)..." << endl;
    }

    return 0;
}
```

You can even turn a **for** loop into a **while** loop, as in this example, adapted from the factorial example in "The **while** Loop" earlier in this chapter—note the compactness of this code:

```
#include <iostream>
using namespace std;

int main()
{
    int value = 6, factorial = 1, temp;

    temp = value;   //make a destructive copy of the data.

    for( ; temp; ) {
        factorial *= temp--;
    }
```

```
    cout << value << "! = " << factorial << endl;

    return 0;
}
```

Here's the result of this code:

```
%factorial
6! = 720
```

A convenient way to specify an "infinite" loop, which will repeat forever unless you use a statement like **break** (see "Using the **break** Statement" later in this chapter), is by using the **for** loop like this:

```
for( ; ; )
{
    // Statements
}
```

This is the same as:

```
while(1)
{
    // Statements
}
```

Nested Loops

C++ lets you nest loops, one within another. Here's an example showing how that works; in this case, I'm finding the average value of the elements in a two-dimensional array by looping over all the elements with two **for** loops:

```
#include <iostream>
using namespace std;

int main()
{
    const int ROWS = 3;
    const int COLS = 3;
```

```
    int array[ROWS][COLS] = {{1, 2, 3},
                              {3, 2, 1},
                              {1, 2, 3}};
    int sum = 0, total = 0;

    for(int outer_index = 0; outer_index < ROWS; outer_index++) {
        for(int inner_index = 0; inner_index < COLS; inner_index++) {
            sum += array[outer_index][inner_index];
            total++;
        }
    }

    cout << "Average array value = " <<
        (static_cast<double> (sum) / total) << endl;

    return 0;
}
```

Here's the result of this code, nestedfor.cpp:

```
%nestedfor
Average array value = 2
```


***NOTE:** Although C++ doesn't put a limit on the levels of nesting, compilers usually have a practical limit, such as nine levels.*

Using the **break** Statement

You can use the **break** statement to end a loop or a **switch** statement. Here's an example in which I'm using the **break** statement to end a loop if a sum becomes greater than 12:

```
#include <iostream>
using namespace std;

int main()
{
    int array[] = {1, 2, 3, 4, 5, 6, 7, 8, 9, 10};
    int sum = 0;
```

```
    for(int loop_index = 0; loop_index <
        sizeof(array) / sizeof(int); loop_index++) {

        sum += array[loop_index];
        if (sum > 12) break;
        cout << "Looping..." << endl;
    }

    cout << "The sum exceeded the maximum value." << endl;

    return 0;
}
```

Here's the result of this code, break.cpp:

```
%break
Looping...
Looping...
Looping...
Looping...
The sum exceeded the maximum value.
```


Note that the **break** statement terminates only the most tightly enclosing loop or **switch** statement. This statement can be a very useful one when you need to end a loop, and I've had frequent occasions to use this statement this way—although note that sometimes the apparent need for a **break** statement in a loop really points out a flaw in the program logic.

Using the **continue** Statement

To skip to the next iteration of a loop, you use the **continue** statement. In general, the **continue** statement forces transfer of control to the next iteration of the smallest enclosing loop. Here's an example in which I'm printing out reciprocals, and I want to avoid trying to print out the reciprocal of 0. If the current loop index equals 0, I'll skip the current iteration and move on to the next one using the **continue** statement:

```
#include <iostream>
using namespace std;
```

```
int main()
{
    for(double loop_index = 5; loop_index > -5; loop_index--) {
        if (loop_index == 0) continue;
        cout << "The reciprocal of " << loop_index <<
            " = " << (1 / loop_index) << endl;
    }

    return 0;
}
```

Here's the result of this code, recip.cpp—note that this output skips over the line where it would try to calculate the reciprocal of 0:


```
%recip
The reciprocal of 5 = 0.2
The reciprocal of 4 = 0.25
The reciprocal of 3 = 0.333333
The reciprocal of 2 = 0.5
The reciprocal of 1 = 1
The reciprocal of -1 = -1
The reciprocal of -2 = -0.5
The reciprocal of -3 = -0.333333
The reciprocal of -4 = -0.25
```

Using the **goto** Statement

You can use the **goto** statement to jump from location to location in your code. This statement is heavily frowned on these days, but it still exists. The reason the use of **goto** is so strongly discouraged is that it can make the flow of your program extremely hard to follow and to debug, creating many different execution paths, sometimes called "spaghetti code." In general, you should stay away from **goto**; if you need to break out of a loop, for example, you should use **break**. If you have multiple nested loops to break out of, you might consider the **goto** statement in some cases, but even then it's usually better to use a ladder of **break** statements.

For the sake of completeness, I'll take a look at **goto** here. You use **goto** with a *label*, as in **goto END_LOOP**. In this case, **END_LOOP** is your own term, called a label, and you use this label followed by a colon to precede a statement you want to jump to. Here's an example, goto.cpp, that shows how this works and uses **goto** to end a loop:

```
#include <iostream>
using namespace std;

int main()
{
    for(int loop_index = 0; loop_index > -5; loop_index--) {
        if(loop_index == 0)
            goto END_LOOP;
        cout << "1 / " << loop_index << " = " << 1 / loop_index;
    }
    exit(0);

END_LOOP: cerr << "Ending loop to avoid dividing by 0." << endl;
    return 0;
}
```

There are one or two points to consider here: First, I'm displaying an error message using **cerr**, not **cout**. You use the **cerr** object to display error messages; by default, **cerr** corresponds to the console, just like **cout**. In addition, I'm using the **exit(0)** statement in the code above to end the program normally as soon as the loop ends to avoid printing out the error message—for more on the **exit** statement, see "Using the **exit** and **abort** Statements," next.

Using the **exit** and **abort** Statements

Both the **exit** and **abort** statements end C++ programs. You can use the **exit** statement to exit programs and return an exit code, just as with the **return** statement. You can use this statement throughout a program to end the program, not just in the **main** function. Here's an example from the previous section; in this case, I'm exiting the program with an **exit** code of 0 to indicate normal program termination, before the error message is displayed:

```
#include <iostream>
using namespace std;
```

```
int main()
{
    for(int loop_index = 0; loop_index > -5; loop_index--) {
        if(loop_index == 0)
            goto END_LOOP;
        cout << "1 / " << loop_index << " = " << 1 / loop_index;
    }
    exit(0);

END_LOOP: cerr << "Ending loop to avoid dividing by 0." << endl;
    return 0;
}
```

You can also use the **abort** statement to end a program if you want to bring things to an abrupt halt, as when a significant error occurs. The difference between **exit** and **abort** is that **exit** allows the normal C++ runtime termination processing to take place (for example, global object destructors will be called—see Chapter 8 for more on destructors), but **abort** just stops the program immediately.

Chapter 5

Pointers and Memory Management

In Depth

In the previous chapters, we've seen one way of handling data—naming memory locations as variables and then referring to the data by name in code. This chapter presents another strategy for handling and addressing data: pointers.

Pointers are extremely important in C++, especially for handling memory. Pointers let you access data in memory not by using names but with the actual memory address of the data in memory. When you have the address of a data item in memory stored in a pointer, you can point to that item, which is how pointers get their names—they're like fingers pointing to locations in memory, instead of names for those locations. The fact that pointers point to memory locations without needing a name makes it easier, in many circumstances, to work with pointers under programmatic control than using named memory locations, because you can change the address that a pointer holds at runtime. Pointers are all about addresses in memory, and that's where I'll start this overview.

Getting Addresses in Memory

C++ has a special operator for getting the address of items in memory—the & operator, also called the *address* or *address-of* or *reference* operator (the & address operator, which takes one operand, is not to be confused with the bitwise & operator, which takes two operands). Here's an example showing how the address operator works; in this case, I'm taking the address of a variable in memory, **apples**, and displaying it:

```
#include <iostream>
using namespace std;

int main()
{
    int apples = 10;

    cout << "I have " << apples << " apples at address " << &apples << endl;

    return 0;
}
```

Here's what I get when I run this program on a PC running Windows:

```
C:\cpp>address
I have 10 apples at address 0065FE00
```

And here's the result on a UNIX system:

```
/home/steve:address
I have 10 apples at address 0xeffffc0c
```

Both of these are typical memory addresses on those systems. What if we were to add another integer to the program and display their addresses like this?

```
#include <iostream>
using namespace std;

int main()
{
    int apples = 10;
    int oranges = 20;

    cout << "I have " << apples << " apples at address " << &apples << endl;
    cout << "I have " << oranges << " oranges at address "
        << &oranges << endl;

    return 0;
}
```


Here's the result of this program, address.cpp, in Windows:

```
%address
I have 10 apples at address 0065FE00
I have 20 oranges at address 0065FDFC
```

And here's the result in UNIX:

```
%address
I have 10 apples at address 0xeffffc0c
I have 20 oranges at address 0xeffffc08
```

The difference in these memory addresses is exactly four bytes, which is the size of an **int** variable on both systems.

That's part of the process of creating a pointer—finding the address of the data in memory you want to point to. The other part of the process—this is C++, after all—is to give the pointer a type, and you do that by declaring it.

Declaring Pointers

Every pointer you use must have a type in C++. For example, a pointer that points to integers is an integer pointer, a pointer to a double is a double pointer, and so on. So when you declare a pointer to an **int**, how do you tell C++ that you're declaring a pointer and not a simple **int** variable? You use an asterisk, *, like this, which makes this a declaration of a pointer to an **int**:

```
int *pointer;
```

In fact, the placement of the * is not fixed here; this is the same declaration (note the spacing):

```
int * pointer;
```

In fact, you can also put the * right after the type specifier, and that's common usage as well, like this:

```
int* pointer;
```

Because you can move the * around, you should note that if you're going to declare more than one pointer, this declaration actually declares only one pointer (**pointer1**) and an **int** (**pointer2**):

```
int* pointer1, pointer2;
```

To declare two pointers in the same statement, you should prefix both items with an asterisk:

```
int *pointer1, *pointer2;
```

Let's see an example putting pointers to work. In this case, I'll create an integer and a pointer to an integer; here's what this declaration looks like:

```
#include <iostream>
using namespace std;

int main()
{
```

```
    int integer, *pointer;
     .
     .
     .
```

Now let's make this pointer point to the integer—and see how we can access the data in the integer using the pointer.

Using Pointers

First, I'll store some data in the integer variable like this:

```
#include <iostream>
using namespace std;

int main()
{
    int integer, *pointer;

    integer = 1;
     .
     .
     .
```


And I can store the address of the integer variable in the pointer with the & address operator:

```
#include <iostream>
using namespace std;

int main()
{
    int integer, *pointer;

    integer = 1;

    pointer = &integer;
     .
     .
     .
}
```

Now the pointer points to the integer variable, and provides us with a way of accessing the data in that variable without using the variable's name. How do we use the pointer to access the data it points to? You use the *dereference operator*, which is also an asterisk, *. To refer to the data pointed to by **pointer**, then, we only have to use ***pointer**. Here's what that looks like in code:

```
#include <iostream>
using namespace std;

int main()
{
    int integer, *pointer;

    integer = 1;

    pointer = &integer;

    cout << "The value of the integer is: " << *pointer;

    return 0;
}
```


The * dereference operator takes the location in the pointer and returns the data at that location, so ***pointer** returns a value of 1, the value in the integer. Here's what this program, intpointer.cpp, looks like at work:

```
%intpointer
The value of the integer is: 1
```

That's how pointers work—after you've stored a data item's address in a pointer, you can use the dereference operator to access the data item's value.

***NOTE:** As we'll see, you can get pointers to more than data items in memory; you can also get pointers to functions, objects, and more.*

In fact, because ***pointer** references the data in **integer**, you can change that data with an assignment like this:

```
#include <iostream>
using namespace std;

int main()
{
```

```
    int integer, *pointer;

    integer = 1;

    pointer = &integer;

    *pointer = 2;

    cout << "The value of the integer is: " << *pointer;

    return 0;
}
```

Here's the result of this new code:

```
%intpointer
The value of the integer is: 2
```

As you can see, pointers simply represent another way of accessing memory—this time with an address, not with a name as with variables. In fact, pointers excel at working with memory, not just because you can store memory addresses in them, but also because you can assign those addresses at runtime—and that's the secret behind dynamic memory allocation in C++.

Handling Memory at Runtime with Pointers

As far as C++ is concerned, memory is divided into three areas:—*automatic storage*, where a function's variables are allocated and stored when you enter the function, *static storage*, where data that is declared *static* is stored (as we'll see in Chapter 7) and left for the duration of the program's runtime, and the *free store* (in C, the free store is called the "heap"). The free store is memory set aside for the use of your code at runtime, and you can allocate and handle space in the free store using the C++ **new** and **delete** operators.

Being able to allocate and free memory at runtime is a great asset to a program. Until now, we've allocated memory using only variables, which means you must indicate to C++ exactly how much memory you want before the program even runs. However, that can be wasteful—what if you need 10 elements in an array 90 percent of the time, but 2,000 elements in the same array 10 percent of the time? Declaring the array as a fixed variable means you'll have to declare it with the full 2,000 elements, which can be very wasteful of space. Allocating it *dynamically* means that you can allocate space for as many elements as you need at runtime, which in this case is far more efficient.

You can allocate memory dynamically with the **new** operator and free it with the **delete** operator. Here's an example; in this case, I'll allocate space for a **double** variable named **pi** with the **new** operator like this:

```
#include <iostream>
using namespace std;

int main()
{
    double * pi = new double;
    .
    .
    .
```

The **new** operator returns a pointer to the newly allocated memory, which is why we had to wait for this chapter to use the **new** operator. In this case, the **new** operator returns a pointer to a **double** variable, because we're asking to allocate space for a **double** value. After you've allocated memory space and gotten a pointer to it—the pointer is named **pi** here—you can access that memory with the pointer, as ***pi** here. Here's how I store a value in the newly allocated memory and display that value:

```
#include <iostream>
using namespace std;

int main()
{
    double * pi = new double;

    *pi = 3.14159;

    cout << "The value of pi = " << *pi << endl;
    .
    .
    .
```

When I'm done with the memory I've allocated, I can free it with the **delete** operator like this (you should use the **delete** operator only on memory allocated with **new**):

```
#include <iostream>
using namespace std;
```

```
int main()
{
    double * pi = new double;

    *pi = 3.14159;

    cout << "The value of pi = " << *pi << endl;

    delete pi;

    return 0;
}
```

Here's what this program looks like when running:

```
%new
The value of pi = 3.14159
```

In fact, there's one more step that we should take—if **new** is unsuccessful at allocating the memory you've asked for, it will return a *null* pointer (which has a value of 0 by convention). In code you release publicly, you should check the pointer returned from **new** to make sure it's not a null pointer, which you can do by comparing it to the constant **NULL**:

```
#include <iostream>
using namespace std;

int main()
{
    double * pi = new double;

    if(pi == NULL) exit(1);

    *pi = 3.14159;

    cout << "The value of pi = " << *pi << endl;

    delete pi;

    return 0;
}
```

***NOTE:** If you don't check the return value from the **new** operator and end up using a null pointer in your code, that code will crash and usually display a message about null pointers at some location in your program, which will be meaningless to the user.*

There's also a form of **new** and **delete** for use with arrays—see "Using **new** and **delete** with Arrays" later in this chapter.

Pointers and Arrays and Pointer Arithmetic

There's a special aspect to pointers that's very important—pointer arithmetic. Say you have a pointer to an array of **double** values in memory. As you know, a pointer points to a memory location, so if you were to add 1 to a pointer, you'd expect it to point to the next memory location—that is, to the next byte following the one originally pointed at. In fact, that's not how it works—each pointer knows its own type, and when you add 1 to it, it's actually incremented by the *size of the element* it points to. For example, a pointer to a **double** is incremented by the size of a **double** (usually eight bytes) when you increment the pointer by 1. This is called pointer arithmetic.

This is a great way to access a sequence of values in memory, because all you have to do is keep adding 1 to a pointer to move from one value to the next, no matter what the size of the item the pointer points to (as long as such items always have the same length). Here's an example; in this case, I'll set up an array of **double** values, which are stored one after the other in memory:

```
#include <iostream>
using namespace std;

int main()
{
    double values[4] = {0.0, 1.0, 2.0, 3.0};
        .
        .
        .
```

Now I'll get a pointer to the first element in the array:

```
#include <iostream>
using namespace std;

int main()
{
    double values[4] = {0.0, 1.0, 2.0, 3.0};
```

```
double *pointer = &values[0];
    .
    .
    .
```

At this point, I can display the value in the first element of the array as ***pointer**, and display it. And using pointer arithmetic, I can also add 1 to the pointer directly to access the next element in the array; that looks like this:

```
#include <iostream>
using namespace std;

int main()
{
    double values[4] = {0.0, 1.0, 2.0, 3.0};

    double *pointer = &values[0];

    cout << "*pointer = " << *pointer << endl;

    cout << "*(++pointer) = " << *(++pointer) << endl;

    return 0;
}
```

Here's what this program, pointermath.cpp, looks like at work; as you can see, the pointer has indeed been incremented from the first element to the second:

```
%pointermath
*pointer = 0
*(++pointer) = 1
```

As you can see, you can move through arrays using pointers. In fact, here's another interesting point—C++ can treat array names as pointers in many ways. For example, the expression **&values[0]** in the code above is actually the same as the name **values** itself—that is, an array name may be treated as a pointer to the first element of the array for many purposes (but not for all purposes—for example, you can't assign a value to an array name as you can to a pointer). The similarities between arrays and pointers is a favorite topic among C++ programmers, and it makes allocating and using arrays at runtime easy; see "Using **new** and **delete** with Arrays" later in this chapter. We'll take a look at this issue in this chapter in detail—see "Similarities between Pointers and Arrays in C++."

Pointers and Structures

There's one more issue to cover in our overview of pointers before getting to the Immediate Solutions: using pointers with structures. A pointer points to a data item in memory—but with a structure, you need more information. What if you want to point to one of the members of a structure, not just the whole structure itself? In that case, you need to specify exactly what member of the structure you want. Up until now, we've used the dot operator, ., to point to a member of a structure like this: ***structure.member***. In fact, the syntax **(*pointer_to _structure).member** will work if you have a pointer to the structure, but C++ has a shortcut that you'll often see used—the arrow operator, ->. When you use the arrow operator, you can use the pointer directly, without having to dereference it with the * operator. All you have to do is to use the expression ***pointer_to_structure->member***, which is the same as **(*pointer_to _structure).member**.

Here's an example. In this case, I'll create a structure variable, **structure1**, and get a pointer to that structure. Then I'll use that pointer directly with the arrow operator to access a text string in the structure—here's what this code looks like, structptr.cpp:

```
#include <iostream>
#include <string>
using namespace std;

int main()
{
    struct structure{
        string text;
        int numbers[100];
    } structure1;

    structure *pointer = &structure1;

    pointer->text = "Hello from the arrow operator.";

    cout << pointer->text << endl;

    return 0;
}
```

How do you access an element in the array of integers that's inside the structure? See "Pointers, Structures, and the -> Operator" later in this chapter. In fact, it's time to turn to the Immediate Solutions section now for the details on pointers.

NOTE: *Working with pointers is one of the topics we'll cover in great depth in this book, handling the special issues that they raise, which many books just gloss over. For example, see "Using Pointers to Functions" in Chapter 6, "Passing Arguments to Functions by Reference" in Chapter 7, "Pointers to Objects and to Object Members" in Chapter 8, "Creating a Copy Constructor" in Chapter 9, "Virtual Methods and Runtime Polymorphism" in Chapter 10, "Using Pointers in Class Templates" in Chapter 11, "Using* ***dynamic_cast*** *with Pointers at Runtime" in Chapter 12, and—well, you get the idea. The upshot is that it's important to get a good understanding of pointers for much of the C++ material that's coming up.*

Immediate Solutions

Finding a Data Item's Address

To create a pointer, you need a memory location to point to, and in C++, you use the & operator, called the *address* or *address-of* or *reference* operator, to get the address of an item in memory. You apply this operator to lvalues. We saw an example in the In Depth section of this chapter, address.cpp, that declared two integers and then found their addresses in memory:

```
#include <iostream>
using namespace std;

int main()
{
    int apples = 10;
    int oranges = 20;

    cout << "I have " << apples << " apples at address " << &apples << endl;
    cout << "I have " << oranges << " oranges at address "
        << &oranges << endl;

    return 0;
}
```


Here's the result of this program, address.cpp, in Windows:

```
%address
I have 10 apples at address 0065FE00
I have 20 oranges at address 0065FDFC
```

And here's the result in UNIX:

```
%address
I have 10 apples at address 0xeffffc0c
I have 20 oranges at address 0xeffffc08
```

The difference in these memory addresses is exactly four bytes, which is the size of an **int** variable on both systems. Knowing how to get an address in memory is only half the process of creating a pointer—pointers are strongly typed in C++, so to create one you first have to declare it. See the next section for the details.

Declaring a Pointer

As we saw in the In Depth section of this chapter, every pointer you use must have a type in C++. For example, a pointer that points to integers is an integer pointer, a pointer to a double is a double pointer, and so on.

For example, you might want to declare a pointer to an **int**—how do you tell C++ that you're declaring a pointer and not an **int** variable? You use an asterisk, *, like this, which makes this a declaration of a pointer to an **int**:

```
int *pointer;
```

As mentioned in the In Depth section of this chapter, the placement of the * is not fixed; this is the same declaration (note the spacing):

```
int * pointer;
```

In fact, you can also put the * right after the type specifier, and some programmers like to do it that way:

```
int* pointer;
```

Here's an important note that we also saw in the In Depth section of this chapter—because you can move the * around, you should know that if you're going to declare more than one pointer, a declaration like this one really declares only one pointer (**pointer1**) and an integer (**pointer2**):

```
int* pointer1, pointer2;
```

If you want to declare two pointers in the same statement, you prefix both items with an asterisk:

```
int *pointer1, *pointer2;
```

Can you declare pointers to pointers? No problem; here's a pointer to a pointer to an **int** value (you can see this pointer to a pointer at work in "Creating and Using Pointers" next in this chapter):

```
int **ptr2ptr;
```

Pointer declarations can become involved, and their syntax a little obscure. For example, is this declaration for a constant pointer to an integer, or a pointer to an integer constant?

```
int * const pointer1;
```

After wrestling with pointer declarations years ago, I finally figured out the way to handle them, which I'm passing on to you (and which I've never seen in any other book on C++). The key is to read them *backwards*. The above declaration, for example, can be read as "pointer1 is a constant pointer to an integer."

How about this one?

```
const int *pointer1;
```

In this case, you'd read this declaration as "pointer1 is a pointer to an integer constant." You can even have declarations like this:

```
const int * const pointer1;
```

As you can now figure out, this is a constant pointer to an integer constant. For more on pointers and constants, by the way, see "Pointers and **const**" later in this chapter. For some details on declaring pointers to multi-dimensional arrays, see "Using **new** and **delete** with Arrays" later in this chapter.

Creating and Using Pointers

There are two steps to creating a pointer, declaring it and placing an address in it. The previous section took a look at declaring pointers, and you can place an address in it with the & ***address*** operator, which is covered in "Finding a Data Item's Address" earlier in this chapter.

We saw this example, intpointer.cpp, in the In Depth section of this chapter; here, I declare a pointer and use the & operator to make it point at an integer variable, and then I use the syntax ***pointer** to access the data the pointer points to:

```
#include <iostream>
using namespace std;

int main()
{
    int integer, *pointer;

    integer = 1;

    pointer = &integer;

    *pointer = 2;

    cout << "The value of the integer is: " << *pointer;

    return 0;
}
```

Here's what this code looked like when running:

```
%intpointer
The value of the integer is: 2
```

You can also initialize a pointer when you declare it, as long as you use the & operator on a memory location that already exists (because declarations are executed left to right, **integer** will exist when we take its address in the second part of the declaration statement):

```
#include <iostream>
using namespace std;

int main()
{
    int integer = 1, *pointer = &integer;

    *pointer = 2;

    cout << "The value of the integer is: " << *pointer;

    return 0;
}
```

__TIP:__ How can you assign a memory location directly to a pointer? Here, **static_cast** *won't work (for example,* **pointer = static_cast <int *> (0xb0000000);** *won't compile). You'll need a stronger cast, like* **reinterpret_cast**, *which reinterprets the bits of a value entirely (like this:* **pointer = reinterpret_cast <int *> (0xb0000000);***). There's usually no reason to do this unless you're working with hardware ports or device buffers (like the keyboard or screen buffers, or the system clock) directly in your code. For more on casts like this, see "Using Static, Reinterpret, and* **const** *Casts" later in this chapter.*

In addition, make sure a pointer actually points to a memory location before you use it—unlike languages like Perl, C++ will not create the memory location a pointer points to when you just use the pointer. For example, this code will cause a problem, because **pi** doesn't point to an actual location in memory until you put an address in it:

```
double * pi;
*pi = 3.14159;
```

Can you use pointers to pointers? Of course—just use double asterisks. Here's an example, ptr2ptr.cpp:

```
#include <iostream>
using namespace std;

int main()
{
    int integer, *pointer, **ptr2ptr;

    integer = 1;

    pointer = &integer;

    ptr2ptr = &pointer;

    cout << "The value of the integer is: " << **ptr2ptr;

    return 0;
}
```

Here's what this program looks like when running:

```
%ptr2ptr
The value of the integer is: 1
```

Using **new** to Allocate Memory

As we saw in the In Depth section of this chapter, you can allocate memory dynamically with the **new** operator and free it with the **delete** operator. Here's an example, new.cpp. Here, I'll allocate space for a **double** variable named **pi** with the **new** operator like this:

```
#include <iostream>
using namespace std;

int main()
{
    double * pi = new double;
        .
        .
        .
```

The **new** operator returns a pointer to the newly allocated memory. In this case, the **new** operator returns a pointer to a **double** variable, because we're asking it to allocate space for a **double** value. The **new** operator will return a null pointer, with the value 0, if it was unsuccessful, so before using the new pointer, you should compare it to the constant **NULL** (note that before exiting a real program in this manner, of course, you should explain why you're exiting):

```
#include <iostream>
using namespace std;

int main()
{
    double * pi = new double;

    if(pi == NULL) exit(1);
        .
        .
        .
```

After you've allocated memory space and gotten a valid pointer to it, you can access that memory with the pointer using this syntax: ***pointer**. Here's how I store a value in the newly allocated memory and display that value:

```
#include <iostream>
using namespace std;
```

```
int main()
{
    double * pi = new double;

    if(pi == NULL) exit(1);

    *pi = 3.14159;

    cout << "The value of pi = " << *pi << endl;

    return 0;
}
```

Here's what this program looks like when running:

```
%new
The value of pi = 3.14159
```

When you're done with the memory you've allocated with the **new** operator, you should free it with the **delete** operator; see the next section for the details.

Related solution:	Found on page:
Using the **exit** and **abort** Statements	195

Using **delete** to Deallocate Memory

When you allocate memory yourself with the **new** operator, you're responsible for managing it yourself. To avoid cluttering up your program with memory you're no longer using, you should delete it with the **delete** operator. To delete allocated memory, you just pass the pointer to that memory to the **delete** operator.

This is especially important when you allocate memory with **new** in a function each time the function is called—don't count on C++ to delete that memory for you. If you call that function repeatedly, the result can be a huge amount of wasted and frozen memory, called a memory leak.

***TIP:** You should use the **delete** operator only on memory allocated with **new.** Don't try to delete memory in automatic or static storage with the **delete** operator.*

For example, here's how I delete the memory allocated in the example in the previous section:

```
#include <iostream>
using namespace std;

int main()
{
    double * pi = new double;

    *pi = 3.14159;

    cout << "The value of pi = " << *pi << endl;

    delete pi;

    return 0;
}
```

As you can see, deleting allocated memory is easy enough. There's also a special form of **delete** you use with arrays—see the next section.

Using **new** and **delete** with Arrays

There are special forms of **new** and **delete** you use with arrays, often referred to as **new[]** and **delete[]**. The **new** operator works as you'd expect with arrays, just add brackets, [and], to indicate how many elements you want to allocate in memory. The arrays you create on the fly like this are called *dynamic arrays*.

For example, here's how I allocate an array of ten **double** values, place a value in one of the array's elements, and display that value:

```
#include <iostream>
using namespace std;

int main()
{
    double * values = new double[10];

    if(values == NULL) exit(1);

    values[5] = 3.14159;
```

```
    cout << "The stored value = " << values[5] << endl;
    .
    .
    .
```

To delete the array when I'm done with it, I just use **delete[]** (not **delete**):

```
#include <iostream>
using namespace std;

int main()
{
    double * values = new double[10];

    if(values == NULL) exit(1);

    values[5] = 3.14159;

    cout << "The stored value = " << values[5] << endl;

    delete[] values;

    return 0;
}
```


Here's what this program, newarray.cpp, looks like when running:

```
%newarray
The stored value = 3.14159
```

When you use **new** to allocate a multi-dimensional array, it returns a pointer to the first element of the array, and the resulting pointer type preserves the size of all but the left-most array dimension. For example:

```
new float[100][200][300];
```

returns a pointer of type **float (*)[200][300]**, and that's the type to use with arrays of this type. For example, the following code, which uses a simple pointer to a **float**, is invalid:

```
float *pointer;
pointer = new float[100][200][300];
```

Here's the way you should write this code:

```
float (*pointer)[200][300];
pointer = new float[100][200][300];
```

In fact, there is a special relationship between pointers and arrays in C++. You may have noticed that I used a pointer as an array name in the code earlier in this section:

```
#include <iostream>
using namespace std;

int main()
{
    double * values = new double[10];

    if(values == NULL) exit(1);

    values[5] = 3.14159;
    .
    .
    .
```

For more on the relationship between pointers and arrays, see the next section, as well as "Passing Arrays to Functions" in Chapter 6.

***TIP:** Unfortunately, when you use **new**, there's no way (yet) to initialize the array you're creating in the same statement. To fill a dynamic array, you must store values in the array after it's been created in the **new** statement.*

Related solution:	Found on page:
Passing Arrays to Functions	264

Similarities between Pointers and Arrays in C++

In C++, pointers and arrays are similar. For example, in the previous section, we saw that you can use a pointer as the name of an array like this:

```
#include <iostream>
using namespace std;
```

```
int main()
{
    double * values = new double[10];

    if(values == NULL) exit(1);

    values[5] = 3.14159;
        .
        .
        .
```

Similarly, you can use an array name as a constant pointer that points to the first element in the array. For example, here's how I create an array, **values**, of ten items and use the name of that array as a constant pointer to the first element of the array:

```
#include <iostream>
using namespace std;

int main()
{
    double values[10];

    *values = 3.14159;

    cout << values[0] << endl;

    return 0;
}
```

In other words, **values** and **&values[0]** are the same thing, as are **values[0]** and ***values**.

The fact that C++ lets you treat array names as pointers in many ways means that you can refer to the elements in an array using pointer notation. As mentioned in the In Depth section of this chapter, and discussed in "Pointer Arithmetic" later in this chapter, when you add 1 to a pointer, the pointer is incremented by the length of the item it points at, not just to the next memory location. That means that the expression **array[*n*]** is actually the same as ***(array + *n*)** (for example, ***(values + 5)** is the same as **values[5]**).

Similarly, if you have a pointer, you can refer to the locations following the current location using array notation—in other words, ***(pointer + *n*)** is the same as **pointer[*n*]**. This is very useful when you've used **new** to allocate an array, as you see in the code at the beginning of this section, where I've allocated an array using **new** and then used the pointer returned by **new** as the name of an array.

However, there are some distinct differences between pointers and array names in C++. An array name is not an lvalue by itself, so you can't add values to it as you can with pointer arithmetic, and you can't assign a pointer to an array name. That is to say, you can only consider an array name a *constant* pointer, not a regular pointer. Note also that the **sizeof** operator gives the size of an array when you apply it to an array, but only the size of the pointer itself when you apply it to a pointer. For more on this topic, see "Pointer Arithmetic, "next in this chapter, as well as "Passing Arrays to Functions" in Chapter 6.

Related solutions:	Found on page:
The **sizeof** Operator	102
Passing Arrays to Functions	264

Pointer Arithmetic

What's pointer arithmetic? It's best explained by example—say that you have a pointer to an array of **double** values in memory. If you were to add 1 to that pointer, you might expect it to point to the next memory location—that is, to the next byte. In fact, that's not how it works—as mentioned in the In Depth section of this chapter, each pointer knows its own type, and when you add 1 to it, it's actually incremented by the size of the element it points to. In this case, that means that a pointer to a **double** is incremented by the size of a **double** (usually eight bytes) when you increment the pointer by 1.

Pointer arithmetic is great when you want to access a sequence of values in memory—all you have to do is to keep adding 1 to a pointer to move from one value to the next. Here's an example we saw briefly in the beginning of this chapter; in this case, I'll set up an array of **double** values, which are stored one after the other in memory:

```
#include <iostream>
using namespace std;
```

```
int main()
{
    double values[4] = {0.0, 1.0, 2.0, 3.0};
    .
    .
    .
```

Now I'll get a pointer to the first element in the array:

```
#include <iostream>
using namespace std;

int main()
{
    double values[4] = {0.0, 1.0, 2.0, 3.0};

    double *pointer = &values[0];
    .
    .
    .
```

At this point, you can access the value in the first element of the array as ***pointer**. With pointer arithmetic, you can add 1 to the pointer to address the next element in the array this way:

```
#include <iostream>
using namespace std;

int main()
{
    double values[4] = {0.0, 1.0, 2.0, 3.0};

    double *pointer = &values[0];

    cout << "*pointer = " << *pointer << endl;

    cout << "*(++pointer) = " << *(++pointer) << endl;

    return 0;
}
```

Here's what this program, pointermath.cpp, looks like when running:

```
%pointermath
*pointer = 0
*(++pointer) = 1
```

If you have a pointer, then, you can refer to item ***n*** in memory following the current item as ***(pointer + *n*)**. In fact, you can refer to the locations following the current one using array notation—in other words, ***(pointer + *n*)** is the same as **pointer[*n*]**. See "Similarities between Pointers and Arrays in C++" earlier in this chapter for more on using pointers with array notation.

Pointers and C-Style Strings

As you recall from Chapter 3, C-style strings are simply arrays of type **char**. Because that's the case, you can use pointers to point to C-style strings; here's an example:

```
#include <iostream>
using namespace std;

int main()
{
    const char *message = "Hello from C++.";
        .
        .
        .
```

The **cout** object is smart enough to know about pointers to C-style strings, so you can display them using **cout** like this:

```
#include <iostream>
using namespace std;

int main()
{
    const char *message = "Hello from C++.";

    cout << message << endl;

    return 0;
}
```

Here's what this code, stringpointer.cpp, looks like at work:

```
%stringpointer
Hello from C++.
```

In fact, many of the standard C library functions that deal with strings handle them with pointers. For example, you can use the **strstr** function to search for the first occurrence of a C-style substring in a C-style string. This function returns a pointer to the found substring in the string (if the substring is not found, **strstr** returns 0). Here's an example, strstr.cpp, that we first saw in Chapter 3; in this case, I search for the substring "ing" in the string "We are building a house." The **strstr** function returns a pointer to the location of the start of the substring, and if I pass that pointer to **cout** as the beginning of a C-style string, it will display all the text including and following "ing":

```
#include <iostream>

using namespace std;
int main()
{
    char string1[] = "We are building a house.";
    char string2[] = "ing";
    char* string3;

    string3 = strstr(string1, string2);

    cout << string3 << endl;

    return 0;
}
```

Here's the result of this program:

```
%strstr
ing a house.
```

You can also use the standard C library function **strcat** to append one string to another; this function returns a pointer to the resulting string. Here's an example showing how to use **strcat**; in this case, I'm concatenating the strings "Hello" and " there" and displaying the result:

```
#include <iostream>

using namespace std;
```

```
int main()
{
    char string1[] = "Hello";
    char string2[] = " there";
    char* string3;

    string3 = strcat(string1, string2);

    cout << string3 << endl;

    return 0;
}
```

Here's the result of this program, strcat.cpp:

```
%strcat
Hello there
```

Related solutions:	Found on page:
Creating C-Style Strings	132
Searching C-Style Strings	135
Concatenating C-Style Strings	135

Pointers, Structures, and the -> Operator

When you want to access a simple data type pointed to by a pointer, there's no problem—you just use an expression like ***pointer**. However, what if the item you're pointing at itself has an internal structure, with internal members? How do you know which one you're pointing at?

Say you have a structure like this one:

```
struct structure{
    string text;
    int numbers[100];
} structure1;
```

Now say you have a pointer, **pointer**, to a variable of this structure type, and you want to access the **text** member in that variable. How do you do it? As discussed in the In Depth section of this chapter, you can use syntax like this: **(*pointer).text**. C++ also supports an alternate syntax that uses the arrow pointer, ->, that you can use without dereferencing the pointer at all, like this: **pointer->text**.

Here's an example, structptr.cpp, putting this to work; in this example, I'm creating a structure variable, getting a pointer to that variable, and then accessing the **text** member in the structure using the pointer directly as **pointer->text**:

```
#include <iostream>
#include <string>
using namespace std;

int main()
{
    struct structure{
        string text;
        int numbers[100];
    } structure1;

    structure *pointer = &structure1;

    pointer->text = "Hello from the arrow operator.";

    cout << pointer->text << endl;

    return 0;
}
```


What if I want to access the array numbers in the structure? I can use an expression like **pointer->numbers[5]** to do that:

```
#include <iostream>
#include <string>
using namespace std;

int main()
{
    struct structure{
        string text;
        int numbers[100];
    } structure1;

    structure *pointer = &structure1;
```

```
    pointer->numbers[5] = 5;
    pointer->text = "Hello from the arrow operator.";

    cout << pointer->text << endl;

    cout << "Here's the value: " << pointer->numbers[5] << endl;
    return 0;
}
```

Here's what this program, structptr.cpp, looks like in action:

```
%structptr
Hello from the arrow operator.
Here's the value: 5
```

You can also store pointers in a structure; here's an example showing how to do that. This example uses a program construct called a *linked list*; in a linked list, each item points to the next item in the list, allowing you to navigate from item to item (in doubly linked lists, each item also points to the previous item). In this case, each item will be a variable of a structure that holds two integers and a pointer to the next structure:

```
#include <iostream>
using namespace std;

int main()
{
    struct structure
    {
        int integer1;
        int integer2;
        struct structure *next;
    } structure1, structure2, structure3;
    .
    .
    .
```

I've created three structures of this type, **structure1**, **structure2**, **structure3**, in this declaration, and I can fill the pointers in **structure1** and **structure2** to point to the next structures in the sequence:

```
#include <iostream>
using namespace std;
```

```
int main()
{
    struct structure
    {
        int integer1;
        int integer2;
        struct structure *next;
    } structure1, structure2, structure3;

    structure1.next = &structure2; //Set up linked list.
    structure2.next = &structure3;
    .
    .
    .
```

After placing a value in **integer1** in the second structure, I can use the pointer in the first structure to access that integer, as in this code:

```
#include <iostream>
using namespace std;

int main()
{
    struct structure
    {
        int integer1;
        int integer2;
        struct structure *next;
    } structure1, structure2, structure3;

    structure1.next = &structure2; //Set up linked list.
    structure2.next = &structure3;

    structure2.integer1 = 5;

    cout << "integer1 in structure2 = "
        << structure1.next->integer1 << endl;

    return 0;
}
```

And here's what this program, linkedlist.cpp, displays when running:

```
%linkedlist
integer1 in structure2 = 5
```

Using **auto_ptr** for Safe Deletes

As you know, you should delete memory that you've allocated with **new** using the **delete** operator. However, under some circumstances, your program may not reach the point where the **delete** operator releases the memory (for example, where an error may have occurred and program flow is returned from a function before all the code in the function is executed).

The C++ standard template library, which we'll see in Chapter 15, has a special template named **auto_ptr** to handle such cases. Using **auto_ptr**, you can allocate memory using pointers in such a way that you don't have to use **delete**; when the pointer is no longer in scope, the memory it points to is automatically returned to the free store (see Chapter 6 for more on scope, which refers to the parts of a program in which an item is visible).

To use **auto_ptr**, you can use the syntax **auto_ptr<*type*> *name* (new *type*)** and include the memory header file, which is where **auto_ptr** is defined. Here's an example where I'm creating a new pointer to a string—note that the code doesn't need to use **delete**, because deleting the allocated memory is handled automatically:

```
#include <iostream>
#include <memory>
#include <string>
using namespace std;

int main()
{
    auto_ptr<string> pointer (new string("Hello from C++"));

    cout << *pointer;

    //no delete needed

    return 0;
}
```

Pointers and **const**

It's worth discussing pointers and constant values, because there are issues here you should know about. In C++, you can have pointers to variables, as we've done throughout this chapter. You can also declare a pointer to a constant value;

in this example, **pointer1** is a pointer to an integer constant (for more on using **const** in pointer declarations, see "Declaring a Pointer" earlier in this chapter):

```
const int * pointer1;
```

In fact, this pointer doesn't have to point to a constant value at all; all you're saying with this declaration is that the pointer will treat the value it points to as a constant (and the compiler will consider it an error if it doesn't). For example, this will work, where the pointer is actually pointing to an **int**, not a constant:

```
#include <iostream>
using namespace std;

int main()
{
    int integer1 = 5;
    const int * pointer1;

    pointer1 = &integer1;

    cout << *pointer1;

    return 0;
}
```


Treating a value as a constant this way can help prevent errors that occur when you inadvertently change that value. You can also have a pointer to a constant value that actually does point to a constant value, like this:

```
#include <iostream>
using namespace std;

int main()
{
    const int integer1 = 5;
    const int * pointer1;

    pointer1 = &integer1;

    cout << *pointer1;

    return 0;
}
```

However, you cannot have a regular pointer that points to a constant, like this—this will generate a compiler error:

```
#include <iostream>
using namespace std;

int main()
{
    const int integer1 = 5;
    int * pointer1;

    pointer1 = &integer1;          //Error.

    cout << *pointer1;

    return 0;
}
```

Here's a summary:

- Regular pointers to variables are allowed.
- Regular pointers to constants are not allowed.
- Pointers to constants that point at constants are allowed.
- Pointers to constants that point at variables are allowed.

You can also create constant pointers. With such pointers, you're indicating you will not change the value in the pointer. Here's an example:

```
#include <iostream>
using namespace std;

int main()
{
    int integer1 = 5;
    int * const pointer1 = &integer1;

    cout << *pointer1;

    return 0;
}
```

And you can also have constant pointers to constants (again, this means you'll be treating the value pointed to as a constant, not necessarily that it is a constant):

```
#include <iostream>
using namespace std;

int main()
{
    int integer1 = 5;
    const int * const pointer1 = &integer1;

    cout << *pointer1;

    return 0;
}
```


Pointers and Casts

Usually, you can't cast between pointer types, however, you can use a pointer of the **void*** type to hold a pointer to *any* non-constant data type. In fact, **void** pointers are sometimes called *generic* pointers.

Here's an example, voidptr.cpp, in which I'll use a **void** pointer to point to an integer value:

```
#include <iostream>
using namespace std;

int main()
{
    int integer = 5;
    void *pointer;

    pointer = &integer;
        .
        .
        .
```

Now I can access the value this pointer points to—but to do that, I need to use a cast to indicate what kind of pointer I want to treat the **void** pointer as (you can't dereference a **void** pointer directly). In this case, I want to treat the void pointer as an integer pointer:

```
#include <iostream>
using namespace std;

int main()
{
    int integer = 5;
    void *pointer;

    pointer = &integer;

    cout << "The value in the integer is "
        << *(static_cast<int *> (pointer)) <<endl;

    return 0;
}
```

Here's what this program, voidptr.cpp, looks like when running:

```
%voidptr
The value in the integer is 5
```

As you can imagine, **void** pointers are useful when the type of data you're pointing at isn't known ahead of time.

Using Static, Reinterpret, and const Casts

As we saw in "Conversion between Data Types" in Chapter 2, there are several different ways you can perform type casts in C++:

- **(*type*)**—Old style cast, considered obsolete.
- **const_cast <*type*> (*expression*)**—This type of cast casts away "const"-ness.
- **dynamic_cast <*type*> (*expression*)**—This type of cast supports runtime identification of class objects addressed by pointer or reference.
- **reinterpret_cast <*type*> (*expression*)**—This type of cast supports low-level reinterpretation of the bit pattern of the expression.
- **static_cast <*type*> (*expression*)**—This type of cast simply makes explicit casts, without runtime type checking, and turns off warning messages.

Now that we know what we're doing with pointers, we can dig into these types of casts more deeply.

You can use **static_cast** to make explicit the kinds of casts that the compiler could actually perform implicitly (although it might issue a warning); here's an example from Chapter 2 where I'm casting from a **float** value to an **int** value:

```
#include <iostream>
using namespace std;
int main()
{
    int sum;
    int ten = 10;
    float pi = 3.14159;

    sum = static_cast <int> (pi) + ten;

    cout << "The integer sum = " << sum << endl;

    return 0;
}
```

You use **const_cast** to cast away the "const"-ness of an expression (also the "volatile"-ness of the expressions—see "All About Storage Class Qualifiers: **const**, **register**, **volatile**, and **mutable**" in Chapter 7). Here's an example in which I'm able to cast away the fact that **const_ptr** is a constant pointer when I assign it to the regular pointer **ptr** (this would be an error otherwise):

```
char *ptr;
const char *const_ptr;
    .
    .
    .
ptr = const_cast <char *> (const_ptr);
```

You use **reinterpret_cast** for those cases when **static_cast** wouldn't work, because **reinterpret_cast** forces the compiler to reinterpret what the actual bits of a value stand for. This is the most powerful cast, and it makes sense to use this cast only if you know what you're doing—for example, if you reinterpret the bits of a **float** as a **long**, you'll just get nonsense.

However, there are times when you should use **reinterpret_cast**, and we already saw one of them in "Creating and Using Pointers" earlier in this chapter. In that case, I wanted to assign a memory location directly to a pointer. Here, **static_cast** wouldn't work.

For example, the following line of code won't compile because the compiler doesn't consider casting from an **unsigned long** to **int*** something it can do implicitly:

```
pointer = static_cast <int *> (0xb0000000);
```

You'll need **reinterpret_cast**, as in this code:

```
pointer = reinterpret_cast <int *> (0xb0000000);
```

NOTE: *As mentioned in "Creating and Using Pointers" earlier in this chapter, there's usually no reason to assign a number directly to a pointer like this unless you're working with hardware ports or device buffers, like the keyboard or screen buffers, or the system clock.*

You use **dynamic_cast** with runtime type information (RTTI), and we'll take a look at that cast in Chapter 12.

Reading Command-Line Arguments

When you start a program on the command line, you can pass command-line arguments to that program. For example, say you start a program named commandline like this:

```
%commandline Hello there C++.
```

The first command-line argument passed to the program is the name of the program itself, "commandline" (some C++ installations preface the name with a path). The second argument is "Hello", the next is "there", and the last is "C++.". To read command-line arguments, you use this special form of the **main** function, as in a new example, commandline.cpp:

```
#include <iostream>
using namespace std;

int main(int argc, char * argv[])
{
      .
      .
      .
}
```

The **argc** argument holds the number of command-line arguments, including the name of the program, and the second argument, **argv**, is a pointer to the **char** arrays holding the command-line arguments. Here's how you can display all the command-line arguments in a loop:

```
#include <iostream>
using namespace std;

int main(int argc, char * argv[])
{
    for (int loop_index = 0; loop_index < argc; loop_index++) {
        cout << argv[loop_index] << endl;
    }

    return 0;
}
```

Here's what you see when you run this example, commandline.cpp:

```
%commandline Hello there C++.
commandline
Hello
there
C++.
```


TIP: *C++ programming in the Macintosh works a little differently here because of the absence of a command line. If you use Symantec C++ or Metrowerks CodeWarrior, you can include console.h and execute the statement* ***argc = ccommand(&argv)****. This displays a dialog box for the command-line arguments, allowing the user to enter those arguments.*

Chapter 6

Functions

If you need an immediate solution to:	*See page:*

In Depth

The building blocks of C++ programs are *functions*. All code is enclosed in functions (although there are a few compiler-specific specialized exceptions to this rule, such as shared code in memory). We already know what functions are—the prime example of a function is the **main** function:

```
#include <iostream>
using namespace std;

// Display a welcoming message.

int main()
{
    cout << "Hello from C++" << endl;

    return 0;
}
```

The empty parentheses after the name of the **main** function is there to indicate that the function is passed no arguments, and the **int** before the **main** function's name is there to indicate that the function returns an integer value. We're going to see how to call functions of our own construction in this chapter. In fact, as you know, C++ comes with many functions built into its various libraries, and we've already seen how to pass arguments to the library functions and make use of their return values, as in this example from Chapter 3 where I'm putting the standard C library function **strlen** to work to find the length of a C-style string:

```
#include <iostream>

using namespace std;
int main()
{
    char string1[] = "Hello";

    cout << "The length of string1 is " << strlen(string1) << " characters."
        << endl;

    return 0;
}
```

In this case, I'm passing a C-style string to **strlen**, and it returns the length of the string (minus the terminating 0 byte) in characters as an integer value, which I'm displaying:

```
%strlen
The length of string1 is 5 characters.
```

As you know, a C-style string is really an array of characters, so what I'm doing here is passing an array to **strlen**, and we'll see how to pass arrays to our own functions in this chapter.

There's a lot to know about functions, so both this and the following chapter are devoted to them. I'll start with an overview about how to define your own functions.

Defining Functions

As you know from working with the **main** function, you *define* your own function with this kind of framework:

```
type name(arguments...)
{
    statements
    return expression;
}
```


Here, ***type*** is the return type of the function—if the function does not return a value, you use the keyword **void** here—***name*** is the name of the function, and ***arguments...*** is the comma-separated argument list, which also specifies the type of each argument (in this format: ***type argument1, type argument2...***). If the function is not passed any arguments, you can either use the keyword **void** in the parentheses or leave the parentheses empty. The body of the function, where the function's code is—***statements*** above—is enclosed in curly braces. If the function returns a value, you can use a **return** statement as shown. The **return** statement need not be the last statement in a function—you may use **return** statements in conditional statements throughout the function, for example—but note that if any code follows the **return** statement at the end of a function, there may be no way of reaching that code, because the program flow of execution may have already exited the function.

A function definition like this tells the C++ compiler what code you want in your function. Here's an example, function.cpp; in this case, I'm creating a function named **greeting** that is passed no arguments and returns none and that simply displays the greeting "Hello from the greeting function."

NOTE: *Don't try to compile the following example just yet—as we'll see, it still needs some additional work.*

```
#include <iostream>
using namespace std;

int main()
{

    return 0;
}

void greeting(void)
{
    cout << "Hello from the greeting function." << endl;
}
```

Because this function is passed no arguments and returns no value, I can call it very simply, like this:

```
#include <iostream>
using namespace std;

int main()
{
    greeting();

    return 0;
}

void greeting(void)
{
    cout << "Hello from the greeting function." << endl;
}
```

When the program flow encounters the function call, program execution transfers to the **greeting** function, executes the code there to display the greeting, and then returns to the point immediately following the function call.

I can also construct a function that you pass arguments to and that returns a value. For example, I can pass two integer values to a function named **adder** and have it return the sum of those arguments as a **long**. Here's what the **adder** function looks like in outline:

```
#include <iostream>
using namespace std;

int main()
{
    greeting();

    return 0;
}

void greeting(void)
{
    cout << "Hello from the greeting function." << endl;
}

long adder(int x, int y)
{
    .
    .
    .
}
```

As you can see, **adder** has two items in its argument list, and I'm specifying the types of those arguments. In this case, the first argument, which I'm naming **x**, is an **int** type argument, and the second argument, which I'm naming **y**, also is an **int** type argument. I'm also specifying the return type from this function as **long**. Naming the arguments passed to functions follows the same rules as you use for naming variables (see "Naming Variables" in Chapter 2 for the details).

Now that I've given names to the arguments passed to the function, I can refer to the values of those arguments in the body of the function using the same names. The order of the arguments is preserved, so the first argument will be named **x** and the second **y**. I can add **x** and **y** and return their sum in this function:

```
#include <iostream>
using namespace std;

int main()
{
    greeting();

    return 0;
}
```

```
void greeting(void)
{
    cout << "Hello from the greeting function." << endl;
}

long adder(int x, int y)
{
    return x + y;
}
```

I can call the new function, **adder**, with two integer arguments and display the return value—the sum of those values—like this:

```
#include <iostream>
using namespace std;

int main()
{
    int value1 = 5, value2 = 10;

    greeting();
    cout << value1 << " + " << value2 << " = "
        << adder(value1, value2)   << endl;

    return 0;
}

void greeting(void)
{
    cout << "Hello from the greeting function." << endl;
}

long adder(int x, int y)
{
    return x + y;
}
```

NOTE: *The type of the arguments you pass to a function must match those declared in the argument list, or the compiler must be able to implicitly convert the types to match; otherwise, you'll get an error.*

Is this code ready to run? No—if you try to compile it, you'll get errors. What's the problem? The problem is that although we *defined* two new functions, we didn't *declare* them, and you do that with *function prototypes*.

Declaring Functions with Prototypes

In the previous section, we took a look at how to define a function. You can also *declare* a function, using a function prototype. In C++, a function prototype tells the compiler about the function so it knows what to expect when you use it. How do you create a prototype? Say you have this general form of a function:

```
type name(arguments...)
{
    statements
    return expression;
}
```

Creating a prototype for this function is easy; you just copy over the first line and add a semicolon after it like this:

```
type name(arguments...);
```

This prototype effectively declares the function, just like declaring a variable, so the compiler knows what arguments and types the function is passed and what type of value it returns. A prototype allows the compiler to perform type checking, and in C++, you must either declare a function (with a prototype) or define it (by giving its full code) before using the function. You usually place the prototypes for the functions you create at the top of the file so the compiler sees them before encountering calls to those functions, like this:

```
type name(arguments...);
    .
    .
    .
type name(arguments...)
{
    statements
    return expression;
}
```

Here's what this looks like in our example, function.cpp—note that the function prototypes appear outside any function, and before any calls to the declared functions appear in code:

```
#include <iostream>
using namespace std;
```

```
void greeting(void);
long adder(int x, int y);

int main()
{
    int value1 = 5, value2 = 10;

    greeting();
    cout << value1 << " + " << value2 << " = " << adder(value1, value2)
        << endl;

    return 0;
}

void greeting(void)
{
    cout << "Hello from the greeting function." << endl;
}

long adder(int x, int y)
{
    return x + y;
}
```

That's all it takes; now this code compiles and runs, calling the two functions **greeting** and **adder**:

```
%function
Hello from the greeting function.
5 + 10 = 15
```

You can avoid using prototypes if you define a function before using it, in which case the compiler knows all about the function before it's called and doesn't need a prototype. (Incidentally, that's why **main** never needs a prototype—you never call **main** yourself, so the compiler never sees any calls to **main** before encountering its definition.)

Here's an example that compiles and runs without the use of prototypes, because I'm defining the **greeting** and **adder** functions before they're ever called:

```
#include <iostream>
using namespace std;

void greeting(void)
{
```

```
    cout << "Hello from the greeting function." << endl;
}

long adder(int x, int y)
{
    return x + y;
}

int main()
{
    int value1 = 5, value2 = 10;

    greeting();
    cout << value1 << " + " << value2 << " = " << adder(value1, value2)
        << endl;

    return 0;
}
```

Although this way of programming works, it's not always possible to place all the functions before they're called (the C++ style is normally to place the **main** function first, because that's where program execution starts and it provides the entry point of the program).

The prototypes for functions are often hidden in header files, along with other declarations. As you know, you frequently have to include header files to use various functions in the C or C++ libraries, and the prototypes of those functions are in those header files.

I can place the prototypes for the **greeting** and **adder** functions in a header file named, say, header; here's the content of that file (some implementations may require you to use an extension for the header file like .h; see "Basic Skills: Using Header Files" in Chapter 1 for more details):

```
void greeting(void);
long adder(int x, int y);
```

And I then include the header file in the rest of the code with an **#include** preprocessor directive:

```
#include <iostream>
#include "header"
using namespace std;
```

```
int main()
{
    int value1 = 5, value2 = 10;

    greeting();
    cout << value1 << " + " << value2 << " = " << adder(value1, value2)
        << endl;

    return 0;
}

void greeting(void)
{
    cout << "Hello from the greeting function." << endl;
}

long adder(int x, int y)
{
    return x + y;
}
```

Scope

Now that we're discussing functions, the idea of scope becomes important. Scope refers to the section of program in which a particular name may be used; for example, the scope of a variable is made up of those parts of your program in which you can legally refer to that variable in code.

The variables declared inside a function are *private* to that function by default. That is, a function provides a private space for variables that you intend to use locally in the function. The fact that such variables are private to the function helps you divide a program into discrete building blocks, because even if you use the same variable name in different functions, those variables won't overlap or conflict. Here's an example, scope.cpp; in this case, I'm declaring and using a variable named **sum** in a function named **adder**, which adds two integer values and returns their sum:

```
#include <iostream>
using namespace std;

long adder(int value1, int value2);

int main()
{
```

```
    return 0;
}

long adder(int value1, int value2)
{
    long sum;

    sum = value1 + value2;
    return sum;
}
```

Now I can call the function **adder** from code in **main**, but I cannot refer directly to the variable named **sum** in the **main** function, because **sum** is declared and is private to another function, **adder**:

```
#include <iostream>
using namespace std;

long adder(int value1, int value2);

int main()
{
    cout << adder(1, 2);
    //cout << sum;                //can't access this variable here!

    return 0;
}

long adder(int value1, int value2)
{
    long sum;

    sum = value1 + value2;
    return sum;
}
```

Variables you declare in functions are called *automatic variables*, because the space for them is automatically allocated every time you call the function. They're stored in a section of memory called the *automatic store*, or automatic storage (which usually corresponds to the program's internal stack).

NOTE: *As discussed in the In Depth section of Chapter 5, memory is divided into three areas—automatic storage, where a function's variables are allocated and stored when you enter the function; static storage, where data that is declared static is stored (as we'll see in Chapter 7) and left for the duration of the program's runtime, and the free store (in C, the free store is called the "heap").*

Here's an example, autostorage.cpp, in which I'll store variables in automatic storage. I start by creating a C++ **string** class variable named **color** with the text "red" in it; because this variable is declared in a function and is not specifically declared static, it'll be allocated in the automatic storage for the **main** function:

```
#include <iostream>
#include <string>
using namespace std;

int main()
{
    string color("red");

    cout << "In main the color is " << color << endl;
    .
    .
    .
```

I can also call a function that uses its own variable of the same name, **color**, but assigns it the color "green", which will be stored in the automatic storage of that function:

```
#include <iostream>
#include <string>
using namespace std;

void function(void);

int main()
{
    string color("red");

    cout << "In main the color is " << color << endl;
    function();

    return 0;
}

void function(void)
{
    string color("green");

    cout << "In the function the color is " << color << endl;
}
```

In fact, variables declared in any code block (as delimited by { and })—not just those defined in a function's code block—are stored in the automatic storage for the code block. You can use such code blocks in conditional statements or loop statements, or by themselves, enclosed in { and } as here, where I'm creating another variable with the name **color**, and this time assigning it the value "blue":

```
#include <iostream>
#include <string>
using namespace std;

void function(void);

int main()
{
    string color("red");

    cout << "In main the color is " << color << endl;
    function();

    return 0;
}

void function(void)
{
    string color("green");

    cout << "In the function the color is " << color << endl;

    {
        string color("blue");
        cout << "In the block the color is " << color << endl;
    }

    cout << "After the block the color is " << color << endl;
}
```

Now, even though I've used the same variable name, **color**, in each code block in the program, each of those variables are local to the code blocks they're in. This means that I've been able to assign a different value to **color** in each code block, as you see when the program, autostorage.cpp, runs:

```
%autostorage
In main the color is red
In the function the color is green
```

```
In the block the color is blue
After the block the color is green
```

NOTE: *In the next chapter, we'll extend the concept of scope to deal with linkage, which specifies how you can use names across files. We'll also see how to create variables with global scope, which you can access with code anywhere in your file.*

As you can see, the idea of scope lets you divide a program into sections, none of which conflicts with the others. For more on scope, see "What Does Scope Mean?" later in this chapter.

That's it for our overview of functions; it's time to start digging into the Immediate Solutions section now—there's far more to see about functions, and we'll also take a look in this and the next chapter at topics like passing arrays and structures to functions, handling a variable number of arguments, inline functions, default arguments, and more.

Immediate Solutions

Defining a Function

To define a function, you indicate the function's name, the names and types of the arguments passed to it, if any, and its return type, like this in general:

```
type name(arguments...)
{
    statements
    return expression;
}
```

As discussed in the In Depth section of this chapter, ***type*** is the return type of the function—if the function does not return a value, you use the keyword **void** here—***name*** is the name of the function, and ***arguments...*** is the comma-separated argument list, which also specifies the type of each argument (in this format: ***type argument1, type argument2...***). If the function is not passed any arguments, you can either use the keyword **void** in the parentheses or leave the parentheses empty. The body of the function, where the function's code is—***statements*** above—is enclosed in curly braces. If the function returns a value, you can use a **return** statement as shown. The **return** statement need not be the last statement in a function—you may use **return** statements in conditional statements throughout the function, for example—but note that if any code follows the **return** statement at the end of a function, there may be no way of reaching that code, because the program flow of execution may have already exited the function.

Here's an example that we saw in the In Depth section of this chapter, function.cpp. In this case, I'm defining two new functions, **greeting** and **adder**. The **greeting** function is passed no arguments and returns none, but the **adder** function is passed two integers and returns a **long**:

```
#include <iostream>
using namespace std;

void greeting(void);
long adder(int x, int y);
```

```
int main()
{
    int value1 = 5, value2 = 10;

    greeting();
    cout << value1 << " + " << value2 << " = " << adder(value1, value2)
        << endl;

    return 0;
}

void greeting(void)
{
    cout << "Hello from the greeting function." << endl;
}

long adder(int x, int y)
{
    return x + y;
}
```

Note that because I've defined these functions after calling them in **main**, I've also added prototypes for these functions at the top of the code—see the next section for all the details on prototypes.

Declaring Functions Using Prototypes

The C++ compiler needs to know about a function before you call it, and you can let the compiler know about a function in two ways—by *defining* it before you call it (see the previous section for more on defining functions), or by *declaring* it using a prototype for the function before you call it.

It's not always possible to define a function before you call it—the function may be in another file, for example, or in a library of such functions—but the compiler still needs to know about the function before you can use it. To let it know about the function in such cases, you use a prototype, which is like a declaration for the function. For example, if this is what your function definition looks like:

```
type name(arguments...)
{
    statements
    return expression;
}
```

then here's the corresponding prototype:

```
type name(arguments...);
```

You can place the prototype in your code before the definition of the corresponding functions, and before any calls are made to that function:

```
type name(arguments...);
    .
    .
    .
type name(arguments...)
{
    statements
    return expression;
}
```

In standard C++, you use a prototype to declare a function, or you must define it before it's called. In ANSI standard C, prototypes are optional, but they're mandatory in C++ if you call a function before defining it, because the C++ compiler needs to know about functions before they are called.

NOTE: *There's another difference between ANSI C and ANSI/ISO standard C++ prototypes: if you leave the parentheses after the function name empty in C++, it means the function is passed no arguments, but in C, it just means you're not specifying the arguments in the argument list.*

Here's how I create prototypes for the functions **greeting** and **adder** for the code from the previous section, where I defined those two functions:

```
#include <iostream>
using namespace std;

void greeting(void);
long adder(int x, int y);

int main()
{
    int value1 = 5, value2 = 10;

    greeting();
    cout << value1 << " + " << value2 << " = " << adder(value1, value2)
        << endl;
```

```
    return 0;
}

void greeting(void)
{
    cout << "Hello from the greeting function." << endl;
}

long adder(int x, int y)
{
    return x + y;
}
```

Using prototypes is easy, because all you have to do is to copy the first line of a function's definition and add a semicolon after it.

All you should remember here is that you must let the compiler know about a function before calling the function. That means using a prototype to declare the function, or defining the function before calling it, as here:

```
#include <iostream>
using namespace std;

void greeting(void)
{
    cout << "Hello from the greeting function." << endl;
}

long adder(int x, int y)
{
    return x + y;
}

int main()
{
    int value1 = 5, value2 = 10;

    greeting();
    cout << value1 << " + " << value2 << " = " << adder(value1, value2)
        << endl;

    return 0;
}
```

It's also worth noting that function prototypes are often stored in header files, which you then include in your code with the **#include** preprocessor directive.

For example, I've been including the iostream header file in nearly every program in the book up to this point, because that header gives the necessary declarations for the functions and objects in the iostream library, like **cout**.

I can place the prototypes of the **greeting** and **adder** functions in a header file, which I'll just name header (some C++ implementations may require you to use an extension for the header file like .h; see "Basic Skills: Using Header Files" in Chapter 1 for more details):

```
void greeting(void);
long adder(int x, int y);
```

Then I use the **#include** preprocessor directive to include that header file with the rest of the code:

```
#include <iostream>
#include "header"
using namespace std;

int main()
{
    int value1 = 5, value2 = 10;

    greeting();
    cout << value1 << " + " << value2 << " = " << adder(value1, value2)
        << endl;

    return 0;
}

void greeting(void)
{
    cout << "Hello from the greeting function." << endl;
}

long adder(int x, int y)
{
    return x + y;
}
```


Related solution:	Found on page:
Basic Skills: Using Header Files	51

Passing Arguments to Functions

You can pass data to a function for that function to use, and that data is passed as *arguments* to the function. You specify the types and names for the arguments passed to a function in both the function's definition and prototype (if it has a prototype) in the *argument list*, which is enclosed in parentheses after the function's name:

```
type name(arguments...);
    .
    .
    .
type name(arguments...)
{
    statements
    return expression;
}
```

The argument list is a comma-separated list of arguments, and each entry in the list specifies the argument's name as well as its type in this format: ***type argument1, type argument2...***. An argument's name is the name you give it so that you can refer to it in the function's code, and such names must obey the naming rules for C++ variables (see "Naming Variables" in Chapter 2 for more details).

In the example function.cpp, which we saw in the In Depth section of this chapter, we defined a function named **adder** that is passed two integer values, adds them, and returns a **long**. Here's what that function looks like in outline:

```
long adder(int x, int y)
{
    .
    .
    .
}
```

As you can see, the argument list here is **int x, int y**, indicating that the function is passed two arguments. The argument list also indicates that the first argument passed to this function is an integer, and I'll refer to it with the name **x** in the function's code, and the second argument is also an integer, and I'll refer to it with the name **y**. Both variables, **x** and **y**, are local to the function. Here's how I put the arguments passed to **adder** to work in code, now that I can refer to them with the names I've given them:

```
#include <iostream>
using namespace std;

void greeting(void);
long adder(int x, int y);

int main()
{
    int value1 = 5, value2 = 10;

    greeting();
    cout << value1 << " + " << value2 << " = " << adder(value1, value2)
        << endl;

    return 0;
}

void greeting(void)
{
    cout << "Hello from the greeting function." << endl;
}

long adder(int x, int y)
{
    return x + y;
}
```

Here are some other examples of argument lists in function prototypes:

```
int draw_circle(int x, int y, int radius);
double calculate_value(double asset_value, float years, float rate);
void display_text(string text, int color);
long find_max(long value1, long value2);
```

It's worth knowing that by default, C++ passes by *value*, which means that what's passed to the function is a *copy* of each value. That doesn't make much difference when you're working with simple variables, but it does when you're working with large structures, because a copy of the entire structure is passed each time you pass it to a function, which can slow things down and strain the program's automatic storage space. Now that you know that structures are passed by value, you might want to pass a pointer to a structure instead, for example (see "Passing Structures to Functions" later in this chapter). And because array names are treated as constant pointers in C++, when you pass an array to a function, what's actually passed is a copy of that pointer—which also has ramifications, because now the code in the function has direct access to the elements in the original array and so might inadvertently change them.

For the details on passing arrays to functions, see "Passing Arrays to Functions." For more details on passing structures to functions, see "Passing Structures to Functions."

NOTE: *You can also pass by reference in C++, which is the alternate way of passing arguments to functions, and we'll take a look at that process in Chapter 7.*

Related solution:	Found on page:
Naming Variables	71

Returning Values from Functions

When you define a function, and when you create a prototype for a function, you must specify the type of the return value of the function, such as **int**, **float**, **double**, and so on. If the function does not return a value, you can use the keyword **void**. You specify the return type of the function just before the function's name in both function definitions and prototypes:

```
type name(arguments...);        //Function prototype
    .
    .
    .
type name(arguments...)         //Function definition
{
    statements
    return expression;
}
```

In C++, functions may be passed multiple arguments, but they may return only a single value, unlike some languages like Perl, which allow you to return multiple values (although the single returned value may be a pointer to an entire array of values—see "Returning Arrays from Functions" later in this chapter).

NOTE: *In older versions of C++, you could omit the type of the return value of a function, because the default was* ***int****. However, in ANSI/ISO standard C++, you must now specify the return type of the functions you define or declare. Some compilers may let you omit the return type, but I encourage you to specify the return type for all functions.*

When you call a function in code (by using the function's name and enclosing any arguments in parentheses after that name), the value of that function call evaluates to the value returned by the function. So how do you actually return a value from a function? You use a **return** statement to return a value. The **return** statement takes the value ***expression***, returns it from the function, and transfers program execution back to the point immediately following the function call:

```
type name(arguments...)
{
    statements
    return expression;
}
```

Note that the type of expression must match the type you declared as the function's return type, or be of a type that the compiler can implicitly cast into that type.

Let's see this at work. We saw this example, function.cpp, in the In Depth section of this chapter—here, two integers are passed to the function **adder**, and **adder** returns their sum. Therefore, in this case, the expression **adder(value1, value2)** is replaced with the sum of the two passed arguments:

```
#include <iostream>
using namespace std;

void greeting(void);
long adder(int x, int y);

int main()
{
    int value1 = 5, value2 = 10;

    greeting();
    cout << value1 << " + " << value2 << " = " << adder(value1, value2)
        << endl;

    return 0;
}

void greeting(void)
{
    cout << "Hello from the greeting function." << endl;
}
```

```
long adder(int x, int y)
{
    return x + y;
}
```

Here are some other examples of return values, as specified by function prototypes:

```
int draw_circle(int x, int y, int radius);
double calculate_value(double asset_value, float years, float rate);
void display_text(string text, int color);
long find_max(long value1, long value2);
```

For the details on returning arrays from functions, see "Returning Arrays from Functions." For more details on returning structures from functions, see "Returning Structures from Functions."

Calling Functions

As we've already seen, when you call a function, you just use the function's name and enclose any arguments you want to pass to the function in parentheses after the name. The function call is itself an expression and it evaluates to the value returned by the function. For example, if the **sqrt** function returns the square root of a value, then the expression **sqrt(4)** evaluates to 2.

You can assign the return value of a function to a variable with the same type (or of a type that the compiler can cast to implicitly):

```
int sum = adder(value1, value2);
```

Sometimes, you might not have any use for the return value of a function, and C++ lets you discard that value, as in this statement, where I am not assigning the return value of **adder** to any variable:

```
adder(value1, value2);
```

For more on calling functions and handling their return values, see the previous section, "Returning Values from Functions." For the details on how to use function pointers to call functions, see "Using Pointers to Functions" later in this chapter.

What Does Scope Mean?

The scope of a name or token in a C++ program is the sum of all the areas in the program in which you can refer to that name or token. In other words, scope represents the window of visibility for names or tokens. The concept of scope becomes important when you start dividing your program into functions, because each function has its own scope.

As mentioned in the In Depth section of this chapter, variables you declare in functions are called automatic variables, because the space for them is automatically allocated every time you call the function. They're stored in a section of memory called automatic storage (which usually corresponds to the program's internal stack). As you know, memory is divided into three areas—automatic storage, where a function's variables are allocated and stored when you enter the function; static storage, where data that is declared static is stored; and the free store.

The scope of automatic variables declared in a function is limited to the function's body, which means that such variables are private to the function. In this example, scope.cpp, the automatic variable **sum** is private to the function **adder** and so cannot be referenced in **main**:

```
#include <iostream>
using namespace std;

int adder(int a, int b);

int main()
{
    cout << adder(1, 2);
    //cout << sum;                  //can't access this variable here!

    return 0;
}

int adder(int a, int b)
{
    int sum;

    sum = a + b;
    return sum;
}
```

As discussed in the In Depth section of this chapter, automatic variables may be declared in any code block, not just functions. This includes conditional and loop statements, and code blocks that are delimited with { and }. The following example, autostorage.cpp, illustrated this point in the In Depth section of this chapter; here, I'm placing variables in automatic storage in functions and a code block, and even though I use the same name for these variables, they're quite separate, as you see when the program runs:

```
#include <iostream>
#include <string>
using namespace std;

void function(void);

int main()
{
    string color("red");

    cout << "In main the color is " << color << endl;
    function();

    return 0;
}

void function(void)
{
    string color("green");

    cout << "In the function the color is " << color << endl;

    {
        string color("blue");
        cout << "In the block the color is " << color << endl;
    }

    cout << "After the block the color is " << color << endl;
}
```

Here's what this example, autostorage.cpp, looks like when running:

```
%autostorage
In main the color is red
In the function the color is green
In the block the color is blue
After the block the color is green
```

Note also that the variables in a code block that encloses another code block are visible in the inner block, unless their name conflicts with a variable in the inner block, in which case the local version of the variable is used. For example, the local redefinition of the color variable in the code block in autostorage.cpp hides the variable of the same name in enclosing block.

NOTE: *Where is automatic storage actually stored? When it runs, your program maintains automatic storage on the program* stack, *which is a special construct designed for this purpose. We'll see more about stacks when we cover the standard C++ templates starting in Chapter 15; you can see an example in which I create a stack for our own use in "The* ***while*** *Loop" in Chapter 4.*

C++ also has a keyword named **auto** that's worth mentioning; using this keyword makes sure a variable is stored in automatic storage, and you can use it if there's any question (the counterpart of **auto** is **static**, which we'll see in Chapter 7, and which explicitly stores variables in static storage):

```
void function(void)
{
    auto string color("green");
        .
        .
        .
```

We'll also take a look at more issues of scope in the next chapter, Chapter 7, as well as the idea of *linkage*, which indicates how you can use variables across files.

Here's an important thing to note about scope: When an automatic variable is no longer in scope, you should not assume that it's still around for you to work with. This means that you should not, for example, return a pointer to an automatic variable from a function if that variable was defined in that function, because if the variable is no longer in scope, it may well have been deallocated and written over. If you want to return a pointer to newly allocated data from a function, you should use the **new** operator to allocate memory in the free store, not in automatic storage. Memory allocated in the free store will stay allocated until you use **delete**, so you can safely return a pointer to memory allocated with **new** from a function.

TIP: *The fact that automatic variables are allocated in a function every time that function is called means that they start off with their initial values every time the function is called. That's bad news if you want those variables to retain their values between function calls, as in a function you call when you want to keep track of a count of some sort. To make variables in functions retain their values between calls to the function, you can declare them* ***static****, as we'll see in the next chapter.*

Related solutions:	*Found on page:*
The **if** Statement	166
The **for** Loop	186

Passing Arrays to Functions

What if you want to pass an entire array to a function? For example, what if you want to write a function that sums all the values in an array and returns their sum? It turns out that this is not so difficult in C++, and we'll take a look at an example, passarray.cpp, that does exactly that—sums the elements of an array.

To add the elements in an array, I'll create a new function named **adder** and pass the array to **adder**, as well as the number of elements in the array to add. To indicate that an argument you are passing to a function is an array, you only need to add [] after the argument's name like this in the prototype for **adder**:

```
#include <iostream>
using namespace std;

long adder(int array[], int number_elements);
    .
    .
    .
```

Now I can create an array in **main** and pass both it and its size to **adder**. After **adder** sums the values in the array, I can display that sum like this:

```
#include <iostream>
using namespace std;

long adder(int array[], int number_elements);

int main()
{
    int data[] = {1, 2, 3, 4};

    int total = adder(data, sizeof(data)/sizeof(int));

    cout << "The total is " << total << endl;

    return 0;
}
```

In the **adder** function, I can simply refer to the passed array as **array[]**, because I've declared it that way in the argument list; here's how I loop over all the elements in the array, find their sum, and return that sum:

```
long adder(int array[], int number_elements)
{
    long sum = 0;

    for (int loop_index = 0; loop_index < number_elements; loop_index++)
        sum = sum + array[loop_index];

    return sum;
}
```

And here's what this program looks like when it's running:

```
%passarray
The total is 10
```

This code looks very much like what you'd expect with simple variables, so why does it merit its own coverage? The answer is that there are several things going on behind the scenes here that you must know about. Recall that C++ treats the names of arrays as constant pointers, so when you pass an array to a function, you're not really passing the array's elements at all, but rather a copy of that constant pointer. Because you can interchange array and pointer notation when indexing elements, I was able to use array notation when accessing members of the array, even though I'm really working with a pointer:

```
long adder(int array[], int number_elements)
{
    long sum = 0;

    for (int loop_index = 0; loop_index < number_elements; loop_index++)
        sum = sum + array[loop_index];

    return sum;
}
```

***NOTE:** Because when you pass an array to a function, what's really passed is a constant pointer to the array, I also needed to pass the number of elements in the array to sum to the function. If I had tried to find the number of elements in the array in the code in **adder** using **sizeof**, I would simply have had returned the size of the pointer.*

Although this interchange of notation between arrays and pointers makes passing arrays to functions very convenient, it also has one ramification you must be aware of—the pointer you're passed points back to the original array, which means that the code in your function can work with the elements in that array directly, possibly changing them inadvertently. To make sure that doesn't happen, you can declare the array parameter with **const**—see the next section for the details.

Function Arguments and **const**

As discussed in the previous section, when you pass a pointer to a function, the code in that function can directly access the data pointed to by that pointer. Sometimes that's just what you want, but other times it's not such a good idea, because the code in the function might inadvertently modify the original data.

One place where it's easy to have problems with pointers passed to functions is where you pass arrays to functions. It's easy to forget that what's actually passed to the function is a constant pointer to the array, which means the code in the function has access to the original array. If you want to make sure the code in the function doesn't alter the data in the original array, you should make the pointer you pass a pointer to constant data, and you do that with **const** (see "Pointers and **const**" in Chapter 5).

It's easy to protect your data in cases like this; here's how I use **const** to modify the example in the previous section to indicate that the code in the function **adder** should treat the data pointed to by the pointer named **array** as constant:

```
#include <iostream>
using namespace std;

int adder(const int array[], int number_elements);

int main()
{
    int data[] = {1, 2, 3, 4};

    int total = adder(data, sizeof(data)/sizeof(int));

    cout << "The total is " << total << endl;

    return 0;
}
```

6. Functions

```
int adder(const int array[], int number_elements)
{
    int sum = 0;

    for (int loop_index = 0; loop_index < number_elements; loop_index++)
        sum = sum + array[loop_index];

    return sum;
}
```

Related solution:	Found on page:
Pointers and **const**	229

Returning Arrays from Functions

Because arrays are passed to functions using pointers, it makes sense to return them the same way. In fact, the easy interchange between pointers and array names makes this process pretty easy.

Here's an example, retarray.cpp, in which I'll return an array from a function named **create_array**. I want to be able to simply assign the return value of **create_array** to an array like this:

```
#include <iostream>
using namespace std;

int main()
{
    new_array = create_array();
        .
        .
        .
```

However, you can't actually assign one array to another in C++, and you can't return a whole array from a function in C++ either, so we'll have to use pointers. That means that **new_array** variable will actually be a regular pointer, not a standard array (note that a standard array name is a constant pointer, which wouldn't work here because we need to assign the return value of the **create_array** function to it):

```
#include <iostream>
using namespace std;

int main()
{
    int *new_array;

    new_array = create_array();
    .
    .
    .
```

However, because you can interchange pointer and array notation, I can also treat **new_array** as an array, which makes it seem that **create_array** has indeed returned an array:

```
#include <iostream>
using namespace std;

int main()
{
    int *new_array;

    new_array = create_array();

    cout << "First element is " << new_array[0] << endl;
    .
    .
    .
}
```

The **create_array** function is going to have to return a pointer to the beginning of an array, and because I'll make that array of type **int**, here's what **create_array** looks like in outline:

```
int* create_array(void)
{
    .
    .
    .
}
```

I can't just declare an automatic variable and return a pointer to that variable, because that variable can't be used when it's out of scope (see "What Does Scope Mean?" earlier in this chapter). Instead, I allocate memory for the array in the free store using **new**, then place values in the array, and return the pointer to the array like this:

```
int* create_array(void)
{
    int *array = new int[3];

    array[0] = 1;
    array[1] = 2;
    array[2] = 3;

    return array;
}
```

There's one more step to remember—now that I've allocated space in memory using **new[]**, I should also delete it using **delete[]**. Here's what the completed program, retarray.cpp looks like:

```
#include <iostream>
using namespace std;

int* create_array(void);

int main()
{
    int *new_array;

    new_array = create_array();

    cout << "First element is " << new_array[0] <<  endl;

    delete[]  new_array;

    return 0;
}

int* create_array(void)
{
    int *array = new int[3];

    array[0] = 1;
```

```
    array[1] = 2;
    array[2] = 3;

    return array;
}
```

Here's what this program looks like when it's running:

```
%retarray
First element is 1
```

As you can see, the easy interchange between pointer and array notation makes this program work in a reasonably straightforward manner. However, you need to know what's going on behind the scenes to write this kind of code.

You can also use the **auto_ptr** template to allocate memory on the free store that doesn't need to be explicitly deleted later—see "Using **auto_ptr** for Safe Deletes" in Chapter 5 for more details.

Related solution:	Found on page:
Using **auto_ptr** for Safe Deletes	229

Passing C-Style Strings to Functions

You can treat C++ **string** class objects as simple variables when it comes to passing them to and returning them from functions, so there's no problem there. Passing and returning C-style strings take a little more thought, however.

C-style strings are arrays of type **char**, so we can use the techniques developed in "Passing Arrays to Functions" earlier in this chapter. Here's an example, passstring.cpp, in which I pass a C-style string to a function named **print_string** and print the string out in that function. I can call **print_string** like this directly, passing a string literal:

```
#include <iostream>
using namespace std;

void print_string(const char * text);

int main()
{
```

```
    print_string("Hello from C++");

    return 0;
}
```

In **print_string**, all I have to do is to remember that what's actually being passed is a pointer to a constant **char**, so I define the function like this (because a string literal is a constant, your compiler will probably complain unless you use **const** here):

```
void print_string(const char * text)
{
    .
    .
    .
}
```

Because C++ understands C-style strings, I can pass the string we want to print directly to **cout** like this in **print_string**:

```
void print_string(const char * text)
{
    cout << text << endl;
}
```

Here's the entire code, passstring.cpp:

```
#include <iostream>
using namespace std;

void print_string(const char * text);

int main()
{
    print_string("Hello from C++");

    return 0;
}

void print_string(const char * text)
{
    cout << text << endl;
}
```

Here's what the program looks like when running:

```
%passstring
Hello from C++
```

Related solution:	Found on page:
Creating C-Style Strings	132

Returning C-Style Strings from Functions

In the previous section, I covered the process of passing C-style strings to functions. Using pointers, you can also return C-style strings from functions, and we'll take a look at how that works here.

In this example, retstring.cpp, the function **return_greeting** will just return a pointer to the C-style string "Hello from C++". As discussed in "Returning Arrays from Functions," you must return a pointer to an array from a function, not the array itself, and because C-style strings are simply arrays of type **char**, there's no problem here. Here's how I store and use the pointer returned from **return_greeting** to display the message returned by that function; note that I'm treating the message itself as I would a string literal—as a constant string:


```
#include <iostream>
#include <cstring>
using namespace std;

int main()
{
    const char *pointer = return_greeting();

    cout << pointer << endl;
        .
        .
        .

}
```

In **return_greeting**, I can't just declare an automatic variable and return a pointer to that, because that variable can't be used when it's out of scope (see "What Does Scope Mean?" earlier in this chapter). Instead, I allocate memory for the C-style string on the free store using **new[]**, allocating space for the message "Hello from C++" like this—recall that **strlen** returns the length of a string, and I must add 1 to allow space for the terminating **'\0'** character.

***NOTE:** If your compiler has problems with the constant return value from this function in the following example, remove the keyword **const** from the return type of the prototype and the function definition.*

```
const char* return_greeting(void)
{
    char *pstring = new char[strlen("Hello from C++") + 1];
        .
        .
        .
}
```

Unfortunately, there's no way to initialize a dynamic array in the **new** statement when you create it, so I'll use **strcpy** separately to fill the C-style string with the message "Hello from C++" and return the pointer to that string from this function, **return_greeting**:

```
const char* return_greeting(void)
{
    char *pstring = new char[strlen("Hello from C++") + 1];

    strcpy(pstring, "Hello from C++");

    return pstring;
}
```

In addition, I'll have to delete the memory set aside for this string with **delete[]** when I'm done using it. Here's what the whole program, retstring.cpp, looks like:

```
#include <iostream>
#include <cstring>
using namespace std;

const char* return_greeting(void);

int main()
{
    const char *pointer = return_greeting();

    cout << pointer << endl;

    delete [] pointer;
```

```
    return 0;
}

const char* return_greeting(void)
{
    char *pstring = new char[strlen("Hello from C++") + 1];
    strcpy(pstring, "Hello from C++");

    return pstring;
}
```

And here's what the program looks like when it's running:

```
%retstring
Hello from C++
```

Related solutions:	Found on page:
Finding a C-Style String's Length	133
Copying C-Style Strings	136

Passing Structures to Functions

By default, arrays are passed to functions as pointers, because array names are treated as constant pointers in C++. However, structures are different—by default, they are passed by value, like simple variables. That means that a copy of the entire structure you're passing to a function is created and passed to the function, and it's stored in automatic storage.

Here's an example, passstructure.cpp. This example uses a structure, **complex_number**, that stores complex numbers, and a function, **add_complex**, that adds complex numbers and returns the sum (for example, if you add a + bi to c + di, you get (a + c) + (b + d)i, where i = the square root of –1). I start this example by defining the structure **complex_number** and the prototype for the function **add_complex**. Then I create two complex numbers and pass them to **add_complex** to add them:

```
#include <iostream>
using namespace std;

struct complex_number
{
```

```
    int real;
    int imaginary;
};

complex_number add_complex(complex_number t1, complex_number t2);

int main()
{
    complex_number c1 = {1, 2};
    complex_number c2 = {3, 4};

    complex_number total = add_complex(c1, c2);
    cout << "Complex number sum = " << total.real;
    cout << " + " << total.imaginary << "i" <<endl;

    return 0;
}
```

All that's left is to create the function **add_complex**. Because structures are passed by value, a complete copy of each passed structure is passed to the function. This means you can treat the structures as you would simple variables—just refer to them by name in your code. After adding the real and imaginary parts of the complex numbers by creating a new complex number named **sum**, all I have to do is to return **sum**:

```
complex_number add_complex(complex_number c1, complex_number c2)
{
    complex_number sum;

    sum.real = c1.real + c2.real;
    sum.imaginary = c1.imaginary + c2.imaginary;

    return sum;
}
```

When I return **sum**, what really is returned is a copy of **sum**, so I don't have to worry about **sum** going out of scope (which would mean I'd have to allocate it on the free store instead of as an automatic variable). Here's what this program, passstructure.cpp, looks like at work:

```
%passstructure
Complex number sum = 4 + 6i
```

***NOTE:** Structures are passed and returned by value, which means that a copy of the structure is created and used. If the structures you pass and return to functions are large and/or numerous, you might be degrading execution time and putting a strain on the automatic store. A better idea is to pass and return pointers to structures instead of the structures themselves; see "Passing Structure Pointers to Functions" later in this chapter.*

Returning Structures from Functions

As discussed in the previous section, "Passing Structures to Functions," structures are passed by value in C++, which means a copy of the structure is created and passed to called functions. Structures are also returned by value, which means that a copy of the entire structure is created and returned. In the example program passstructure.cpp, created in the previous section, we saw that this means you can simply return a structure directly with the **return** statement, because what's actually returned is a copy of the structure:

```
#include <iostream>
using namespace std;

struct complex_number
{
    int real;
    int imaginary;
};

complex_number add_complex(complex_number t1, complex_number t2);

int main()
{
    .
    .
    .
}

complex_number add_complex(complex_number c1, complex_number c2)
{
    complex_number sum;

    sum.real = c1.real + c2.real;
    sum.imaginary = c1.imaginary + c2.imaginary;

    return sum;
}
```

The reason this is safe is that because a copy of the structure named **sum** is returned, you don't have to worry about **sum** going out of scope when the function call returns. The **sum** structure does go out of scope, but what's been returned from the function is a copy of that structure, so there's no problem.

NOTE: *Structures are passed and returned by value, which means that a copy of the structure is created and used. If the structures you pass and return to functions are large and/or numerous, you might be degrading execution time and putting a strain on the automatic store. A better idea is to pass and return pointers to structures instead of the structures themselves; see "Passing Structure Pointers to Functions" next in this chapter.*

Passing Structure Pointers to Functions

Because structures are passed and returned by value, you can end up using a lot of memory if you pass or return large structures to or from functions. To avoid degrading program performance, it's often better to pass or return pointers to structures instead of the structures themselves.

Here's an example, structureptr.cpp, that uses the **complex_number** example structure developed in the two previous sections in this chapter. This structure holds complex numbers; in this program, I'll add a function, **magnitude**, that calculates the magnitude of a complex number (the magnitude of a complex number is the square root of the sum of the squares of the real and imaginary parts). To illustrate passing structures with pointers, I'll pass a pointer to a complex number to **magnitude**, as you see in that function's prototype:


```
#include <iostream>
#include <cmath>
using namespace std;

struct complex_number
{
    int real;
    int imaginary;
};

double magnitude(complex_number * c);
    .
    .
    .
```

Here's the whole code, structureptr.cpp—all I need to do is to make sure I pass a pointer to a complex number to **magnitude**, and use the arrow operator with that pointer to access the real and imaginary parts of the complex number:

```
#include <iostream>
#include <cmath>
using namespace std;

struct complex_number
{
    int real;
    int imaginary;
};

double magnitude(complex_number * c);

int main()
{
    complex_number complex = {3, 4};

    cout << "Maginitude of the complex number: "
        << magnitude(&complex) << endl;

    return 0;
}

double magnitude(complex_number* c)
{
    return sqrt(c->real * c->real + c->imaginary * c->imaginary);
}
```

Here's what this program looks like at work:

```
%structureptr
Maginitude of the complex number: 5
```

Using Recursion

One important concept when working with functions is recursion, or the ability of functions to call themselves. Using recursion is appropriate when you can divide a task into a sequence of programmatically identical steps, each of which depends on the result from a previous step. That's not going to be the clearest of concepts if it's new to you, so let's take a look at an example.

The traditional example to illustrate recursion is to calculate factorials, so let's do it. The factorial of a positive integer is simply the product of that integer and all the smaller positive integers, down to 1. That is, six factorial, which is designated 6!, is the same as 6 * 5 * 4 * 3 * 2 * 1 = 720. An interesting fact is that 6! = 6 * 5!, and in fact, n! = n * (n – 1)!. That's perfect for recursion—for example, if you have a function named **factorial** that calculates factorials, then this function can call itself to make the whole process easier—for example, when you call **factorial(*n*)**, the code in **factorial** just needs to multiply ***n*** by **factorial(*n* – 1)**. The only fact we need to add to the code is that 1! = 1, so that **factorial(1)** should just return 1 (this stops the code from trying to figure out 0!, then –1!, and so on infinitely).

Here's what the code, factorial.cpp, looks like; in this case, I'm calling the **factorial** function to figure out 6!:

```
#include <iostream>
using namespace std;

int factorial(int value);

int main()
{
    cout << "6! = " << factorial(6) << endl;

    return 0;
}
```

Here's what the **factorial** function looks like; when it's called with a value of ***n***, it should return 1 if ***n*** equals 1, and it should return the product of ***n*** with **(*n* – 1)!** otherwise—note that it figures out **(*n* – 1)!** by calling itself:

```
int factorial(int value)
{
    if (value == 1) {
        return value;
    } else {
        return value * factorial(value - 1);
    }
}
```

Here's what this code looks like at work:

```
%factorial
6! = 720
```

That's all it takes to get recursion working. Even if you take nothing else away from the idea of recursion, you should remember that in C++, functions can call themselves. In programming terms, this means that functions are *re-entrant*. Each time a function is called, space for the automatic variables in the function is allocated in the automatic store. Every time a function calls itself subsequently, additional space is allocated, so any new values stored in the most recent function call won't conflict with the values stored for the previous call (each set of automatic variables stored this way is named a *call frame*).

Using Pointers to Functions

As mentioned briefly in Chapter 5, C++ supports pointers to functions. This may seem a little odd, because we're used to using pointers only with data in memory, but it becomes a little more plausible if you consider that compiled code is also stored in memory. A pointer to a function, then, points to the location that program execution is transferred to when the function is called.

You can use a declaration to create a pointer to a function; for example, if this is the prototype of the function you want a pointer to:

```
type function_name(argument1, argument2...);
```

then this is how you could declare a pointer to this function:

```
type (*pointer_to_function)(argument1, argument2...);
```

In C++, function names may be treated as constant pointers to a function, just as array names may be treated as constant pointers to arrays. That means that to get a pointer to a function, you can use the function name itself, as in this assignment:

```
pointer_to_function = function_name;
```

Now you can use the pointer to the function to call the function, like this:

```
return_value = (*pointer_to_function)(argument1, argument2...);
```

NOTE: *Why do you need the parentheses around* ****pointer_to_function*** *in this code? The parentheses are there because the * operator has lower precedence than the parentheses operator, so* ****pointer_to_function(argument1, argument2...)*** *is technically a function that returns a pointer, not a function call. On the other hand, see the comments at the end of this section on removing both the parentheses around* ****pointer_to_function*** *and the * in ANSI/ISO C++.*

Here's an example, functionpointer.cpp, that puts function pointers to work. In this case, I'll create a function named **printem** that displays a string passed to it. Instead of calling **printem** directly, however, I'll create a new function, **caller_function**. I'll pass a pointer that points to **printem** to **caller_function**, and the code in **caller_function** will use that pointer to call **printem**. In this way, we'll see not only how to use function pointers but also the syntax you use to pass function pointers to other functions.

When I call **caller_function**, I'll pass both the string I want **printem** to display and a pointer to **printem**. To pass a pointer that points to **printem**, all I have to do is to pass the name **printem** itself, this way:

```
#include <iostream>
#include <string>
using namespace std;

int main()
{
    caller_function("Hello from C++", printem);

    return 0;
}
```

Now I've passed the string to print, "Hello from C++", and a pointer to the **printem** function to **caller_function**. Here's how I define **caller_function**; note the way you specify the function pointer argument in the argument list—you must specify both the return value and argument list of the function pointed to, using syntax like this:

```
void caller_function(string text, void (*pointer_to_function)(string))
{
    .
    .
    .
}
```

Now I can use the function pointer to call **printem** and pass the **text** argument to that function like this:

```
void caller_function(string text, void (*pointer_to_function)(string))
{
    (*pointer_to_function)(text);
}
```

All that's left is to write the **printem** function, which prints out text sent to it, and that looks like this:

```
void printem(string text)
{
    cout << text << endl;
}
```

Here's the whole code, functionpointer.cpp:

```
#include <iostream>
#include <string>
using namespace std;

void printem(string text);
void caller_function(string text, void (*pointer_to_function)(string text));

int main()
{
    caller_function("Hello from C++", printem);

    return 0;
}

void printem(string text)
{
    cout << text << endl;
}

void caller_function(string text, void (*pointer_to_function)(string))
{
    (*pointer_to_function)(text);
}
```

And here's what this program looks like when you run it:

```
%functionpointer
Hello from C++
```

There's one last point to cover on function pointers. ANSI/ISO C++ allows you a shortcut that's worth knowing about. Because you can treat function names as constant pointers to functions, ANSI/ISO C++ also now lets you treat pointers to functions as function names. That means that this syntax:

```
return_value = (*pointer_to_function)(argument1, argument2...);
```

is actually the same as this syntax—note that I've removed the * and parentheses from ***(*pointer_to_function)***:

```
return_value = pointer_to_function(argument1, argument2...);
```

Some purists object to this syntax, but it's now legal.

Chapter 7

Functions: Overloading, References, Linkage, and Templates

In Depth

We got our start with functions in the previous chapter, but there's no way to cram all that C++ functions can do in one chapter. In this chapter, we'll take a look at the remaining topics, and we'll find that Chapter 6 just skimmed the surface. Here, we'll see how to use references and overload functions, all about scope and linkage to other files, and how to use function templates. We'll also look at inline functions, default arguments, overloading function templates, handling a variable number of function arguments, using storage class specifiers like **register**, **volatile**, and **mutable**, and more. It's all here, and there's a lot to see.

References

One of the most important topics we'll see in this chapter is how to use references. In the previous chapter, we saw that, by default, C++ passes arguments to functions by value. That means that a copy is made of each argument, and the copy is supplied to the code in the function. We also saw that sometimes it's useful to give the code in a function direct access to the data it's supposed to work on, especially if you're working with large data structures and don't want to pass copies of them each time you call a function. If the code in the function has access to the data you want to work on, it can change that data in place.

As you know from our work with passing arrays to functions, one way to give the code in a function access to your original data is to pass a pointer to that data. For example, take a look at this program, addone.cpp; in this case, I just want a function, **add_one_ptrs**, to accept a pointer to a **long** value and to use the pointer to increment that **long** value. Here's how I use **add_one_ptrs** to add 1 to the value in a variable named **salary**—note that I'm passing a pointer to this value to **add_one_ptrs**:

```
#include <iostream>
using namespace std;

void add_one_ptrs(long * n);
```

```
int main()
{
    long salary = 250000;

    cout << "Current salary: $" << salary << endl;

    add_one_ptrs(&salary);

    cout << "After the first raise: $" << salary << endl;

    return 0;
}
```

In the function **add_one_ptrs**, I simply need to dereference the pointer and increment the value it points to:

```
void add_one_ptrs(long * n)
{
    (*n)++;
}
```

Passing a pointer to **add_one_ptrs** gives the code in that function access to the **salary** variable directly. However, there's an easier way of doing this—you can pass values by *reference*, not by value. When you pass a reference to a variable to a function, that function has direct access to the variable without needing to dereference any pointers. To show how it works, I'll add another function, **add_one_refs**, to addone.cpp. This new function will pass its arguments by reference, not value.

In C++, the & operator does double duty as the address operator and the symbol you use for references. Here's how I use & to indicate that I want arguments passed by reference in **add_one_refs**:

```
#include <iostream>
using namespace std;

void add_one_refs(long & n);
void add_one_ptrs(long * n);
    .
    .
    .
```

Note the similarity between this new prototype and the one I used for the function that takes pointers, **add_one_ptrs**. However, there is a significant difference—now that I'm passing a reference, all the behind-the-scenes pointer work is now done automatically. That means that all I need to do is pass the variable I want **add_one_refs** to work on, **salary**, directly to that function, without finding its address:

```
#include <iostream>
using namespace std;

void add_one_refs(long & n);
void add_one_ptrs(long * n);

int main()
{
    long salary = 250000;

    cout << "Current salary: $" << salary << endl;

    add_one_ptrs(&salary);

    cout << "After the first raise: $" << salary << endl;

    add_one_refs(salary);

    cout << "After the second raise: $" << salary << endl;

    return 0;
}
```

Now, in the code for **add_one_refs**, I can simply work with the passed variable directly, and because that variable was passed by reference, any changes I make to the variable here will actually be made to the data in the variable itself—contrast this to **add_one_ptrs** below it, where I have to dereference the passed pointer before I can work with the original data directly:

```
void add_one_refs(long & n)
{
    n++;
}

void add_one_ptrs(long * n)
{
    (*n)++;
}
```

That's all it takes—when you use & in front of an argument in a function's argument list, that argument is passed by reference, which means you have direct access to it and don't have to go through the additional steps of creating and dereferencing a pointer. Here's what this program, addone.cpp, looks like when you run it:

```
%addone
Current salary: $250000
After the first raise: $250001
After the second raise: $250002
```

Function Overloading

Another important function topic is how to *overload functions*. This topic is one of my favorites, because it allows you to customize code in a way that makes programs a lot easier to work with. An overloaded function can handle different numbers and types of arguments; for example, you might overload a function, **print_this**, that displays text so that you can pass it a C-style string, or a C++ **string** object, or a single **char**, or even an ASCII character code. When you overload **print_this** correctly, it can handle all those data types, and that makes **print_this** a very useful general-purpose function.

To overload a function for different argument lists, you just define the function several times, each with a different argument list. When you overload functions, argument lists are called *signatures*, so you define the function a number of times, each with a different signature. When you call a function, the C++ compiler checks the arguments you're passing and determines if they match any of the function signatures you've defined. If not, the compiler checks if it can make any implicit data conversions that would match any signature. If there's no match, or if two signatures match equally well, you'll get a compiler error.

To show how this works, I'll create the **print_this** function in an example, functionoverload.cpp, and overload that function so you can pass it a single **char**, a C-style string, the ASCII code for a single character, or a C++ string object. To do that, I just need to define the function with multiple signatures:

```
#include <iostream>
#include <string>
using namespace std;

void print_this(char the_char){cout << the_char;}
void print_this(char* the_C_string){cout << the_C_string;}
```

```
void print_this(int ASC_code){cout << static_cast<char> (ASC_code);}
void print_this(string the_string) {cout << the_string;};
     .
     .
     .
```

This defines the various forms of the overloaded function, **print_this**. Now the compiler can figure out which of the forms of this function it should use based on the data you pass to it, as in this code:

```
#include <iostream>
#include <string>
using namespace std;

void print_this(char the_char){cout << the_char;}
void print_this(char* the_C_string){cout << the_C_string;}
void print_this(int ASC_code){cout << static_cast<char> (ASC_code);}
void print_this(string the_string) {cout << the_string;};

int main()
{
    print_this(97);                    // ASCII code for 'a'
    print_this('b');                   // Char
    print_this("c");                   // C-style String
    print_this(string("d"));           // C++-style String

    return 0;
}
```

This code uses **print_this** to display the ASCII code for '**a**', the character '**b**', a C-style string “c”, and a C++ string object that holds “d”. Here’s the result when you run this example, functionoverload.cpp:

```
%functionoverload
abcd
```


If you go on to work in C++ a great deal, you’ll find yourself overloading functions all the time—see “Overloading a Function” for more details on this topic.

Storage Classes, Scope, and Linkage

In the previous chapter, I started discussing the idea of scope, those areas in a program where a specific item is “visible” and may be used in code. There’s plenty more to be said on this topic, however, and we’ll see a great deal more in this chapter.

As you know, memory in a C++ program is divided into three areas—automatic storage, where a function's variables are allocated and stored when you enter the function; static storage, where data that is declared static is stored and left for the duration of the program's runtime; and the free store. These three areas, automatic storage, static storage, and the free store are called the three different *storage classes.*

Storage Classes

In Chapter 5, we took a look at the free store, using **new** and **delete** as well as **new[]** and **delete[]**, to allocate and deallocate space there as needed.

In Chapter 6, we took a look at automatic storage, and the issues of scope that the use of automatic variables raised. In particular, automatic variables are allocated in the automatic storage for the block in which they're declared, and their scope is limited to that block and any enclosed blocks (as long as an enclosing block doesn't declare a variable of the same name, which overrides the enclosing declaration locally).

In this chapter, we'll take a look at the third storage class, static storage. When you store data in a program's static storage, that data persists throughout the lifetime of the program. That means you don't have to worry about static data being reset every time you call a function, for example, as happens with automatic storage. For more on this aspect of static storage, see "Creating Local Static (Persistent) Variables" in this chapter.

Scope

I'll also have more to say about scope in this chapter. Variables can have *local* (or *block*) scope, or they can have *global* (or *file*) scope which makes them available throughout the entire code in a file, and we'll see how to use global scope in this chapter. When you declare a variable outside any function, that variable is called *external.* External variables are global in a file and may be used in any function that follows the variable's declaration and hasn't declared a variable of the same name (which would override the global variable). The storage class of data can also affect its scope; for example, automatic variables can have local scope, but not global scope. However, static variables can have either local scope or global scope.

Linkage

We'll also see a new concept in this chapter—*linkage.* Linkage refers to an item's ability to be used in different files in the same program. External variables also have external linkage, which means they are available to other files in the same program. Variables with internal linkage, by contrast, are not available in other files in the same program. The storage class of data affects its linkage; for example, you cannot have a global automatic variable, which means there's no such thing as an external automatic variable. That means that automatic variables can have only internal linkage, which restricts them to the file in which they're defined.

In C++, the concepts of scope, linkage, and storage classes are entangled together in a way that's not systematic and often hard to keep straight. To shed light on all this, I've put together an overview:

- *Automatic variables* are local to a block and so have local scope, internal linkage.
- *External variables* are declared outside any function, are available to all files in a program, and have global scope, external linkage.
- *External static variables* are external variables declared with the **static** keyword and are available to all code in the file, but they are restricted to the file they're defined in and so have global scope, internal linkage.
- *External constant variables* are external variables declared with the **const** keyword and are available to all code in the file, but they are restricted to the file they're defined in and have global scope, internal linkage. (They're given internal linkage so you can place them in headers and share them across multiple files without conflict.)
- *Static variables* are automatic variables declared with the **static** keyword, are confined to a block, and so have local scope, internal linkage.

NOTE: *Why haven't I mentioned the free store in the bulleted items above? I haven't because you handle memory allocated in the free store with pointers, and those pointers themselves must be declared in one of the other two storage classes, automatic or static. That means that the pointers to memory in the free store must follow the rules in the bulleted items above, which determine their scope and linkage.*

Here are two examples to make this all clearer. The first example is called external.cpp and declares an external variable, **color**, outside any function, which makes that variable external and gives it global scope and external linkage:

```
#include <iostream>
#include <string>
using namespace std;

string color("red");
    .
    .
    .
```

If I had made this a static external variable by using the **static** keyword, **color** would still have global scope, but now it would have internal linkage, which means it would be restricted to the current file only:

```
#include <iostream>
#include <string>
using namespace std;

static string color("red");
    .
    .
    .
```

Because **color** is global, it's available throughout the file, as in this case, where I'm displaying its value in the **main** function:

```
#include <iostream>
#include <string>
using namespace std;

string color("red");

int main()
{
    cout << "Global color: " << color << endl;

    return 0;
}
```

However, if I have another function, **local**, which defines its own variable named **color**, the local variable takes precedence, and we can see when I print that variable out:

```
#include <iostream>
#include <string>
using namespace std;

string color("red");

void local();

int main()
{
    cout << "Global color: " << color << endl;
```

```
    local();

    return 0;
}

void local()
{
    string color("blue");

    cout << "Local color: " << color << endl;
}
```

Here's what this program, external.cpp, looks like when running—as you can see, the local version of **color** overrode the global one:

```
%external
Global color: red
Local color: blue
```

TIP: *How can you access the value in the global variable color inside the local function? See "Creating Variables with Global Scope" later in this chapter.*

This example, external.cpp, took a look at scope, and the next example will take a look at linkage. This next example is made up of two files, file1.cpp and file2.cpp. In file1.cpp, I declare and initialize a variable, **value1**, making it an external variable:

```
#include <iostream>
using namespace std;

int value1 = 1;            // external variable definition
    .
    .
    .
```

Because it's an external variable, it has global scope and external linkage. The fact that it has external linkage means that it can be accessed in other files in the same program, as we'll see. First, I'll display the value in **value1** from code in file1.cpp:

```
#include <iostream>
using namespace std;

int value1 = 1;            // external variable definition
```

```
int main()
{
    cout << "In file one..." << endl;
    cout << "value1: " << value1 << endl;
    .
    .
    .
}
```

Next, I'll call a function named **second_file_values**, defined in the other file, file2.cpp, which will display the value of **value1** as seen in that file:

```
#include <iostream>
using namespace std;

int value1 = 1;              // external variable definition

void second_file_values();

int main()
{
    cout << "In file one..." << endl;
    cout << "value1: " << value1 << endl;

    second_file_values();

    return 0;
}
```

In the second file, file2.cpp, I'll create the function **second_file_values** and display **value1** as it's seen in the second file:

```
#include <iostream>
using namespace std;

void second_file_values()
{
    cout << "In file two..." << endl;
    cout << "value1: " << value1 << endl;
}
```

There's one more step to take; when the compiler compiles file2.cpp, it will be confused, because I'm using **value1** without ever having declared it. To avoid having the compiler think that I just forgot to declare **value1**, I need to tell it that **value1** is defined in another file, and I do that with the keyword **extern**:

```
#include <iostream>
using namespace std;

extern int value1;          // value1 defined in other file

void second_file_values()
{
    cout << "In file two..." << endl;
    cout << "value1: " << value1 << endl;
}
```

That's all it takes. Now you compile and link both file1.cpp and file2.cpp together; for example, using g++, in a command line that looks like this:

```
%g++ file1.cpp file2.cpp
```

See "Basic Skills: Compiling a Program" in Chapter 1 for more on compiling and linking multiple files. Now when I run the program, you can see that **value1** is indeed visible in the code in both file1.cpp and file2.cpp:

```
%file1
In file one...
value1: 1
In file two...
value1: 1
```


As I said, the concepts of storage class, scope, and linkage are entangled together in C++—for example, the **static** keyword has two uses, one for storage class and one for linkage (you use **static** to place automatic variables in the persistent static storage class, but you also use it with external variables to change their linkage from external to internal). It takes a little while to unravel things, so you might find yourself going through the material in this chapter more than once.

Function Templates

The fourth major topic in this chapter is how to use *function templates*. As you know, C++ is a strongly typed language, so if you define a long, involved function that handles integers, you can't call it with floating point variables. You can overload the function to handle both integers and floating point numbers, but that means defining the function twice, which is a little irksome if there are no code changes except for the type of the arguments.

That's why C++ provides function templates. Using a function template, you can define a function using an abstract, non-specific data type and then use that template to create functions that use specific data types, like **int** or **float**. In other words, a function template lets you leave the data type it works on unspecified, and you specify the data type when you use the template to create a function. In this way, templates are part of C++'s generic programming initiative.

Here's an example, functiontemplate.cpp, that shows how this works. In this case, I'll define a function template named **add_one** that simply adds 1 to a number passed to it by reference. To create a function template, you need to use a name to stand for the data type that will ultimately be used in the function, and many programmers simply use the name **T**, so I will too. Here's how you start the new template, using the keyword **template**, and the keyword **typename** to stand for any type:

```
template <typename T>
    .
    .
    .
```

Besides **typename**, you can also use the keyword **class** (and in fact, older C++ compilers won't know about the newer keyword **typename**). Now that you've indicated that you're creating a template using the data type **T**, you can define the function that uses that data of that type this way:

```
template <typename T>
void add_one(T &n)
{
    n++;
}
```

You can now use this function template to create functions, and you do that by using the function on data of a certain type and letting the compiler create the corresponding version of the function. To put this template to use, I start by creating a prototype for the function template as in the following example (note that this function template prototype is much like a function prototype—you just omit the function body and add a semicolon at the end):

```
#include <iostream>
using namespace std;

template <typename T>
void add_one(T &n);
```

```
int main()
{
    .
    .
    .
}

template <typename T>
void add_one(T &n)
{
    n++;
}
```

Next I set up a **long** variable, **salary**, and use **add_one** to raise that salary by 1 like this:

```
#include <iostream>
using namespace std;

template <typename T>
void add_one(T &n);

int main()
{
    long long_salary = 250000;

    cout << "Current long salary: $" << long_salary << endl;

    add_one(long_salary);

    cout << "After the long raise: $" << long_salary << endl;

    return 0;
}

template <typename T>
void add_one(T &n)
{
    n++;
}
```

When the compiler sees the expression **add_one(long_salary)**, it uses the function template to create a function body for **add_one** that handles long variables. Similarly, if I call **add_one** with a **double**, the compiler creates a version of **add_one** for **double** variables:

```
#include <iostream>
using namespace std;

template <typename T>
void add_one(T &n);

int main()
{
    long long_salary = 250000;

    cout << "Current long salary: $" << long_salary << endl;

    add_one(long_salary);

    cout << "After the long raise: $" << long_salary << endl;

    double double_salary = 250000.0;

    cout << "Current double salary: $" << double_salary << endl;

    add_one(double_salary);

    cout << "After the double raise: $" << double_salary << endl;

    return 0;
}

template <typename T>
void add_one(T &n)
{
    n++;
}
```

And that's all you need—here's what this example, functiontemplate.cpp, looks like when running:

```
%functiontemplate
Current long salary: $250000
```

```
After the long raise: $250001
Current double salary: $250000
After the double raise: $250001
```

As you can see, the compiler was able to use the function template to create versions of the **add_one** function for both **long** and **double** variables.

There's plenty of additional material in this chapter on templates, and on other topics as well, such as inline functions, default arguments, temporary variables and so on. In fact, it's time to turn to the Immediate Solutions section of the chapter now.

Immediate Solutions

Creating Inline Functions

C++ supports *inline functions* to let you save a little execution time in your code. With normal functions, the compiler puts a jump instruction into your code when you call the function. This means that arguments and automatic variables have to be set up on the stack and program execution has to be transferred to the function itself, and so on. On the other hand, when you use an inline function, the compiler actually puts the entire code for the function directly into the code (that is, "inline") when the function is called. That means that no jump is needed, and you can save a little time. To create an inline function, you use the keyword **inline**.

You usually use only small amounts of code in inline functions; here's an example, inline.cpp, showing how to create an inline function. In this case, I'll create a function named **sq** that squares numeric arguments like this:

```
#include <iostream>
using namespace std;

inline int sq(int value) {return value * value;}
    .
    .
    .
```

Note the keyword **inline** here, making this an inline function. Now when **sq** is called, the entire code of that function is placed into the code directly:

```
#include <iostream>
using namespace std;

inline int sq(int value) {return value * value;}

int main()
{
    int data = 5;

    cout << data << " squared = " << sq(5) << endl;
```

```
    return 0;
}
```

Here's what this example, inline.cpp, looks like at work:

```
%inline
5 squared = 25
```

Inline functions are often placed in header files. They have internal linkage (as opposed to regular functions, which have external linkage), which means they're local to the file they're in and so won't clash with other files that also include the same header file. See "Linkage and Functions" later in this chapter for more details.

Specifying Default Arguments

C++ allows you to specify *default arguments* in functions. Using default arguments, you can specify a default value for the various arguments in a function, and that value will be used if no other value was passed for that argument.

You specify a default value for an argument by following the argument's name with **= *default_value*** in the function prototype's argument list. Here's an example, default.cpp, in which I'm setting the default value for the argument **operand2** to 1 for the function **adder**, which adds its arguments and returns their sum:

```
#include <iostream>
using namespace std;

long adder(int operand1, int operand2 = 1);

int main()
{
    .
    .
    .
}

long adder(int operand1, int operand2)
{
    return operand1 + operand2;
}
```

Now when I call **adder**, I can pass either two arguments or one; if I pass one argument, the second argument will be set to its default value, which is 1:

```
#include <iostream>
using namespace std;

long adder(int operand1, int operand2 = 1);

int main()
{
    cout << "5 + 7 = " << adder(5, 7) << endl;
    cout << "5 + 1 = " << adder(5) << endl;

    return 0;
}

long adder(int operand1, int operand2)
{
    return operand1 + operand2;
}
```

Here's what this program, default.cpp, looks like when running—note that when I pass a single value of 5, the default value, 1, is added to it:

```
%default
5 + 7 = 12
5 + 1 = 6
```

Here's an important point: If you assign a default value for one argument in a function's argument list, you also need to assign default arguments for all the arguments to the right of that argument in the argument list as well:

```
int calculate(int value1, int value2 = 2, int value3 = 3, int value4 = 4);
```

The reason for this convention is that you specify which arguments are to be set to their defaults by omitting them in the function call, and when you start omitting arguments, the compiler won't know which are missing unless you omit all the remaining arguments as well.

Handling a Variable Number of Arguments

C++ has a set of macros that let you create functions with a variable number of arguments. This way of doing things has largely been superceded by function overloading, but I'll take a look at it here in a program named varargs.cpp for completeness.

To use these macros, you include the cstdarg header file. In this case, I'll create a function named **adder** that will add a variable number of arguments as long as you pass the number of arguments to add as the first argument. To indicate that this function takes one integer followed by a variable number of arguments, you give this function the argument list **int...**. In **adder**, I use the macro **va_list** to get a list of the arguments passed to the function and the **va_start** macro to initialize the list. Every time I use the **va_arg** macro from then on, I get a new argument from the list, and when done, I use the **va_end** macro. It looks like this in varargs.cpp:

```
#include <iostream>
#include <cstdarg>
using namespace std;

int adder(int...);

int main()
{
    cout << "The sum = " << adder(3, 1, 2, 3) << endl;

    return 0;
}

int adder(int number ...)
{
    int result = 0;
    va_list list;
    va_start(list, number);

    for(int loop_index = 0;loop_index < number; loop_index++){
        int integer = va_arg(list, int);
        result += integer;
    }

    va_end(list);
```

```
    return result;
}
```

Here's what this example, varargs.cpp, looks like when running:

```
%varargs
The sum = 6
```


Related solution:	Found on page:
Creating Preprocessor Macros	54

Creating Reference Variables

References are one of the important topics in C++, and I discussed them in the In Depth section of this chapter. Besides passing arguments by reference to functions, you can also create reference *variables*. A reference variable is much like an alias for another variable, and you declare it with & like this: **int & *variable_name***.

Here's an example, reference.cpp. In this case, I'll create a variable named **couches** and alias a reference variable, **sofas**, to it—you initialize a reference variable simply by assigning another variable to it. These two variables will then refer to the same location in memory from then on. In other words, **sofas** will be an alias for **couches**. In the example program, reference.cpp, I'll display the addresses both variables refer to (which should be the same), the values in the variables, and then the values after one of the variables is incremented:

```
#include <iostream>
using namespace std;

int main()
{
    int couches = 101;
    int & sofas = couches;

    cout << "Address of couches: " << &couches << endl;
    cout << "Address of sofas: " << &sofas << endl;

    cout << "Number of couches: " << couches << endl;
    cout << "Number of sofas: " << sofas << endl;
```

```
    couches++;

    cout << "Number of couches: " << couches << endl;
    cout << "Number of sofas: " << sofas << endl;

    return 0;
}
```

Here's what this program, references.cpp, looks like when running—note that not only do both variables refer to the same location in memory, but when one is incremented, they both hold the new value:

```
%references
Address of couches: 0065FE00
Address of sofas: 0065FE00
Number of couches: 101
Number of sofas: 101
Number of couches: 102
Number of sofas: 102
```

You can also create constant references, and references to constant values. You read such declarations backwards, just as you do with pointers; here are some examples:

```
const long & ref;          //Reference to a long constant
long & const ref;          //Constant reference to a long
const long & const ref;    //Constant reference to a long constant
```


Related solution:	Found on page:
Declaring a Pointer	211

Passing Arguments to Functions by Reference

As discussed in the In Depth section of this chapter, you can pass arguments to functions by reference if you simply place & in front of the argument in the function's argument list. Here's an example we first saw in the In Depth section of this chapter, addone.cpp. Here, I'm incrementing the value in a variable named **salary** in two ways—using pointers and using references. As you can see here, the two techniques are similar, but you don't need to create and dereference pointers when you pass by reference:

```
#include <iostream>
using namespace std;

void add_one_refs(long & n);
void add_one_ptrs(long * n);

int main()
{
    long salary = 250000;

    cout << "Current salary: $" << salary << endl;

    add_one_ptrs(&salary);

    cout << "After the first raise: $" << salary << endl;

    add_one_refs(salary);

    cout << "After the second raise: $" << salary << endl;

    return 0;
}

void add_one_refs(long & n)
{
    n++;
}

void add_one_ptrs(long * n)
{
    (*n)++;
}
```


Here's what this program, addone.cpp, looks like when it's running—note that I was able to change the value in the variable **salary** from code in both functions **add_one_ptrs** using pointers and **add_one_refs** by passing **salary** by reference:

```
%addone
Current salary: $250000
After the first raise: $250001
After the second raise: $250002
```

In C++, you can actually use constant references (declared with **const**) if you don't want to alter the data the reference refers to. However, passing a constant reference really ends up having the same effect as passing by value (see the previous section for more on declaring constant references).

Temporary Variables and Reference Arguments

When you pass by reference, things work smoothly if you pass an lvalue, because it's no problem to create a reference to an lvalue. But what if you pass an rvalue, such as a constant or a mixed expression that does not correspond to a location in memory? For example, what if you have a function, **add_one_refs**, whose arguments are passed by reference, and instead of passing a variable such as **salary**, you pass an expression that doesn't correspond to a memory location, such as **salary + 1**:

```
#include <iostream>
using namespace std;

void add_one_refs(long & n);

int main()
{
    long salary = 250000;

    add_one_refs(salary + 1);

    cout << "After the raise: $" << salary << endl;

    return 0;
}

void add_one_refs(long & n)
{
    n++;
}
```

In cases like these, the C++ compiler creates a *temporary variable* that corresponds to the expression you're passing. This is okay except for one thing: What if the code in the called function attempts to change the data passed to it by reference? In that case, it'll try to change the data in the temporary variable, which means any changes will be lost. Compilers often give you a warning that something like this is happening, as in this case with Borland C++, when I try to compile the code above:

```
tempvars.cpp:
Warning W8030 tempvars.cpp 10: Temporary used for parameter 'n' in call to
'add_one_refs(long &)' in function main()
```

If you're not changing the data passed by reference, you can ignore this warning, or to suppress the warning, you can pass a reference to a constant instead so the compiler knows you won't try to change the original data. Note, however, that some compilers (like Visual C++) are "phasing out" (as they put it) the use of temporary variables, so they will consider this code in error.

Related solution:	Found on page:
Basic Skills: Storing Data	34

Using References to Structures

Passing by reference was originally added to C++ so you could handle large structures with functions without having to pass a copy of the entire structure to the function. Here's an example, structurereference.cpp, showing how that works. In this case, I'm creating a structure named **person** that holds a person's first name, last name, and salary. To give a person a raise, I can pass structures of that type to a function named **raise**, which adds 1 to the value in the **salary** member of the structure.

To show how you can return a reference from a function, I'll have **raise** do just that—return a reference to the structure it was passed. That means that if you want to give a person two raises, all you have to do is to pass the return value of **raise** back to **raise** again. Here's what this example looks like—note the syntax for the prototype of **raise**, indicating that this function not only is passed a reference but also returns a reference:

```
#include <iostream>
using namespace std;

struct person
{
    char first_name[40];
    char last_name[40];
    long salary;
};

person & raise(person & personref);
```

```
int main()
{
    person dan =
    {
        "Dan",
        "DeFoe",
        14000,
    };

    cout << "Dan\'s salary: $" << dan.salary << endl;

    raise(dan);
    cout << "After the first raise: $" << dan.salary << endl;

    raise(raise(dan));
    cout << "After two more raises: $" << dan.salary << endl;

    return 0;
}

person & raise(person & person_ref)
{
    person_ref.salary++;

    return person_ref;
}
```

Note that, as mentioned, because the **raise** function returns a reference, you can pass its return value right back to **raise** again if you wish, giving a person two raises as in the code above. Here's what this example, structurereference.cpp, looks like when it runs:

```
%structurereference
Dan's salary: $14000
After the first raise: $14001
After two more raises: $14003
```

In fact, because **raise** does return a reference, you can even assign a value to the return value of **raise** if you wish, which looks pretty unusual, resulting in statements like this one:

```
raise(structure1) = raise(structure2);
```

NOTE: When functions return references, the item referenced must not have gone out of scope, so unless you return the same reference that was originally passed to the function, use the ***new*** *operator to allocate space for the referenced item in the free store (and use* ***delete*** *later to delete it).*

Overloading a Function

As discussed in the In Depth section of this chapter, C++ allows you to overload functions, which means that you can call the one function with multiple argument lists—that is, argument lists with different numbers of arguments as well as different types of arguments. For example, you might overload a function, **print_this**, that displays text so that you can pass it a C-style string, a C++ **string** object, a single **char**, or even an ASCII character code. That makes **print_this** a very useful general-purpose function, callable with all kinds of data.

To overload a function for different argument lists, you simply define the function several times, each with a different argument list. As mentioned in the In Depth section of this chapter, when you overload functions, argument lists are called *signatures*, so you define the function a number of times, each with a different signature.

When you call an overloaded function, the C++ compiler checks the arguments you're passing and determines if they match any of the function signatures you've defined. If not, the compiler checks if it can make any implicit data conversions that would match any signature. If there's no match, or if two signatures match equally well, you'll get a compiler error. Table 7.1 shows the typical kinds of standard conversions that the compiler tries to make when converting from the type of arguments you pass to those actually declared in a function's argument list ("type" refers to any data type in that table).

Table 7.1 Standard conversions allowed for overloaded argument list matches.

Passed Argument Type	Argument Type in Argument List
type	type &
type &	type
type[]	*type
type(args...)	type(*)(args...)
type	const or volatile type
type*	const or volatile type*

Function overloading is also called *function polymorphism* or "many form-ism," and we'll use overloading more when dealing with classes and objects. In general, you overload a function when you want to execute the same task while passing different argument lists.

Here's an example, functionoverload.cpp, that we saw in the In Depth section of this chapter. In this example, I created the **print_this** function, mentioned at the beginning of this section, and overloaded that function so you can pass it a single **char**, a C-style string, the ASCII code for a single character, or a C++ **string** object. To overload a function, you just define it several times with distinct signatures, so here's what the code for functionoverload.cpp looks like:

```
#include <iostream>
#include <string>
using namespace std;

void print_this(char the_char){cout << the_char;}
void print_this(char* the_C_string){cout << the_C_string;}
void print_this(int ASC_code){cout << static_cast<char> (ASC_code);}
void print_this(string the_string) {cout << the_string;};

int main()
{
    print_this(97);                 // ASCII code for 'a'
    print_this('b');                // Char
    print_this("c");                // C-style String
    print_this(string("d"));        // C++-style String

    return 0;
}
```

This code uses **print_this** to display the ASCII code for '**a**', the character '**b**', a C-style string "c", and a C++ string object that holds "d". Here's the result when you run this example, functionoverload.cpp:

```
%functionoverload
abcd
```

***NOTE:** In this code, I'm taking advantage of the fact that the << operator is itself overloaded for the **cout** object, allowing **cout** to display text stored in all different types of formats, which makes the code for each form of **print_this** very compact. The fact that you can overload operators is a very powerful aspect of C++, which we'll see about in Chapter 9.*

Of course, you can overload functions with all kinds of argument lists, as long as each such signature is unique, not just those with a single argument. For example, say you want to create a function named **draw_ellipse** that will draw both ellipses and circles. To draw an ellipse, you can pass the length of the ellipse's major and minor axes, but to draw a circle, all you'll need is the circle's radius. That means you can overload **draw_ellipse** as these prototypes indicate:

```
void draw_ellipse(ellipse_major_axis, ellipse_minor_axis);
void draw_ellipse(circle_radius);
```

Now when you call **draw_ellipse** with two arguments, the C++ compiler will know you want to use the two-argument form of that function, and if you call it with one argument, the compiler knows you want to use the one-argument form.

Understanding Storage Classes, Scope, and Linkage

The concepts of storage classes, scope, and linkage become important when you're working with functions, and I discussed these topics in the In Depth section of this chapter. Here's what these terms mean:

- *Storage class* refers to type of storage used for a memory item and can be automatic, static, or free store.
- *Scope* refers to the areas of a program in which an item is visible and may be used in code. Scope can be local (also called block), which means that an item is visible in the code block in which it's defined only, or global (also called file-wide), which means that it has file-wide scope and is visible throughout the file.
- *Linkage* can be internal or external; if an item has internal linkage, it is restricted to the current file, but if it has external scope, it can be accessed across multiple files in the same program.

We'll take a look at these three topics in more detail now.

Storage Class

The storage class of an item determines how it's stored; here are the possibilities:

- *Automatic storage* corresponds to the program's stack and is where a function's variables are allocated and stored when you enter the function.
- *Static storage* is where data that is declared static is stored and left for the duration of the program's lifetime.
- *Free store* is the memory where items you allocate with **new** and **new[]** are stored.

Scope

Here's an overview of how scope works:

- *Automatic variables* are local and have local scope.
- *External variables* are declared outside any function and have global scope.
- *External static variables* are declared with the **static** keyword outside any function and have global scope.
- *External constant variables* are declared with the **const** keyword outside any function and have global scope.
- *Static variables* are automatic variables declared with the **static** keyword and are confined to a block, so they have local scope.

Linkage

And here's an overview of how linkage works:

- *Automatic variables* have internal linkage.
- *External variables* are declared outside any function. They are available to all files in a program and have external linkage.
- *External static variables* are declared with the **static** keyword and are available to all code in the file, but they are restricted to the file they're defined in, which means they have internal linkage.
- *External constant variables* are declared with the **const** keyword and are available to all code in the file, but they are restricted to the file they're defined in, which means they have internal linkage. They're given internal linkage so you can place them in headers and share them across multiple files without conflict.
- *Static variables* are automatic variables declared with the **static** keyword, are confined to a block and so have internal linkage.

That's how the concepts of storage class, scope, and linkage break down in overview. I'll take a look at these concepts in more detail over the next few sections.

Creating Variables with Global Scope

How do you give a variable global (file-wide) scope in C++? You do that by making the variable external, which means you declare it outside any function. To see this in action, take a look at this example program, external.cpp; we originally saw this example in the In Depth section of this chapter, but I'll add more code here. I start by declaring a variable named **color** set to "red" that is external and therefore global:

```
#include <iostream>
#include <string>
using namespace std;

string color("red");
    .
    .
    .
```

In the **main** function, I can refer to this global variable, and I can also declare it with the keyword **extern** to explicitly show that I'm using the external variable **color** (this declaration is optional, and although legal, confuses some compilers we tried it on—omit it if it causes problems with your compiler):

```
#include <iostream>
#include <string>
using namespace std;

string color("red");

void local();

int main()
{
    extern string color;            //Optional declaration

    cout << "Global color: " << color << endl;
    .
    .
    .
```

And I can also create a new function named **local** that also declares a variable named **color**, but this time set to "blue". This local variable overrides the global one, so **color** has the value "blue" in **local**. How can you get access to the global variable **color** in local? You can refer to the global variable with the scope resolution operator **::** as **::color** (we'll see why this works when we work with classes):

```
#include <iostream>
#include <string>
using namespace std;
```

```
string color("red");

void local();

int main()
{
    extern string color;            //Optional declaration

    cout << "Global color: " << color << endl;

    local();

    return 0;
}

void local()                    // uses local variable
{
    string color("blue");

    cout << "Local color: " << color << endl;

    cout << "Global color: " << ::color << endl;
}
```

Here's what this program, external.cpp, looks like when running—note that we are able to access the global variable even in the **local** function:

```
%external
Global color: red
Local color: blue
Global color: red
```

External variables like this also have external linkage; on the other hand, if you declare a variable external static, that variable has internal, not external linkage; see "Using Internal and External Linkage with Multiple Files" next in this chapter for the details.

In addition, you should note that constant global variables (that is, those declared with **const**) have internal, not external linkage, so you can place them in headers shared across multiple files. Because they have internal linkage, they won't conflict when you include the same header in multiple files.

NOTE: *Although using global variables can seem very convenient, you should limit their use for one very important reason—unintentional conflict with other variables. Cluttering up the global space in a program with variables is considered poor programming form—the whole idea behind scope is to let you divide your program up into private spaces to avoid such unintentional conflicts, and making many variables global defeats that purpose.*

Using Internal and External Linkage with Multiple Files

The whole idea behind linkage is to let you specify how items are to be handled across multiple files. An item with external linkage can be used across several files, while an item with internal linkage is restricted to the file it's defined in. To use external linkage, you declare the item in one file and declare it again with the **extern** keyword in all other files you want to use it in. On the other hand, if you declare an external item as static, it has only internal linkage.

Here's an example made up of two files, file1.cpp and file2.cpp; we saw these files in the In Depth section of this chapter, but I'll go into more detail here. In file1.cpp, I'll create two external variables and one external static variable. I'll display their values with code in **main** and also call a function in the second file, **second_file_values**, like this:

```
#include <iostream>
using namespace std;

int value1 = 1;
int value2 = 2;
static int value3 = 3;

void second_file_values();

int main()
{
    cout << "In file one..." << endl;
    cout << "value1: " << value1 << endl;
    cout << "value2: " << value2 << endl;
    cout << "value3: " << value3 << endl;

    second_file_values();

    return 0;
}
```

In file2.cpp, I'll declare **value1** as **extern**, which indicates to the compiler that **value1** is defined externally (in file1.cpp in this case). I'll also declare and initialize an external static variable **value2** in file2.cpp; this variable has internal linkage, and overrides **value2** from file1.cpp. Finally, I'll declare and initialize an external variable named **value3**; because the variable named **value3** in file1.cpp has internal linkage, it doesn't conflict with file2.cpp's **value3**. I'll also display all three variables in the function called from file1.cpp, **second_file_values**:

```
#include <iostream>
using namespace std;

extern int value1;
static int value2 = 4;
int value3 = 5;

void second_file_values()
{
    cout << "In file two..." << endl;
    cout << "value1: " << value1 << endl;
    cout << "value2: " << value2 << endl;
    cout << "value3: " << value3 << endl;
}
```

That's all it takes. Now you compile and link both file1.cpp and file2.cpp together (for more details on this process, see "Basic Skills: Compiling a Program" in Chapter 1); for example, using g++, with a command line that looks like this:

```
%g++ file1.cpp file2.cpp
```

Now, when you run the code, this is what you see, showing that **value1** has been shared across files, that **value2** was overridden by a local version of the same variable in file2.cpp, and that **value3** has internal linkage in file1.cpp, so it doesn't conflict with the variable with the same name in file2.cpp:


```
%file1
In file one...
value1: 1
value2: 2
value3: 3
In file two...
value1: 1
value2: 4
value3: 5
```

Note that constant global variables (that is, external variables declared with **const**) have internal, not external linkage, so you can place them in headers shared across multiple files. In other words, because they have internal linkage, they won't conflict when you include the same header in multiple files. Here's another note: When you use **static** with external variables, it makes their linkage internal—but when you use **static** with automatic variables, it changes their storage class to **static**. See the next section for the details.

Creating Local Static (Persistent) Variables

There are two ways to use the keyword **static** with variables in C++—with external variables and with automatic variables. When you use **static** with external variables, it makes their linkage internal, but when you use **static** with automatic variables, it changes their storage class to **static**. Unlike data in automatic storage, data in static storage persists throughout the lifetime of the program.

That's a useful thing to know. For example, say you want to keep a running count by calling a function named **totaller**—the first time you call **totaller** it should return 1, the next time it should return 2, and so on. Here's what the first attempt at implementing such a counter function might look like:

```
#include <iostream>
using namespace std;

int totaller();

int main()
{
    cout << "After first call, totaller returns " << totaller() << endl;

    cout << "After second call, totaller returns " << totaller() << endl;

    return 0;
}

int totaller()
{
    int total = 0;              // automatic local variable

    total++;
```

```
    return total;
}
```

But here's what this program displays when it runs:

```
%static
After first call, totaller returns 1
After second call, totaller returns 1
```

Note that **totaller** always returns 1; the problem is that the variable in **totaller**, **total**, is an automatic variable, which is re-initialized every time the **totaller** function is called. That means **total** starts off at 0, is incremented and then returned as 1, which is fine—but the next time you call the function, **total** starts off at 0 again.

To fix this problem, you can use a variable declared with the **static** keyword, because that variable is stored in static storage and so *persists* while the program is running. To do that, I'll add a new function, **summer**, to the program like this:

```
#include <iostream>
using namespace std;

int totaller();
int summer();

int main()
{
    cout << "After first call, totaller returns " << totaller() << endl;
    cout << "After first call, summer returns " << summer() << endl;

    cout << "After second call, totaller returns " << totaller() << endl;
    cout << "After second call, summer returns " << summer() << endl;

    return 0;
}

int totaller()
{
    int total = 0;                    // automatic local variable

    total++;

    return total;
}
```

```
int summer()
{
    static int sum = 0;            // static local variable

    sum++;

    return sum;
}
```

Here's the new result of this program, static.cpp—as you can see, storing the count in static storage has fixed the problem:

```
%static
After first call, totaller returns 1
After first call, summer returns 1
After second call, totaller returns 1
After second call, summer returns 2
```

***TIP:** Older C++ compilers did not allow you to initialize arrays unless they were static, so if you've been having problems initializing automatic arrays, now you know the solution—make them static. ANSI/ISO standard C++-compliant compilers do not have this problem.*

Linkage and Functions

Linkage is also defined for functions in C++. By default, functions must be defined outside any other function, and so they have global (file-wide) scope and external linkage. In other words, you can define a function in one file and use it in another. We saw an example of that in "Using Internal and External Linkage with Multiple Files" earlier in this chapter with the function **second_file_values**.

You can, however, give a function internal linkage, confining it to one file, if you use the **static** keyword:

```
static int call_me(int n);
```

Because functions have external linkage by default, you can't include them in a header if you share that header among the files in a program—because the compiler would think you're defining the same function more than once. However, inline functions have been specifically designed to have internal linkage, so they are local, and there's no problem including them in headers that are included in multiple files in the same program. For more on inline functions, see "Creating Inline Functions" earlier in this chapter.

Mixed-Language Linking

On occasion, you might want to link your code with compiled files that were written in other languages, such as C, or even use libraries of functions that were originally written in another language. To do so, you must let the compiler and linker know what you're doing.

There are two reasons the compiler and linker need to know that you're using code written in another language—first, some other languages, by default, pass by reference instead of by value like C++, and second, compilers actually change the name of your functions when they're compiled. This name change is called *name mangling*.

In C++, for example, name mangling lets the compiler differentiate between the various overloaded forms of a function. You might have a function named **calculate(int m, int n)** that's also overloaded as **calculate(double m, double n)**; to keep these two forms of the function separate, the C++ compiler might name them something like **calculate__ii** and **calculate__dd**. Because different languages use different name-mangling schemes, the linker must know what language the compiled code you're calling was written in, if it wasn't C++.

By default, C++ programs use C++ linkage, so if you're sticking with C++, you don't have to worry about language linkage. To link to compiled code originally written in C, however, you can specify C linkage like this (note that you also must declare the function with **extern**, because the function definition is outside the current file):

```
extern "C" long make_money(int);      //Use C linkage
```

Here's how you'd specify C++ linkage if you wanted to:

```
extern "C++" long make_money(int);    //Use C++ linkage
```

All About Storage Class Qualifiers: **const, register, volatile,** and **mutable**

C++ supports several qualifiers you can use to specify more information about the storage class of variables when you declare those variables: **const**, **register**, **volatile**, and **mutable**.

We're already familiar with **const**, which you use to give data a constant value. I won't add much to our coverage of **const** here except to say that by default, external variables have external linkage, but if you use **const** to declare them, they have internal linkage.

The **register** storage class qualifier acts as a *request* to the compiler to store the variable in one of the CPU's internal registers for quick access. If you store data in memory, it must be fetched from memory every time you want to use it, but if you store it in the CPU's registers, it's already loaded and ready to be used, saving time. That's useful if you use the same variable over and over again in quick succession, but creating code that keeps a value constantly in one register of the CPU is often very hard to do (all registers are normally used because there are only a very limited number available), which is why this qualifier is only a request to the compiler, not an instruction.

Bear in mind that CPU registers are typically 32 bits long (although in some machines, they are 64), so don't ask the compiler to make a **double** register variable. Here's an example:

```
register int count;
```

The **volatile** storage class qualifier indicates that the value in a variable can change under non-programmatic control. For example, a variable might correspond to a hardware location that's updated by the computer automatically, not by your code, such as the system clock. In multithreaded programs, which are supported by some compilers but which are not standard C++, there are multiple threads of execution, and one thread might have changed the value in a variable that you're about to read, so such a variable should be declared volatile. (What the **volatile** keyword really does, for the most part, is to tell the compiler not to optimize the handling and location of the volatile data in such a way that assumes its value doesn't change.)

The **mutable** storage class qualifier specifies that a particular member of a structure or class can be altered even if used in a variable that has been declared constant. For example, I'm making the **salary** member of this structure mutable, and even though I declare a variable of this structure type with **const**, the **salary** member is not constant, and so might be changed:

```
struct person
{
    char first_person[40];
    char last_person[40];
```

```
    mutable int salary;
};

const person ralph = {"Ralph", "Kramden", 14000};
ralph.salary -= 100;
```

Creating Function Templates

As discussed in the In Depth section of this chapter, you can use function templates to create multiple functions in which the code is the same—except for the type of the data the function handles. In other words, you can think of a function template as a sort of cookie cutter for functions, and each such function will operate on a different data type. Function templates are often stored in header files as opposed to the functions themselves being stored there (because if you include the header in multiple files in the same program, the compiler can think you're defining the same function a number of times and there can be a conflict).

You use the keyword **template** to define a function template and use a placeholder for the type of data you want the function to operate on; many programmers use the letter **T**, and I'll do the same here. For example, here's how I set up a function template for a function named **sq**, which squares its argument:

```
template <class T>
T sq(T data)
{
    return data * data;
}
```

You can also use the keyword **typename** instead of **class** to refer to the data type the function will handle (note that older compilers won't recognize the keyword **typename**):

```
template <typename T>
T sq(T data)
{
    return data * data;
}
```

Now when you use the function **sq** in code, the C++ compiler will *instantiate* the correct version of that function, depending on the data type you're using:

```
long long_result = sq(int_value, int_value);
double double_result = sq(float_value, float_value);
```

You can also include arguments of a fixed data type in the argument list of the function you're creating a template for, like this, where I'm adding an integer argument:

```
template <class T>
T adder(T data, int n)
{
    return data + n;
}
```

Here's an example we saw at the beginning of this chapter, in the In Depth section, named functiontemplate.cpp. In this case, I created a template for a function named **add_one** that adds 1 to its argument—which is passed by reference—and then used that function with both **long** and **double** values. Note that you create a prototype for a function template just as you would for a function—you omit the function body and terminate the prototype with a semicolon:

```
#include <iostream>
using namespace std;

template <typename T>
void add_one(T &n);

int main()
{
    long long_salary = 250000;

    cout << "Current long salary: $" << long_salary << endl;

    add_one(long_salary);

    cout << "After the long raise: $" << long_salary << endl;

    double double_salary = 250000.0;

    cout << "Current double salary: $" << double_salary << endl;

    add_one(double_salary);

    cout << "After the double raise: $" << double_salary << endl;
```

```
    return 0;
}

template <typename T>
void add_one(T &n)
{
    n++;
}
```

Here's the result of the program, functiontemplate.cpp:

```
%functiontemplate
Current long salary: $250000
After the long raise: $250001
Current double salary: $250000
After the double raise: $250001
```

Overloading Function Templates

As with functions, you can overload function templates. In fact, the process is practically the same—you simply define a number of function templates with different function signatures. Here's an example, templateoverload.cpp; in this case, I'm overloading the **add_one** function we used in the previous section. This function adds 1 to its argument, but I'm also declaring a version that takes an integer argument and adds that to its argument instead of 1:

```
#include <iostream>
using namespace std;

template <typename T>
void add_one(T &n);

template <typename T>
void add_one(T &n, int m);

int main()
{
    long salary = 250000;

    cout << "Current salary: $" << salary << endl;

    add_one(salary);
```

```
    cout << "After the raise: $" << salary << endl;

    add_one(salary, 10);

    cout << "After the new raise: $" << salary << endl;

    return 0;
}

template <typename T>
void add_one(T &n)
{
    n++;
}

template <typename T>
void add_one(T &n, int m)
{
    n += m;
}
```

Here is what this program, templateoverload.cpp, looks like at work—as you can see, the two-argument version of the overloaded template was used when appropriate:

```
%templateoverload
Current salary: $250000
After the raise: $250001
After the new raise: $250011
```


Creating Explicit Function Instantiations

Although C++ instantiates functions from function templates as needed, you can also create *explicit* function instantiations, which instantiate a function without waiting for the compiler to do so. To create an explicit function instantiation, you simply give the data type you want the instantiation to handle, such as **int** in this case:

```
template swap<int>(int, int);
```

Here's how I add an explicit function instantiation to an example named explicitfunctiontemplate.cpp (note that not all compilers will support explicit function instantiations):

```
#include <iostream>
using namespace std;

template <typename T>
void add_one(T &n);

void add_one<int>(int);

int main()
{
    long salary = 250000;

    cout << "Current salary: $" << salary << endl;

    add_one(salary);

    cout << "After the long raise: $" << salary << endl;

    return 0;
}

template <typename T>
void add_one(T &n)
{
    n++;
}
```

Here's what explicitfunctiontemplate.cpp looks like when running:

```
%explicitfunctiontemplate
Current salary: $250000
After the long raise: $250001
```


Creating Explicit Function Template Specializations

Sometimes, a function template is perfect for all the data types you want to use—except for one or two data types. For example, the function **add_one** we've used over the previous few sections adds 1 to its argument, which is fine for numeric types. However, it's inappropriate for string types, so you might want to create a specific non-template version of **add_one** that displays an error if **add_one** is called with a string. Such a specific version of a function that doesn't use the function's normal template is called an *explicit specialization*. If a function call exactly matches the argument list you've given in a specialization, the compiler will use the specialization instead of the function's template.

To create a specialization, you simply define the function you want to use for a specific argument list instead of the template and put **template <>** in front of the function's prototype and definition. Here's an example, specialization.cpp; in this case, I'll use a function template for **add_one** unless a reference to a string is passed, in which case I'll use an explicit specialization that displays an error:

```
#include <iostream>
#include <string>
using namespace std;

template <typename T>
void add_one(T &n);

template <> void add_one(string &s);

int main()
{
    int int_value = 0;
    string string_value("Hello from C++");

    add_one(int_value);

    cout << "The new int_value = " << int_value << endl;

    add_one(string_value);

    return 0;
}

template <typename T>
void add_one(T &n)
{
    n++;
}
```

```
template <> void add_one(string &s)
{
    cout << "Sorry, adding one to the string \"" << s
        << "\" is not defined." << endl;
}
```

Here's what this program, specialization.cpp, looks like at work:

```
%specialization
The new int_value = 1
Sorry, adding one to the string "Hello from C++" is not defined.
```

Chapter 8

Classes and Objects

In Depth

One of the big attractions of C++ has always been *object-oriented programming*, and in fact, OOP has become such a buzzword that legions of C programmers migrated to C++ whether they needed to or not. As you know, the original big change from C to C++ was the introduction of object-oriented programming. C itself was a terrific innovation from earlier days, but eventually C ran into limitations, as previous programming languages had before it. As programs grew longer, C programs became more unwieldy, because there was no easy way to cut a long C program up into truly self-contained components. C programming is *procedural*, which means you can break a program up into functions, but as programs got really long, that wasn't enough—imagine managing a program with several hundred functions in it and having to keep in mind what they all do.

To allow programmers to cut long programs up into more autonomous units, C++ added OOP to C (in fact, Bjarne Stroustrup, the creator of C++, heads AT&T Lab's Large-Scale Programming Research Department). With object-oriented programming, the motto is "divide and conquer." You can divide a program into parts that you can think of as easily conceptualized parts. For example, imagine if you had a complex system that you used to keep food cold. You might watch the temperature of the food using a thermometer, and when the temperature got high enough, you could throw a switch to start the compressor and work the valves so the coolant circulates, then start a fan to blow air over the cooling vanes, and so on. That's one way to do it; another is to connect all those operations together and so make them automatic, wrapping the whole into an easily conceptualized unit—a refrigerator. Now all the internals are hidden from view, and all you have to do is to put food in or take it out. The process of breaking your problem into easily handled concepts is called *abstraction*.

Objects are able to hide their internal programming details from the rest of the program, reducing all the interdependencies that spring up in a long C program by setting up a well-defined and controllable interface that handles the connection between the object and the rest of the code. Now you can think of the object in an easy way—for example, you might have an object that handles all the interaction with the screen, an object you call **screen**. You can use that object in ways we'll see throughout this book to manipulate what it's intended to work on, in this case, the screen display. After creating that object, you know that the screen is handled by that object, and you can put it out of mind—no longer does every part of the code have to set up its own screen handling; no longer do you need to keep in mind what four hundred screen-handling functions do; you can use the **screen** object instead. Hiding the details and data in objects is called *encapsulation*, and it helps you handle large-scale programming tasks.

When C added object-oriented programming, it became C++, which lets programmers deal with longer programs, and object-oriented code helped solve many other problems as well. For example, supporting objects made it easier for the manufacturers that supply software to provide you with lots of pre-written code, ready to use. To create an object, you use a *class*, which acts like a template or cookie cutter for that object; that is, a class is to an object what a cookie cutter is to a cookie. In other words, you can think of a class as an object's *type* (much like a variable's type might be the integer type).

Now that C++ supports classes, software manufacturers started providing huge libraries of classes, ready for you to start creating objects from. For example, one of the most popular libraries of C++ classes is the Microsoft Foundation Class (MFC) library that comes with Microsoft's Visual C++, and programmers found the MFC library a tremendous improvement over the old days. When you wrote a Windows program in C, you needed about five pages of solid code just to display a blank window. However, using a class in the MFC library, you could simply create an object of the kind of window you wanted to use—with a border, without a border, as a dialog box, and so on. All the functionality of the kind of window you wanted to create was already built into the object, so all it took to create that window was one line of code—the line where you create the new window object from the class you've selected.

This chapter, then, is all about object-oriented programming (OOP). I first discussed it in Chapter 1, and now that we've come up through the basics of C++ syntax, we're ready to work with it in a formal way. In OOP, the idea is that you encapsulate data and methods into objects, making each object semi-autonomous, enclosing private (that is, purely internal) data and methods in a way that stops them from cluttering the general namespace. The object can then interact with the rest of the program through a well-defined interface defined by its public (that is, externally callable) methods. The idea behind encapsulation is to take a complex system that demands a lot of attention and to turn it into an object that handles all its own work internally and can be easily conceptualized. If the first dictum of object-oriented programming is divide and conquer, the second is surely out of sight out of mind—a process called *data hiding*.

Object-oriented programming revolves around a few key concepts: classes, objects, data members, methods, inheritance, and data hiding. Here's what those terms mean in overview:

- A *class* is a template from which you can create objects. The definition of the class includes the formal specifications for the class and any data and methods in it. That is, a class is an object's *type*.
- An *object* is an instance of a class, much the way a variable is an instance of a data type. If you think of a class as the type of an object, an object is an instance of a class. Objects encapsulate methods and instance variables.
- *Data members* are those variables that are part of a class, and what you use to store the data the object uses.
- *Methods* are functions built into a class and therefore into the objects created from that class.
- *Inheritance* is the process of deriving one class, called the *derived* class, from another, the *base* class, and being able to make use of the base class's data and methods in the derived class.
- *Data hiding* is all about hiding your data inside objects. In fact, objects and classes are often designed around data, and OOP is often considered data-centric (and the process of encapsulation is often called *data encapsulation*). You can make data *private* (visible only to code in the same class), *protected* (visible only inside the same class and classes derived from it), or *public* (visible to code inside and outside the class). You can also make methods *private*, *protected*, or *public*.

All these concepts are important to object-oriented programming, and we'll get more details on each of them in this and the next few chapters.

Creating Classes and Objects

It's time to get to some code. Here, I'm going to create a class and show how the concept of classes springs naturally from what we've already done. Say, for example, that you've decided to take up bird watching, and you want to keep track of how many of each bird you've seen. Naturally, you turn to C++ to implement this process.

Starting with a Structure

You could keep track of the birds you see with individual variables, such as **name_of_bird1**, **number_of_bird1_seen**, **name_of_bird2**, **number_of_bird2_seen**, and so on, but that would become unwieldy as you tried to track dozens of birds.

Instead, basing your work on what we've already done, you might create a structure named, say, **bird_structure**, that allows you to store all you need for each type of bird. Here's how that looks in an example named birdstructure.cpp:

```
#include <iostream>
#include <string>
using namespace std;

struct bird_structure
{
    string name;
    int number_seen;
};
    .
    .
    .
```

Now the name and number of a particular bird are stored inside variables of this new **bird_structure** type. You can create variables of this type and place values in the data members of the structure, like this, where I'm creating a variable named **orioles** and initializing the number of orioles seen to 0:

```
#include <iostream>
#include <string>
using namespace std;

struct bird_structure
{
    string name;
    int number_seen;
};

int main()
{
    bird_structure orioles;

    orioles.name = "oriole";
    orioles.number_seen = 0;
    .
    .
    .
```

Now when you see an oriole, you can increment the **number_seen** data member and display the new result:

```
#include <iostream>
#include <string>
using namespace std;

struct bird_structure
{
    string name;
    int number_seen;
};

int main()
{
    bird_structure orioles;

    orioles.name = "oriole";
    orioles.number_seen = 0;

    orioles.number_seen++;

    cout << "Number of " << orioles.name << "s seen: "
        << orioles.number_seen << endl;

    return 0;
}
```

Here's what you see when you run this code:

```
%birdstructure
Number of orioles seen: 1
```

This code runs as it should, but it can be improved. The internal details of the **bird_structure** are all too visible from the OOP point of view—for example, in this code, you have to remember that this structure uses an internal data member named **number_seen** to store the number of birds seen and to increment it yourself. Wouldn't it be better, the OOP programmer asks, if all those internal details were hidden from view, and you could simply call well-defined functions that make up a systematic interface to that data? In that way, you wouldn't be responsible for all the data management tasks like error checking, watching for overflow, and so on. For example, the OOP programmer says, what about adding a function named **increment_count** to each structure which, when called, would increment the internal count automatically?

Adding Methods to a Structure

That would be nice, you think, if you could add a function to a structure. It turns out that in C++, you can. For example, you can define this new function, **increment_count**, inside the structure itself:

```
#include <iostream>
#include <string>
using namespace std;

struct bird_structure
{
    string name;
    int number_seen;
    void increment_count(){number_seen++;}
};
    .
    .
    .
```

This is not something you can do in C, but you can in C++. This new function, **increment_count**, is now a member function of **bird_structure**, and you can access it using the dot operator, ., just as you can access the structure's data members. For example, if you see an oriole, you can call the **oriole** structure's **increment_count** method like this:

```
#include <iostream>
#include <string>
using namespace std;

struct bird_structure
{
    string name;
    int number_seen;
    void increment_count(){number_seen++;}
};

int main()
{
    bird_structure orioles;

    orioles.name = "oriole";
    orioles.number_seen = 0;
```

```
    orioles.increment_count();

    cout << "Number of " << orioles.name << "s seen: "
        << orioles.number_seen << endl;

    return 0;
}
```

Here's what you see when you run this code, as before:

```
%birdstructure
Number of orioles seen: 1
```

From the OOP point of view, this is a step in the right direction, because we're hiding some of the internal data handling inside the structure. However, note that we still have to initialize the internal data member **number_seen** and use it directly to display the number of orioles seen:

```
#include <iostream>
#include <string>
using namespace std;

struct bird_structure
{
    string name;
    int number_seen;
    void increment_count(){number_seen++;}
};

int main()
{
    bird_structure orioles;

    orioles.name = "oriole";
    orioles.number_seen = 0;

    orioles.increment_count();

    cout << "Number of " << orioles.name << "s seen: "
        << orioles.number_seen << endl;

    return 0;
}
```

It's time to hide the data inside **bird_structure** even further—and for that, we have to make it a class. In fact, in C++, structures *are* classes (and so are unions, for that matter), except that all their internal members are *public*—that is, accessible to code outside the structure. To make the internal data really internal, we have to change **bird_structure** into **bird_class**.

Hiding Data in Classes

Data and methods inside classes are *private*—accessible to code inside the class only—by default, which points out the data-hiding nature of classes. Changing **bird_structure** into **bird_class** is easy—all we have to do besides changing the name is change the word **structure** to **class**:

```
#include <iostream>
#include <string>
using namespace std;

class bird_class
{
public:
    string name;
    int number_seen;
    void increment_count(){number_seen++;}
};
    .
    .
    .
```

Note that I've also used the keyword **public** here to indicate that I want the members of this class to be public, at least for now. If I were to make them **private**, they'd be accessible only to code inside the class. That's how *class scope* works—all the members of a class are accessible to any code in the class. From outside the class, all **public** members of the class are visible, no **private** members of the class are visible, and any members declared **protected** are accessible only in code in classes based on the present class. As we'll see in the Immediate Solutions sections in this chapter, you use the ., ->, and :: operators to access the members of an object from outside that object.

Recall that a class is a *type*, and you can create objects using that type. That works just as it did with structures, which means here's what our first class-based program, birdclass.cpp, looks like:

```
#include <iostream>
#include <string>
using namespace std;

class bird_class
{
public:
    string name;
    int number_seen;
    void increment_count(){number_seen++;}
};

int main()
{
    bird_class orioles;

    orioles.name = "oriole";
    orioles.number_seen = 0;

    orioles.increment_count();

    cout << "Number of " << orioles.name << "s seen: "
        << orioles.number_seen << endl;

    return 0;
}
```

Notice, however, that I'm still accessing the internal data members of this new class directly; for example, here's how I initialize the internal data member **number_seen** to 0:

```
#include <iostream>
#include <string>
using namespace std;

class bird_class
{
public:
    string name;
    int number_seen;
    void increment_count(){number_seen++;}
};
```

```
int main()
{
    bird_class orioles;

    orioles.name = "oriole";
    orioles.number_seen = 0;
        .
        .
        .
```

Classes and objects are largely about data hiding, so it would be better if we handle everything having to do with the internal data **number_seen** inside the class itself. However, classes are *types*, not lvalues, so they have no place to store data—which means you can't initialize **number_seen** to 0 when you declare it in the class like this:

```
#include <iostream>
#include <string>
using namespace std;

class bird_class
{
private:
    int number_seen = 0;
public:
    string name;
    void increment_count(){number_seen++;}
};
    .
    .
    .
```

Instead, you initialize the data in objects using special methods called *constructors*.

***NOTE:** Actually, it's not entirely true that you can't initialize data in a class definition. A little-known fact is that you can set items you declare as **static const** to constant values, like this: **static const int zero = 0;** in class definitions. You can also use an enumeration to define values in a class definition like this: **enum {constant1 = 1, constant2 = 2};**.*

Initializing Data with Constructors

An object's constructor is a method that's run when the object is being allocated in memory, which means you can initialize the data in the object at that time. A constructor is just a method of the class like any other, except that it has the same name as the class and it has no return value (see "Creating Constructors" later in this chapter for the details). As with any other method, constructors can accept arguments, so here's how I declare a constructor for **bird_class** in a new program, birdclassconstructor.cpp, that allows you to pass the name of the bird to track:

```
#include <iostream>
#include <string>
using namespace std;

class bird_class
{
public:
    string name;
    int number_seen;
    void increment_count(){number_seen++;}
    bird_class(string text);
};
```

I could define the body of the new constructor inside the class definition, as I have for the **increment_count** method, but that gets awkward if there are more than a few lines of code. You can define the body of a method *outside* the class definition if you use the scope resolution operator, ::, to indicate which class the method belongs to. Here's how that looks when I'm putting code in the constructor for **bird_class** to store the name of the bird to track and initializing **number_seen** to 0:

```
#include <iostream>
#include <string>
using namespace std;

class bird_class
{
public:
    string name;
    int number_seen;
    void increment_count(){number_seen++;}
    bird_class(string text);
};
```

```
bird_class::bird_class(string text)
{
    name = text;
    number_seen = 0;
}
    .
    .
    .
```

Now you can use this new constructor to create new objects with, and you can pass the name of the bird you want to track to the constructor when you create an object of **bird_class** like this:

```
#include <iostream>
#include <string>
using namespace std;

class bird_class
{
public:
    string name;
    int number_seen;
    void increment_count(){number_seen++;}
    bird_class(string text);
};

bird_class::bird_class(string text)
{
    name = text;
    number_seen = 0;
}

int main()
{
    bird_class orioles("oriole");

    orioles.increment_count();

    cout << "Number of " << orioles.name << "s seen: "
        << orioles.number_seen << endl;

    return 0;
}
```

Using this new constructor, then, we've been able to initialize the data in an object without having to set the internal member **number_seen** to 0 explicitly in the **main** function.

Managing Private Data

There's one last place we use the internal data member **number_seen** outside objects of the **bird_class**, and that's when we display the number of birds seen:

```
cout << "Number of " << orioles.name << "s seen: "
    << orioles.number_seen << endl;
```

To make **number_seen** entirely private to **bird_class**, I'll add a *data access method* named **get_count** to this class, which returns the value in **number_seen**. When you make the data in objects private, you can provide data access methods like **get_count** to control the access that code outside the object has to the object's internal data (see "Creating Data Access Methods" later in this chapter for more details). When I add the **get_count** method to **bird_class**, I can make **number_seen** a **private** data member of that class, which means it'll be inaccessible outside that class, as you see in the new program birdclass2.cpp:

```
#include <iostream>
#include <string>
using namespace std;

class bird_class
{
private:
    int number_seen;
public:
    string name;
    void increment_count(){number_seen++;}
    int get_count(){return number_seen;}
    bird_class(string text);
};

bird_class::bird_class(string text)
{
    name = text;
    number_seen = 0;
}

int main()
{
    bird_class orioles("oriole");

    orioles.increment_count();
```

```
    cout << "Number of " << orioles.name << "s seen: "
        << orioles.get_count() << endl;

    return 0;
}
```

And that's all it takes—now the data member **number_seen** is private to objects of **bird_class**, and we've hidden that data. You can see how this process can be invaluable in objects on a larger scale—imagine, for example, that you're working with an object that handles the screen and the data in screen registers and data buffers, as well as setting scan rates, locking vertical hold, and so on. Instead of handling all those details yourself, or worrying that other parts of the program might interfere with that data by mistake, it would be a lot easier if such an object simply *exposed* a number of easy-to-use methods like **display_text** or **draw_circle**. Dividing everything up into autonomous components like this is a big part of what OOP is all about. It's time to get to the Immediate Solutions now and see all this at work.

Immediate Solutions

Defining a Class

To define a class, you use this syntax (I'll add more to this syntax diagram in Chapter 10 on class inheritance—see "Deriving a Class from a Base Class" in that chapter for more details):

```
class name
{
private:
    private data members and methods
protected:
    protected data members and methods
public:
    public data members and methods
}[object_list...];
```

You can make data and methods in the class **private** (visible only to code in the same class), **protected** (visible only inside the same class and classes derived from it), or **public** (visible to code inside and outside the class).

Can you also declare a class? For example, can you use a class "prototype" like this to introduce the compiler to the class before it's been defined?:

```
class name;
```

Yes you can, but such declarations are of limited utility, because the compiler doesn't know anything about what's in this class. Class declarations are useful when you want to create and use pointers to objects of a class before defining the class, because the compiler doesn't need to know what's in a class before creating a pointer to objects of that class. It turns out that there are some occasions when declaring a class is necessary—see "Creating Friend Methods" in Chapter 9 for an example.

Here's an example that we saw in the In Depth section of this chapter, birdclass.cpp, showing how to define a class; in this case, I define a class named **bird_class** and then declare an object of that class like this:

```
#include <iostream>
#include <string>
using namespace std;

class bird_class
{
public:
    string name;
    int number_seen;
    void increment_count(){number_seen++;}
};

int main()
{
    bird_class orioles;

    orioles.name = "oriole";
    orioles.number_seen = 0;

    orioles.increment_count();

    cout << "Number of " << orioles.name << "s seen: "
        << orioles.number_seen << endl;

    return 0;
}
```

It's worth noting that C++ treats classes much as it treats other types; for example, class definitions have internal linkage, so they can be put in header files and included in multiple files of the same program without conflict.

Related solution:	Found on page:
Creating Friend Methods	426

Creating an Object

A class is the type of an object, which is to say that a class is to an object what a cookie cutter is to a cookie. To create an object of a certain class, you simply declare the object as a variable of the class type like this:

```
#include <iostream>
#include <string>
```

```
using namespace std;

class bird_class
{
public:
    string name;
    int number_seen;
    void increment_count(){number_seen++;}
};

int main()
{
    bird_class orioles;

    orioles.name = "oriole";
    orioles.number_seen = 0;

    orioles.increment_count();

    cout << "Number of " << orioles.name << "s seen: "
        << orioles.number_seen << endl;

    return 0;
}
```

As with structures, you can also declare an object or objects at the end of the class definition:

```
#include <iostream>
#include <string>
using namespace std;

class bird_class
{
public:
    string name;
    int number_seen;
    void increment_count(){number_seen++;}
}orioles;

int main()
{
    orioles.name = "oriole";
    orioles.number_seen = 0;
```

```
    orioles.increment_count();

    cout << "Number of " << orioles.name << "s seen: "
        << orioles.number_seen << endl;

    return 0;
}
```

As we've also seen in the In Depth section of this chapter, you can also use a constructor, which is a class method with the same name as the class and no return value, to initialize an object. When declaring the object, you can pass arguments to the constructor as we've seen (if you don't define a constructor, the compiler creates a default constructor for you, so you can create objects without passing any arguments to the class's constructor). Here's the example:

```
#include <iostream>
#include <string>
using namespace std;

class bird_class
{
public:
    string name;
    int number_seen;
    void increment_count(){number_seen++;}
    bird_class(string text);
};

bird_class::bird_class(string text)
{
    name = text;
    number_seen = 0;
}

int main()
{
    bird_class orioles("oriole");

    orioles.increment_count();

    cout << "Number of " << orioles.name << "s seen: "
        << orioles.number_seen << endl;

    return 0;
}
```

You can also use the **new** operator to create objects with, in which case you get a pointer to the new object:

```
bird_class *orioles = new bird_class("oriole");
```

Creating Data Members

You can store data in objects by creating data members. Data members of a class are just like the data members of a structure, and you declare and use them in almost the same way, as we've seen:

```
#include <iostream>
#include <string>
using namespace std;

class bird_class
{
public:
    string name;
    int number_seen;
    void increment_count(){number_seen++;}
};

int main()
{
    bird_class orioles;

    orioles.name = "oriole";
    orioles.number_seen = 0;

    orioles.increment_count();

    cout << "Number of " << orioles.name << "s seen: "
        << orioles.number_seen << endl;

    return 0;
}
```

As discussed in the In Depth section of this chapter, the main difference between using data members in classes and structures is that all data in a structure is public, while data members in classes are all private by default. You can make data members in a class private, protected, or public by explicitly declaring them so with the keywords **private**, **protected**, and **public**.

Creating Methods

The functions you define as part of a class are called methods, and there are two primary ways of defining methods in a class—internally and externally. To define a method inside the class definition, you simply place the method definition inside the class definition, as we've seen in the program birdclass.cpp in the In Depth section of this chapter:

```
#include <iostream>
#include <string>
using namespace std;

class bird_class
{
public:
    string name;
    int number_seen;
    void increment_count(){number_seen++;}
};

int main()
{
    bird_class orioles;

    orioles.name = "oriole";
    orioles.number_seen = 0;

    orioles.increment_count();

    cout << "Number of " << orioles.name << "s seen: "
        << orioles.number_seen << endl;

    return 0;
}
```

Defining a method inside the class definition actually makes that function inline (see "Creating Inline Functions" in Chapter 7 and "Creating Inline Methods" later in this chapter). You can also place a new method's *declaration* in the class definition, and its *definition* outside, as long as you preface the method definition with the name of the class it's part of, as well as the scope resolution operator, ::. Here's how that looks in this case:

```
#include <iostream>
#include <string>
using namespace std;
```

```
class bird_class
{
public:
    string name;
    int number_seen;
    void increment_count();
};

void bird_class::increment_count()
{
    number_seen++;
}

int main()
{
    bird_class orioles;

    orioles.name = "oriole";
    orioles.number_seen = 0;

    orioles.increment_count();

    cout << "Number of " << orioles.name << "s seen: "
        << orioles.number_seen << endl;

    return 0;
}
```

The methods in classes are all private by default. You can make the methods in a class private, protected, or public by explicitly declaring them so with the keywords **private**, **protected**, or **public**. Note that the methods you declare like this must all be called on an object, like this: **orioles.get_count()**; or **pointer_to_orioles->get_count()**. You can, however, also call static methods using only the class name, with no object needed. See "Static Methods" later in this chapter for more details.

Related solution:	Found on page:
Creating Inline Functions	301

Using Access Specifiers

Using the access specifiers **private**, **protected**, and **public**, you can set the access of a class's members. You can make members *private* (visible only to code in the same class), *protected* (visible only inside the same class and classes derived from it), or *public* (visible to code inside and outside the class). By default, all the members of a class are private, and all the members of a structure are public.

Here's an example showing how to use access specifiers that we saw in birdclass2.cpp in the In Depth section of this chapter, where I declared some members private and some public. The members declared after an access specifier use the corresponding access (so note that the **private** declaration here is not needed, because all members of a class are private by default):

```
#include <iostream>
#include <string>
using namespace std;

class bird_class
{
private:
    int number_seen;
public:
    string name;
    void increment_count(){number_seen++;}
    int get_count(){return number_seen;}
    bird_class(string text);
};

bird_class::bird_class(string text)
{
    name = text;
    number_seen = 0;
}

int main()
{
    bird_class orioles("oriole");

    orioles.increment_count();
```

```
    cout << "Number of " << orioles.name << "s seen: "
        << orioles.get_count() << endl;

    return 0;
}
```

Creating Data Access Methods

A crucial part of OOP is data hiding, as discussed in the In Depth section of this chapter. When you hide data inside an object, you can provide data access methods to allow code outside the object access to that data. In that way, you can control access to that data, making sure, for example, that values you consider illegal are not stored. You usually implement data access methods in pairs, as "get" and "set" methods, where the get method gets a data item's value, and the set method sets it.

Here's an example, birdclassdataaccess.cpp. In this case, I'll add the get and set methods, **get_number** and **set_number**, to allow access to the number of birds seen, **number_seen**, in **bird_class**:

```
#include <iostream>
#include <string>
using namespace std;

class bird_class
{
private:
    int number_seen;
public:
    string name;
    void increment_count(){number_seen++;}
    bird_class(string text);
    int bird_class::get_number();
    void bird_class::set_number(int new_number);
};

bird_class::bird_class(string text)
{
    name = text;
    number_seen = 0;
}
```

```
int bird_class::get_number()
{
    return number_seen;
}

void bird_class::set_number(int new_number)
{
    number_seen = new_number;
}

int main()
{
    bird_class orioles("oriole");

    orioles.increment_count();

    cout << "Number of " << orioles.name << "s seen: "
        << orioles.get_number() << endl;

    return 0;
}
```

Now code outside objects of **bird_class** can use **get_number** and **set_number** to access the object's internal data, which is stored in the private data member **number_seen**. Note also that you can have data access methods return an error if appropriate.

Creating Constructors

As discussed in the In Depth section of this chapter, you can use constructors to initialize the data in an object as that object is being created. A constructor is a special method with the same name as the class itself, and with no return value. You can overload constructors (see "Overloading Methods and Constructors" later in this chapter for more details). When you declare objects, you can pass values to the constructor to be used to initialize that object. Here's the example we saw in the In Depth section of this chapter, birdclassconstructor.cpp:

```
#include <iostream>
#include <string>
using namespace std;
```

```
class bird_class
{
public:
    string name;
    int number_seen;
    void increment_count(){number_seen++;}
    bird_class(string text);
};

bird_class::bird_class(string text)
{
    name = text;
    number_seen = 0;
}

int main()
{
    bird_class orioles("oriole");

    orioles.increment_count();

    cout << "Number of " << orioles.name << "s seen: "
        << orioles.number_seen << endl;

    return 0;
}
```

Here's something that not many C++ programmers know—you can also use a list of *initializers* when writing a constructor to assign values to data members. Each initializer has the form ***name(value)***, where ***name*** is the name of the data member you're initializing and ***value*** is the value you want to give it. You can place a comma-separated list of initializers after a colon and preceding the curly braces in a constructor definition. For example, this constructor is the same as the one we've just seen:

```
#include <iostream>
#include <string>
using namespace std;

class bird_class
{
public:
    string name;
    int number_seen;
    void increment_count(){number_seen++;}
```

```
    bird_class(string text);
};

bird_class::bird_class(string text) : name(text), number_seen(0){}

int main()
{
    bird_class orioles("oriole");

    orioles.increment_count();

    cout << "Number of " << orioles.name << "s seen: "
        << orioles.number_seen << endl;

    return 0;
}
```

There is a special shortcut you can use if a class has a one-argument constructor (which is not supported universally by all compilers):

```
#include <iostream>
#include <string>
using namespace std;

class bird_class
{
public:
    string name;
    int number_seen;
    void increment_count(){number_seen++;}
    bird_class(string text);
};

bird_class::bird_class(string text)
{
    name = text;
    number_seen = 0;
}

int main()
{
    bird_class orioles = "oriole";
        .
        .
        .
}
```

You can also use the **new** operator to return a pointer to a new object and pass arguments to the constructor like this:

```
bird_class *orioles = new bird_class("oriole");
```

NOTE: *If you don't provide a constructor, the compiler will provide a default one for you—see the next section for the details.*

The Default Constructor

If you don't provide a constructor for a class, the compiler will provide one for you—the *default constructor*. The default constructor takes no arguments, and it exists so that you can create objects of your new class. For example, we saw the default constructor at work in the program birdclass.cpp in the In Depth section of this chapter:

```
#include <iostream>
#include <string>
using namespace std;

class bird_class
{
public:
    string name;
    int number_seen;
    void increment_count(){number_seen++;}
};

int main()
{
    bird_class orioles;

    orioles.name = "oriole";
    orioles.number_seen = 0;

    orioles.increment_count();

    cout << "Number of " << orioles.name << "s seen: "
        << orioles.number_seen << endl;

    return 0;
}
```

If you do provide a normal constructor, the compiler will not create a default (no-argument) constructor for you, so if you still want one, you have to create one yourself. You can do that simply by creating a constructor with no arguments, as in this example, birdclassdefaultconstructor.cpp:

```
#include <iostream>
#include <string>
using namespace std;

class bird_class
{
public:
    string name;
    int number_seen;
    void increment_count(){number_seen++;}
    bird_class(string text);
    bird_class();
};

bird_class::bird_class(string text)
{
    name = text;
    number_seen = 0;
}

bird_class::bird_class()
{
    name = "Robin";
    number_seen = 0;
}

int main()
{
    bird_class orioles;

    orioles.name = "oriole";

    orioles.increment_count();

    cout << "Number of " << orioles.name << "s seen: "
        << orioles.number_seen << endl;

    return 0;
}
```

***NOTE:** You might not want a default constructor—for example, you might not want to let anyone create objects from your class unless they explicitly initialize them with data not available to you when you created the class, such as the person's email address.*

Creating Destructors

Besides constructors, C++ also supports *destructors*. A destructor does much the opposite of a constructor—while constructors initialize an object, destructors are run automatically (you never call them yourself) when an object is being destroyed (as when an object allocated in automatic storage is going out of scope). The code in the destructor allows you to clean up after the object, such as by deleting memory allocated with **new**. Destructors also differ from constructors two other ways—they have the same name as the class, but the name begins with a tilde (~), and you do not pass them any arguments (which makes sense because the program framework calls them, not you).

Here's an example, birdclassdestructor.cpp. In this case, I'm creating a destructor, **~bird_class**, that will delete memory allocated with **new** in the constructor:

```
#include <iostream>
#include <string>
using namespace std;

class bird_class
{
public:
    string *name;
    int number_seen;
    void increment_count(){number_seen++;}
    bird_class(string text);
    ~bird_class();
};

bird_class::bird_class(string text)
{
    name = new string(text);
    number_seen = 0;
}

bird_class::~bird_class()
{
    delete name;
```

```
}

int main()
{
    bird_class orioles("oriole");

    orioles.increment_count();

    cout << "Number of " << *(orioles.name) << "s seen: "
        << orioles.number_seen << endl;

    return 0;
}
```

And that's all there is to it. You can also see a destructor at work in the example in the next section.

A Stack Example

For some reason, nearly all the C++ books I've read have a stack example to illustrate how you use classes and objects, so here's ours, stack.cpp. This example is complete with constructor, destructor, hidden data, and **push** and **pop** methods. As is normal with stacks, you use **push** to place a value onto the stack, and **pop** to retrieve a value, much like working with plates in a stack in a cafeteria. This example pushes ten numbers on the stack and then pops them—notice that the values are popped in an order that's the reverse of the order in which they were pushed:

```
#include <iostream>
#include <string>
using namespace std;

class stack_class
{
    int max_values;
    int *data_buffer;
    int stack_top;     // When stack_top is -1, stack is empty
public:
    stack_class(int mem_required);
    ~stack_class(void);
    int pop(int & pop_to);
    int push(int push_this);
```

```
};

stack_class::stack_class(int mem_required)
{
    stack_top = -1;
    max_values = mem_required;
    data_buffer = new int[mem_required];  // Allocate memory
}

stack_class::~stack_class(void)
{
    cout << "Deallocating memory.\n";
    delete[] data_buffer;                   // Get rid of memory
}

int stack_class::pop(int & pop_to)
{
    if(stack_top == -1)      // Stack is empty -- return error
        return 0;
    else                     // Else return data
        pop_to = data_buffer[stack_top--];
        return 1;
}

int stack_class::push(int push_this)
{
    if(stack_top >= max_values)     // Stack is full -- return error
        return 0;
    else                            // Else store data
        data_buffer[++stack_top] = push_this;
        return 1;
}

int main()
{
    stack_class stack(200);
    int loop_index, popped_value;

    cout << "Pushing values now...\n";       // Push values first

    for(loop_index = 0; loop_index < 10; loop_index++){
        stack.push(loop_index);
        cout << "Pushed value--> " << loop_index << "\n";
    }
```

```
    cout << "Popping values now...\n";      // Now pop values

    while(stack.pop(popped_value)){
        cout << "Popped value--> " << popped_value << "\n";
    }

    return 0;
}
```

Note that **pop** pops its value by reference, so you can check the return value of this method for errors (it returns false if the stack is empty). Here's what this program displays when you run it:

```
Pushing values now...
Pushed value--> 0
Pushed value--> 1
Pushed value--> 2
Pushed value--> 3
Pushed value--> 4
Pushed value--> 5
Pushed value--> 6
Pushed value--> 7
Pushed value--> 8
Pushed value--> 9
Popping values now...
Popped value--> 9
Popped value--> 8
Popped value--> 7
Popped value--> 6
Popped value--> 5
Popped value--> 4
Popped value--> 3
Popped value--> 2
Popped value--> 1
Popped value--> 0
Deallocating memory.
```


Creating Inline Methods

As we saw in Chapter 7 (see "Creating Inline Functions"), an inline function's code is inserted inline in a compiled file, which means that program execution doesn't have to jump to a new location to execute that function. It turns out that if you place the definition (not just the declaration) of a function inside the class definition, that function is made inline by default:

```
#include <iostream>
#include <string>
using namespace std;

class bird_class
{
public:
    string name;
    int number_seen;
    void increment_count(){number_seen++;}
};

int main()
{
    bird_class orioles;

    orioles.name = "oriole";
    orioles.number_seen = 0;

    orioles.increment_count();

    cout << "Number of " << orioles.name << "s seen: "
        << orioles.number_seen << endl;

    return 0;
}
```

In fact, you can also define a method outside the class definition and make that method inline if you use the **inline** keyword:

```
#include <iostream>
#include <string>
using namespace std;

class bird_class
{
public:
    string name;
    int number_seen;
    void increment_count();
};
```

```
inline void bird_class::increment_count()
{
    number_seen++;
}

int main()
{
    bird_class orioles;

    orioles.name = "oriole";
    orioles.number_seen = 0;

    orioles.increment_count();

    cout << "Number of " << orioles.name << "s seen: "
        << orioles.number_seen << endl;

    return 0;
}
```


Related solution:	Found on page:
Creating Inline Functions	301

Passing and Returning Objects

By default, when you pass or return an object from a function or method, a copy of the object is passed. However, you'll often see functions or methods written like this, where I'm not only passing an object to the function or method, but I'm passing it by constant reference and returning it by reference:

```
class_type & function_name(const class_type & object)
{
     .
     .
     .
}
```

Why do programmers prefer this way of passing and returning objects? Because this way, the program doesn't have to make an entire copy of the object each time you pass it and return it. And if appropriate, you can pass constant references to objects to guarantee that you won't change the original object. (There are additional reasons that we'll see when discussing virtual functions in Chapter 10.)

***NOTE:** Of course, you should return a reference only to an object that will stay in scope when the function or method returns; you can return a reference to an object that was passed to you by reference, for example. If the object you want to return won't be in scope after the function or method returns, you should probably return the object itself, in which case a copy of the object will be returned.*

By the way, if you're passing or returning objects that contain pointers, see "Creating a Copy Constructor" in Chapter 9 for some important details.

Related solution:	Found on page:
Creating a Copy Constructor	415

Storing Class Definitions in Header Files

You can store class definitions in header files without worrying about compiler errors concerning multiple definitions, even if you include that header in multiple files in your program. Classes are handled this way in C++ because they're considered types, and you might need to use the same type in a number of files.

Here's a quick example in which I'm placing a class definition in a header file, birdclassheader, and using that header in another file. Here's what birdclassheader looks like:

```
class bird_class
{
public:
    string name;
    int number_seen;
    void increment_count(){number_seen++;}
    bird_class(string text);
};

bird_class::bird_class(string text)
{
    name = text;
    number_seen = 0;
}
```

Here's birdclassheaders.cpp, the file that makes use of birdclassheader:

```
#include <iostream>
#include <string>
using namespace std;
#include "birdclassheader"

int main()
{
    bird_class orioles("oriole");

    orioles.increment_count();

    cout << "Number of " << orioles.name << "s seen: "
        << orioles.number_seen << endl;

    return 0;
}
```

Note that I've placed birdclassheader in the same directory as birdclassheaders.cpp, so I include that header with the statement **#include "birdclassheader"**. If you were to store this header file in your C++ installation's directory for include files, you could of course include it as:

```
#include <birdclassheader>
```

(But it's best to reserve this syntax for system header files). Here is what this program displays when running:

```
%birdclassheaders
Number of orioles seen: 1
```


Constant Methods

What if you declare an object with **const**—making it a constant object—and then try to invoke an object method? The C++ compiler will generate an error unless you also declare the method itself with **const**. We've solved this kind of problem before by declaring arguments to functions as constant references or constant pointers, but the syntax here is different. What if your method accepts no arguments, for example? How do you still declare the whole method as constant, assuring the compiler that the method won't change the object?

You do this by placing the keyword **const** *after* the argument list of the method, like this in the example birdclassconstmethod.cpp:

```
#include <iostream>
#include <string>
using namespace std;

class bird_class
{
private:
    int number_seen;
public:
    string name;
    void increment_count(){number_seen++;}
    bird_class(string text);
    int bird_class::get_number() const;
};

bird_class::bird_class(string text)
{
    name = text;
    number_seen = 1;
}

int bird_class::get_number() const
{
    return number_seen;
}

int main()
{
    const bird_class orioles("oriole");

    cout << "Number of " << orioles.name << "s seen: "
        << orioles.get_number() << endl;

    return 0;
}
```

Here's what this example, birdclassconstmethod.cpp, looks like when running:

```
%birdclassconstmethod
Number of orioles seen: 1
```

Using the **this** Pointer

Say you have two objects of the **bird_class** that we've been using in this chapter, and you want to compare them. You might, for example, want to determine which bird you've seen more of—orioles or robins. To be able to compare objects like this, you might want to add a new method to **bird_class** named **compare**. If you had two objects of this class, **orioles** and **robins**, you might invoke **compare** like this: **orioles.compare(robins)**, and this method would return the object (either **orioles** or **robins**) with the larger number of birds.

Implementing this example, birdclasscompare.cpp, will demonstrate the use of the **this** pointer, which is built into every object and which points to the current object. In this case, I'll pass a constant object to **compare** by reference, and return a reference to the object with the most number of birds. Here's what the prototype of **compare** looks like:

```
const bird_class & compare(const bird_class & other_bird);
```

Because **compare** is invoked like this: **orioles.compare(robins)**, we'll be working with two objects in this method—the current object (**orioles** here) and the passed object (**robins** here). To compare these two objects, we need only compare the **number_seen** data member of each object, like this:

```
const bird_class & bird_class::compare(const bird_class & other_bird)
{
    if(number_seen > other_bird.number_seen)
        .
        .
        .
}
```

If **number_seen** is greater in the current object, we want to return the current object from **compare**—but how do we do that? The current object doesn't even know its own name, so how can we return it from **compare**? That is, we can't say **return orioles;**. It turns out that every object has a built-in pointer named **this** that points to the current object. To return the current object, then, we only need to return ***this** (if we had wanted to return a pointer to the current object, we could have returned **this** itself):

```
const bird_class & bird_class::compare(const bird_class & other_bird)
{
    if(number_seen > other_bird.number_seen)
        return *this;
```

```
        .
        .
        .
}
```

If, on the other hand, the object we were passed has more birds, we should return that object, which we can do by name:

```
const bird_class & bird_class::compare(const bird_class & other_bird)
{
    if(number_seen > other_bird.number_seen)
        return *this;
    else
        return other_bird;
}
```

Here's what the whole program, birdclasscompare.cpp, looks like—note that to display the name of the object with more birds, I need only to use the **name** data member of the object returned from **compare**:

```
#include <iostream>
#include <string>
using namespace std;

class bird_class
{
public:
    string name;
    int number_seen;
    void increment_count(){number_seen++;}
    bird_class(string text);
    const bird_class & compare(const bird_class & other_bird);
};

bird_class::bird_class(string text)
{
    name = text;
    number_seen = 0;
}

const bird_class & bird_class::compare(const bird_class & other_bird)
{
    if(number_seen > other_bird.number_seen)
        return *this;
    else
```

```
        return other_bird;
}

int main()
{
    bird_class orioles("oriole");
    bird_class robins("robin");

    orioles.increment_count();

    cout << "Type of most birds seen: "
        << orioles.compare(robins).name << endl;

    return 0;
}
```

Here's what you see when you run this program:

```
%birdclasscompare
Type of most birds seen: oriole
```

Arrays of Objects

Arrays of objects work more or less as you'd expect them to. For example, you can declare an array of objects like this: **bird_class birds[3];**, and you can invoke methods of each individual object in the array like this: **birds[2].increment _count();**. However, there are one or two subtleties here—for example, what if you want to use a constructor to initialize each object separately?

Here's an example, birdclassarray.cpp, showing how this works. To initialize each object in an array of objects, you can call the associated class's constructor for each object in an initialization list, like this:

```
#include <iostream>
#include <string>
using namespace std;

class bird_class
{
public:
    string name;
    int number_seen;
```

```
    void increment_count(){number_seen++;}
    bird_class(string text);
};

bird_class::bird_class(string text)
{
    name = text;
    number_seen = 0;
}

int main()
{
    bird_class birds[3] = {bird_class("oriole"),
                           bird_class("robin"),
                           bird_class("blue jay")};

    birds[2].increment_count();

    cout << "Number of " << birds[2].name << "s seen: "
        << birds[2].number_seen << endl;

    return 0;
}
```

This is an extension of the normal technique you use to initialize an array.

NOTE: *If you initialize only the first few objects in an array with an initialization statement like the one I've used here, all the objects following use their class's default constructor.*

Related solution:	Found on page:
Initializing Arrays	128

Overloading Methods and Constructors

Just as with functions, you can overload methods and constructors. When you overload a method or constructor, you redefine the method or constructor using a different argument list, or signature (see "Overloading a Function" in Chapter 7). The compiler decides which overloaded version of the method or constructor to use based on the type and number of arguments you pass and whether or not it can find a form of the method or constructor with the same signature.

Here's an example, birdclassoverload.cpp, which overloads the **increment_count** method. Normally, you don't pass this method any arguments, because it simply increments the number seen of a certain bird by 1. However, I'll add a new form of this method so you can pass it an integer and increment the count by a number greater than 1 if you wish. Here's what the code, birdclassoverload.cpp, looks like:

```
#include <iostream>
#include <string>
using namespace std;

class bird_class
{
public:
    string name;
    int number_seen;
    void increment_count(){number_seen++;}
    void increment_count(int n){number_seen += n;}
    bird_class(string text);
};

bird_class::bird_class(string text)
{
    name = text;
    number_seen = 0;
}

int main()
{
    bird_class orioles("oriole");

    orioles.increment_count(10);

    cout << "Number of " << orioles.name << "s seen: "
        << orioles.number_seen << endl;

    return 0;
}
```

Here's what birdclassoverload.cpp displays when you run it:

```
%birdclassoverload
Number of orioles seen: 10
```

You can also overload constructors, as we've seen when we added a default constructor to **bird_class** in birdclassdefaultconstructor.cpp:

```
#include <iostream>
#include <string>
using namespace std;

class bird_class
{
public:
    string name;
    int number_seen;
    void increment_count(){number_seen++;}
    bird_class(string text);
    bird_class();
};

bird_class::bird_class(string text)
{
    name = text;
    number_seen = 0;
}

bird_class::bird_class()
{
    name = "Robin";
    number_seen = 0;
}

int main()
{
    bird_class orioles;

    orioles.name = "oriole";

    orioles.increment_count();

    cout << "Number of " << orioles.name << "s seen: "
        << orioles.number_seen << endl;

    return 0;
}
```

Related solution:	Found on page:
Overloading a Function	311

Creating Static Data Members

As we saw in Chapter 7, there are two ways to use the keyword **static** with variables in C++—when you use **static** with external variables, it makes their linkage internal, but when you use **static** with automatic variables, it changes their storage class to **static**. So it might not surprise you that there are two ways to use **static** with classes and objects (actually, all these ways of using **static** are related, although it might not seem so at first glance). When you use **static** with *data members* in a class, all objects of that class share the same memory location, as we'll see in this section. When you declare a *method* **static**, on the other hand, it becomes a class (not object) method, which means you can invoke it simply with the class name, as we'll see in the next section.

When you declare a data member *static*, it acts much like a union (see "Creating Unions" in Chapter 3). The C++ compiler allocates only one memory location for that data member, no matter how many objects you instantiate, and all the objects share the same location for that data member. This is very useful if you want all the objects of a certain class to share some specific data and can provide a way of communicating between those objects.

Here's an example, birdclassstaticdata.cpp. I'll use the class **bird_class** that we've been using throughout this chapter and make the data member that stores the number of birds seen, **number_seen**, static—which means that all objects of this class will share the same value in **number_seen**. In this way, I'll be able to keep track of the total number of birds seen by all objects, no matter how many such objects there are:

```
#include <iostream>
#include <string>
using namespace std;

class bird_class
{
public:
    static int number_seen;
    string name;
    void increment_count(){number_seen++;}
    bird_class(string text);
};
        .
        .
        .
```

You need to initialize static variables outside the class definition, and if you don't, your compiler will complain that there has been no memory allocated for that variable. Here's how I initialize **number_seen** outside the class definition—note that I use the scope resolution operator, ::, like this:

```
#include <iostream>
#include <string>
using namespace std;

class bird_class
{
public:
    static int number_seen;
    string name;
    void increment_count(){number_seen++;}
    bird_class(string text);
};

int bird_class::number_seen = 0;
    .
    .
    .
```

Now I can create two objects of **bird_class**, increment the number of each bird seen, and then display **number_seen**, which will hold 2. Here's the code, birdclassstaticdata.cpp:

```
#include <iostream>
#include <string>
using namespace std;

class bird_class
{
public:
    static int number_seen;
    string name;
    void increment_count(){number_seen++;}
    bird_class(string text);
};

int bird_class::number_seen = 0;

bird_class::bird_class(string text)
{
```

```
    name = text;
    number_seen = 0;
}

int main()
{
    bird_class orioles("oriole");
    bird_class robins("robin");

    orioles.increment_count();
    robins.increment_count();

    cout << "Number of birds seen: " << bird_class::number_seen << endl;

    return 0;
}
```

Here's what this example, birdclassstaticdata.cpp, displays when you run it:

```
%birdclassstaticdata
Number of birds seen: 2
```

There are two other advantages of static data members—you can declare them to be of the same class of which they are members (which you can't with other data members), and they can be used as a default argument to a method of the class that they're part of.

TIP: *If you declare items as* ***static const****, you can initialize those items to constant values inside a class definition like this:* ***static const int zero = 0;****. There's no other type of data item you can initialize inside a class definition (except an enumeration like this:* ***enum {constant1 = 1, constant2 = 2};****), which is why you need constructors.*

Related solutions:	Found on page:
Creating Unions	151
Creating Local Static (Persistent) Variables	319

Static Methods

When you declare a method **static**, it becomes a class (not object) method, which means you can invoke it simply with the class name, even if you don't have an object of that class. This is useful if you have a class full of utility methods and you don't want to create an object of that class before using those methods.

Here's an example; in this case, I'll add a method named **info** to the **bird_class** that we've been using throughout this chapter. This method will be a class method, not one you use on objects; in particular, I'll use **info** to return information about **bird_class** itself:

```
#include <iostream>
#include <string>
using namespace std;

class bird_class
{
public:
    int number_seen;
    string name;
    void increment_count(){number_seen++;}
    bird_class(string text);
    static string info() {return string("This is the bird_class");}
};
    .
    .
    .
```

Now I can invoke the new static **info** method using just the class name and the scope resolution operator, ::, like this—no object needed:

```
#include <iostream>
#include <string>
using namespace std;

class bird_class
{
public:
    int number_seen;
    string name;
    void increment_count(){number_seen++;}
    bird_class(string text);
    static string info() {return string("This is the bird_class");}
};

bird_class::bird_class(string text)
{
    name = text;
    number_seen = 0;
}
```

```
int main()
{
    cout << bird_class::info() << endl;

    return 0;
}
```

Here's what you see when you run this program, birdclassstaticmethods.cpp:

```
%birdclassstaticmethods
This is the bird_class
```

NOTE: *Because static methods are not part of any object in memory, they can access only static data members of the class.*

Pointers to Objects and to Object Members

There are two C++ operators that are designed to assist work with pointers to the members of an object, and they are .* and ->*. The C++ standard calls these the pointer-to-member operators. Here's an example, birdclasspointers.cpp, that introduces these operators. This topic is all about dealing with pointers to the members of an object, so in this case, I'll use a pointer to the **bird_class** class's **increment_count** method.

I start by declaring an object of **bird_class**, which we've used throughout this chapter, and naming that object **orioles**. Then I use the **new** operator to get a pointer to a new object of the same class and name that pointer **robins_pointer**:

```
#include <iostream>
#include <string>
using namespace std;

class bird_class
{
public:
    string name;
    int number_seen;
    void increment_count(){number_seen++;}
    bird_class(string text);
};

bird_class::bird_class(string text)
```

```
{
    name = text;
    number_seen = 0;
}

int main()
{
    bird_class orioles("oriole");
    bird_class *robins_pointer = new bird_class("robin");
    .
    .
    .
```

Next in **main**, I'll get a pointer that points to the **bird_class** class's **increment_count** method. Usually, you can create a pointer to a function like this (see "Using Pointers to Functions" in Chapter 6):

```
type (*pointer_to_function)(argument1, argument2...);
```

When you work with a method, however, you need to indicate which class the method belongs to, so you use this syntax:

```
int main()
{
    bird_class orioles("oriole");
    bird_class *robins_pointer = new bird_class("robin");

    void (bird_class::*pointer)(void);
    .
    .
    .
```

Now that I've declared **pointer** as a pointer to the **bird_class** class's **increment_count** method, I can initialize that pointer like this:

```
int main()
{
    bird_class orioles("oriole");
    bird_class *robins_pointer = new bird_class("robin");

    void (bird_class::*pointer)(void);
    pointer = &bird_class::increment_count;
    .
    .
    .
```

To invoke the **increment_count** function using **pointer**, I can use the .* operator with the **orioles** object, using the expression **orioles.*pointer**. This operator, .*, treats **pointer** as a pointer to a member of **orioles** and dereferences that pointer (note that you have to use an expression like **orioles.*pointer** here, not **orioles.(*pointer)**):

```
int main()
{
    bird_class orioles("oriole");
    bird_class *robins_pointer = new bird_class("robin");

    void (bird_class::*pointer)(void);
    pointer = &bird_class::increment_count;

    (orioles.*pointer)();
    .
    .
    .
```

If you don't have an object, but rather a pointer to an object, you use the ->* operator to point to a member of that object. Here's how I use ->* with the pointer **robins_pointer**:

```
int main()
{
    bird_class orioles("oriole");
    bird_class *robins_pointer = new bird_class("robin");

    void (bird_class::*pointer)(void);
    pointer = &bird_class::increment_count;

    (orioles.*pointer)();
    (robins_pointer->*pointer)();

    cout << "Number of " << orioles.name << "s seen: "
        << orioles.number_seen << endl;
    cout << "Number of " << robins_pointer->name << "s seen: "
        << robins_pointer->number_seen << endl;

    return 0;
}
```

At the end of this code, I display the incremented number of birds. Here's what this program, birdclasspointers.cpp, displays when you run it:

```
%birdclasspointers
Number of orioles seen: 1
Number of robins seen: 1
```


Related solution:	Found on page:
Using Pointers to Functions	280

Chapter 9

Friend Functions, Operator Overloading, and Copy Constructors

If you need an immediate solution to:	*See page:*

In Depth

We got our start with object-oriented programming (OOP) in the previous chapter, but of course there's no way to cram all of C++ OOP into one chapter. In this chapter, we're going to flesh out our understanding of object-oriented programming with some essential topics: friend functions, copy constructors, how to overload operators, friend classes, friend methods, conversions between classes and other types, nesting classes, and more.

We'll need a simple class to demonstrate the new techniques in this chapter, so here's the **product** class, which you can use to track inventory in a grocery store. This class lets you create objects that store the number and name of a certain product, like oranges, in an internal data member named **number**, and you can access that data member with the access methods **get_number** and **set_number**. In addition, there's a public data member called **name** that holds the name of the product (I'm making this data member public to make things simpler, but in a class you release for public consumption, you should make the data member **name** private and use data access methods to handle it). There's also a constructor that you can pass the name of the product (like "oranges") and the number of the product in stock (such as 200). Here's what this class looks like in productclass.cpp—in this case, I'm simply creating an object of this class, and storing and then displaying the data in that object:

```
#include <iostream>
#include <string>
using namespace std;

class product
{
    int number;
public:
    string name;
    int get_number(){return number;}
    void set_number(int n){number = n;}
    product(string text, int count);
};

product::product(string text, int count)
```

```
{
    name = text;
    number = count;
}

int main()
{
    product oranges("oranges", 200);

    cout << "Number of " << oranges.name << ": "
        << oranges.get_number() << endl;

    return 0;
}
```

As you can see, this is a very simple class, and it'll be easy to augment it throughout this chapter, because there's no better way to understand programming concepts than by seeing them at work. Here's what you see if you run productclass.cpp:

```
%productclass
Number of oranges: 200
```

Friend Functions

The first topic we'll take a look at in this chapter is how to use *friend functions*. If you declare a function a friend of a class, that function has access to the public, protected, and private members of that class. This is useful in many circumstances, such as when you have many classes and don't want to have to define the same utility method for each class—instead, you can create a function and make it a friend of all the classes. You might think that friend functions oppose the fundamental OOP concept of data hiding, but in fact, all you're doing is extending the class when you add a friend to it.

Here's a short example, productclassfriend.cpp, that shows how this works. In this case, I'll declare a function named **display**, which displays the data inside an object, a friend of the **product** class by declaring it in the **product** class definition and by using the keyword **friend** in front of that declaration. That means **display** has access to all the internal data in objects of the **product** class, so when I pass a **product** object to that function, it can display the product's name and number without using any data access methods:

```
#include <iostream>
#include <string>
using namespace std;
```

```
class product
{
    int number;
public:
    string name;
    int get_number(){return number;}
    void set_number(int n){number = n;}
    product(string text, int count);
    friend void display(product p);
};

product::product(string text, int count)
{
    name = text;
    number = count;
}

void display(product p)
{
    cout << "Number of " << p.name << ": " << p.number << endl;
}

main()
{
    product oranges("oranges", 200);

    display(oranges);

    return 0;
}
```

Here's what this code, productclassfriend.cpp, looks like when you run it:

```
%productclassfriend
Number of oranges: 200
```

You should be careful of friend functions, because they can provide significant "leaks" in data hiding; however, there are times when you need them and they are very useful. See "Conversions, Friends, and Operator Overloading" later in this chapter for an example. Besides friend functions, we'll also take a look at friend classes and friend methods in this chapter—see "Creating Friend Classes" and "Creating Friend Methods."

Overloading Operators

One of the nicest features of C++ OOP is that you can overload operators to handle objects of your classes (you can't do this in some other OOP-centric languages, like Java). There are some restrictions, though—overloaded operators must be used with at least one operand that is of the overloaded type, you can't create entirely new operators, change an operator from unary to binary or the other way around, and you cannot overload the **sizeof**, ., ::, .*, ?:, **typeid**, **const_cast**, **dynamic_cast**, **reinterpret_cast**, or **static_cast** operators. You can, however, overload all the other operators, including operators like **new** and **delete**, and += and *=.

For example, what if you want a handy way to increment the number of oranges stored in a **product** class object named **oranges**? Being able to use an expression like **oranges++** would be great, but you have to tell C++ what such an expression means and how to implement it.

Here's an example, productclassincrement.cpp, that does that. To overload the ++ operator to handle objects of a specific class, you must define a new method in that class: **operator++**, which takes no arguments and returns the incremented object. Because this method is a method of an object, it has access to the object's internal data, which means that I can implement **operator++** like this:

```
#include <iostream>
#include <string>
using namespace std;

class product
{
    int number;
public:
    string name;
    int get_number(){return number;}
    void set_number(int n){number = n;}
    product(string text, int count);
    product operator++(void);
};

product::product(string text, int count)
{
    name = text;
    number = count;
}
```

```
product product::operator++(void)
{
    number++;
    return *this;
}

int main()
{
    product oranges("oranges", 200);

    ++oranges;

    cout << "Number of " << oranges.name << ": "
        << oranges.get_number() << endl;

    return 0;
}
```

This works fine—except for one thing: It turns out that the **operator++(void)** method overloads ++ only as a prefix operator (as in **++oranges**), not as a postfix operator (as in **oranges++**). How do you overload ++ as a postfix operator? You must define a new method, **operator++(int)**, in addition to **operator++(void)**. The **int** argument is a complete dummy and serves only to let the compiler distinguish between ++ as a prefix or postfix operator. This points out an annoying facet of operator overloading in C++—it's not systematic. Many operators have their own peculiar way that you must use to overload them, and for that reason, we'll take a look at how to overload a number of operators in this chapter, such as +, ++, <<, >>, [] (the array index operator), **new**, **delete**, and so on. The process used to overload each of these operators is different. Here, then, is how I also overload ++ as a postfix operator for objects of the **product** class:

```
#include <iostream>
#include <string>
using namespace std;

class product
{
    int number;
public:
    string name;
    int get_number(){return number;}
    void set_number(int n){number = n;}
    product(string text, int count);
    product operator++(void);
```

```
    product operator++(int);
};

product::product(string text, int count)
{
    name = text;
    number = count;
}

product product::operator++(void)
{
    number++;
    return *this;
}

product product::operator++(int)
{
    number++;
    return *this;
}

int main()
{
    product oranges("oranges", 200);

    oranges++;

    cout << "Number of " << oranges.name << ": "
        << oranges.get_number() << endl;

    return 0;
}
```

Here's what this example, productclassincrement.cpp, looks like when you run it:

```
%productclassincrement
Number of oranges: 201
```

TIP: *When you overload operators like **new** and **delete**, how do you get access to the original, non-overloaded versions of **new** and **delete**? You can refer to them as **::new** and **::delete**.*

Conversions to and from Objects

Operator overloading lets you instruct the compiler how to handle your objects with operators, and there's even more customization you can do: You can also instruct the compiler how to perform conversions on your objects. For example, what if you have a **product** class object named **oranges** that is storing the name "oranges" and the number of oranges on hand, 200, and someone assigns **oranges** to an integer variable? Or what if someone assigns a string to the **oranges** object? What should the compiler do?

In C++, you can instruct the compiler exactly what to do. Here's an example, productclassconversion.cpp; in this case, I'll do just as discussed in the previous paragraph—create a **product** class object named **oranges**, assign a string to **oranges**, then assign an integer to **oranges**. So how do you let the compiler know what to do if you assign a **string** to **oranges**? You can do that by creating a constructor for the **product** class that takes only a **string** argument. Here's what that looks like in productclassconversion.cpp—note that I'm assigning a **string** to the **oranges** object in **main**, and the new constructor will use that **string** as the product name to be stored in the object:

```
#include <iostream>
#include <string>
using namespace std;

class product
{
    int number;
public:
    string name;
    int get_number(){return number;}
    void set_number(int n){number = n;}
    product();
    product(string text);
};

product::product()
{
    name = "";
    number = 0;
}

product::product(string text)
{
    name = text;
```

```
    number = 0;
}

int main()
{
    product oranges;
    string product_name("oranges");

    oranges = product_name;

    oranges.set_number(200);
    .
    .
    .
}
```

***TIP:** What if you don't want the compiler to use a constructor implicitly like this to convert other data types to objects of your class? You can preface the compiler's declaration with the keyword **explicit**, which means it'll be used only for explicit conversions. See "Conversions to and from Objects" in the Immediate Solutions section.*

Now we've instructed the compiler how to convert a string into a **product** object. But what if we want to go the other way and assign, say, a **product** object to an integer? To tell the compiler how to convert your objects to other data types, you must add a new operator method named **operator *type***, where ***type*** is the name of the type you want to allow the compiler to convert your objects to. For example, if I were to assign **oranges** to an integer, I'd want the integer to be assigned the number of oranges stored. I can do that by declaring a new method named **operator int** and having that function return the number as stored in the **product** class object. Here's what it looks like in code:

```
#include <iostream>
#include <string>
using namespace std;

class product
{
    int number;
public:
    string name;
    int get_number(){return number;}
    void set_number(int n){number = n;}
    product();
    product(string text);
```

```
    operator int() const;
};

product::product()
{
    name = "";
    number = 0;
}

product::product(string text)
{
    name = text;
    number = 0;
}

product::operator int() const
{
    return number;
}

int main()
{
    product oranges;
    string product_name("oranges");

    oranges = product_name;

    oranges.set_number(200);

    int number_of_oranges = oranges;

    cout << "Number of " << oranges.name << ": " << number_of_oranges
        << endl;

    return 0;
}
```

Here's what this code, productclassconversion.cpp, looks like at work—note that we have set both the name and number of the product using conversions we've defined ourselves:

```
%productclassconversion
Number of oranges: 200
```

Copy Constructors

There's another important topic in this chapter—copy constructors. Copy constructors become important when you have objects that store pointers as data members. (As you already know, pointers often introduce complications that you have to think twice about in C++, and that may well be why they've been omitted from languages like Java and Microsoft's C#—the C# promotional material even goes so far as to call pointers "the root of all evil.")

Say, for example, that you have an object with data members that are pointers and return that object from a method. Even though the original object goes out of scope when you return from the method, you might think you're safe, because what's really being returned is a copy of the object. But what about the pointers in the copy of the object? If those pointers point to items inside the old object, or to items in automatic storage that were allocated in the method, those items are also out of scope. That means the returned object will be left pointing to items that are no longer in scope and that might be written over at any time.

In fact, this kind of problem can arise any time you make a copy of an object than has pointers as data members—even if the items the pointers point to don't go out of scope, there can still be a problem, because the new object's pointers still point to the old object's data. And that can be disastrous if the pointers in the new object should be pointing to data connected with the new object, not the old one.

If you want to create a new object and initialize it from an existing object, it's often the case that you must make sure the pointers in the new object point to items associated with the new object, not the old one. Copying over an old object's pointers by mistake can occur in many hidden ways, such as when the program passes or returns a copy of the object to a function or method, when it creates a temporary copy of the object (as some compilers do when assigning objects an intermediate value while performing operations on multiple objects), or when you explicitly create and initialize an object using another object of the same class.

By default, when the program needs to create a copy of an object, it uses the object's *default copy constructor*, which just copies over each member in the old object into the new one. But that's a problem when you have pointers in the old object that must be changed to create a new object, so you can create your own copy constructor (resetting needed pointers and other data that shouldn't just be copied over is called making a *deep copy*). Here's an example, productclasscopyconstructor.cpp, that shows how this works. In this case, I'll change the **product** class so that we save the product's name as a pointer (called **name**) to a **char** array that is created and initialized in the class's constructor:

```
#include <iostream>
#include <cstring>
using namespace std;

class product
{
    int number;
public:
    char *name;
    int get_number(){return number;}
    void set_number(int n){number = n;}
    product(char *text, int count);
};

product::product(char *text, int count)
{
    name = new char[40];
    strcpy(name, text);
    number = count;
}
    .
    .
    .
```

Now when we make copies of objects of this class, we want to make sure we change the **name** pointer to point to a **char** array in the new object, and not just make a copy of the old pointer, which points to the **char** array in the old object. I'll do that with a copy constructor. You create a copy constructor for a class by defining a constructor that takes a constant reference to an object of the same class. In the copy constructor, I'll explicitly create a new **char** array for **name** to point at and use **strcpy** (see "Copying C-Style Strings" in Chapter 3 for more details on **strcpy**) to copy over the product's name from the original object. Now I'm free to create a **product** class object named **oranges** and use that object to initialize a new object, **also_oranges**:

```
#include <iostream>
#include <cstring>
using namespace std;
```

```
class product
{
    int number;
public:
    char *name;
    int get_number(){return number;}
    void set_number(int n){number = n;}
    product(char *text, int count);
    product(const product &other_product);
};

product::product(char *text, int count)
{
    name = new char[40];
    strcpy(name, text);
    number = count;
}

product::product(const product &other_product)
{
    name = new char[40];
    strcpy(name, other_product.name);
    number = other_product.number;
}

int main()
{
    product oranges("oranges", 200), also_oranges(oranges);

    cout << "Number of " << also_oranges.name << ": "
        << also_oranges.get_number() << endl;

    return 0;
}
```

Here's what you see when you run productclasscopyconstructor.cpp—note that **also_oranges** has indeed been initialized from **oranges**:

```
%productclasscopyconstructor
Number of oranges: 200
```

TIP:** If you wish, you can also modify the code above to confirm that both **oranges.name** and **also_oranges.name** point to different locations in memory, but if you do, don't forget to cast those pointers to type **void first, or **cout** will simply display the text pointed to by these pointers (because their type is **char***).*

And that's all the overview we need for this chapter—it's time to get to the Immediate Solutions.

***TIP:** In general, when you create a class that allocates memory using **new** and therefore stores pointer to that new memory, you should give that class a copy constructor, a destructor to deallocate the allocated memory, and an explicit assignment operator method. All these topics are covered in this chapter.*

Immediate Solutions

Creating Friend Functions

When you declare a function a friend of a class, that function has access to the internal data members of that object (that is, all its public, protected, and private data members).

Here's an example, productclassfriend.cpp, that we saw in the In Depth section of this chapter, which shows this works. In this case, I'll declare a function named **display** a friend of the **product** class. That means **display** has access to all the internal data in objects of the **product** class, so I'm able to access even the private **number** member in **product** objects passed to **display**, as you see here:

```
#include <iostream>
#include <string>
using namespace std;

class product
{
    int number;
public:
    string name;
    int get_number(){return number;}
    void set_number(int n){number = n;}
    product(string text, int count);
    friend void display(product p);
};

product::product(string text, int count)
{
    name = text;
    number = count;
}

void display(product p)
{
    cout << "Number of " << p.name << ": " << p.number << endl;
}
```

```
main()
{
    product oranges("oranges", 200);

    display(oranges);

    return 0;
}
```

Here's what this code, productclassfriend.cpp, looks like when you run it:

```
%productclassfriend
Number of oranges: 200
```

For more friend functions, see "Conversions, Friends, and Operator Overloading" later in this chapter.

Overloading Unary Operators Like ++ and --

As discussed in the In Depth section of this chapter, you overload operators by creating new operator methods, and you can use methods of a class or non-member functions to do so. (Note, however, that you can't overload =, ( ), [], or -> with a non-member function.) We'll take a look at overloading operators with methods in this and the next few sections, and then with non-member functions in "Conversions, Friends, and Operator Overloading" later in this chapter.

This section is about overloading unary operators, like ++ and --, which take one operand. To overload a unary operator, you can create a class method like this, where ***op*** is the symbol for the operator itself—note also that this method must return an object of the class you're overloading the operator for:

```
type operatorop()
{
    .
    .
    .
}
```

In this case, ***type*** is the return type of the operator, which can be an object or a simple data type. Here's how to overload the ++ operator for the **product** class, as we saw in the program productclassincrement.cpp in the In Depth section of this chapter. You start by creating a new method, **operator++(void)**; in that method, I just need to increment the internal count stored in the object and return the object:

```
#include <iostream>
#include <string>
using namespace std;

class product
{
    int number;
public:
    string name;
    int get_number(){return number;}
    void set_number(int n){number = n;}
    product(string text, int count);
    product operator++(void);
};

product::product(string text, int count)
{
    name = text;
    number = count;
}

product product::operator++(void)
{
    number++;
    return *this;
}

int main()
{
    product oranges("oranges", 200);

    ++oranges;

    cout << "Number of " << oranges.name << ": "
        << oranges.get_number() << endl;

    return 0;
}
```

As discussed in the In Depth section of this chapter, this code overloads ++ only when it's used as a prefix operator, like this: **++oranges**. To overload ++ as a postfix so I can use it in expressions like **oranges++**, I also have to overload **operator++(int)**, where the **int** argument is a dummy:

```
#include <iostream>
#include <string>
using namespace std;

class product
{
    int number;
public:
    string name;
    int get_number(){return number;}
    void set_number(int n){number = n;}
    product(string text, int count);
    product operator++(void);
    product operator++(int);
};

product::product(string text, int count)
{
    name = text;
    number = count;
}

product product::operator++(void)
{
    number++;
    return *this;
}

product product::operator++(int)
{
    number++;
    return *this;
}

int main()
{
    product oranges("oranges", 200);

    oranges++;
```

```
    cout << "Number of " << oranges.name << ": "
        << oranges.get_number() << endl;

    return 0;
}
```

Here's what this example, productclassincrement.cpp, looks like when you run it:

```
%productclassincrement
Number of oranges: 201
```

Overloading Binary Operators Like + and -

In the previous section, we took a look at overloading unary operators. Overloading binary operators, which take two operands, works differently. For example, what if we overload the + operator using a method named **operator+** for the **product** class and add two **product** objects, **apples** and **oranges** like this: **apples** + **oranges**? In this case, the **operator+** method of the **apples** object will be called, and the **oranges** object is passed to that method. In general, this is what an operator method looks like to overload a binary operator, ***op***:

```
type operatorop(class_name second_operand)
{
    .
    .
    .
}
```

In this case, ***type*** is the return type of the operator, which could be an object or a simple data type. You'll often see operator overloading methods written to pass and return values by reference, like this: ***type* & operator*op*(*class_name* & *second_operand*)**. The compiler will also match this method to the ***op*** operator. You can also use the **const** keyword to indicate that you don't intend changing the passed object, like this: ***type* & operator*op*(const *class_name* & *second_operand*)**. And, of course, if the item you're passing to the method has itself been declared with **const**, you have to declare that argument in the argument list using **const**. In fact, programmers often pass objects to functions and methods using constant references as a matter of efficiency, because that way you don't have to make a copy of the object (see "Passing and Returning Objects" in Chapter 8). I'll use these techniques in this chapter when appropriate (for example, I won't return a reference to an object when I'm returning an object in automatic storage, because in that case, I really want to return a copy of the object). There are other reasons to use these techniques as well when working with inheritance, as we'll see in the next chapter.

Let's take a look at an example, productclassaddition.cpp, that adds two **product** objects, **apples** and **oranges**. To overload the + operator for the **product** class, I create a new method **operator+**, that takes one argument: an object of the **product** class. In the expression **apples + oranges**, the object passed to **operator+** will be **oranges**. The **operator+** method must return an object that represents the sum of its operands, so in this case, I'll concatenate the names of the added products and sum their numbers. To do that, I'll create a new object and return that object from **operator+**:

```
#include <iostream>
#include <string>
using namespace std;

class product
{
    int number;
public:
    string name;
    int get_number(){return number;}
    void set_number(int n){number = n;}
    product(string text, int count);
    product operator+(const product & second_product);
};

product::product(string text, int count)
{
    name = text;
    number = count;
}

product product::operator+(const product & second_product)
{
    product temp("", 0);
    temp.name = name + " and " + second_product.name;
    temp.set_number(number + second_product.number);
    return temp;
}
```

```
int main()
{
    product oranges("oranges", 200);
    product apples("apples", 300);

    product apples_and_oranges = apples + oranges;

    cout << "Number of " << apples_and_oranges.name << ": "
        << apples_and_oranges.get_number() << endl;

    return 0;
}
```

Here's the result of this program, productclassaddition.cpp, so far:

```
%productclassaddition
Number of apples and oranges: 500
```

What about adding other types to objects of the **product** class? For example, what if you want to add an integer to **oranges** like this: **oranges + 5**? You can overload the + operator to add integers to **product** class objects like this, where I'll add the integer to the number stored internally in the **product** object:

```
#include <iostream>
#include <string>
using namespace std;

class product
{
    int number;
public:
    string name;
    int get_number(){return number;}
    void set_number(int n){number = n;}
    product(string text, int count);
    product operator+(const product & second_product);
    product operator+(int n);
};

product::product(string text, int count)
{
    name = text;
    number = count;
}
```

```
product product::operator+(const product & second_product)
{
    product temp("", 0);
    temp.name = name + " and " + second_product.name;
    temp.set_number(number + second_product.number);
    return temp;
}

product product::operator+(int n)
{
    product temp("", 0);
    temp.name = name;
    temp.set_number(number + n);
    return temp;
}

int main()
{
    product oranges("oranges", 200);
    product apples("apples", 300);

    product apples_and_oranges = apples + oranges;

    cout << "Number of " << apples_and_oranges.name << ": "
        << apples_and_oranges.get_number() << endl;

    apples = apples + 5;

    cout << "Number of " << apples.name << ": "
        << apples.get_number() << endl;

    return 0;
}
```

Here's what the program displays when you run it now:

```
%productclassaddition
Number of apples and oranges: 500
Number of apples: 305
```

You can add integers and other data types to objects of the **product** class because in expressions like **apples + 5**, the value 5 is passed to the **operator+** method of the **apples** object. But what about expressions like **5 + apples**? The number 5 doesn't have an **operator+** method, so this is not going to work. To handle expressions like this, where the **product** object comes second, see "Conversions, Friends, and Operator Overloading" later in this chapter.

Overloading the << Operator

You can overload the << operator in C++. The << operator works on a stream named **ostream**, the output stream from our program, so the prototype for the function **operator<<** looks like this:

```
ostream &operator<<(ostream &stream, const product & p);
```

Here, we're passed a reference to **ostream** (which I name **stream**) and a **product** object (the object we want to send to the screen with <<). Inside **operator<<**, I can use **cout** to send text to the terminal. After I do, I also have to return a reference to the same stream we received as a parameter, because << can be *chained*—in other words, expressions like this are legal:

```
cout << apples << oranges;
```

Let's see this at work. In this example, productclassinsertion.cpp (<< is called the *insertion* operator, because it inserts data into streams), I'll display the name and number of a product in a **product** object like this—note that I'm making the **operator<<** function a friend of the **product** class, so that this function has access to the internal data of the **product** class (it's standard to make **operator<<** a friend of the class you're overloading it for):

```
#include <iostream>
#include <string>
using namespace std;

class product
{
    int number;
public:
    string name;
    int get_number(){return number;}
    void set_number(int n){number = n;}
    product(string text, int count);
    friend ostream &operator<<(ostream &stream, const product & p);
};

product::product(string text, int count)
{
    name = text;
    number = count;
}

ostream &operator<<(ostream &stream, const product & p)
```

```
{
    cout << "Number of " << p.name << ": " << p.number << endl;
    return stream;
}

int main()
{
    product oranges("oranges", 200);

    cout << oranges << endl;

    return 0;
}
```

Now you can send objects of the **product** class to the terminal with << directly; here's how that looks when you run the program productclassinsertion.cpp:

```
%productclassinsertion
Number of oranges: 200
```

Besides <<, you can also overload >>; see the next topic for the details.

Overloading the >> Operator

You can overload >>, the extraction operator, in C++. The >> operator works on a stream named **istream**, the input stream to our program, so the prototype for the function **operator>>** looks like this:

```
istream &operator>>(istream &stream, const product & p);
```

Here, we're passed a reference to **istream** (which I name **stream**) and a reference to a **product** object (the object we want to store data in with >>). Inside **operator>>**, I can use **cin** to read data from the keyboard. After I do, I also have to return a reference to the same stream we got as a parameter, because >> can be chained—in other words, expressions like this are legal:

```
cin >> apples >> oranges;
```

The **product** class stores two data items—the name and number of the product, so I have to overload the >> operator to read two data items. I start this new example, productclassextraction.cpp (the >> operator is called the extraction operator, because it extracts data from streams), by making the **operator>>** function a friend of the **product** class:

```
#include <iostream>
#include <string>
using namespace std;

class product
{
    int number;
public:
    string name;
    int get_number(){return number;}
    void set_number(int n){number = n;}
    product(string text, int count);
    friend ostream &operator<<(ostream &stream, const product & p);
    friend istream &operator>>(istream &stream, product & p);
};
    .
    .
    .
```

Now I can define the body of the **operator>>** function to read and store the two data items we need—note that because **operator>>** is a friend of the **product** class, I can access the internal data in the **product** class directly. In this program, I'll prompt the user to enter data values for an object named **oranges**, use the overloaded >> operator to store that data in **oranges**, and then use the overloaded << operator (see the previous section) to display the new data. Here's what the code looks like:

```
#include <iostream>
#include <string>
using namespace std;

class product
{
    int number;
public:
    string name;
    int get_number(){return number;}
    void set_number(int n){number = n;}
    product(string text, int count);
    friend ostream &operator<<(ostream &stream, const product & p);
    friend istream &operator>>(istream &stream, product & p);
};
```

```
product::product(string text, int count)
{
    name = text;
    number = count;
}

istream &operator>>(istream &stream, product & p)
{
    cin >> p.name >> p.number;
    return stream;
}

ostream &operator<<(ostream &stream, const product & p)
{
    cout << "Number of " << p.name << ": " << p.number << endl;
    return stream;
}

main()
{
    product oranges("", 0);

    cout << "Please enter the product name and number: ";

    cin >> oranges;

    cout << oranges << endl;

    return 0;
}
```

Here's what this program, productclassextraction.cpp, displays when you run it:

```
%productclassextraction
Please enter the product name and number: oranges 200
Number of oranges: 200
```


Overloading the [] Operator

In C++, you can overload the [], or array index, operator. This operator lets you use array indices on your objects and return data as needed from the object's internal store. Overloading this operator gives you the chance to do any appropriate calculation on that data before you return it.

Overloading the [] operator is not difficult; as you might expect, you overload this operator with a method named **operator[]**. This method is passed the array index that was used on the object; here's what the prototype for **operator[]** looks like:

```
type operator[](int index);
```

Note that this method returns a reference to the data specified by the array ***index***.

Here's an example, productclassarray.cpp. In this case, I'll expand the **product** class we've been using throughout the chapter so that it can keep track of product inventory in three different locations by supporting the [] operator—for example, **oranges[0]** might be your stock of oranges in San Francisco, **oranges[1]** your stock of oranges in Boston, and **oranges[3]** your stock of oranges in Paris. In this example, then, I'll store three product counts in the object and initialize them in the constructor like this:

```
#include <iostream>
#include <string>
using namespace std;

class product
{
    int number[3];
public:
    string name;
    product(string text, int count0, int count1, int count2);
};

product::product(string text, int count0, int count1, int count2)
{
    name = text;
    number[0] = count0;
    number[1] = count1;
    number[2] = count2;
}
        .
        .
        .
```

Now I can overload the [] operator for the **product** class. In this case, I'll return a reference to the value stored for each of the three possible array indices, as needed.

That looks like this in **operator[]**—note also that I pass three integers to the object's constructor and can now use the [] operator on that object in **main**:

```
#include <iostream>
#include <string>
using namespace std;

class product
{
    int number[3];
public:
    string name;
    product(string text, int count0, int count1, int count2);
    int operator[](int index) {return number[index];}
};

product::product(string text, int count0, int count1, int count2)
{
    name = text;
    number[0] = count0;
    number[1] = count1;
    number[2] = count2;
}

int main()
{
    product oranges("oranges", 200, 300, 400);

    cout << "Number of " << oranges.name << ": " << oranges[0] << endl;

    return 0;
}
```

And here's what this program, productclassarray.cpp, displays when you run it:

```
%productclassarray
Number of oranges: 200
```


Overloading the = Operator

In C++, you can overload the = operator, and that's often a good thing to do when your objects store pointers internally. The overloaded = operator is used when you assign an object to another this way:

```
apples = oranges;
```

C++ compilers can also use an overloaded assignment operator when you initialize one object from another:

```
product apples = oranges;
```

Usually this kind of initialization from another object is performed with the copy constructor, but C++ compilers can also use the copy constructor to create a temporary object and the = operator to assign a value to that temporary object.

If you don't overload it, the = assignment operator simply copies an object member by member, just like the default copy constructor. However, there's the same problem here as with default copy constructors—if an object contains pointers, you shouldn't necessarily simply copy those pointers over to the new object, because the copied pointers will still point to the old object's data (see the In Depth section of this chapter for more about when making copies of objects that store pointers can cause problems). To fix problems of this kind, you can overload the = operator with a method like this:

```
class_type operator=(class_type second_object);
```

In an expression such as **also_oranges** = **oranges**, the **operator=** method of **also_oranges** will be called, and **oranges** is passed to this method.

Here's an example, productclassequals.cpp, that shows how this works. In this case, I'll change the **product** class to store the name of the product using a pointer to a **char** array:

```
#include <iostream>
#include <cstring>
using namespace std;

class product
{
    int number;
public:
    char *name;
    int get_number(){return number;}
    void set_number(int n){number = n;}
    product();
    product(char *text, int count);
};
```

```
product::product(char *text, int count)
{
    name = new char[40];
    strcpy(name, text);
    number = count;
}
    .
    .
    .
```

To overload the = operator to handle objects of this class, I add the method **operator=** like this, and use **strcpy** (see "Copying C-Style Strings" in Chapter 3 for more details on **strcpy**) to copy over the **char** array in the original object to the new object. Now I can assign one **product** object to another, like this:

```
#include <iostream>
#include <cstring>
using namespace std;

class product
{
    int number;
public:
    char *name;
    int get_number(){return number;}
    void set_number(int n){number = n;}
    product();
    product(char *text, int count);
    product & operator=(const product & second_product);
};

product::product(char *text, int count)
{
    name = new char[40];
    strcpy(name, text);
    number = count;
}

product::product()
{
    name = new char[40];
    number = 0;
}
```

```
product & product::operator=(const product & second_product)
{
    strcpy(name, second_product.name);
    number = second_product.number;
    return *this;
}

int main()
{
    product oranges("oranges", 200), also_oranges;

    also_oranges = oranges;

    cout << "Number of " << also_oranges.name << ": "
        << also_oranges.get_number() << endl;

    return 0;
}
```

This example, productclassequals.cpp, displays the name and number of oranges in the new object, **also_oranges**, and as you can see, the assignment operator has worked:

```
%productclassequals
Number of oranges: 200
```


Related solution:	Found on page:
Copying C-Style Strings	136

Overloading the **new** and **delete** Operators

You can overload the **new** and **delete** operators in C++. The overloaded **new** operator returns a pointer of type **void***, and it's passed an argument of type **size_t**, a special type created to hold sizes. The **delete** operator is passed a pointer of type **void***:

```
void *operator new(size_t size);
void operator delete(void *p);
```

You can also overload **new[]** and **delete[]**:

```
void *operator new[](size_t size);
void operator delete[](void *p);
```

In the overloaded **new** operator, you allocate memory for the new object and return a **void*** pointer to that memory (the program framework initializes the object and stores it in that memory for you). Here's how that looks in an example, productclassnew.cpp; in this case, I'll overload **new** to allocate the memory for an object of the **product** class and use **delete** to delete that memory. Here's what the code looks like:

```
#include <iostream>
#include <string>
using namespace std;

class product
{
    int number;
public:
    string name;
    int get_number(){return number;}
    product(string text, int count);
    void *operator new(size_t size);
    void operator delete(void *p);
};

product::product(string text, int count)
{
    name = text;
    number = count;
}

void *product::operator new(size_t size)
{
    cout << "Allocating memory..." << endl;
    void *p = new char[size];
    return p;
}

void product::operator delete(void *p)
{
    cout << "Deleting memory..." << endl;
    delete[] (void *) p;
}
```

```
int main()
{
    product *orange_pointer = new product("oranges", 200);

    cout << "Number of " << orange_pointer->name << ": "
        << orange_pointer->get_number() << endl;

    delete orange_pointer;

    return 0;
}
```

After you've overloaded **new** and **delete**, how can you access the original, non-overloaded, **new** and **delete**? That's simple enough—you can refer to them as **::new** and **::delete**.

Creating a Copy Constructor

As discussed in the In Depth section of this chapter, copy constructors become important when you have objects that store pointers as data members. If you have pointers in an object and make a copy of that object, the pointers in the copy point to the same data as the pointers in the original object. That might not be what you want, because you might want the pointers in the new object to use new data, not point to the old object's data.

This kind of a problem can occur when the program creates a copy of an object, such as when it passes or returns a copy of the object to a function or method, when it creates a temporary copy of the object, or when you explicitly create and initialize an object using another object of the same class. By default, when the program needs to create a copy of an object, it uses the object's *default copy constructor*, which simply copies over each member in the old object into the new one. That, of course, is a problem when you have pointers in the old object that must be re-initialized in the new object, so in such cases, you should create your own copy constructor. As mentioned in the In Depth section of this chapter, resetting pointers and other data that shouldn't simply be copied over is called making a *deep copy*.

We saw an example in the In Depth section, productclasscopyconstructor.cpp, that shows how this works. In this case, I'll change the **product** class, so that we save the product's name as a pointer to a **char** array, and change the **product** class's normal constructor to handle that kind of **char** array:

```
#include <iostream>
#include <cstring>
using namespace std;

class product
{
    int number;
public:
    char *name;
    int get_number(){return number;}
    void set_number(int n){number = n;}
    product(char *text, int count);
};

product::product(char *text, int count)
{
    name = new char[40];
    strcpy(name, text);
    number = count;
}
        .
        .
        .
```

When we copy over objects of this class, we don't just want to make a copy of the **name** pointer, because that pointer will point to the **name** in the old object, not the new one. We need a copy constructor. To create a copy constructor for a class, you simply create a constructor that is passed a constant reference to an object of the same class. In that constructor, you can reset any pointers or other data as needed to create the new copy of the object. In this case, that means allocating a new **char** array to hold the name of the product and using **strcpy** to copy the old name to the new. I can use the copy constructor by, for example, initializing one object from another of the same class:

```
#include <iostream>
#include <cstring>
using namespace std;

class product
{
    int number;
```

```
public:
    char *name;
    int get_number(){return number;}
    void set_number(int n){number = n;}
    product(char *text, int count);
    product(const product & other_product);
};

product::product(char *text, int count)
{
    name = new char[40];
    strcpy(name, text);
    number = count;
}

product::product(const product & other_product)
{
    name = new char[40];
    strcpy(name, other_product.name);
    number = other_product.number;
}

int main()
{
    product oranges("oranges", 200), also_oranges(oranges);

    cout << "Number of " << also_oranges.name << ": "
        << also_oranges.get_number() << endl;

    return 0;
}
```

Using copy constructors is such a subtle point that it's easy to forget. However, if your objects store pointers, bear in mind they are good candidates for copy constructors, especially because it's up to the C++ implementation when to use copy constructors and when not— and you might not get the results you're expecting if you don't provide copy constructors.

Conversions to and from Objects

C++ offers a great deal of support for objects, making them as close to the built-in data types as it can. Part of that support is to let you specify how you want the compiler to perform conversions on your objects. For example, what if you have a **product** class object named **oranges** that is storing the name "oranges" and the number of **oranges** on hand, 200, and someone assigns **oranges** to an integer variable? Or what if someone assigns a string to **oranges**? What should the compiler do?

We saw how to let the compiler know what to do in an example named productclassconversion.cpp in the In Depth section of this chapter. In that example, I created an object named **oranges**, assigned a string to **oranges**, and then assigned an integer to **oranges**. We'll take a look at more of the details here.

Conversions to Objects

How do you let the compiler know what to do if you assign a **string** to **oranges**? To do that, you create a constructor for the **product** class that takes only a **string** argument. Here's what that looks like in productclassconversion.cpp—note that I'm assigning a **string** to the **oranges** object in **main**, and the new constructor will use that **string** as the product name to be stored in the object:

```
#include <iostream>
#include <string>
using namespace std;

class product
{
    int number;
public:
    string name;
    int get_number(){return number;}
    void set_number(int n){number = n;}
    product();
    product(string text);
};

product::product()
{
    name = "";
    number = 0;
}

product::product(string text)
{
    name = text;
    number = 0;
}
```

```
int main()
{
    product oranges;
    string product_name("oranges");

    oranges = product_name;
        .
        .
        .
}
```

What if you have a constructor that accepts a string argument, but you don't want to let the compiler use it to make implicit conversions? In that case, you use the keyword **explicit** to let the compiler know that it should use this constructor only to make conversions made explicitly with a cast (some compilers will only let you use **explicit** with constructors that are defined in-class—that is, inside the class definition):

```
#include <iostream>
#include <string>
using namespace std;

class product
{
    int number;
public:
    string name;
    int get_number(){return number;}
    void set_number(int n){number = n;}
    product();
    explicit product(string text){name = text; number = 0;}
};

product::product()
{
    name = "";
    number = 0;
}
        .
        .
        .
```

Conversions from Objects

You can also specify how to convert your objects to various data types using special methods. For example, to specify how to convert an object to a variable of type **int**, you'd declare a method named **operator int**. To convert an object to a variable of type **double**, that method would be **operator double**, and so on. Here's how I enable conversions of objects of the **product** class to integers and make use of the new conversion in **main** in productclassconversion.cpp:

```
#include <iostream>
#include <string>
using namespace std;

class product
{
    int number;
public:
    string name;
    int get_number(){return number;}
    void set_number(int n){number = n;}
    product();
    product(string text);
    operator int() const;
};

product::product()
{
    name = "";
    number = 0;
}

product::product(string text)
{
    name = text;
    number = 0;
}

product::operator int() const
{
    return number;
}

int main()
{
    product oranges;
```

```
    string product_name("oranges");

    oranges = product_name;

    oranges.set_number(200);

    int number_of_oranges = oranges;

    cout << "Number of " << oranges.name << ": " << number_of_oranges
        << endl;

    return 0;
}
```

And here's what you see when you run productclassconversion.cpp—as you can see, we've successfully converted from a string to a **product** object, and from a **product** object to an integer:

```
%productclassconversion
Number of oranges: 200
```

Conversions, Friends, and Operator Overloading

As we saw in "Overloading Binary Operators like + and -" earlier in this chapter, when you overload a binary operator in expressions like **a + b**, the **operator+** method of **a** is called and passed a reference to **b**. This is fine for expressions like **apples + oranges**, where **apples** and **oranges** are objects, or even **apples + 5**, but not expressions like **5 + apples**, because the first operand is not an object that can have an **operator+** method.

You can, however, fix this problem using friend functions, because a friend function will be passed *both* operands. For example, if you make **operator+** a friend function, you can declare a version of **operator+** that accepts an integer argument first and a **product** object second. Doing so enables you to use expressions like **5 + apples**, as you see in this example, productclassaddition2.cpp:

```
#include <iostream>
#include <string>
using namespace std;

class product
{
    int number;
```

```
public:
    string name;
    int get_number(){return number;}
    void set_number(int n){number = n;}
    product(int count);
    product(string text, int count);
    friend product operator+(int n, const product & product2);
};

product::product(int count)
{
    number = count;
}

product::product(string text, int count)
{
    name = text;
    number = count;
}

product operator+(int n, const product & product2)
{
    product temp("", 0);
    temp.name = product2.name;
    temp.set_number(n + product2.number);
    return temp;
}

main()
{
    product apples("apples", 300);

    apples = 5 + apples;

    cout << "Number of " << apples.name << ": "
        << apples.get_number() << endl;

    return 0;
}
```

Here's what you see when you run this new program, productclassaddition2.cpp:

```
%productclassaddition2
Number of apples: 305
```

Although it seems you'd have to define a new version of **operator+** for every possible combination of operands this way, you can make this whole process easier if you allow conversions from various data types to your objects. For example, say you define a friend function named **operator+** and pass it two objects of the **product** class. If you also provide conversion methods from various data types to the **product** class, the compiler converts those data types as needed and passes them to the **operator+** function, so you need only one **operator+** function. Here's an example, productclassaddition3.cpp, showing how that works—in this case, I'm letting **operator+** handle two **product** class objects, but I'm also providing a conversion constructor from integers to **product** objects, which means I'm now able to handle expressions like **apples + oranges**, **apples + 5**, and **5 + apples**:

```
#include <iostream>
#include <string>
using namespace std;

class product
{
    int number;
public:
    string name;
    int get_number(){return number;}
    void set_number(int n){number = n;}
    product(int count);
    product(string text, int count);
    friend product operator+(const product & product1,
        const product & product2);
};

product::product(int count)
{
    number = count;
}

product::product(string text, int count)
{
    name = text;
    number = count;
}

product operator+(const product & product1, const product & product2)
{
    product temp("", 0);
    if(!product1.name.empty())
        temp.name = product1.name;
```

```
    if(!product2.name.empty())
        temp.name = product2.name;
    if(!product1.name.empty() && !product2.name.empty())
        temp.name = product1.name + " and " + product2.name;
    temp.set_number(product1.number + product2.number);
    return temp;
}

main()
{
    product oranges("oranges", 200);
    product apples("apples", 300);

    product apples_and_oranges = apples + oranges;

    cout << "Number of " << apples_and_oranges.name << ": "
        << apples_and_oranges.get_number() << endl;

    apples = apples + 5;

    cout << "Number of " << apples.name << ": "
        << apples.get_number() << endl;

    apples = 5 + apples;

    cout << "Number of " << apples.name << ": "
        << apples.get_number() << endl;

    return 0;
}
```

Here's what you see when you run this program, productclassaddition3.cpp:

```
%productclassaddition3
Number of oranges: 500
Number of apples: 305
Number of apples: 310
```


Creating Friend Classes

Besides functions, you can also declare classes as friends of other classes. If a class is a friend of another class, it has access to all that class's internal members. Here's an example, productclassfriendclass.cpp; in this program, I'm creating a new class named **inventory** and making it a friend of the **product** class. The **inventory** class has only one method—**get_number**, and when you pass it an object of the **product** class, it returns the number stored in the private data member **number** in that object. In **main**, I can use an **inventory** class object to get the number of oranges as stored in a **product** class object like this:

```
#include <iostream>
#include <string>
using namespace std;

class product
{
    friend class inventory;
    int number;
public:
    string name;
    int get_number(){return number;}
    void set_number(int n){number = n;}
    product(string text, int count);
};

class inventory
{
public:
    int get_number(product p);
};

int inventory::get_number(product p)
{
    return p.number;
}

product::product(string text, int count)
{
    name = text;
    number = count;
}

int main()
{
    product oranges("oranges", 200);
    inventory i;

    cout << "Number of " << oranges.name << ": "
        << i.get_number(oranges) << endl;
```

```
    return 0;
}
```

Here's what you see when you run this code, productclassfriendclass.cpp:

```
%productclassfriendclass
Number of oranges: 200
```

Creating Friend Methods

Besides friend classes and friend functions, you can also make specific methods friends of a class. Here's an example, productclassfriendmethod.cpp. In this example, I'm making the method **get_number** in the **inventory** class a friend of the **product** class, and then I'm using that method to access the internal data of a **product** class object—note that I have to declare the **product** class before using it in the **inventory** class's **get_number** method (and I can't have simply put the **product** class first, because that class declares the **inventory** class's **get_number** method as a friend, and the compiler would have complained that it hasn't seen the **inventory** class):

```
#include <iostream>
#include <string>
using namespace std;

class product;

class inventory
{
public:
    int get_number(product p);
};

class product
{
    friend int inventory::get_number(product p);
    int number;
public:
    string name;
    int get_number(){return number;}
    void set_number(int n){number = n;}
    product(string text, int count);
};
```

```
int inventory::get_number(product p)
{
    return p.number;
}

product::product(string text, int count)
{
    name = text;
    number = count;
}

int main()
{
    product oranges("oranges", 200);
    inventory i;

    cout << "Number of " << oranges.name << ": "
        << i.get_number(oranges) << endl;

    return 0;
}
```

Here's what you see when you run this program, productclassfriendmethod.cpp:

```
%productclassfriendmethod
Number of oranges: 200
```

Creating Nested and Local Classes

You put one class inside another in C++. Here's an example, productclassnested.cpp; in this case, I'm defining a new class, **value**, inside the **product** class and using an object of the **value** class to store the number of the product in inventory. Now to access the number of an object, I can use the **value** class's data access methods **set_value** and **get_value**:

```
#include <iostream>
#include <string>
using namespace std;

class product
{
    class value
```

```
    {
    public:
        int internal_value;
        int get_value(){return internal_value;}
        void set_value(int n){internal_value = n;}
    };
    value number;
public:
    string name;
    int get_number(){return number.get_value();}
    void set_number(int n){number.set_value(n);}
    product(string text, int count);
};

product::product(string text, int count)
{
    number.set_value(count);
    name = text;
}

int main()
{
    product oranges("oranges", 200);

    cout << "Number of " << oranges.name << ": "
        << oranges.get_number() << endl;

    return 0;
}
```

Here's what you see when you run this program, productclassnested.cpp:

```
%productclassnested
Number of oranges: 200
```

You can also use objects of the **value** class outside the **product** class, but then you must use the **value** class's fully qualified name: **product::value**.

In addition, you can define classes inside a function body, and such classes are called *local classes*. These classes are allocated in automatic storage, so they cannot have static members. Also, a class nested inside a local class can be referred to outside the nesting class, but only inside the scope of the local class.

Chapter 10

Class Inheritance

In Depth

One of the major attractions of the C++ packages sold by independent vendors is the pre-written classes that come with those packages. For example, the Microsoft Foundation Classes that come with Microsoft's Visual C++ offer a tremendous amount of support for Windows programmers, with literally thousands of classes. However, none of that would work if you couldn't customize those classes in some way by making them behave as you want and adding your own code. This chapter is all about *reusing* code in C++ through *class inheritance*, one of the main pillars of OOP, and the reason that you can customize and use the classes supplied by independent vendors.

Class inheritance allows you to reuse your classes by deriving new classes from old ones and customizing the new classes as you want. I'll start with some examples, beginning with an introduction to the simple class we'll use in this chapter, the **animal** class.

The animal Class

To see how inheritance works, we'll need an example class to work with, and so I'll introduce the **animal** class here. This class simply supports a few methods, **eat**, **sleep**, and **breathe**, which display the messages "Eating...", "Sleeping...", and "Breathing...":

```
#include <iostream>
using namespace std;

class animal
{
public:
    void eat();
    void sleep();
    void breathe();
};

void animal::eat(){cout << "Eating..." << endl;}
void animal::sleep(){cout << "Sleeping..." << endl;}
void animal::breathe(){cout << "Breathing..." << endl;}
    .
    .
    .
```

The methods of this class are common to all animals; for example, you can declare an object named **cat** that eats, sleeps, and breathes like this:

```
#include <iostream>
using namespace std;

class animal
{
public:
    void eat();
    void sleep();
    void breathe();
};

void animal::eat(){cout << "Eating..." << endl;}
void animal::sleep(){cout << "Sleeping..." << endl;}
void animal::breathe(){cout << "Breathing..." << endl;}

int main()
{
    animal cat;

    cat.eat();
    cat.breathe();
    cat.sleep();

    return 0;
}
```

When you run this code, animalclass.cpp, here's what you see:

```
%animalclass
Eating...
Breathing...
Sleeping...
```

The **animal** class methods are common to all animals, but very basic. Using this class alone, you can't tell a cat from a canary, and as time goes on, you might find that tedious. If you stick with the **animal** class for the long term, you might find yourself wanting to customize it in some way to more accurately reflect the behavior of various animals—for example, a fish doesn't breathe in the same way a giraffe does.

One way to customize this class for various animals is to copy the class over into dozens of classes and tailor each to a specific animal. However, if the code in the **animal** class were lengthy, or if it maintained a great deal of internal data, it might not be a good idea to write separate classes for each type of animal. If you had to change the code in one method, you'd have to modify each class separately.

Instead, you can take what all the animals have in common and put it into a *base class*. In this case, the **animal** class, with its basic **eat**, **sleep**, and **breathe** methods common to all animals, will be our base class. Using inheritance, you can then derive new classes from that base class, and those *derived classes* can be tailored to each animal while still retaining the functionality of the **eat**, **sleep**, and **breathe** methods from the base class, **animal**. For example, an elephant can stampede, but goldfish rarely do, which means you might derive an **elephant** class from the **animal** class and add a method named **stampede**, while the **goldfish** class won't have such a method. Now the **elephant** class has **eat**, **sleep**, **breathe**, and **stampede** methods, and all you had to do was to develop the **stampede** method—the **eat**, **sleep**, and **breathe** methods were already there for you to use from the **animal** class.

Inheritance

Here's how you use inheritance to develop the **elephant** class. This class is based on the **animal** class, so I include the definition of the **animal** class in this new example, animalclassinheritance.cpp:

```
#include <iostream>
using namespace std;

class animal
{
public:
    void eat();
    void sleep();
    void breathe();
};

void animal::eat(){cout << "Eating..." << endl;}
void animal::sleep(){cout << "Sleeping..." << endl;}
void animal::breathe(){cout << "Breathing..." << endl;}
    .
    .
    .
```

Now I'll derive the **elephant** class from the **animal** class and add two new methods: the **trumpet** and **stampede** methods. To indicate that **elephant** is based on **animal**, I add **: public animal** (note the colon) to the declaration of **elephant**:

```
#include <iostream>
using namespace std;

class animal
{
public:
    void eat();
    void sleep();
    void breathe();
};

class elephant : public animal
{
public:
    void trumpet();
    void stampede();
};

void animal::eat(){cout << "Eating..." << endl;}
void animal::sleep(){cout << "Sleeping..." << endl;}
void animal::breathe(){cout << "Breathing..." << endl;}

void elephant::trumpet(){cout << "Trumpeting..." << endl;}
void elephant::stampede(){cout << "Stampeding..." << endl;}
    .
    .
    .
```

This means that **elephant** is derived from **animal**, so **elephant** inherits all that's in the **animal** class; **elephant** now has **eat**, **sleep**, **breathe**, **trumpet**, and **stampede** methods. If I declare an object named **jumbo** of the **elephant** class, I can now use all those methods:

```
#include <iostream>
using namespace std;

class animal
```

```
{
public:
    void eat();
    void sleep();
    void breathe();
};

class elephant : public animal
{
public:
    void trumpet();
    void stampede();
};

void animal::eat(){cout << "Eating..." << endl;}
void animal::sleep(){cout << "Sleeping..." << endl;}
void animal::breathe(){cout << "Breathing..." << endl;}

void elephant::trumpet(){cout << "Trumpeting..." << endl;}
void elephant::stampede(){cout << "Stampeding..." << endl;}

int main()
{
    elephant jumbo;

    jumbo.breathe();
    jumbo.trumpet();
    jumbo.stampede();

    return 0;
}
```

Here's what you see when you run this example, animalclassinheritance.cpp:

```
%animalclassinheritance
Breathing...
Trumpeting...
Stampeding...
```

In this way, we've been able to create a derived class from a base class, and we've added some additional methods to it.

NOTE: *Remember that you can store class definitions in header files. For simplicity's sake, I won't do that often in this chapter (for an example, however, see "Creating Class Libraries" later in this chapter), but if you're going to be reusing your classes across many files, bear that in mind, because that's the way professionals frequently code.*

Here's some of what you can do using inheritance:

- You can add functionality to an existing class by adding your own methods, as we've seen.
- You can add data members to an existing class.
- You can change how an existing class method works by redefining it. This is called *overriding* a base class method.

Inheritance is based on "is-a" relationships; in this case, that relationship can be expressed as "An elephant is a type of animal." (Another frequent relationship you see between classes is a "has-a" relationship, in which an object is a member of another object—see "Creating Has-a Relationships" later in this chapter.)

There are a few methods that you should know are *not* inherited when you create a derived class—constructors, destructors, and assignment operator methods are all not inherited. Derived classes, however, can use the constructors, destructors, and assignment operator methods of their base classes, as well as adding their own. For example, if the base class has an assignment operator method, the compiler will use that method for the derived class as well, which is fine unless the derived class also adds its own data members (in which case you should create a new **operator=** method for the derived class). We'll take a look at using constructors and destructors with inheritance in this chapter.

NOTE: *Here's something else worth knowing: you can assign objects of a derived class to objects of a base class (although any members that were added in the derived class will not be retained after the assignment), but you can't assign a base class object to a derived class object unless you've defined a conversion method—see "Conversions to and from Objects" in Chapter 9 for more on conversion methods.*

Access Specifiers

As you recall, the members of a class can be declared private, public, or protected. Private members are not available outside objects of the class, public members are available outside the class, and protected members are available only to classes derived from the current one. Which access specifiers you use has implications for how inheritance works with your classes. To see how this works, take a look at the code in a new example, animalclassaccess.cpp; in this case, I've made the **animal** class's **eat** method private, its **run** method protected, and the **sleep** and **breathe** methods public:

```
#include <iostream>
using namespace std;
```

```
class animal
{
private:
    void eat();
protected:
    void run();
public:
    void sleep();
    void breathe();
};
    .
    .
    .
```

Note what happens when I derive the **elephant** class from **animal**; the private method **eat** is not available to **elephant**, but the protected **run** method and the public **sleep** and **breathe** methods are. Because the protected **run** method is available only to classes derived from **animal**, it's not available publicly from **elephant** objects. To make the **animal** class's **run** method available publicly from **elephant** objects, I can define a new public method named **run** in **elephant** to call the **animal** class's **run** method. How do you specify that you want to call a base class's method? You use the scope resolution operator, ::, like this: **animal::run**, as you see here:

```
#include <iostream>
using namespace std;

class animal
{
private:
    void eat();
protected:
    void run();
public:
    void sleep();
    void breathe();
};

class elephant : public animal
{
public:
    void run();
    void trumpet();
```

```
    void stampede();
};

void animal::eat(){cout << "Eating..." << endl;}
void animal::run(){cout << "Running..." << endl;}
void animal::sleep(){cout << "Sleeping..." << endl;}
void animal::breathe(){cout << "Breathing..." << endl;}

void elephant::run(){animal::run();}
void elephant::trumpet(){cout << "Trumpeting..." << endl;}
void elephant::stampede(){cout << "Stampeding..." << endl;}

int main()
{
    elephant jumbo;

    jumbo.run();
    jumbo.breathe();
    jumbo.trumpet();
    jumbo.stampede();

    return 0;
}
```

Here's what you see when you run this example, animalclassaccess.cpp:

```
%animalclassaccess
Running...
Breathing...
Trumpeting...
Stampeding...
```

Using the access specifiers **public**, **private**, and **protected**, you can specify in your base classes just what you want to make available to derived classes. However, that still leaves plenty of questions about the connection between base and derived classes unanswered—for example, what if both base and derived classes have constructors? Which of them is called, and in which order?

Inheritance and Constructors

If a base class doesn't have an explicitly defined constructor, its default constructor is called each time you create an object of a class derived from that class. But what happens if the base class does have an explicit constructor? For example, suppose I add a constructor to the **animal** class that stores the name of the animal this way:

```
class animal
{
private:
    string name;
public:
    void eat();
    void sleep();
    void breathe();
    animal(string s);
};

animal::animal(string s){name = s;}
```

Now the **animal** class has a constructor that takes a string argument (and because a constructor has been created, the C++ compiler no longer creates a default constructor for this class). When you create an object of the **elephant** class, which is derived from **animal**, how do you pass data back to the **animal** class's constructor? To do that, you add a list of initializers to the **elephant** class's constructor (see "Creating Constructors" in Chapter 8 for more on initializers). For example, if I write the **elephant** class's constructor to take a string argument, I can pass that same string argument back to the **animal** class's constructor like this, in animalclassconstructor.cpp:

```
#include <iostream>
#include <string>
using namespace std;

class animal
{
private:
    string name;
public:
    void eat();
    void sleep();
    void breathe();
    animal(string s);
};

class elephant : public animal
{
```

```
public:
    void trumpet();
    void stampede();
    elephant(string s);
};

void animal::eat(){cout << "Eating..." << endl;}
void animal::sleep(){cout << "Sleeping..." << endl;}
void animal::breathe(){cout << "Breathing..." << endl;}
animal::animal(string s){name = s;}

void elephant::trumpet(){cout << "Trumpeting..." << endl;}
void elephant::stampede(){cout << "Stampeding..." << endl;}
elephant::elephant(string s) : animal(s)
{
    cout << "Initializing name to " << s << endl;
}

int main()
{
    elephant jumbo("Jumbo");

    jumbo.breathe();
    jumbo.trumpet();
    jumbo.stampede();

    return 0;
}
```

That's the way you pass arguments back to base class constructors, using initializers as in **elephant::elephant(string s) : animal(s)**, which passes the string argument back to the **animal** class's constructor. Here's what you see when you run this program, animalclassconstructor.cpp:

```
%animalclassconstructor
Initializing name to Jumbo
Breathing...
Trumpeting...
Stampeding...
```

For more details, see "Using Constructors with Inheritance" later in this chapter.

Overriding Base Class Members

You can also customize a base class by redefining its members in a derived class. This process is called *overriding* (not to be confused with overloading). When you override a base class's member, you redefine the member, whether it's a data member or a method. For example, the **animal** class has a method named **breathe** that prints "Breathing...", but if you derive a class named **fish** from the **animal** class, you might think it more appropriate if that method were to print out "Bubbling...". To override the base class's method, you simply redefine the method—that's all there is to it. For instance, here's how I override the **breathe** method in the **fish** class in a new example, animalclassoverride.cpp:

```
#include <iostream>
using namespace std;

class animal
{
public:
    void eat();
    void sleep();
    void breathe();
};

class fish : public animal
{
public:
    void breathe();
};

void animal::eat(){cout << "Eating..." << endl;}
void animal::sleep(){cout << "Sleeping..." << endl;}
void animal::breathe(){cout << "Breathing..." << endl;}
void fish::breathe(){cout << "Bubbling..." << endl;}

int main()
{
    fish bigfish;
    bigfish.breathe();

    return 0;
}
```

Here's what you see when you run this example, animalclassoverride.cpp—note that the overridden **breathe** method displays "Bubbling...", not "Breathing...":

```
%animalclassoverride
Bubbling...
```

As you can see, the **fish** class's **breathe** method has overridden the base class's **breathe** method. In this way, you can still use a base class, even if a few methods or data members are inappropriate and so need to be redefined differently in the derived class. Here's an important note: overriding a base class's method hides all the methods of the same name in the base class, not just those with the same argument list. In other words, overriding is not like overloading—when you override a method, all overloaded versions of that method are also overridden. For more information, see "Overriding Base Class Members" later in this chapter.

Virtual Methods, Early and Late Binding

We haven't discussed what happens to pointers when we work with base and derived classes, and there's a lot to discuss. Pointers to base class objects can also be used to point to derived class objects (although you can't reference members in the derived class that are not in the base class when you use a base class pointer). Because one pointer can point to various different derived objects as well, this process is called *polymorphism*.

Here's an example, animalclasspolymorphism.cpp. In this case, I'll add an **animal** object named **animal_object** to the **fish** class example we just saw in the previous section, as well as a pointer to the **animal** class, named **pointer**. I can use **pointer** to point to objects of both the **animal** and **fish** classes, like this, where I'm calling the **breathe** method in each case:

```
#include <iostream>
using namespace std;

class animal
{
public:
    void eat();
    void sleep();
    void breathe();
};

class fish : public animal
{
public:
    void breathe();
};
```

```
void animal::breathe(){cout << "Breathing..." << endl;}
void animal::eat(){cout << "Eating..." << endl;}
void animal::sleep(){cout << "Sleeping..." << endl;}
void fish::breathe(){cout << "Bubbling..." << endl;}

int main()
{
    animal animal_object;
    fish bigfish;
    animal *pointer;

    pointer = &animal_object;

    pointer->breathe();

    pointer = &bigfish;

    pointer->breathe();

    return 0;
}
```

Here's what you see when you run this code:

```
%animalclasspolymorphism
Breathing...
Breathing...
```

Note what's happened here—although the **animal** class pointer can point to objects of both the **animal** class and the derived **fish** class, when you call the **breathe** method, it's the base class's **breathe** method that's called in both cases. That's because the compiler knows that the pointer points to the **animal** class, so it uses that class's methods by default, a process called *early* or *static* binding.

However, you can make the program wait until it actually runs before deciding what version of **breathe** to call, which is called *late* or *dynamic* binding. To use late binding with **breathe**, you use the keyword **virtual** when declaring it, making it a *virtual method*. Now if **pointer** holds a pointer to an **animal** class object and you use it to call **breathe**, **animal::breathe** will be called. But if **pointer** holds a pointer to a **fish** class object and you use it to call **breathe**, **fish::breathe** will be called, not **animal::breathe**. Using late binding, the program determines what class's members a pointer points to at runtime, not at compile time.

Here's how that works in animalclasspolymorphism.cpp—note that I'm making **breathe** a virtual method:

```
#include <iostream>
using namespace std;

class animal
{
public:
    void eat();
    void sleep();
    virtual void breathe();
};

class fish : public animal
{
public:
    void breathe();
};

void animal::breathe(){cout << "Breathing..." << endl;}
void animal::eat(){cout << "Eating..." << endl;}
void animal::sleep(){cout << "Sleeping..." << endl;}
void fish::breathe(){cout << "Bubbling..." << endl;}

int main()
{
    animal animal_object;
    fish bigfish;
    animal *pointer;

    pointer = &animal_object;

    pointer->breathe();

    pointer = &bigfish;

    pointer->breathe();

    return 0;
}
```

Now when you run this code, you'll see this result—note that when you place a pointer to a **fish** object in **pointer** and call **pointer->breathe**, the **fish** class's version of **breathe** is called:

```
%animalclasspolymorphism
Breathing...
Bubbling...
```

NOTE: *Although you can use a base class pointer to point to a derived class object, you can't use that base class pointer to access members that are in the derived class but not in the base class—trying to do so results in a compiler error.*

That's an introduction to polymorphism as well as inheritance; there's more coming up in the Immediate Solutions, and we'll turn to that now.

Immediate Solutions

Deriving a Class from a Base Class

You can derive a class from a base class with this syntax—here, ***access_specifier*** can be **public**, **private**, or **protected**, and ***base_class*** is the name of the base class:

```
class name [: access_specifier base_class [, access_specifier
base_class...]]
{
private:
    private data members and methods
protected:
    protected data members and methods
public:
    private data members and methods
}[object_list...];
```

We saw an example in the In Depth section of this chapter, animal-classinheritance.cpp, in which I derived a class named **elephant** from a base class named **animal**:

```
#include <iostream>
using namespace std;

class animal
{
public:
    void eat();
    void sleep();
    void breathe();
};

class elephant : public animal
{
public:
    void trumpet();
    void stampede();
};
```

```
void animal::eat(){cout << "Eating..." << endl;}
void animal::sleep(){cout << "Sleeping..." << endl;}
void animal::breathe(){cout << "Breathing..." << endl;}

void elephant::trumpet(){cout << "Trumpeting..." << endl;}
void elephant::stampede(){cout << "Stampeding..." << endl;}
        .
        .
        .
```

I then created an object of the **elephant** class and used its methods:

```
#include <iostream>
using namespace std;

class animal
{
public:
    void eat();
    void sleep();
    void breathe();
};

class elephant : public animal
{
public:
    void trumpet();
    void stampede();
};

void animal::eat(){cout << "Eating..." << endl;}
void animal::sleep(){cout << "Sleeping..." << endl;}
void animal::breathe(){cout << "Breathing..." << endl;}

void elephant::trumpet(){cout << "Trumpeting..." << endl;}
void elephant::stampede(){cout << "Stampeding..." << endl;}

int main()
{
    elephant jumbo;

    jumbo.breathe();
    jumbo.trumpet();
    jumbo.stampede();
```

```
    return 0;
}
```

The **elephant** class has inherited the methods of the **animal** class, as you can see when the example runs:

```
%animalclassinheritance
Breathing...
Trumpeting...
Stampeding...
```

However, that's just skimming the surface of inheritance—take a look at the following sections for more.

Using Access Specifiers

You can specify the access a derived class has to a base class's members using access specifiers. In particular, the members of a class can be declared private, public, or protected. Private members are not available outside objects of the class, public members are available outside the class, and protected members are available only to classes derived from the current one.

For instance, we saw the example named animalclassaccess.cpp in the In Depth section of this chapter. In that case, the **animal** class has private, protected, and public methods:

```
#include <iostream>
using namespace std;

class animal
{
private:
    void eat();
protected:
    void run();
public:
    void sleep();
    void breathe();
};
    .
    .
    .
```

The public members of the base class will also be public in the derived class. The private members of the base class cannot be accessed in the derived class, but the protected and public members can. The protected members cannot be accessed outside the derived class—for example, because **run** is a protected **animal** class method, I have to provide a public method in the derived class that calls **animal::run** to make that method accessible:

```
#include <iostream>
using namespace std;

class animal
{
private:
    void eat();
protected:
    void run();
public:
    void sleep();
    void breathe();
};

class elephant : public animal
{
public:
    void run();
    void trumpet();
    void stampede();
};

void animal::eat(){cout << "Eating..." << endl;}
void animal::run(){cout << "Running..." << endl;}
void animal::sleep(){cout << "Sleeping..." << endl;}
void animal::breathe(){cout << "Breathing..." << endl;}

void elephant::run(){animal::run();}
void elephant::trumpet(){cout << "Trumpeting..." << endl;}
void elephant::stampede(){cout << "Stampeding..." << endl;}

int main()
{
    elephant jumbo;
```

```
    jumbo.run();
    jumbo.breathe();
    jumbo.trumpet();
    jumbo.stampede();

    return 0;
}
```

Here's what you see when you run this example, animalclassaccess.cpp:

```
%animalclassaccess
Running...
Breathing...
Trumpeting...
Stampeding...
```

There's another place you can use access specifiers with inheritance—when you define a derived class. In the code above, for example, I've used public inheritance, as indicated with the public access specifier:

```
class elephant : public animal
{
public:
    void run();
    void trumpet();
    void stampede();
};
```

However, you can also be more restrictive with the members of the base class, using private or protected inheritance—see "Using Private Inheritance" and "Using Protected Inheritance" later in this chapter.

Using Constructors with Inheritance

If a base class doesn't have an explicitly defined constructor, its default constructor is called each time you create an object of a class derived from that class. But what happens if the base class does have an explicit constructor? In that case, you can specify the arguments you want to pass back to that constructor using initializers.

Here's an example we first saw in the In Depth section of this chapter, animalclassconstructor.cpp. In this case, I've added a constructor that takes a string argument to the **animal** and **elephant** classes. To pass the argument back to the **animal** class's constructor, I use an initializer like this:

```
#include <iostream>
#include <string>
using namespace std;

class animal
{
private:
    string name;
public:
    void eat();
    void sleep();
    void breathe();
    animal(string s);
};

class elephant : public animal
{
public:
    void trumpet();
    void stampede();
    elephant(string s);
};

void animal::eat(){cout << "Eating..." << endl;}
void animal::sleep(){cout << "Sleeping..." << endl;}
void animal::breathe(){cout << "Breathing..." << endl;}
animal::animal(string s){name = s;}

void elephant::trumpet(){cout << "Trumpeting..." << endl;}
void elephant::stampede(){cout << "Stampeding..." << endl;}
elephant::elephant(string s) : animal(s)
{
    cout << "Initializing name to " << s << endl;
}

int main()
{
    elephant jumbo("Jumbo");
```

```
    jumbo.breathe();
    jumbo.trumpet();
    jumbo.stampede();

    return 0;
}
```

That's how you pass arguments back to base class constructors, using initializers like this: **elephant::elephant(string s) : animal(s)**, which passes the string **s** back to the **animal** class's constructor. Here's what you see when you run this program, animalclassconstructor.cpp:

```
%animalclassconstructor
Initializing name to Jumbo
Breathing...
Trumpeting...
Stampeding...
```

The base class's constructor is called before the derived class's constructor (because the derived class might rely on the base class members being fully initialized). Destructors are called in reverse order—derived class first, then base class. You can pass multiple arguments to base class constructors, of course, including those that are not in the derived class constructor's argument list. Here's an example:

```
elephant::elephant(string s, int n) : animal(s, n, -512)
{
    cout << "Initializing name to " << s << endl;
}
```

TIP: *If you are initializing an object from another object, you should call the base class's copy constructor.*

For more on this process, take a look at multiple inheritance in the next chapter.

Overriding Base Class Members

You can customize a base class in a derived class by overriding the base class's members. When you override a base class member, whether a data member or a method, you redefine it, and the new version will become the default version in the derived class. However, you can still access the overridden member as ***base_class::member***.

When you override a base class method, all versions of that method, no matter what argument list they use, are overridden. So as you can see, overriding is very different from overloading. For instance, here's an example, animalclass-override.cpp, from the In Depth section of this chapter. In this case, the **animal** class has a method named **breathe** that I override in the derived class **fish**. The **animal::breathe** method displays "Breathing...", but the **fish::breathe** method displays "Bubbling...":

```
#include <iostream>
using namespace std;

class animal
{
public:
    void eat();
    void sleep();
    void breathe();
};

class fish : public animal
{
public:
    void breathe();
};

void animal::eat(){cout << "Eating..." << endl;}
void animal::sleep(){cout << "Sleeping..." << endl;}
void animal::breathe(){cout << "Breathing..." << endl;}
void fish::breathe(){cout << "Bubbling..." << endl;}
        .
        .
        .
```

Now when I call the **breathe** method in an object of the **fish** class, the overridden version is used:

```
#include <iostream>
using namespace std;

class animal
{
public:
    void eat();
    void sleep();
```

```
    void breathe();
};

class fish : public animal
{
public:
    void breathe();
};

void animal::eat(){cout << "Eating..." << endl;}
void animal::sleep(){cout << "Sleeping..." << endl;}
void animal::breathe(){cout << "Breathing..." << endl;}
void fish::breathe(){cout << "Bubbling..." << endl;}

int main()
{
    fish bigfish;
    bigfish.breathe();

    return 0;
}
```

Here's what you see when you run this example:

```
%animalclassoverride
Bubbling...
```

Note that you can still access the **animal** class's **breathe** method even in the **fish** class, if you use the expression **animal::breathe**.

Related solution:	*Found on page:*
Overloading Methods and Constructors	372

Virtual Methods and Runtime Polymorphism

As discussed in the In Depth section of this chapter, you can store a pointer or reference to a derived class in a pointer or reference to the base class. In other words, a pointer or reference can point to or refer to objects not just of one class, but also to objects of classes derived from that class. If those objects support methods, you can make the program wait until runtime to decide what version of those methods it should call—those in the base class or the derived class. This process is called runtime polymorphism, and it's useful because your code can decide at runtime what methods it wants to call.

This is better seen with an example, and we first saw this at work in animalclasspolymorphism.cpp, in the In Depth section of this chapter. In this case, I create an object of the **animal** class, a pointer to the **animal** class, and an object of the **fish** class, which is derived from the **animal** class. The **animal** and **fish** classes each have a different version of a method named **breathe**, and I've declared that method virtual in the base class to indicate that the compiler should handle it with runtime polymorphism:

```
#include <iostream>
using namespace std;

class animal
{
public:
    void eat();
    void sleep();
    virtual void breathe();
};

class fish : public animal
{
public:
    void breathe();
};

void animal::breathe(){cout << "Breathing..." << endl;}
void fish::breathe(){cout << "Bubbling..." << endl;}
        .
        .
        .
```

That means that **pointer->breathe** calls **animal::breathe** when **pointer** points to an **animal** object, but it calls **fish::breathe** when **pointer** points to a **fish** object:

```
#include <iostream>
using namespace std;

class animal
{
public:
```

```
    void eat();
    void sleep();
    virtual void breathe();
};

class fish : public animal
{
public:
    void breathe();
};

void animal::breathe(){cout << "Breathing..." << endl;}
void animal::eat(){cout << "Eating..." << endl;}
void animal::sleep(){cout << "Sleeping..." << endl;}
void fish::breathe(){cout << "Bubbling..." << endl;}

int main()
{
    animal animal_object;
    fish bigfish;
    animal *pointer;

    pointer = &animal_object;

    pointer->breathe();

    pointer = &bigfish;

    pointer->breathe();

    return 0;
}
```

Here's what this example looks like when running; note that the program used **animal::breathe** when the pointer pointed to an **animal** object, but it used **fish::breathe** when the pointer pointed to a **fish** object:

```
%animalclasspolymorphism
Breathing...
Bubbling...
```

***NOTE:** Because you can use runtime polymorphism with virtual methods, one style of programming says you should declare all methods you want overridden to be virtual, and none of the methods you don't want overridden.*

Note also that constructors can't be virtual, nor can friend methods or friend functions (because friends are not actual members of the current class). However, it's often a good idea to make *destructors* virtual, especially if your class serves as a base class and objects of classes derived from it are allocated with **new**. In that case, the program uses the pointer returned from **new** to point to your object, which means that static binding applies to the object's destructor, unless you make the destructor virtual. If you leave static binding in effect, the base class's destructor will be the only one called, but if the destructor is virtual, the destructor of the appropriate derived class will be called.

Also, as noted in the In Depth section of this chapter, although you can use a base class pointer to point to a derived class object, you can't use that pointer to access members that are in the derived class but that are *not* members of the base class. Trying to do so will give you a compiler error.

Related solution:	Found on page:
Using **dynamic_cast** with Pointers at Runtime	528

Creating Abstract Classes and Pure Virtual Methods

You can leave a base class method *unimplemented* if you make it a *pure virtual method*. When a class has one or more pure virtual methods, it's called an *abstract class*, and you can't instantiate objects of that class directly. Instead, you have to derive your own class from that abstract class, explicitly overriding any pure virtual functions.

TIP: *If you want programmers to have to override certain methods in a class, such as those that need information customized for a particular installation, you should make those methods pure virtual—that's what pure virtual methods were created for.*

You create a pure virtual method by using **= 0** in place of a method body. Here's an example, animalclassabstractclass.cpp, that shows how this works. In this case, I'll make the **breathe** method in the **animal** class a pure virtual method:

```
#include <iostream>
using namespace std;
```

```
class animal
{
public:
    void eat();
    void sleep();
    virtual void breathe() = 0;
};
    .
    .
    .
```

Now the **animal** class is an abstract class, and you can't create objects of this class—you can only use it as a base class. To create a non-abstract derived class from this class, you must override the **breathe** method like this:

```
#include <iostream>
using namespace std;

class animal
{
public:
    void eat();
    void sleep();
    virtual void breathe() = 0;
};

class fish : public animal
{
public:
    void breathe();
};

void animal::eat(){cout << "Eating..." << endl;}
void animal::sleep(){cout << "Sleeping..." << endl;}
void fish::breathe(){cout << "Bubbling..." << endl;}

int main()
{
    fish bigfish;

    bigfish.breathe();

    return 0;
}
```

Here's what this example, animalclassabstractclass.cpp, displays when you run it:

```
%animalclassabstractclass
Bubbling...
```

Creating Has-a Relationships

As mentioned in the In Depth section of this chapter, inheritance is based on "is-a" relationships. For example, say you derive the **elephant** class from the **animal** class:

```
#include <iostream>
using namespace std;

class animal
{
public:
    void eat();
    void sleep();
    void breathe();
};

class elephant : public animal
{
public:
    void trumpet();
    void stampede();
};
```

Here, the relationship between animal and elephant is an "is-a" relationship; that is, elephant "is-a" type of animal. There are other types of relationships between objects, however, such as "has-a" relationships. In that case, one object contains another. Here's an example, animalclasscontainment.cpp. Here, I'll create a new class named **legs** with one method, **walk**:

```
#include <iostream>
using namespace std;

class legs
{
public:
    void walk(){cout << "Walking..." << endl;}
```

```
};
    .
    .
    .
```

Then I embed an object of the **legs** class in the **animal** class—in other words, **animal** "has-a" **legs**:

```
#include <iostream>
using namespace std;

class legs
{
public:
    void walk(){cout << "Walking..." << endl;}
};

class animal
{
    legs l;
    .
    .
    .
```

Now I'm free to use this object's **walk** method in the methods of the **animal** class:

```
#include <iostream>
using namespace std;

class legs
{
public:
    void walk(){cout << "Walking..." << endl;}
};

class animal
{
    legs l;
public:
    void eat();
    void sleep();
    void breathe();
    void walk(){l.walk();}
};
```

```
void animal::eat(){cout << "Eating..." << endl;}
void animal::sleep(){cout << "Sleeping..." << endl;}
void animal::breathe(){cout << "Breathing..." << endl;}

int main()
{
    animal jumbo;

    jumbo.eat();
    jumbo.breathe();
    jumbo.sleep();
    jumbo.walk();

    return 0;
}
```

Here's what you see when you run this program, animalclasscontainment.cpp:

```
%animalclasscontainment
Eating...
Breathing...
Sleeping...
Walking...
```

You can also use contained objects in a constructor initialization list like this, where I'm assigning the contained object **name** the string "James":

```
person::person() : name("James")
{
    .
    .
    .
}
```

Using Private Inheritance

When you derive a class from a base class, you use this syntax—***access_specifier*** can be **public**, **private**, or **protected**, and ***base_class*** is the name of the base class:

```
class name [: access_specifier base_class [, access_specifier
```

```
base_class...]]
{
private:
    private data members and methods
protected:
    protected data members and methods
public:
    private data members and methods
}[object_list...];
```

I've used public inheritance throughout this chapter—that is, I use the access specifier **public** when specifying how to derive a new class from a base class:

```
class elephant : public animal
{
public:
    void trumpet();
    void stampede();
};
```

Here, the private members of **animal** are not available in **elephant**, but the public members of **animal** become public in **elephant**, and the protected members of **animal** become protected in **elephant**.

However, there are two other possible access specifiers—**private** and **protected**. We'll take a look at **private** in this section and **protected** in the next. When you use private inheritance, the public and protected members of the base class become *private* members of the derived class. In fact, you can think of private inheritance as implementing a has-a relationship (see the previous topic) more than a is-a relationship, because the base class is far more contained than in public inheritance.

Here's an example, animalclassprivateinheritance.cpp; in this code, I'll derive the **elephant** class from the **animal** class using private inheritance. Note that the methods of the **animal** class are no longer available from an object of the **elephant** class, because those methods are now private, so if I want to call one, I have to implement that call from code inside the **elephant** class, as with the **breathe** method:

```
#include <iostream>
using namespace std;
```

```
class animal
{
protected:
    void breathe();
public:
    void eat();
    void sleep();
};

class elephant : private animal
{
public:
    void trumpet();
    void stampede();
    void breathe();
};

void animal::eat(){cout << "Eating..." << endl;}
void animal::sleep(){cout << "Sleeping..." << endl;}
void animal::breathe(){cout << "Breathing..." << endl;}

void elephant::trumpet(){cout << "Trumpeting..." << endl;}
void elephant::stampede(){cout << "Stampeding..." << endl;}
void elephant::breathe(){animal::breathe();}

int main()
{
    elephant jumbo;

    jumbo.breathe();
    jumbo.trumpet();
    jumbo.stampede();

    return 0;
}
```

Here's what the program animalclassprivateinheritance.cpp displays when you run it:

```
%animalclassprivateinheritance
Breathing...
Trumpeting...
Stampeding...
```

Besides private inheritance, you can also use protected inheritance—see the next section.

***TIP:** Want to use private inheritance but still keep a few members of the base class public, not private, in the derived class? Take a look at "Defining Access with **using**" later in this chapter.*

Using Protected Inheritance

When you derive a class from a base class, you use this syntax—***access_specifier*** can be **public**, **private**, or **protected**, and ***base_class*** is the name of the base class:

```
class name [: access_specifier base_class [, access_specifier
base_class...]]
{
private:
    private data members and methods
protected:
    protected data members and methods
public:
    private data members and methods
}[object_list...];
```

We've already seen public and private inheritance in this chapter, and we'll take a look at protected inheritance in this section. When you derive a base class using the **protected** access specifier, the public and protected members of the base class become protected members of the derived class (the private members of the base class are not available to the derived class). Protected inheritance is often a good technique to use when you derive a class based on a class that was not written for inheritance, because it converts public members of the base class, which you might not want to expose, to protected members of the derived class.

Here's an example, animalclassprotectedinheritance.cpp. In this case, I'll use protected inheritance, which means that any public or protected members of the **animal** class become protected members of the **elephant** class. That, in turn, means they're not available from outside **elephant**, so if I want to call an **animal** class method using an **elephant** class object, I have to call that method using code in the **elephant** object, as with the **breathe** method:

```
#include <iostream>
using namespace std;
```

```
class animal
{
public:
    void eat();
    void sleep();
    void breathe();
};

class elephant : protected animal
{
public:
    void trumpet();
    void stampede();
    void breathe();
};

void animal::eat(){cout << "Eating..." << endl;}
void animal::sleep(){cout << "Sleeping..." << endl;}
void animal::breathe(){cout << "Breathing..." << endl;}

void elephant::trumpet(){cout << "Trumpeting..." << endl;}
void elephant::stampede(){cout << "Stampeding..." << endl;}
void elephant::breathe(){animal::breathe();}

int main()
{
    elephant jumbo;

    jumbo.breathe();
    jumbo.trumpet();
    jumbo.stampede();

    return 0;
}
```

Here's what you see when you run this program, animalclass-protectedinheritance.cpp:

```
%animalclassprotectedinheritance
Breathing...
Trumpeting...
Stampeding...
```

TIP: *Want to use protected inheritance but still keep a few members of the base class public, not protected, in the derived class? Take a look at "Defining Access with* ***using****" next in this chapter.*

Defining Access with **using**

What if you use private or protected inheritance but suddenly realize that you still want to leave some public members of the base class public in the derived class? Do you have to switch to public inheritance and worry about members that then become public but that you'd rather leave private or protected? No—you can use the keyword **using** to declare the access of specific base class members in the derived class. This keyword allows you to redefine the access of individual base class members in a derived class.

Here's an example, animalclassusing.cpp. In this case, I'll use private inheritance when I derive the **elephant** class from the **animal** class this way:

```
#include <iostream>
using namespace std;

class animal
{
public:
    void eat();
    void sleep();
    void breathe();
};

class elephant : private animal
{
        .
        .
        .
```

Using private inheritance makes all the public methods of the **animal** class private. But what if you want to make the animal class's **breathe** method public in **elephant**? You can do that by declaring **breathe** with **using** in the public section of the **elephant** class definition (note that I declare **breathe** using its fully qualified name, but no argument list):

```
#include <iostream>
using namespace std;
```

```
class animal
{
public:
    void eat();
    void sleep();
    void breathe();
};

class elephant : private animal
{
public:
    void trumpet();
    void stampede();
    using animal::breathe;
};
    .
    .
    .
```

That's how it works—you use **using** to redefine the access of a base class's member and specify the kind of access you want, **public**, **protected**, or **private**. Now **breathe** becomes a public method of the **elephant** class, so I can call it directly:

```
#include <iostream>
using namespace std;

class animal
{
public:
    void eat();
    void sleep();
    void breathe();
};

class elephant : private animal
{
public:
    void trumpet();
    void stampede();
    using animal::breathe;
};

void animal::eat(){cout << "Eating..." << endl;}
void animal::sleep(){cout << "Sleeping..." << endl;}
```

```
void animal::breathe(){cout << "Breathing..." << endl;}

void elephant::trumpet(){cout << "Trumpeting..." << endl;}
void elephant::stampede(){cout << "Stampeding..." << endl;}

int main()
{
    elephant jumbo;

    jumbo.breathe();
    jumbo.trumpet();
    jumbo.stampede();

    return 0;
}
```

Here's what you see when you run this code, animalclassusing.cpp:

```
%animalclassusing
Breathing...
Trumpeting...
Stampeding...
```

Here's one thing to note—you used to be able to redefine access without the **using** keyword, like this:

```
class elephant : private animal
{
public:
    void trumpet();
    void stampede();
    animal::breathe;
};
```

However, this way of doing things is now *deprecated*, that is, it's being phased out.

Creating Class Libraries

When you create a number of classes designed to be used as base classes, you should consider creating a class library. Many of the big C++ compiler packages come with class libraries, and you can derive your own classes from the classes in those libraries.

How class libraries are implemented varies by system. Typically, the code in a class library is compiled code that you can use with your compiler's linker. The details depend on your installation; in this section, we'll take a look at creating a class library using Borland C++. Here, I'll create a class library file named animal.lib that will contain the compiled definition and methods of the **animal** class. Here's the file that defines the **animal** class and its methods, animalclasssource.cpp:

```
#include <iostream>
using namespace std;

class animal
{
public:
    void eat();
    void sleep();
    void breathe();
};

void animal::eat(){cout << "Eating..." << endl;}
void animal::sleep(){cout << "Sleeping..." << endl;}
void animal::breathe(){cout << "Breathing..." << endl;}
```

After compiling this file into animalclasssource.obj, I can use the library tool, tlib, that comes with Borland C++ to create the library file animal.lib:

```
%tlib animal.lib +animalclasssource.obj
```

I'm ready to use this class library now. First, I define a header file, animal, that will tell the compiler about the **animal** class:

```
class animal
{
public:
    void eat();
    void sleep();
    void breathe();
};
```

To put the class library to work, you include this header file, animal, in your code, as I've done here in an example named animalclassuselib.cpp. After you've included the header, you can make use of the **animal** class as you like:

```
#include <iostream>
#include "animal"
using namespace std;

class elephant : public animal
{
public:
    void trumpet();
    void stampede();
};

void elephant::trumpet(){cout << "Trumpeting..." << endl;}
void elephant::stampede(){cout << "Stampeding..." << endl;}

int main()
{
    elephant jumbo;

    jumbo.breathe();
    jumbo.trumpet();
    jumbo.stampede();

    return 0;
}
```

Finally, when I compile animalclassuselib.cpp, I also link in animal.lib so the linker can find the compiled version of the **animal** class (the compiler switches below tell the compiler where to search for include and system library files, and they turn warnings on):

```
%bcc32 -Ic:\bcc\include -w -Lc:\bcc\lib animalclassuselib.cpp animal.lib
```

And that's all you need. Storing your classes in class library files can save you considerable development time, and if you're building a number of base classes, creating pre-compiled class libraries is something you should consider.

Chapter 11

Multiple Inheritance and Class Templates

In Depth

In the previous chapter, we took a look at the issue of code reuse through inheritance, and this chapter continues that theme. In this chapter, we'll continue on to discuss inheriting multiple base classes and how to create *class templates* that let you instantiate classes using various data types. These topics are central to both the major thrusts that differentiate C++ from C—object-oriented programming and generic programming.

Multiple Inheritance

Using multiple inheritance, you can create a single derived class from several base classes. For example, you might have a class named **zoo** that inherits various animal classes, or a class named **staff** that inherits various employee classes—**manager**, **vice_president**, **director**, and so on.

In C++, multiple inheritance is actually a little controversial (in fact, some programmers want multiple inheritance removed from C++), because with multiple base classes, it's easy to have conflicts with both classes and methods. For example, if you have a class named **zoo** that inherits both the **anaconda** and **zebra** classes, each base class might define a different version of the method **walk**, which would then conflict. Part of our coverage of multiple inheritance will be to see how C++ deals with such conflicts.

***NOTE:** Some other languages, like Java, don't really support multiple inheritance, for the reason mentioned here—to avoid conflicts. Instead, Java uses interfaces made up of unimplemented methods to offer some multiple inheritance support.*

How do you implement multiple inheritance? You indicate that a new class is derived from multiple base classes simply by giving a comma-separated list of those base classes when you derive the new class. For example, here's how to create the **zoo** class, based on the **anaconda** and **zebra** classes in an example named animalclassmultipleinheritance.cpp—note that you can specify **public**, **protected**, or **private** inheritance for each base class:

```
#include <iostream>
using namespace std;
```

```
class anaconda
{
public:
    void slither() {cout << "Slithering..." << endl;}
};

class zebra
{
public:
    void saunter() {cout << "Sauntering..." << endl;}
};

class zoo : public anaconda, public zebra
{
public:
    void close() {cout << "Sorry, we're closed..." << endl;}
};

int main()
{
    zoo z;

    z.slither();
    z.saunter();

    return 0;
}
```

The **anaconda** class has a method named **slither**, and the **zebra** class has a method named **saunter**—and because both those classes are base classes of **zoo**, a **zoo** object can call both those methods, as you see when you run the program:

```
%animalclassmultipleinheritance
Slithering...
Sauntering...
```

What if both the **anaconda** class and the **zebra** class define the same method, called **eat**? If you have a **zoo** object named **z**, which method would **z.eat** refer to? As far as the compiler is concerned, there's no problem here at all—because there is no way for it to decide between **anaconda::eat** and **zebra::eat**, the call is ambiguous, and the compiler will give you an error and quit. On the other hand, conflicts can be a little more complicated—for example, what if both the **anaconda** class and the **zebra** class are themselves based on the same class, like the **animal** class we saw in Chapter 10? When you create an object of the **zoo** class in that case, *two* internal objects of the **animal** class will be created, one inside **anaconda** and one inside **zebra**. If you call an **animal** class method, the compiler will have no way to distinguish between the two **animal** objects, and again the call will be ambiguous. This time, however, C++ offers a way to fix the problem.

Virtual Base Classes

In this case, there really shouldn't be a conflict, because the **animal** class methods are the same no matter which of the two internal **animal** objects you use. C++ allows you create just one shared internal object if you make that object's class *virtual*. Take a look at this code, animalclassvirtualbaseclass.cpp, to see how this works—in this case, I'll derive the **anaconda** and **zebra** classes from the same base class, **animal**, and use virtual inheritance with the keyword **virtual** to create **anaconda** and **zebra**:

```
#include <iostream>
using namespace std;

class animal
{
public:
    void eat() {cout << "Eating..." << endl;};
    void sleep() {cout << "Sleeping..." << endl;};
    void breathe() {cout << "Breathing..." << endl;};
};

class anaconda : public virtual animal
{
    void walk() {cout << "Slithering..." << endl;}
};

class zebra : public virtual animal
{
    void walk() {cout << "Sauntering..." << endl;}
};

class zoo : public anaconda, public zebra
{
public:
    void close() {cout << "Sorry, we're closed..." << endl;}
};

int main()
{
```

```
    zoo z;

    z.eat();
    z.breathe();
    z.sleep();

    return 0;
}
```

Now when you create a **zoo** object, only one internal **animal** object is created, even though both **zoo** base classes, **anaconda** and **zebra**, share that class as a base class. Because there's only one **animal** base class, there's no ambiguity when you use the **eat**, **breathe**, and **sleep** methods, so the program runs without problem:


```
%animalclassvirtualbaseclass
Eating...
Breathing...
Sleeping...
```

NOTE: *Why do you use the keyword* ***virtual*** *here instead of one that would really fit, like* ***shared****? You use* ***virtual*** *here partly because you use virtual when defining methods that are designed to be overridden (see "Virtual Methods and Runtime Polymorphism" in Chapter 10), but also partly because the C++ community is very resistant to new keywords. In any case, we're stuck with* ***virtual*** *here. In fact, this keyword is one of my pet peeves—creating only one shared object instead of multiple ones in cases like this should actually be C++'s default behavior, because there's no other possible interpretation.*

Things can get complex here too, however—for example, what if you use constructors in the **anaconda** and **zebra** classes to pass back different arguments to the **animal** class's constructor? Because the program can create only one shared object if the two internal **animal** objects are really identical, C++ disables the automatic passing of arguments through intermediate classes to a shared base class when the base class is virtual. In such cases, the program will call the base class's default (that is, without argument) constructor. However, you can specify arguments for the shared base class object directly—see "Virtual Base Classes and Constructors" later in this chapter for more information on what happens here.

Class Templates

We saw function templates in Chapter 7 and, as you recall, you can use a function template to instantiate functions, much the way you use a cookie cutter to cut cookies. Like function templates, class templates are parameterized—that is, you create class templates to work with unspecified data types, and you specify the data type only when you instantiate a class with the template.

Here's an example, classtemplate.cpp. Creating a class template works much like creating a function template—you use the **template** keyword and give a name, such as **T**, to the type you're creating the template to work with (**T** is called a *type parameter*). In classtemplate.cpp, I'll create a template for an array class named **Array**. When you call this class's constructor, you pass the number of elements in the array to the constructor, and each element will be of the type **T**. I'll also override the [] operator so you can use objects of this class as you would any array (in fact, we'll even be able to use this class template recursively to create multidimensional arrays—see "Using Class Templates Recursively and As Base Classes" later in this chapter). I start by indicating that I'm creating a class template for the **Array** class based on the unspecified type I'm naming **T**:

```
#include <iostream>
using namespace std;

template <class T>
class Array
{
        .
        .
        .
}
```

In the **Array** class itself, I'll allocate the memory for the new array using **new** and store the pointer to the new array as **ptr_to_array**, as well as the number of items in the array. Here's what that looks like—note that you pass the number of elements you want in the array to the constructor as an integer, so I'm making the constructor explicit to avoid unintentional "conversions" from integers (see "Conversions to and from Objects" in Chapter 9)—note that you begin the definition of class methods outside the class template with **template<*parameter_list*>**:

```
#include <iostream>
using namespace std;

template <class T>
class Array
{
    T *ptr_to_array;
    int number;
public:
    explicit Array(int number_of_elements);
```

```
    T& operator[](int index) {return ptr_to_array[index];}
};

template <class T>
Array<T>::Array(int number_of_elements)
{
    number = number_of_elements;
    ptr_to_array = new T[number];
}
    .
    .
    .
```


Now I'm ready to create an object of the **Array** class. To do that, I only need to specify the type of elements I want in the array and pass the number of elements I want to allocate space for to the constructor, and then I'm free to use the new **Array** object with the [] operator:

```
#include <iostream>
using namespace std;

template <class T>
class Array
{
    T *ptr_to_array;
    int number;
public:
    explicit Array(int number_of_elements);
    T& operator[](int index) {return ptr_to_array[index];}
};

template <class T>
Array<T>::Array(int number_of_elements)
{
    number = number_of_elements;
    ptr_to_array = new T[number];
}

int main()
{
    const int student_number = 5;
    Array<float> scores(10);

    scores[student_number] = 85;
```

```
    cout << "Student number " << student_number << " scored "
        << scores[student_number] << endl;

    return 0;
}
```


Here's what this program, classtemplate.cpp, displays when you run it:

```
%classtemplate
Student number 5 scored 85
```

NOTE: *You might have noticed that because we're storing the array data using a pointer, the* ***Array*** *class should have a copy constructor, an assignment operator, and a destructor. Right you are—see "Using Pointers in Class Templates" later in this chapter.*

You can also use multiple type parameters in a class template—see "Using Class Templates with Multiple Types" later in this chapter. In fact, class templates are very versatile in C++; you can use friend methods in them:

```
template <class T>
class animal
{
    friend friend_method();
       .
       .
       .
};
```

You can even use nested classes in class templates if you wish. We'll see all the details in the Immediate Solutions section, and we'll move on to that section now.

Immediate Solutions

Inheriting Multiple Base Classes

You can derive a class from multiple base classes in C++ just by specifying a list of base classes—each their own access specifier—in a comma-separated list when you create the derived class:

```
class name [: access_specifier base_class [, access_specifier base_class...]]
{
private:
    private data members and methods
protected:
    protected data members and methods
public:
    private data members and methods
}[object_list...];
```

We saw an example, animalclassmultipleinheritance.cpp, in the In Depth section of this chapter. In that example, I derived a class named **zoo** from two base classes, **anaconda** and **zebra**:

```
#include <iostream>
using namespace std;

class anaconda
{
public:
    void slither() {cout << "Slithering..." << endl;}
};

class zebra
{
public:
    void saunter() {cout << "Sauntering..." << endl;}
};

class zoo : public anaconda, public zebra
{
```

```
public:
    void close() {cout << "Sorry, we're closed..." << endl;}
};
```


Now I can use this new class, **zoo**, and all the methods it's inherited from **anaconda** and **zebra**:

```
#include <iostream>
using namespace std;

class anaconda
{
public:
    void slither() {cout << "Slithering..." << endl;}
};

class zebra
{
public:
    void saunter() {cout << "Sauntering..." << endl;}
};

class zoo : public anaconda, public zebra
{
public:
};

int main()
{
    zoo z;

    z.slither();
    z.saunter();

    return 0;
}
```

Here's what you see when you run animalclassmultipleinheritance.cpp—note that the **zoo** object in this program has access to both the **anaconda::slither** method and the **zebra::saunter** method:

```
%animalclassmultipleinheritance
Slithering...
Sauntering...
```

As mentioned in the In Depth section of this chapter, one of the biggest problems with multiple inheritance is the conflicts it can create—for example, what if two base classes define a method with the same name and argument list? Take a look at the next section for the details.

Specifying Base Class Method Calls

What if multiple base classes define the same method? How do you handle such conflicts? That's one of the issues you have to face in multiple inheritance, and we'll take a look at it here. For example, say that the **anaconda** and **zebra** classes that are the base classes of the **zoo** class both define the same method, **walk**, but with different code? Which one should the compiler choose when you call **walk** from a **zoo** object? If the methods have different argument lists, the compiler has no problem, but what happens if **anaconda::walk** and **zebra::walk** have the same signatures?

There are two main ways to resolve the problem: First, you can use the scope resolution operator to specify which method to call. For example, if you have a **zoo** object named **z** and want to call **anaconda::walk**, you can call it as **z.anaconda::walk**. Second, you can define a **walk** method in the **zoo** class itself that specifically calls the base class method you want. Here's how those techniques are implemented in a new example, animalclassmultiplemethods.cpp:

```
#include <iostream>
using namespace std;

class anaconda
{
public:
    void walk() {cout << "Slithering..." << endl;}
};

class zebra
{
public:
    void walk() {cout << "Sauntering..." << endl;}
};

class zoo : public anaconda, public zebra
{
public:
```

```
    void walk() {zebra::walk();}
};

int main()
{
    zoo z;

    z.anaconda::walk();
    z.walk();

    return 0;
}
```


Here's what you see when you run this code, animalclassmultiplemethods.cpp:

```
%animalclassmultiplemethods
Slithering...
Sauntering...
```

Using Virtual Base Classes

Something you have to be careful about with multiple inheritance is the conflicts between base classes. For example, what if you create the **zoo** class from two base classes, **anaconda** and **zebra**, and the two base classes are themselves both derived from the **animal** class? When you create an object of the **zoo** class, two internal objects of the **animal** class will be created, and if you call any **animal** class methods from the **zoo** object, the compiler won't know which **animal** object to use. To fix that, you make **animal** a virtual base class, which means that only one shared internal object of that class will be created.

To indicate that a base class is shared and only one internal object of that class should be created, you use virtual inheritance, using the **virtual** keyword. Here's an example, animalclassvirtualbaseclass.cpp, that we saw in the beginning of this chapter showing how to use **virtual** to make base classes virtual:

```
#include <iostream>
using namespace std;

class animal
{
public:
    void eat() {cout << "Eating..." << endl;};
```

```
    void sleep() {cout << "Sleeping..." << endl;};
    void breathe() {cout << "Breathing..." << endl;};
};

class anaconda : public virtual animal
{
    void walk() {cout << "Slithering..." << endl;}
};

class zebra : public virtual animal
{
    void walk() {cout << "Sauntering..." << endl;}
};
    .
    .
    .
```

Now I can use the **animal** class methods without conflict, even though it's a base class of both **anaconda** and **zebra**:

```
#include <iostream>
using namespace std;

class animal
{
public:
    void eat() {cout << "Eating..." << endl;};
    void sleep() {cout << "Sleeping..." << endl;};
    void breathe() {cout << "Breathing..." << endl;};
};

class anaconda : public virtual animal
{
    void walk() {cout << "Slithering..." << endl;}
};

class zebra : public virtual animal
{
    void walk() {cout << "Sauntering..." << endl;}
};

class zoo : public anaconda, public zebra
{
public:
    void close() {cout << "Sorry, we're closed..." << endl;}
```

```
};

int main()
{
    zoo z;

    z.eat();
    z.breathe();
    z.sleep();

    return 0;
}
```

Here's what you see when you run animalclassvirtualbaseclass.cpp:

```
%animalclassvirtualbaseclass
Eating...
Breathing...
Sleeping...
```

Using virtual inheritance in this way lets you avoid conflicts between shared base classes. But what if the base classes have constructors? See the next section.

Virtual Base Classes and Constructors

The previous section discussed how to use virtual base classes, but there's more to talk about. For example, what if you use constructors in the **anaconda** and **zebra** classes to pass back different arguments to the **animal** class's constructor? Because the program can create only one shared object if the two **animal** objects are really identical, C++ *disables* the automatic passing of arguments through intermediate classes to a shared base class when the base class is virtual. In such cases, the program will call the base class's default (that is, without argument) constructor instead. For example, say that this is the **zoo** class's constructor, which passes back the weight and name of the animal to the **anaconda** and **zebra** constructors:

```
zoo(int weight, string name) : anaconda(weight, name), zebra(weight,name){}
```

In this case, the **anaconda** and **zebra** constructors won't be allowed to pass back data like the weight and name to the **animal** class constructor. However, you *can* specify arguments for a virtual base class's constructor if you call it explicitly.

Here's an example, animalclassmultipleconstructors.cpp, where I do that. In this case, I've added constructors to all the classes like this:

```
#include <iostream>
#include <string>
using namespace std;

class animal
{
    string name;
public:
    void eat() {cout << "Eating..." << endl;};
    void sleep() {cout << "Sleeping..." << endl;};
    void breathe() {cout << "Breathing..." << endl;};
    animal(string s) {name = s;}
};

class anaconda : public virtual animal
{
    int weight;
public:
    void walk() {cout << "Slithering..." << endl;}
    anaconda(int w, string s) : animal(s){weight = w;}
};

class zebra : public virtual animal
{
    int weight;
public:
    void walk() {cout << "Sauntering..." << endl;}
    zebra(int w, string s) : animal(s){weight = w;}
};
        .
        .
        .
```

Now note how I call the **animal** class's constructor explicitly with the **name** argument when defining the **zoo** class's constructor, and note that I call it before the **anaconda** or **zebra** constructors:

```
#include <iostream>
#include <string>
using namespace std;
```

```
class animal
{
    string name;
public:
    void eat() {cout << "Eating..." << endl;};
    void sleep() {cout << "Sleeping..." << endl;};
    void breathe() {cout << "Breathing..." << endl;};
    animal(string s) {name = s;}
};

class anaconda : public virtual animal
{
    int weight;
public:
    void walk() {cout << "Slithering..." << endl;}
    anaconda(int w, string s) : animal(s){weight = w;}
};

class zebra : public virtual animal
{
    int weight;
public:
    void walk() {cout << "Sauntering..." << endl;}
    zebra(int w, string s) : animal(s){weight = w;}
};

class zoo : public anaconda, public zebra
{
public:
    zoo(int weight, string name) : animal(name), anaconda(weight, name),
        zebra(weight,name){}
};

int main()
{
    zoo z(1000, "Franklin");

    z.eat();
    z.breathe();
    z.sleep();

    return 0;
}
```

Here's what you see when you run animalclassmultipleconstructors.cpp:

```
%animalclassmultipleconstructors
Eating...
Breathing...
Sleeping...
```


Dominance of Virtual Base Classes

Besides those we've seen in this chapter, C++ defines another rule to resolve conflicts between virtual base classes in multiple inheritance—*dominance*. The rule here is that class members in a derived class that conflict with members in a virtual base class *dominate* the base class's members.

Here's an example, animalclassdominance.cpp, to make this clearer. In this case, the virtual base class **animal** defines a method named **eat**, and so does the **anaconda** class derived from it. In this case, **anaconda::eat** dominates **animal::eat**:

```
#include <iostream>
using namespace std;

class animal
{
public:
    void eat() {cout << "Eating..." << endl;};
    void sleep() {cout << "Sleeping..." << endl;};
    void breathe() {cout << "Breathing..." << endl;};
};

class anaconda : public virtual animal
{
public:
    void eat() {cout << "Swallowing..." << endl;}
};

class zebra : public virtual animal
{
public:
    void walk() {cout << "Sauntering..." << endl;}
};
```

```
class zoo : public anaconda, public zebra
{
public:
    void close() {cout << "Sorry, we're closed..." << endl;}
};

int main()
{
    zoo z;

    z.eat();

    return 0;
}
```

You can see that **anaconda::eat** dominates **animal::eat** when you run this code:

```
%animalclassdominance
Swallowing...
```

Defining Class Templates

You use class templates to create templates for classes using unspecified data types, and you specify the data type only when you instantiate a class with the template. Creating a class template works much like creating a function template—you use the **template** keyword and give a name, like **T**, to the type you're creating the class for (**T** is called a type parameter):

```
template <parameter_list>
class name
{
    .
    .
    .
}
```

In the classtemplate.cpp example we saw in the In Depth section of this chapter, I created a template for an array class named **Array**. When you call this class's constructor, you pass the number of elements to place in the array, and each element will be of the type **T**. I'll also override the [] operator so you can use objects of this class as you would any array. I start by setting up the class template itself with the keyword **template**, and follow it with the parameters I want to use in the template, enclosed by < and >. In this case, I want to use only one parameter, **T**, which specifies the type of the elements that will be stored in the array:

```
template <class T>
class Array
{
    T *ptr_to_array;
    int number;
public:
    explicit Array(int number_of_elements);
    T& operator[](int index) {return ptr_to_array[index];}
};
    .
    .
    .
```

This is a template for a class named **Array<T>**. Now you can define the class methods; to define a method outside the class template, you preface the definition with **template *<parameter_list>*** this way:

```
template <class T>
class Array
{
    T *ptr_to_array;
    int number;
public:
    explicit Array(int number_of_elements);
    T& operator[](int index) {return ptr_to_array[index];}
};

template <class T>
Array<T>::Array(int number_of_elements)
{
    number = number_of_elements;
    ptr_to_array = new T[number];
}
```

How do you use this template to instantiate a class? Take a look at the next section.

NOTE: *Because class templates define only types and you can compile only instantiations, you can't place templates in files by themselves and compile those files (unless your compiler supports the* ***export*** *keyword). Class templates are great in header files, though.*

Using a Class Template

In the previous section, I created a class template for the **Array** class, and I'll put it to use in this section. To instantiate a class from that template, you have to specify the type or types you want it to use (such as **float**)—unlike with function templates, which can use the function arguments you specify to decide how to instantiate a function. Here's how that looks in the example classtemplate.cpp—in this case, I'm creating an array of floating point values named **scores** with 10 elements:

```
#include <iostream>
using namespace std;

template <class T>
class Array
{
    T *ptr_to_array;
    int number;
public:
    explicit Array(int number_of_elements);
    T& operator[](int index) {return ptr_to_array[index];}
};

template <class T>
Array<T>::Array(int number_of_elements)
{
    number = number_of_elements;
    ptr_to_array = new T[number];
}

int main()
{
    const int student_number = 5;
    Array<float> scores(10);

    scores[student_number] = 85;

    cout << "Student number " << student_number << " scored "
        << scores[student_number] << endl;

    return 0;
}
```

Here's what this program, classtemplate.cpp, displays when you run it:

```
%classtemplate
Student number 5 scored 85
```

Here, I've used an implicit template instantiation—that is, the compiler will instantiate the correct version of the **Array** class based on the declaration of the **scores** array. You can also instantiate classes explicitly—see "Creating Explicit Template Specializations" later in this chapter.

Using Pointers in Class Templates

What if you want to store pointers in the class you're creating templates for? Such classes follow the same rules as any other classes that store pointers—they'll need a copy constructor, an assignment operator, and a destructor. Here's how I modify the classtemplate.cpp example we've seen in the previous two sections so that the template for the **Array** class supports those items:

```
#include <iostream>
using namespace std;

template <class T>
class Array
{
    T *ptr_to_array;
    int number;
public:
    Array(int number_of_elements);
    Array(const Array & a);
    ~Array();
    T& operator= (const Array & a);
    T& operator[](int index) {return ptr_to_array[index];}
};

template <class T>
Array<T>::Array(int number_of_elements)
{
    number = number_of_elements;
    ptr_to_array = new T[number];
}
```

```
template <class T>
Array<T>::Array(const Array & a)
{
    number = a.number;
    T *ptr_to_array = new T[number];

    for(int loop_index = 0; loop_index < number; loop_index++) {
        ptr_to_array[loop_index] = a.ptr_to_array[loop_index];
    }
}

template <class T>
T& Array<T>::operator= (const Array & a)
{
    if(this == &a) return *this;
    delete[] ptr_to_array;

    number = a.number;
    T *ptr_to_array = new T[number];

    for(int loop_index = 0; loop_index < number; loop_index++) {
        ptr_to_array[loop_index] = a.ptr_to_array[loop_index];
    }
    return *this;
}

template <class T>
Array<T>::~Array()
{
    delete[] ptr_to_array;
}

int main()
{
    const int student_number = 5;
    Array<float> scores(10);

    scores[student_number] = 85;

    cout << "Student number " << student_number << " scored "
        << scores[student_number] << endl;

    return 0;
}
```

Now the code works as before, but it's much safer, because the pointers inside objects of the **Array** class are handled properly.

Note also that you can use the **Array** class to store pointers—there's no problem with that, but if you copy an **Array** object into another, the second object's pointers will point to the same data as the first **Array** object's pointers.

NOTE: *For an example showing how to store pointers in the* ***Array*** *class, see "Using Different Object Types with the Same Type Parameter" later in this chapter.*

Using Non-Type Arguments in Class Templates

What if you want to pass, say, an integer value to a class template? For example, the **Array** class template we've developed over the previous few sections lets you specify the type of elements you want to store in the array:

```
template <class T>
class Array
{
      .
      .
      .
}
```

But what if you want to pass an integer to this template to specify, for example, the initial value each element that the array should have? Can you do something like this?

```
template <class T, int initial_value>
class Array
{
      .
      .
      .
}
```

Yes, you can, and here's an example, classtemplatenontype.cpp, that shows how. When you include non-type parameters in a template, you name those parameters and then you can refer to them just as if they were passed to code in a class method. In this case, you can set the initial value of array elements by specifying a value for the **initial_value** parameter, which I use in the array's constructor (for the sake of simplicity, this parameter is of type **int**, from which it's easiest for the compiler to make implicit conversions to other types). Note that I now create an array with the declaration **Array<float, 50> scores(10)**, which gives each of the 10 **float** elements the initial value of 50:

```
#include <iostream>
using namespace std;

template <class T, int initial_value>
class Array
{
    T *ptr_to_array;
    int number;
public:
    explicit Array(int number_of_elements);
    Array(const Array & a);
    ~Array();
    T& operator= (const Array & a);
    T& operator[](int index) {return ptr_to_array[index];}
};

template <class T, int initial_value>
Array<T, initial_value>::Array(int number_of_elements)
{
    number = number_of_elements;
    ptr_to_array = new T[number];

    for(int loop_index = 0; loop_index < number; loop_index++) {
        ptr_to_array[loop_index] = initial_value;
    }
}

template <class T, int initial_value>
Array<T, initial_value>::Array(const Array & a)
{
    number = a.number;
    T *ptr_to_array = new T[number];

    for(int loop_index = 0; loop_index < number; loop_index++) {
        ptr_to_array[loop_index] = a.ptr_to_array[loop_index];
    }
}
```

```
template <class T, int initial_value>
T& Array<T, initial_value>::operator= (const Array & a)
{
    if(this == &a) return *this;
    delete[] ptr_to_array;

    number = a.number;
    T *ptr_to_array = new T[number];

    for(int loop_index = 0; loop_index < number; loop_index++) {
        ptr_to_array[loop_index] = a.ptr_to_array[loop_index];
    }
    return *this;
}

template <class T, int initial_value>
Array<T, initial_value>::~Array()
{
    delete[] ptr_to_array;
}

int main()
{
    const int student_number = 5;
    Array<float, 50> scores(10);

    cout << "Student number " << student_number << " scored "
        << scores[student_number] << endl;

    return 0;
}
```

Here's what you see when you run this example, classtemplatenontype.cpp:

```
%classtemplatenontype
Student number 5 scored 50
```

Here's another example, classtemplatesetnumber.cpp. In the example we've already seen, classtemplate.cpp, you set the number of elements in the array by passing that number to the **Array** class's constructor like this, where I'm creating an array of 10 float elements:

```
Array<float> scores(10);
```

However, you can also pass the number of elements to create in the array as a non-type template parameter, making this declaration look like this instead:

```
Array<float, 10> scores;
```

Here's what the code for classtemplatesetnumber.cpp looks like; note that I've added a non-type parameter to the class template, **number_of_elements**, and I use that parameter in the constructor to create the array:

```
#include <iostream>
using namespace std;

template <class T, int number_of_elements>
class Array
{
    T *ptr_to_array;
public:
    explicit Array();
    Array(const Array & a);
    ~Array();
    T& operator= (const Array & a);
    T& operator[](int index) {return ptr_to_array[index];}
};

template <class T, int number_of_elements>
Array<T, number_of_elements>::Array()
{
    ptr_to_array = new T[number_of_elements];
}

template <class T, int number_of_elements>
Array<T, number_of_elements>::Array(const Array & a)
{
    number_of_elements = a.number_of_elements;
    T *ptr_to_array = new T[number_of_elements];

    for(int loop_index = 0; loop_index < number_of_elements; loop_index++) {
        ptr_to_array[loop_index] = a.ptr_to_array[loop_index];
    }
}

template <class T, int number_of_elements>
T& Array<T, number_of_elements>::operator= (const Array & a)
{
    if(this == &a) return *this;
```

```
    delete[] ptr_to_array;

    number_of_elements = a.number_of_elements;
    T *ptr_to_array = new T[number_of_elements];

    for(int loop_index = 0; loop_index < number_of_elements; loop_index++) {
        ptr_to_array[loop_index] = a.ptr_to_array[loop_index];
    }
    return *this;
}

template <class T, int number_of_elements>
Array<T, number_of_elements>::~Array()
{
    delete[] ptr_to_array;
}

int main()
{
    const int student_number = 5;
    Array<float, 10> scores;

    scores[student_number] = 85;

    cout << "Student number " << student_number << " scored "
        << scores[student_number] << endl;

    return 0;
}
```

Now this program runs just as classtemplate.cpp did, except that I've moved the parameter specifying the number of elements in the array from the class's constructor to the class template:

```
%classtemplatesetnumber
Student number 5 scored 85
```

Using Class Templates with Multiple Types

You're not restricted to using only one type parameter in a class template—you can use multiple type parameters, which means that you can use class templates as templates for classes based on more than one data type.

Here's an example, classtemplatenamed.cpp, that allows you to specify a name for the array. In this case, the class template takes two type parameters; the first one sets the type of the elements in the array, and the second one sets the type for the name of the array (I'll use **string** for this type). You can implement this example simply by adding a new type parameter, **T2**, to the template and using **T2** to declare the **name** member of the array (I'm making **name** public in this example for brevity's sake, but in release code, you should make it private and add access methods):

```
#include <iostream>
#include <string>
using namespace std;

template <class T, class T2>
class Array
{
    T *ptr_to_array;
    int number;
public:
    T2 name;
    explicit Array(int number_of_elements);
    Array(const Array & a);
    ~Array();
    T& operator= (const Array & a);
    T& operator[](int index) {return ptr_to_array[index];}
};

template <class T, class T2>
Array<T, T2>::Array(int number_of_elements)
{
    number = number_of_elements;
    ptr_to_array = new T[number];
}

template <class T, class T2>
Array<T, T2>::Array(const Array & a)
{
    number = a.number;
    T *ptr_to_array = new T[number];

    for(int loop_index = 0; loop_index < number; loop_index++) {
        ptr_to_array[loop_index] = a.ptr_to_array[loop_index];
    }
}
```

```
template <class T, class T2>
T& Array<T, T2>::operator= (const Array & a)
{
    if(this == &a) return *this;
    delete[] ptr_to_array;

    number = a.number;
    T *ptr_to_array = new T[number];

    for(int loop_index = 0; loop_index < number; loop_index++) {
        ptr_to_array[loop_index] = a.ptr_to_array[loop_index];
    }
    return *this;
}

template <class T, class T2>
Array<T, T2>::~Array()
{
    delete[] ptr_to_array;
}

int main()
{
    const int student_number = 5;
    Array<float, string> scores(10);

    scores.name = "Students";

    scores[student_number] = 85;

    cout << "In the " << scores.name << " array, student number "
         << student_number << " scored " << scores[student_number] << endl;

    return 0;
}
```

Now I've been able to name the array "Students", and I can use that name when I display data from the array when I run classtemplatenamed.cpp:

```
%classtemplatenamed
In the Students array, student number 5 scored 85
```

Using Different Object Types with the Same Type Parameter

One of the problems with templates is that when you declare them for a certain type, you're stuck using only that type in instantiations of that template:

```
template <class T>
class Array
{
     .
     .
     .
}
```

Or are you? There is a way to get around this, using runtime polymorphism. As you recall from Chapter 10, runtime polymorphism means that you can load pointers to derived classes into pointers of a base class type (see "Virtual Methods and Runtime Polymorphism" in that chapter). For example, if I have a class named **student** and a class named **exchange_student** derived from that class, then pointers of the **student** type can also hold pointers to **exchange_student** objects. Because the same pointer can point to different types of objects, runtime polymorphism lets you use a class template declared for a single type of object with derived objects as well. All you have to do is instantiate the template using pointers to the base class.

Here's an example, classtemplatemulticlass.cpp. In this example, I'll create the **student** class, derive a new class, **exchange_student**, from that class, and use pointers to objects of both classes in an array created with the array template we've developed throughout this chapter. Here's how I create the **student** and **exhange_student** classes, as well as the array template:

```
#include <iostream>
#include <string>
using namespace std;

template <class T>
class Array
{
    T *ptr_to_array;
    int number;
public:
    explicit Array(int number_of_elements);
    Array(const Array & a);
```

```
    ~Array();
    T& operator= (const Array & a);
    T& operator[](int index) {return ptr_to_array[index];}
};

template <class T>
Array<T>::Array(int number_of_elements)
{
    number = number_of_elements;
    ptr_to_array = new T[number];
}

template <class T>
Array<T>::Array(const Array & a)
{
    number = a.number;
    T *ptr_to_array = new T[number];

    for(int loop_index = 0; loop_index < number; loop_index++) {
        ptr_to_array[loop_index] = a.ptr_to_array[loop_index];
    }
}

template <class T>
T& Array<T>::operator= (const Array & a)
{
    if(this == &a) return *this;
    delete[] ptr_to_array;

    number = a.number;
    T *ptr_to_array = new T[number];

    for(int loop_index = 0; loop_index < number; loop_index++) {
        ptr_to_array[loop_index] = a.ptr_to_array[loop_index];
    }
    return *this;
}

template <class T>
Array<T>::~Array()
{
    delete[] ptr_to_array;
}
```

```
class student
{
public:
    int score;
};

class exchange_student : public student
{
public:
    string home_school;
};
```

Now, in the **main** function, I create a pointer to a **student** object, a pointer to an **exchange_student** object, and an array of 10 elements, each of which is of type **student***, that is, a pointer to the base class:

```
int main()
{
    student *dan = new student;
    exchange_student *jerry = new exchange_student;
    Array<student *> students(10);
    .
    .
    .
```

Next, I'll store data in each new object and store the pointers to each object—even though one is a **student** object and one an **exchange_student** object—in the array. Here's how that looks; after storing the student's data in the array, I display that data to confirm it's been stored accurately:

```
int main()
{
    student *dan = new student;
    exchange_student *jerry = new exchange_student;
    Array<student *> students(10);

    dan->score = 80;
    jerry->score = 85;

    students[0] = dan;
    students[1] = jerry;

    cout << "Dan's score is " << students[0]->score << endl;
    cout << "Jerry's score is " << students[1]->score << endl;
```

```
    return 0;
}
```

Here's what this example, classtemplatemulticlass.cpp, displays when you run it:

```
%classtemplatemulticlass
Dan's score is 80
Jerry's score is 85
```

In this way, even though you can't store data items of different types in the same array, you can at least store pointers to those different types in the same array.

Related solution:	Found on page:
Virtual Methods and Runtime Polymorphism	453

Using Class Templates Recursively and as Base Classes

C++ allows you to use template classes as base classes. In fact, you can use template classes with the normal inheritance syntax, like this:

```
template <class T>
class new_array : public array<T>
{
    .
    .
    .
}
```

You can also use template classes as components in other template classes:

```
template <class T>
class new_array
{
public:
    array<T> old_array;
    .
    .
    .
}
```

You can use class templates recursively if you're careful how you develop them. For example, you can use the **Array** class template we've created in this chapter recursively, which means that you can create multi-dimensional arrays that you can use like this: **scores[0][1]**. Using class templates recursively often takes a little extra thought, but in this case, we're all set, because the [] operator returns a reference to its data:

```
T& operator[](int index) {return ptr_to_array[index];}
```

Multi-dimensional arrays are actually arrays of arrays, which is what makes it possible to use the **Array** class template recursively. In an expression like **scores[0][1]**, the [] operator is called twice—the first time it returns a reference to a one-dimensional array, and the second time it returns a reference to the specific element in that array that's been indexed.

This example is called classtemplaterecursion.cpp, and I'll start it with the **Array** class template:

```
#include <iostream>
using namespace std;

template <class T, int number_of_elements>
class Array
{
    T *ptr_to_array;
public:
    explicit Array();
    Array(const Array & a);
    ~Array();
    T& operator= (const Array & a);
    T& operator[](int index) {return ptr_to_array[index];}
};

template <class T, int number_of_elements>
Array<T, number_of_elements>::Array()
{
    ptr_to_array = new T[number_of_elements];
}

template <class T, int number_of_elements>
Array<T, number_of_elements>::Array(const Array & a)
```

```
{
    number_of_elements = a.number_of_elements;
    T *ptr_to_array = new T[number_of_elements];

    for(int loop_index = 0; loop_index < number_of_elements; loop_index++) {
        ptr_to_array[loop_index] = a.ptr_to_array[loop_index];
    }
}

template <class T, int number_of_elements>
T& Array<T, number_of_elements>::operator= (const Array & a)
{
    if(this == &a) return *this;
    delete[] ptr_to_array;

    number_of_elements = a.number_of_elements;
    T *ptr_to_array = new T[number_of_elements];

    for(int loop_index = 0; loop_index < number_of_elements; loop_index++) {
        ptr_to_array[loop_index] = a.ptr_to_array[loop_index];
    }
    return *this;
}

template <class T, int number_of_elements>
Array<T, number_of_elements>::~Array()
{
    delete[] ptr_to_array;
}
    .
    .
    .
```

Now in the **main** function, I can use the **Array** class template recursively to create a multi-dimensional array named **scores**:

```
int main()
{
    Array<Array<float, 3>, 10> scores;
    .
    .
    .
```

Because we've designed the [] operator of this class template to return reference values, we can call it twice in succession. And because this operator returns a reference, we can set the actual data referred to by such a reference like this:

```
int main()
{
    Array<Array<float, 3>, 10> scores;

    scores[0][1] = 85;
    .
    .
    .
```

This stores the value 85 in **scores[0][1]**, as you can see when we display that value:

```
int main()
{
    Array<Array<float, 3>, 10> scores;

    scores[0][1] = 85;

    cout << "The student scored " << scores[0][1] << endl;

    return 0;
}
```

Here's what you see when you run this example, classtemplaterecursion.cpp:

```
%classtemplaterecursion
The student scored 85
```

As you can see, you can use template classes in the same ways that you can use standard classes—you can use them in inheritance, as components in other classes, and recursively, and you can even nest them.

Creating Explicit Template Specializations

When you declare an object using a class template, the compiler makes an *implicit class instantiation* of the required class using the type or types you specify:

```
int main()
{
```

```
    const int student_number = 5;
    Array<float, 10> scores;
    .
    .
    .
}
```


However, the compiler does not instantiate a class implicitly until it needs an object of that class. On the other hand, there are times when you might want a class instantiation without having an object, such as when you're coding in multiple files and you need to tell the compiler about members of the **Array** class in a file that does not have any **Array** objects in it (for example, you might need to declare a pointer that can point to a structure defined in the class). To create an explicit instantiation of a class from a class template, you can use the keyword **template** and specify the type parameter or parameters needed in an explicit declaration that looks like this:

```
template Array<float>;
```

This instantiates a class named **Array<float>**. You can also provide values for non-type parameters like this:

```
template Array<float, 100>;
```

This instantiates a class named **Array<float, 100>**.

You can also create *explicit specializations* of class templates, just as you can with function templates. An explicit specialization is a class definition for a particular type, and the compiler will use that specialization for that type instead of the general template. For example, your template might handle the type parameters **float**, **int**, and **double** without problem, but you might want to handle C-style strings, type **char***, in a different way. In that case, you'd create a specialization of your template for the **char*** type.

Here's an example, classtemplatespecialization.cpp, that introduces a specialization for the **Array** class template we've developed in this chapter. I'll add a specialization here that will block any attempts to instantiate an **Array** class based on the C++ **string** class.

You create an explicit specialization with the **template** keyword like this:

```
template <>
class name<specialized_parameter_list>
{
    .
```

```
    .
    .
}
```

This creates a specialization for the parameters listed between < and >. Here's how I create a specialization for the **string** class for the **Array** class template in classtemplatespecialization.cpp—in this specialization, I'm simply providing a constructor that sends an error message to the error output stream object **cerr**, but you can add whatever class members you want to specializations:

```
#include <iostream>
#include <string>
using namespace std;

template <class T>
class Array
{
    T *ptr_to_array;
    int number;
public:
    explicit Array(int number_of_elements);
    Array(const Array & a);
    ~Array();
    T& operator= (const Array & a);
    T& operator[](int index) {return ptr_to_array[index];}
};

template <>
class Array<string>
{
public:
    explicit Array(int number_of_elements){cerr <<
        "Sorry, I don't do strings.";};
};

template <class T>
Array<T>::Array(int number_of_elements)
{
    number = number_of_elements;
    ptr_to_array = new T[number];
}

template <class T>
Array<T>::Array(const Array & a)
{
```

```
    number = a.number;
    T *ptr_to_array = new T[number];

    for(int loop_index = 0; loop_index < number; loop_index++) {
        ptr_to_array[loop_index] = a.ptr_to_array[loop_index];
    }
}

template <class T>
T& Array<T>::operator= (const Array & a)
{
    if(this == &a) return *this;
    delete[] ptr_to_array;

    number = a.number;
    T *ptr_to_array = new T[number];

    for(int loop_index = 0; loop_index < number; loop_index++) {
        ptr_to_array[loop_index] = a.ptr_to_array[loop_index];
    }
    return *this;
}

template <class T>
Array<T>::~Array()
{
    delete[] ptr_to_array;
}
```

Now I can attempt to instantiate an **Array** class based on the C++ **string** class like this in the **main** function:

```
int main()
{
    Array<string> scores(10);

    return 0;
}
```

However, this declaration makes our specialized template display an error message; here's what you see when you run this example, classtemplatespecialization.cpp:

```
%classtemplatespecialization
Sorry, I don't do strings.
```

Besides explicit specializations like this one, you can also create partial specializations—see the next section for the details.

Related solution:	Found on page:
Creating Explicit Function Template Specializations	328

Creating Partial Template Specializations

In the previous section, we saw that an explicit class template specialization is a class definition for a particular type, and the compiler will use that specialization for that type instead of the general template. In an explicit specialization, you specify all the parameters in a class template's parameter list—however, C++ also allows you to create *partial specializations*, where you specify only the parameters you want the specialization to match. In a partial specialization, for example, you might specify the type of only one of the type parameters in a class template.

Here's an example, classtemplatepartialspecialization.cpp. In this case, I'll modify the two-type-parameter template we developed in "Using Class Templates with Multiple Types" earlier in this chapter by adding a partial specialization. The template we developed there took two type parameters, **T** and **T2**:

```
template <class T, class T2>
class Array
{
     .
     .
     .
};
```

When you create a partial specialization, you leave the parameters you want unspecified in the template's parameter list, while specifying the types of others in the name of the class. For example, here's what the code looks for a partial specialization where the **T2** type parameter is the **string** class type:

```
template <class T>
class Array<T, string>
{
     .
     .
     .
};
```

I'll use this partial specialization in classtemplatepartialspecialization.cpp to send an error to the error output stream object **cerr** if **T2** is type **string**. And to make sure this happens, I'll attempt to instantiate a class by setting **T2** to **string** in the **main** function.

NOTE: *Not all C++ compilers will support partial specializations like this (one of the major compilers we used while checking code did not), so this might not work for you.*

```
#include <iostream>
#include <string>
using namespace std;

template <class T, class T2>
class Array
{
    T *ptr_to_array;
    int number;
public:
    T2 name;
    explicit Array(int number_of_elements);
    Array(const Array & a);
    ~Array();
    T& operator= (const Array & a);
    T& operator[](int index) {return ptr_to_array[index];}
};

template <class T>
class Array<T, string>
{
public:
    explicit Array(int number_of_elements){cerr <<
        "Sorry, I don't do strings.";};
};

template <class T, class T2>
Array<T, T2>::Array(int number_of_elements)
{
    number = number_of_elements;
    ptr_to_array = new T[number];
}

template <class T, class T2>
Array<T, T2>::Array(const Array & a)
{
```

```
    number = a.number;
    T *ptr_to_array = new T[number];

    for(int loop_index = 0; loop_index < number; loop_index++) {
        ptr_to_array[loop_index] = a.ptr_to_array[loop_index];
    }
}

template <class T, class T2>
T& Array<T, T2>::operator= (const Array & a)
{
    if(this == &a) return *this;
    delete[] ptr_to_array;

    number = a.number;
    T *ptr_to_array = new T[number];

    for(int loop_index = 0; loop_index < number; loop_index++) {
        ptr_to_array[loop_index] = a.ptr_to_array[loop_index];
    }
    return *this;
}

template <class T, class T2>
Array<T, T2>::~Array()
{
    delete[] ptr_to_array;
}

int main()
{
    Array<float, string> scores(10);

    return 0;
}
```

Here's what the program classtemplatepartialspecialization.cpp displays when you run it:

```
%classtemplatepartialspecialization
Sorry, I don't do strings.
```

As you can see, the compiler used the partial specialization to handle the case where the second type parameter is the C++ **string** class. Using specializations like this provides one way to customize your templates the way you want them.

Chapter 12

Runtime Type Information, Namespaces, and Exceptions

In Depth

This chapter is all about three important C++ topics: runtime type information, namespaces, and exceptions. Each of these topics is a major one in C++. *Runtime type information*, or RTTI, is a collection of technologies that allows you to identify an item's type at runtime, which is very useful when you deal with runtime polymorphism. *Namespaces* give you the ability to divide your code into regions that maintain their own symbol tables, which means that the names you declare in one namespace can't interfere with those you declare in another. Using namespaces becomes important when programs become very long, or when you're importing code from class libraries that declare names that might conflict with those in your code. The biggest topic in this chapter, however, is how to work with C++ *exceptions*. Exceptions provide you with a way of handling what otherwise might be serious errors in a program. For example, your code might try to allocate space for 1,000,000,000 floating point values, something that few machines have the memory for. In this case, your program might well crash unless you provide code to handle such a runtime problem, and that's what exception handling is all about. I'll start this chapter with an overview of each topic, beginning with RTTI.

Runtime Type Information (RTTI)

There are three components to runtime type information (RTTI—you'll also see people calling this runtime type *identification*):

- The **dynamic_cast** operator, which creates a pointer to a derived type using the contents of a pointer to a base type, if possible. If that's not possible, **dynamic_cast** returns 0, a null pointer.
- The **typeid** operator, which returns data that identifies the type of an object.
- The **type_info** structure, which is designed to store information about the type of an object as returned by **typeid**.

All these items have their place in C++ programming. For example, runtime polymorphism has added a lot to C++, but that utility comes at a cost. You can point to derived objects with a base class pointer, and if you're using virtual methods, the correct version of a method you invoke with that pointer will be selected automatically. However, say you're passed a pointer in a function. How can you tell what type that pointer points to? If it's important to know which virtual method is going to be called, it's important to know what kind of object the pointer points to, and with the **dynamic_cast** operator, you can check that.

The dynamic_cast Operator

We've already seen the static, reinterpret, and **const** casts that are supported in C++ (see "Using Static, Reinterpret, and **const** Casts" in Chapter 5), and now that we've discussed inheritance and are discussing runtime type information, we can take a look at dynamic casts using the **dynamic_cast** operator.

Dynamic casts let you convert the pointer in a base class pointer variable (recall that the pointer in such a variable might be of the base class or a class derived from that class) to a derived class, if possible. It's safe to do that only if the pointer in question is *already* of the class you're casting to, or you're casting to a base class of the pointer's class. You can't cast a base class pointer to a class derived from the base class, because some members might have been added in the derived class, and C++ would have no idea what to do if you tried to reference one of those members. On the other hand, it is safe to cast a pointer to another pointer of the same class, or to a base class of that class. The **dynamic_cast** operator lets you know at runtime if a cast is safe or not.

NOTE: *As you recall from Chapter 10, although you can use a base class pointer to point to a derived class object, you can't use that base class pointer to access members that are in the derived class but not in the base class—trying to do so results in a compiler error.*

For example, take a look at this code—here, class **a** is a base class and class **b** is a class derived from **a**. Both classes support a virtual method, **display**, but with different code:

```
class a
{
public:
    virtual void display(){/*code...*/};
};

class b : public a
{
public:
    virtual void display(){/*code...*/};
};
```

I can pass pointers of class **a** to a function named **check** like this:

```
class a
{
public:
    virtual void display(){/*code...*/};
};

class b : public a
{
public:
    virtual void display(){/*code...*/};
};

void check(a *pointer)
{
        .
        .
        .
}
```

However, a pointer to class **a** can really hold a pointer to either class **a** or class **b**. So, if I use the pointer passed to **check**, which **display** method will be called, the one in the **a** class or the **b** class? Say I only want to call **b::display**. In that case, I need to see if the pointer is really a pointer to a **b** class object, which I can check with **dynamic_cast**. If **dynamic_cast** can cast the pointer to type **b***, it's safe to call **b::display**. Otherwise, **dynamic_cast** returns 0, which means the pointer was to an **a** class object. Here's how I can implement this safely in code:

```
class a
{
public:
    virtual void display(){/*code...*/};
};

class b : public a
{
public:
    virtual void display(){/*code...*/};
};

void check(a *pointer)
{
```

```
    b *b_pointer = dynamic_cast<b *> (pointer);
    if(b_pointer)
        b_pointer->display();
}
```

NOTE: *Visual C++ seems to require that you specifically enable runtime type information checking with the* ***/GR*** *switch when compiling this code.*

The **dynamic_cast** operator uses runtime type information stored for each pointer to determine if a cast like this is safe or not, which is an issue that's often important when you're working with runtime polymorphism.

The typeid Operator and the type_info Class

Besides **dynamic_cast**, the other part of RTTI consists of the **typeid** operator and the **type_info** class. The **typeid** operator returns an object of the **type_info** class, and you can use that object to identify the type of data items at runtime.

The members of the **type_info** class vary by compiler—manufacturers always seem eager to add their own data members and methods to this class. However, there are a few members that all **type_info** classes have, regardless of manufacturer—a constructor, a copy constructor, a destructor, an assignment operator, and a method called **name**. The **name** method returns the name of the type of item you're examining.

You can pass either a generic type or class (such as **int**), or an actual variable (such as **integer1**), to **typeid**. As you might recall from Chapter 2, we already took a look at **typeid** in an example named typeid.cpp (see "What Type Is a Given Variable?" in Chapter 2). Here's what that example looked like—here, I'm using **typeid** to determine the type of an integer, **integer1**:

```
#include <iostream>
#include <typeinfo>
using namespace std;

int main()
{
    int integer1 = 200;

    cout << "The type of integer1 is: " << typeid(integer1).name() << endl;

    return 0;
}
```

Here's the result of this program, typeid.cpp, where we learn that **integer1**'s type is **int**:

```
%typeid
The type of integer1 is: int
```

The **typeid** operator is more useful with pointers, because a base class pointer can hold a pointer to a derived object and you can use **typeid** to determine the type a pointer actually points to. For example, say that I use the **animal** class introduced in Chapter 10, and I derive a class from **animal** named **fish** in an example named animalclasstypeid.cpp:

```
#include <iostream>
using namespace std;

class animal
{
public:
    void eat();
    void sleep();
    virtual void breathe();
};

class fish : public animal
{
public:
    void breathe();
    void swim();
};

void animal::breathe(){cout << "Breathing..." << endl;}
void animal::eat(){cout << "Eating..." << endl;}
void animal::sleep(){cout << "Sleeping..." << endl;}
void fish::breathe(){cout << "Bubbling..." << endl;}
void fish::swim(){cout << "Swimming..." << endl;}
    .
    .
    .
```

Now I can create a pointer to the base class, **animal_pointer**, and an object of the derived class, **fish_object**. I can store the address of **fish_object** in **animal_pointer**, of course, but how can I find out what type of object **animal_pointer** is really pointing to, an **animal** object or a **fish** object? That's easy enough, using **typeid**—all I need to do is take a look at the pointer's class as returned by **typeid(*animal_pointer)**. Here's what the code looks like—note that you should include the typeinfo header, which defines the **type_info** class, to use **typeid**:

```
#include <iostream>
#include <typeinfo>
using namespace std;

class animal
{
public:
    void eat();
    void sleep();
    virtual void breathe();
};

class fish : public animal
{
public:
    void breathe();
    void swim();
};

void animal::breathe(){cout << "Breathing..." << endl;}
void animal::eat(){cout << "Eating..." << endl;}
void animal::sleep(){cout << "Sleeping..." << endl;}
void fish::breathe(){cout << "Bubbling..." << endl;}
void fish::swim(){cout << "Swimming..." << endl;}

int main()
{
    animal *animal_pointer;
    fish fish_object;

    animal_pointer = &fish_object;

    cout << "The type of the object is "
        << typeid(*animal_pointer).name() << endl;

    return 0;
}
```

Here's what you see when you run this code, animalclasstypeid.cpp:

```
%animalclasstypeid
The type of the object is fish
```

NOTE: *The actual class name displayed can vary by C++ installation; for example, if you use g++, you'll see "4fish", not "fish".*

As you see, the **typeid** operator allowed us to determine that the class of the object the animal pointer actually pointed to was **fish**, not **animal**. Determining the actual type of an object a pointer points to this way can be invaluable when you use runtime polymorphism.

You can also compare types directly, using a **type_info** object's **name** method:

```
if(typeid(*animal_pointer).name() == typeid(*fish_pointer).name())
{
      .
      .
      .
}
```

Namespaces

As already mentioned, namespaces let you divide your program up into regions that maintain their own symbol tables, and these regions are called *declarative regions*. The idea behind namespaces is to avoid having the names you declare conflict with others defined in the same program, because the names in one namespace are independent of those in another.

There is one namespace that every C++ program comes with currently—the *global namespace*. The global namespace is a default namespace for your program, and all global items are part of this namespace. In earlier versions of C++, everything was part of this default namespace, but now the items in the standard C++ library have been made part of the **std** namespace. When you place this line in your code:

```
#include <iostream>
using namespace std;
      .
      .
      .
```

what you're really doing is *importing* the symbols in the **std** namespace into the global namespace. When you import a symbol into the global namespace, it becomes available throughout your code. If you don't import a symbol in another namespace, you'd have to qualify it with its namespace name this way: ***namespace*::*name***, such as **std::cout**. If you look in the standard C++ library header files, you'll see this namespace declaration in each of them, which places the items declared in the header in the **std** namespace:

```
namespace std {
    .
    .
    .
}
```

That's how you create a namespace—with the **namespace** keyword. Here's an example, namespace.cpp, in which I create a namespace called **NS** and place a string named **data** in it:

```
#include <iostream>
#include <string>
using namespace std;

namespace NS {
    string data("NS namespace data");
}
    .
    .
    .
```


I can also add a variable in the global namespace, also named **data**, but with different text:

```
#include <iostream>
#include <string>
using namespace std;

namespace NS {
    string data("NS namespace data");
}

string data("Global namespace data");
    .
    .
    .
```

You can break up a namespace into multiple regions, but if you give them the same name, all the names in them are in the same namespace. To show how that works, I'll add a new text string, **data2**, to the **NS** namespace:

```
#include <iostream>
#include <string>
using namespace std;
```

```
namespace NS {
    string data("NS namespace data");
}

string data("Global namespace data");

namespace NS {
    string data2("Additional NS namespace data");
}
    .
    .
    .
```

Finally, I can create one more version of **data**, this time a local version in **main**:

```
#include <iostream>
#include <string>
using namespace std;

namespace NS {
    string data("NS namespace data");
}

string data("Global namespace data");

namespace NS {
    string data2("Additional NS namespace data");
}

int main()
{
    string data("Local data");
    .
    .
    .
```

At this point, I can display all the various **data** variables. You can refer to the local data simply as **data** and the **data** in the NS namespace as **NS::data**:

```
int main()
{
    string data("Local data");
    cout << data << endl;
```

```
    cout << NS::data << endl;
        .
        .
        .
```

What would happen if I added a **using namespace NS** statement next? In that case, the symbols in the **NS** namespace would be imported into the global namespace—but note that global symbols are overridden by local symbols, so **data** still refers to the local version, *not* the one in the **NS** namespace. However, now I can refer to the **NS** variable **data2** simply as **data2**, not **NS::data2**:


```
int main()
{
    string data("Local data");
    cout << data << endl;

    cout << NS::data << endl;

    using namespace NS;
    cout << data << endl;             // Overwritten by local data
    cout << data2 << endl;
        .
        .
        .
```

And I can also explicitly refer to the data variable in the global namespace as **::data**, like this:

```
int main()
{
    string data("Local data");
    cout << data << endl;

    cout << NS::data << endl;

    using namespace NS;
    cout << data << endl;             // Overwritten by local data
    cout << data2 << endl;

    cout << ::data << endl;

    return 0;
}
```

Here's what you see when you run namespace.cpp:

```
%namespace
Local data
NS namespace data
Local data
Additional NS namespace data
Global namespace data
```


Being able to section your code into namespaces is very popular with programmers, and some even want to put everything into namespaces, eliminating the global, or default, namespace entirely.

Exceptions

The C++ exception mechanism exists to allow you to handle runtime problems. These problems are not usually logic errors in your code (that is, bugs), but rather, problems that can arise at runtime. For example, the user might direct your code to open a file that doesn't exist, in which case, your code could *throw* an exception. A different part of your code could *catch* and handle the exception. Let's take a look at an example, dividebyzero.cpp. As you can tell from this example's name, the code here will divide a number by zero if the user asks it to, which is an arithmetic problem. All I do here is to ask the user to enter two floating point numbers and divide them:

```
#include <iostream>
#include <string>
using namespace std;

int main ()
{
   float op1, op2;

   cout << "Enter the two floating point numbers to divide: ";
   cin >> op1 >> op2;

   cout << op1 << "/" << op2 << " = " << op1/op2 << endl;

   return 0;
}
```

If the user enters 1 as the first number and 0 as the second number, the program will try to divide 1 by 0. In general, the executable files generated by C++ installations do not handle this problem well. Some compilers generate code to simply ignore the problem; some programs will crash. In either case, dividing 1 by 0 yields an undefined result as far as your code goes, and we should have some way of avoiding that problem.

The way to handle problems like this is with exceptions. Here are the general steps you follow:

1. Put sensitive code in a **try** block.
2. Throw exceptions as needed with **throw** statements.
3. Catch and handle the exceptions in a **catch** block.

Here's an example, except.cpp, to show how this works. In this case, I'll place the sensitive code that could execute a division by zero inside a **try** block, which you implement as a code block that begins with the **try** keyword:

```
#include <iostream>
#include <string>
using namespace std;

int main ()
{
    float op1, op2;

    cout << "Enter the two floating point numbers to divide: ";
    cin >> op1 >> op2;

    try
    {
        cout << op1 << "/" << op2 << " = " << op1/op2 << endl;
    }
    .
    .
    .
```

If the number we're dividing by is zero, I won't execute this code—instead, I'll have the code throw an exception with the **throw** statement:

```
#include <iostream>
#include <string>
using namespace std;

int main ()
{
    float op1, op2;
```

```
    cout << "Enter the two floating point numbers to divide: ";
    cin >> op1 >> op2;

    try
    {
        if(op2 != 0)
            cout << op1 << "/" << op2 << " = " << op1/op2 << endl;
        else
            throw string("Error: division by zero.");
    }
    .
    .
    .
```

If the **throw** statement is executed, it will throw an exception of type **string**, whose content is the message "Error: division by zero." To handle such exceptions, if they occur, I can catch them with a **catch** block, which you implement with the **catch** keyword. You indicate the type of the exception you want to catch, which is **string** in this example, and deal with the exception in the code block following the **catch** keyword. Here, I'll just display the exception's internal message, like this:

```
#include <iostream>
#include <string>
using namespace std;

int main ()
{
    float op1, op2;

    cout << "Enter the two floating point numbers to divide: ";
    cin >> op1 >> op2;

    try
    {
        if(op2 != 0)
            cout << op1 << "/" << op2 << " = " << op1/op2 << endl;
        else
            throw string("Error: division by zero.");
    }
    catch (string s)
```

```
    {
        cout << s << endl;
    }

    return 0;
}
```

You can also specify that exceptions should be passed to **catch** blocks by reference, if you wish, like this: **catch (string & s)**, which will catch the same exceptions as the code above. Here's what you see when you run this code, except.cpp—note that the exception was thrown and caught in this example:

```
%except
Enter the two floating point numbers to divide: 1 0
Error: division by zero.
```

***NOTE:** Many other languages, such as Java, and some C++ implementations, like Microsoft's Visual C++, have many exceptions already built in, and dividing by zero would usually throw one of those exceptions. However, standard C++ has only eight standard exceptions built in (see "The Standard Exceptions" in this chapter), and for various reasons standard C++ does not consider arithmetic overflows exceptions, so you have to create your own. (Interestingly, one of the main reasons that dividing by zero does not throw an exception in C++ is because of multithreading, which is not even supported in standard C++).*

In this example, the exception was a **string** object, but you can create your own exception objects with specialized methods to hold error messages, codes, and more. We'll take a look at all that and more in the Immediate Solutions section, and it's time to start that section now.

Immediate Solutions

Using **dynamic_cast** with Pointers at Runtime

As we saw in the In Depth section of this chapter, one runtime type information technique is to use **dynamic_cast** to see if a pointer cast is safe. That's often important to determine if you want to use a pointer to call a method, because a base class pointer can hold a pointer to a derived object, and if the method you want to call is virtual, each class will have its own version of the method. To determine what type of pointer you're dealing with, and so what method you'll actually be calling, you can check the pointer with the **dynamic_cast** operator.

You can't cast a base class pointer to a class derived from that base class, but it is safe to cast a pointer to another pointer of the same class, or to a base class of that class. The **dynamic_cast** operator lets you know at runtime if a cast is safe or not, and this is often useful if you want to know which overridden version of a method will be called. Here's an example we saw in the In Depth section of this chapter—in this case, classes **a** and **b** have different versions of a method named **display**, and if you pass a pointer to class **a** to the function named **check**, that pointer can be to either class **a** or **b**. If you only want to call the **b** class's version of **display**, you can use **dynamic_cast** to see if the pointer really is to a **b** class object:

```
#include <iostream>
using namespace std;

class a
{
public:
    virtual void display(){/*code...*/};
};

class b : public a
{
public:
    virtual void display(){/*code...*/};
};

void check(a *pointer)
{
```

```
    b *b_pointer = dynamic_cast<b *> (pointer);
    if(b_pointer)
        b_pointer->display();
}
```

The **dynamic_cast** operator uses runtime type information stored for each pointer to determine if a cast like this is safe or not, which is an issue that's often important when you're working with runtime polymorphism. Here's a more extensive example, animalclassdynamiccast.cpp. In this example, I'll use the **animal** class from Chapter 10 and derive a class from **animal** named **fish**. In this code, I'll try to use **dynamic_cast** to cast a **fish** pointer to an **animal** pointer, which will work, and an **animal** pointer to a **fish** pointer, which won't work:


```
#include <iostream>
using namespace std;

class animal
{
public:
    void eat();
    void sleep();
    virtual void breathe();
};

class fish : public animal
{
public:
    void breathe();
    void swim();
};

void animal::breathe(){cout << "Breathing..." << endl;}
void animal::eat(){cout << "Eating..." << endl;}
void animal::sleep(){cout << "Sleeping..." << endl;}
void fish::breathe(){cout << "Bubbling..." << endl;}
void fish::swim(){cout << "Swimming..." << endl;}

int main()
{
    animal animal_object;
    animal *animal_pointer;

    fish fish_object;
    fish *fish_pointer;
```

```
    //Cast from fish to animal
    fish_pointer = &fish_object;
    animal_pointer = dynamic_cast<animal *>(fish_pointer);

    if(fish_pointer)
        cout << "Made the conversion fish* to animal*." << endl;
    else
        cout << "Could not make the conversion fish* to animal*." << endl;

    //Cast from animal to fish
    animal_pointer = &animal_object;
    fish_pointer = dynamic_cast<fish *>(animal_pointer);

    if(fish_pointer)
        cout << "Made the conversion animal* to fish*." << endl;
    else
        cout << "Could not make the conversion animal* to fish*." << endl;

    return 0;
}
```

Here's what you see when you run this code, animalclassdynamiccast.cpp:

```
%animalclassdynamiccast
Made the conversion fish* to animal*.
Could not make the conversion animal* to fish*.
```

Related solution:	Found on page:
Using Static, Reinterpret, and **const** Casts	233

Using the **typeid** Operator and the **type_info** Class

Besides the **dynamic_cast** operator, RTTI also includes the **typeid** operator and the **type_info** class. When you apply the **typeid** operator to an item, that operator returns an object of the **type_info** class, and you can use that object to get information about the item. This is useful when you're working with pointers and runtime polymorphism to see what kind of object a pointer points to. Here's an example, animalclasstypeid.cpp, that we saw in the In Depth section of this chapter. In this case, I'm using the **animal** class and deriving a class named **fish** from it. Next, I'll point to a **fish** object using an **animal** pointer. How can you determine what kind of object this **animal** pointer really points to? You can use the **typeid** operator to return a **type_info** object and use the **name** method of that object to find the name we need—note that you should include the typeinfo header, which defines the **type_info** class, to use **typeid**:

```
#include <iostream>
#include <typeinfo>
using namespace std;

class animal
{
public:
    void eat();
    void sleep();
    virtual void breathe();
};

class fish : public animal
{
public:
    void breathe();
    void swim();
};

void animal::breathe(){cout << "Breathing..." << endl;}
void animal::eat(){cout << "Eating..." << endl;}
void animal::sleep(){cout << "Sleeping..." << endl;}
void fish::breathe(){cout << "Bubbling..." << endl;}
void fish::swim(){cout << "Swimming..." << endl;}

int main()
{
    animal *animal_pointer;
    fish fish_object;

    animal_pointer = &fish_object;

    cout << "The type of the object is "
        << typeid(*animal_pointer).name() << endl;

    return 0;
}
```

Here's what you see when you run this code, animalclasstypeid.cpp:

```
%animalclasstypeid
The type of the object is fish
```

As you can see, even though we had an **animal** pointer, the object pointed to was really of the **fish** class, as **typeid** reported. As noted in the In Depth section of this chapter, the actual class name displayed can vary by C++ installation; for example, if you use g++, you'll see "4fish", not "fish".

Creating a Namespace

As discussed in the In Depth section of this chapter, you can use namespaces to divide your code into declarative regions, and the names in those regions won't conflict. To declare a namespace, you use the **namespace** keyword and enclose the code you want in the namespace in a code block following that keyword. We saw an example in the In Depth section of this chapter, namespace.cpp. In that example, I created a namespace named **NS** and declared a **string** variable named **data** in that namespace:

```
#include <iostream>
#include <string>
using namespace std;

namespace NS {
    string data("NS namespace data");
}
    .
    .
    .
```

I also added another variable named **data** to the global namespace for the program:

```
#include <iostream>
#include <string>
using namespace std;

namespace NS {
    string data("NS namespace data");
}

string data("Global namespace data");
    .
    .
    .
```

You can add code to a namespace throughout your program—just create a new namespace block like this, which adds a new string variable, **data2**, to the **NS** namespace:

```
#include <iostream>
#include <string>
using namespace std;

namespace NS {
    string data("NS namespace data");
}

string data("Global namespace data");

namespace NS {
    string data2("Additional NS namespace data");
}
    .
    .
    .
```

And in the **main** function, I can also add a local variable named **data**. In **main**, the local **data** will override both the global **data** and the data in the **NS** namespace, but I can still access the global data as **::data**, and **data** in the **NS** namespace as **NS::data**:

```
#include <iostream>
#include <string>
using namespace std;

namespace NS {
    string data("NS namespace data");
}

string data("Global namespace data");

namespace NS {
    string data2("Additional NS namespace data");
}

int main()
{
    string data("Local data");
    cout << data << endl;
```

```
    cout << NS::data << endl;

    cout << ::data << endl;

    return 0;
}
```

Here's what you see when you run the code for namespace.cpp so far:

```
%namespace
Local data
NS namespace data
Global namespace data
```

You can also nest namespaces, and even use *unnamed* namespaces like this:

```
namespace {
    string data("NS namespace data");
}
```

In this case, the variable data is treated as an external static variable (see "Understanding Storage Classes, Scope, and Linkage" in Chapter 7).

It's a little tedious to have to qualify each name in the **NS** namespace with **NS::**, so C++ provides an alternative—you can import all the names in a namespace into the global namespace with the **using** directive. See the next section for the details.

Related solution:	Found on page:
Understanding Storage Classes, Scope, and Linkage	313

Working with Namespaces and the **using** Directive

You can import names from a namespace into the global namespace with the **using** directive. There are two ways to work with **using**—you can import individual names from a namespace, like this:

```
using Thanksgiving::turkey;
```

Or you can import all the names in a namespace at once. Here's an example, namespace.cpp, that I'm adapting from the previous section, which imports all the names in a namespace at once. If I add the **using namespace NS** statement to the code in **main**, all the symbols from the **NS** namespace—**data** and **data2**—are imported, and I don't need to refer to them with the **NS** qualifier. However, note that the code in **main** already defines a variable named **data**, and that local variable will take precedence when I display the results of this code:

```
#include <iostream>
#include <string>
using namespace std;

namespace NS {
    string data("NS namespace data");
}

string data("Global namespace data");

namespace NS {
    string data2("Additional NS namespace data");
}

int main()
{
    string data("Local data");
    cout << data << endl;

    cout << NS::data << endl;

    using namespace NS;
    cout << data << endl;                //Overwritten by local data
    cout << data2 << endl;

    cout << ::data << endl;

    return 0;
}
```

Here's what you see when you run namespace.cpp:

```
%namespace
Local data
NS namespace data
Local data
Additional NS namespace data
Global namespace data
```

Related solution:	Found on page:
Understanding Storage Classes, Scope, and Linkage	313

Creating and Throwing Exceptions

Using exceptions, you can let your program recover from problems that might otherwise prove fatal. As mentioned in the In Depth section of this chapter, to handle exceptions, you place sensitive or problematic code (such as code that might read a file as directed by the user, which would cause a problem if that file didn't exist) in a **try** block, throw exceptions as needed with the **throw** statement, and handle those exceptions in **catch** blocks.

The rest of this chapter is dedicated to exception handling. We got started with exception handling in the In Depth section of this chapter with the example except.cpp. In that example, I asked the user for two numbers and divide them; if we end up dividing by zero, the code should throw an exception, which the program should handle without aborting. I start by placing the sensitive code in a **try** block:

```
#include <iostream>
#include <string>
using namespace std;

int main ()
{
   float op1, op2;

   cout << "Enter the two floating point numbers to divide: ";
   cin >> op1 >> op2;

   try
   {
      cout << op1 << "/" << op2 << " = " << op1/op2 << endl;
   }
    .
    .
    .
```

If the user is trying to divide by zero, we throw an exception; in this case, the exception will be a **string** object holding the text "Error: division by zero.":

```
#include <iostream>
#include <string>
using namespace std;

int main ()
{
   float op1, op2;

   cout << "Enter the two floating point numbers to divide: ";
   cin >> op1 >> op2;

   try
   {
      if(op2 != 0)
          cout << op1 << "/" << op2 << " = " << op1/op2 << endl;
      else
          throw string("Error: division by zero.");
   }
    .
    .
    .
```


Now I set up a **catch** block to handle exceptions of the **string** class and display an error message in that **catch** block:

```
#include <iostream>
#include <string>
using namespace std;

int main ()
{
   float op1, op2;

   cout << "Enter the two floating point numbers to divide: ";
   cin >> op1 >> op2;

   try
   {
      if(op2 != 0)
          cout << op1 << "/" << op2 << " = " << op1/op2 << endl;
      else
          throw string("Error: division by zero.");
   }
```

```
    catch (string s)
    {
        cout << s << endl;
    }

    return 0;
}
```

Here's what you see when the user tries to divide by 0:

```
%except
Enter the two floating point numbers to divide: 1 0
Error: division by zero.
```

This is just the beginning of exception handling—take a look at the remaining sections in this chapter for more details.

Throwing Exceptions from Functions

If you throw an exception in a function and don't catch that exception in the function, control returns to the point immediately following the function call in the calling code, and the program looks for a **catch** block after that point. If there is a **catch** block of the same type as the exception, the code in the **catch** block is executed.

You can indicate what type or types of exceptions a function can return when you define the function (although this is not required). This allows the compiler to check if the code is going to return any exceptions of incorrect types (see "Handling Uncaught Exceptions" later in this chapter), and it also lets you know what kinds of exceptions to handle.

Here's an example, exceptprototypes.cpp. In this code, I'll use a function named **divider** to divide two numbers, and if a division by zero occurs, the code in that function will throw a **string** object exception. Because there is no catch block in **divider**, control will transfer back to the **catch** block following the call to **divider** in **main**. Note that I'm adding the keywords **throw (string)** when defining **divider** to indicate that this function can throw an exception of type **string**:

```
#include <iostream>
#include <string>
using namespace std;
```

```
float divider(float op1, float op2) throw (string)
{
    if(op2 != 0)
        return op1 / op2;
    else
        throw string("Error: division by zero.");
}

int main ()
{
   float op1, op2;

   cout << "Enter the two floating point numbers to divide: ";
   cin >> op1 >> op2;

   try
   {
        float result = divider(op1, op2);
        cout << op1 << "/" << op2 << " = " << result << endl;
   }
   catch (string s)
   {
      cout << s << endl;
   }

   return 0;
}
```

Note that you can also specify that a function can throw more than one exception type; for example, here's how I indicate that the **divider** function can throw either a **string** or **double*** exception:

```
float divider(float op1, float op2) throw (string, double*)
{
    if(op2 != 0)
        return op1 / op2;
    else
        throw string("Error: division by zero.");
}
```

For more on handling functions and exceptions, take a look at the next section.

"Unwinding" the Stack

When you throw an exception in a function and don't handle that exception in that function, control returns up the *call stack*, looking for a **catch** block. The call stack is what the program uses to keep track of function calls, and to handle an exception, the program moves back up the call stack, searching for a **catch** block.

Here's an example, exceptstack.cpp, that shows how this works. In this case, I'll call a function, **divider**, to divide two numbers. The **divider** function will itself call another function, **do_work**, to perform the division, and that function will throw an exception. Because there's no **catch** block in **do_work**, this exception will travel back up the call stack to **divider**. But because there's no **catch** block in **divider**, the exception will travel back to **main** and be handled there. (What happens to uncaught exceptions? See "Handling Uncaught Exceptions" later in this chapter.) Here's what the code looks like:

```
#include <iostream>
#include <string>
using namespace std;

float do_work(float op1, float op2) throw (string)
{
    if(op2 != 0)
        return op1 / op2;
    else
        throw string("Error: division by zero.");
}

float divider(float op1, float op2) throw (string)
{
    return do_work(op1, op2);
}

int main ()
{
   float op1, op2;

   cout << "Enter the two floating point numbers to divide: ";
   cin >> op1 >> op2;

   try
   {
       float result = divider(op1, op2);
       cout << op1 << "/" << op2 << " = " << result << endl;
   }
```

```
   catch (string s)
   {
      cout << s << endl;
   }

   return 0;
}
```

Here's what you see when you run this code, exceptstack.cpp—note that the exception has indeed travelled up the call stack and been handled in **main**:

```
%exceptstack
Enter the two floating point numbers to divide: 1 0
Error: division by zero.
```


Throwing Custom Objects

The examples in this chapter have thrown an exception of the **string** class so far, but you can throw exceptions using objects you create. This is often the best way to support exceptions, because you can add your own methods and data members to such objects.

Here's an example, exceptobject.cpp, putting this into practice. In this case, I'll create a class named **Exception** that can hold an error message in an internal data member and has a constructor and one method—**get_error**, which returns the error message:

```
#include <iostream>
#include <string>
using namespace std;

class Exception
{
   string error_message;
public:
   string get_error(){return error_message;}
   Exception(string s);
};

Exception::Exception(string s){error_message = s;}
   .
   .
   .
```

Now when an error occurs in the **try** block, I can create an object of the **Exception** class, passing an error message to this class's constructor. In the **catch** block, I can use the **Exception** object's **get_error** method to display that error message:

```
#include <iostream>
#include <string>
using namespace std;

class Exception
{
    string error_message;
public:
    string get_error(){return error_message;}
    Exception(string s);
};

Exception::Exception(string s){error_message = s;}

int main ()
{
   float op1, op2;

   cout << "Enter the two floating point numbers to divide: ";
   cin >> op1 >> op2;

   try
   {
      if(op2 != 0)
          cout << op1 << "/" << op2 << " = " << op1/op2 << endl;
      else
          throw Exception("Error: division by zero.");
   }
   catch (Exception e)
   {
      cout << e.get_error() << endl;
   }

   return 0;
}
```

Here's what you see when you run this example, exceptobject.cpp:

```
%exceptobject
Enter the two floating point numbers to divide: 1 0
Error: division by zero.
```

Handling Multiple Exception Objects in Multiple **catch** Blocks

One of the virtues of defining your own exception classes is that you can use multiple **catch** blocks to catch different types of exceptions. In this example, exceptmultipleobject.cpp, I'll define two exception classes, **Exception** and **Divide_by_zero_exception**:

```
#include <iostream>
#include <string>
using namespace std;

class Exception
{
    string error_message;
public:
    string get_error(){return error_message;}
    Exception(string s);
};

Exception::Exception(string s){error_message = s;}

class Divide_by_zero_exception
{
    string error_message;
public:
    string get_error(){return error_message;}
    Divide_by_zero_exception();
};

Divide_by_zero_exception::Divide_by_zero_exception()
{error_message = "Error: division by zero.";}
    .
    .
    .
```

Now I can use multiple **catch** blocks to catch exceptions of these two classes:

```
#include <iostream>
#include <string>
using namespace std;

class Exception
{
    string error_message;
public:
    string get_error(){return error_message;}
    Exception(string s);
};

Exception::Exception(string s){error_message = s;}

class Divide_by_zero_exception
{
    string error_message;
public:
    string get_error(){return error_message;}
    Divide_by_zero_exception();
};

Divide_by_zero_exception::Divide_by_zero_exception()
{error_message = "Error: division by zero.";}

int main ()
{
   float op1, op2;

   cout << "Enter the two floating point numbers to divide: ";
   cin >> op1 >> op2;

   try
   {
      if(op2 != 0)
          cout << op1 << "/" << op2 << " = " << op1/op2 << endl;
      else
          throw Divide_by_zero_exception();
   }
   catch (Exception e)
   {
      cout << e.get_error() << endl;
   }
```

```
    catch (Divide_by_zero_exception e)
    {
        cout << e.get_error() << endl;
    }

    return 0;
}
```

Here's what you see when you run this program, exceptmultipleobject.cpp:

```
%exceptmultipleobject
Enter the two floating point numbers to divide: 1 0
Error: division by zero.
```

Here's something to note—if the **Divide_by_zero_exception** class were derived from **Exception**, the first **catch** block would hide the second one.

Using the **exception** Class

C++ actually comes with a built-in exception class named **exception**, and you can use this class as the base class for your own exception classes. The **exception** class has a method named **what** that returns an error message, and when you derive a class from the **exception** class, you override that method. Here's how that looks in an example, exceptexceptionobject.cpp, where I'm deriving a class named **Divide_by_zero_exception** from **exception**—note that you include the exception header file to use the **exception** class:

```
#include <iostream>
#include <exception>
using namespace std;

class Divide_by_zero_exception : public exception
{
    char* error_message;
public:
    const char* what(){return error_message;}
    Divide_by_zero_exception(){error_message = "Error: division by zero.";}
};
    .
    .
    .
```

Now I can throw exceptions of the **Divide_by_zero_exception** class and use its **what** method to display the error message:

```
#include <iostream>
#include <exception>
using namespace std;

class Divide_by_zero_exception : public exception
{
    char* error_message;
public:
    const char* what(){return error_message;}
    Divide_by_zero_exception(){error_message = "Error: division by zero.";}
};

int main ()
{
   float op1, op2;

   cout << "Enter the two floating point numbers to divide: ";
   cin >> op1 >> op2;

   try
   {
      if(op2 != 0)
         cout << op1 << "/" << op2 << " = " << op1/op2 << endl;
      else
         throw Divide_by_zero_exception();
   }
   catch (Divide_by_zero_exception e)
   {
      cout << e.what() << endl;
   }

   return 0;
}
```

Here's what you see when you run exceptexceptionobject.cpp:

```
%exceptexceptionobject
Enter the two floating point numbers to divide: 1 0
Error: division by zero.
```

The Standard Exceptions

Some languages come with plenty of predefined exceptions. In fact, some C++ implementations like Visual C++ come with dozens of predefined exceptions that are thrown by the many library functions that the implementation adds to standard C++. However, standard C++ itself defines only eight standard exceptions, which you'll find in Table 12.1.

To see one of these exceptions, **bad_alloc**, at work, look at the next section.

Table 12.1 The standard C++ exceptions.

Exception	Thrown By	Header File
bad_alloc	**new**	new
bad_cast	**dynamic_cast**	typeinfo
bad_typeid	**typeid**	typeinfo
bad_exception	**exception specification**	exception
out_of_range	**at, bitset<>::operator[]**	stdexcept
invalid_argument	**bitset constructor**	stdexcept
overflow_error	**bitset<>::to_ulong**	stdexcept
ios_base::failure	**ios_base::clear**	ios

Handling the **bad_alloc** Exception

C++ now gives language implementations their choice of how to handle bad allocation attempts with **new**—a C++ implementation can either return a null pointer or throw a **bad_alloc** exception. The **bad_alloc** exception is one of the few that are built into standard C++, and here's an example, exceptbadalloc.cpp, that shows how it works.

In a **try** block, I start by trying to allocate enough space for 1,000,000,000 floating point values, something considerably beyond the capacity of my machine:

```
#include <iostream>
#include <new>
using namespace std;
```

```
int main()
{
    float* float_pointer;

    try {
        float_pointer = new float[1000000000];
        float_pointer[0] = 3.14159;
    }
    .
    .
    .
```

The **new** operator throws the built-in **bad_alloc** exception when I try to allocate this huge amount of memory, and I can handle that exception in a **catch** block:

```
#include <iostream>
#include <new>
using namespace std;

int main()
{
    float* float_pointer;

    try {
        float_pointer = new float[1000000000];
        float_pointer[0] = 3.14159;
    }
    catch (bad_alloc & b)
    {
        .
        .
        .
    }
    .
    .
    .
```

The **bad_alloc** exception is based on the **exception** class, so you can use the **what** method to find out what went wrong (see "Using the **exception** Class" earlier in this chapter for more on the **exception** class):

```
#include <iostream>
#include <new>
using namespace std;
```

```
int main()
{
    float* float_pointer;

    try {
        float_pointer = new float[1000000000];
        float_pointer[0] = 3.14159;
    }
    catch (bad_alloc & b)
    {
        cout << b.what() << endl;
    }

    return 0;
}
```


Here's what you see when you run this example, exceptbadalloc.cpp:

```
%exceptbadalloc
bad alloc exception thrown
```

Note that the message you'll see is implementation dependent—for example, programs compiled with g++ simply display "bad_alloc". In fact, this code, compiled withVisual C++, did not throw an error but caused an invalid memory page fault and was simply shut down by the operating system.

Handling Uncaught Exceptions

What happens if an exception is thrown that doesn't match the exceptions given in any catch block? If an exception doesn't match any **catch** block, it's considered an *uncaught* exception, and it'll usually terminate your program. It turns out that you can specify how to handle otherwise uncaught exceptions—you can use the library function **set_terminate** to register a handler function for such exceptions.

Here's an example, exceptuncaught.cpp; in this case, I'll create a function named **stopper** to handle uncaught exceptions by displaying a message and quitting, returning an error code to the operating system:

```
#include <iostream>
#include <string>
using namespace std;
```

```
void stopper()
{
    cout << "Exception uncaught, so quitting" << endl;
    exit(1);
}
        .
        .
        .
```


Now I register this function with **set_terminate** and create an uncaught exception by throwing a **string** exception when the user tries to divide by zero; note that you include the exception header file to work with **set_terminate**:

```
#include <iostream>
#include <exception>
#include <string>
using namespace std;

void stopper()
{
    cout << "Exception uncaught, so quitting" << endl;
    exit(1);
}

int main ()
{
   float op1, op2;

   cout << "Enter the two floating point numbers to divide: ";
   cin >> op1 >> op2;

   set_terminate(stopper);

   try
   {
      if(op2 != 0)
          cout << op1 << "/" << op2 << " = " << op1/op2 << endl;
      else
          throw string("Error: division by zero.");
   }
   catch(float){}

   return 0;
}
```

Here's what you see when you run exceptuncaught.cpp and try to divide by zero:

```
%exceptuncaught
Enter the two floating point numbers to divide: 1 0
Exception uncaught, so quitting
```

You can also use the C++ function **set_unexpected** to indicate how to handle *unexpected* exceptions. When a function throws an exception that is not in its exception specification (see "Throwing Exceptions from Functions" earlier in this chapter), that exception is considered unexpected. By default, if there is an unexpected exception, the program calls a function named **unexpected**. That function calls the **terminate** function by default, which calls **abort** (see "Using the **exit** and **abort** Statements" in Chapter 4). Just as you can change the behavior of **terminate** with **set_terminate**, so you can change the behavior of **unexpected** with **set_unexpected**.

The function you register with **set_unexpected** has two choices—it can throw an exception, or it can end the program by calling **terminate**, **exit**, or **abort**. If that function throws an exception, the program checks to see if the new exception matches any **catch** block; in other words, you can convert the exception to a new type of exception. If the new exception does not match any **catch** block, however, the program terminates—it does not call the handler function a second time for the same exception. One thing you can do in the handler function is to convert the exception to the **bad_exception** type—see "The Standard Exceptions" earlier in this chapter. If you then provide a **catch** block for the **bad_exception** type, then you're able to catch all exceptions, unexpected or not:

```
catch (bad_exception & e)
{
    .
    .
    .
}
```

See also "Creating Catch-All Handlers" later in this chapter.

Related solution:	Found on page:
Using the **exit** and **abort** Statements	195

Nesting **try** Blocks and Rethrowing Exceptions

As you might imagine, you can nest **try** blocks in C++, which is useful if a sensitive section of code itself contains a small subset that you want to put in a **try**/**catch** block to handle exceptions without leaving the enclosing **try** block. You can also *rethrow* exceptions from a **catch** block to be handled by the **catch** block of an enclosing **try** block. To rethrow an exception, you just use the **throw** statement by itself.

Here's an example, exceptrethrow.cpp, that illustrates both points—nesting **try** blocks and rethrowing an exception. Here, I start by creating an exception class named **Divide_by_zero_exception**:

```
#include <iostream>
#include <string>
using namespace std;

class Divide_by_zero_exception
{
    string error_message;
public:
    string get_error(){return error_message;}
    Divide_by_zero_exception(){error_message = "Error: division by zero.";}
};
    .
    .
    .
```

Now I'll divide two numbers provided by the user inside two **try** blocks (there's no real reason to do this here except as illustration):

```
#include <iostream>
#include <string>
using namespace std;

class Divide_by_zero_exception
{
    string error_message;
public:
    string get_error(){return error_message;}
    Divide_by_zero_exception(){error_message = "Error: division by zero.";}
};
```

```
int main ()
{
    float op1, op2;

    cout << "Enter the two floating point numbers to divide: ";
    cin >> op1 >> op2;

    try
    {
        try
        {
            if(op2 != 0)
                cout << op1 << "/" << op2 << " = " << op1/op2 << endl;
            else
                throw Divide_by_zero_exception();
        }
    }
    .
    .
    .
```

And I'll add two **catch** blocks to handle exceptions—note that the inner **catch** block just rethrows the exception to the outer **catch** block:

```
#include <iostream>
#include <string>
using namespace std;

class Divide_by_zero_exception
{
    string error_message;
public:
    string get_error(){return error_message;}
    Divide_by_zero_exception(){error_message = "Error: division by zero.";}
};

int main ()
{
    float op1, op2;

    cout << "Enter the two floating point numbers to divide: ";
    cin >> op1 >> op2;
```

```
    try
    {
        try
        {
            if(op2 != 0)
                cout << op1 << "/" << op2 << " = " << op1/op2 << endl;
            else
                throw Divide_by_zero_exception();
        }
        catch (Divide_by_zero_exception e)
        {
            cout << "Rethrowing the exception." << endl;
            throw;
        }
    }
    catch (Divide_by_zero_exception e)
    {
        cout << e.get_error() << endl;
    }

    return 0;
}
```

Here's what you see when you run this program, exceptrethrow.cpp, and try to divide by zero—you can see the messages displayed by both the inner and outer **catch** blocks here:

```
%exceptrethrow
Enter the two floating point numbers to divide: 1 0
Rethrowing the exception.
Error: division by zero.
```

Creating Catch-All Handlers

Can you create a **catch** block that handles any kind of exception? Yes, you can. To do that, you give a **catch** block the exception specification "**...**". Here's an example, exceptany.cpp, with a **catch** block that will catch any type of exception:

```
#include <iostream>
#include <string>
using namespace std;
```

```
int main ()
{
   float op1, op2;
   string s;

   cout << "Enter the two floating point numbers to divide: ";
   cin >> op1 >> op2;

   try
   {
      if(op2 != 0)
          cout << op1 << "/" << op2 << " = " << op1/op2 << endl;
      else {
          s = "Error: division by zero.";
          throw s;
      }
   }
   catch (...)
   {
      cout << s << endl;
   }

   return 0;
}
```

That's all it takes; here's what you see when you run this example, exceptany.cpp:

```
%exceptany
Enter the two floating point numbers to divide: 1 0
Error: division by zero.
```

Chapter 13

I/O Streams

In Depth

This chapter is all about input and output, I/O, in C++. Unlike other languages, C++ uses I/O *streams* to handle input and output from your programs. I/O is considered a stream of data moving to or from your program to or from other devices, such as the keyboard, screen, or a hard disk. In fact, support for I/O is not built into the C++ language (for example, **cin** and **cout** are not built-in keywords) but instead is supported by the **iostream** and **fstream** classes. The C language comes with a standard library of functions for I/O, and C++ comes with both those functions and the **iostream** and **fstream** classes.

The **iostream** classes are designed for the kind of I/O we've been doing so far, and the **fstream** classes are for working with files of the kind you store on disk. For example, the **cout** object is an object of the **ostream** class, the **cin** object is an object of the **istream** class, and both **istream** and **ostream** are part of the **iostream** classes. To be able to work with console I/O, we've already used **cout** and **cin** throughout this book, but to really understand what's going on, we'll dig deeper into those objects and their associated classes in this chapter. In the next chapter, we'll work with I/O specifically targeted to files on disk.

It's worth noting that the I/O streams in C++ have evolved over time, so their design is anything but systematic. In fact, the C++ I/O support is a real hodgepodge of classes and methods, and what's most important is knowing what's available—including the seemingly random, but very important, collection of stream methods. I'll start that examination in this chapter.

All About Streams and Buffers

C++ treats input and output as a stream of bytes. We've already seen the **cin** and **cout** objects throughout this book, which are objects of the **istream** and **ostream** classes. You can use the >> operator to extract data from an input stream and the << operator to insert data into an output stream, or use the other stream methods we'll see in this chapter. Input data can come from the keyboard, files on disk, another program, even the Internet, and so on. Output data can go to the screen, files, another program, the Internet, and so on.

Treating I/O in terms of streams lets C++ treat input from the keyboard in much the same way as from a file on disk and output to the screen in much the same way as to a file on disk. In fact, one often calls input sources or output targets *files*, no matter what they really are. In this way, C++ programmers often think of input as a stream of bytes from a "file," even if it's really coming from the keyboard or the Internet. And output goes to another "file," even if that really means the screen. If you really need to make the distinction between an actual file on disk and an I/O device, you can use the terms *physical files* for actual disk files and *logical files* for general I/O sources and targets. With this terminology, then, input consists of connecting a stream from a file to your program, and output consists of connecting a stream from your program to a file.

I/O is often *buffered* in C++. A buffer holds data in storage on its way into or out of a program. Because writing and reading data often go at different rates, this is very useful. A typical buffer size is 1,024 bytes, or some multiple of that number, and read and write operations can handle that many bytes at once. You can see the utility of this: imagine you're reading data from a disk—you wouldn't want to perform 1,024 individual read operations from the disk, you'd want to read that many bytes all at once. Buffering comes in handy in other ways as well; for example, what the user types at the keyboard is buffered until the user presses ENTER. One of the main reasons for the buffer is so that the user can correct errors before sending data to your program.

In fact, we've already worked with I/O buffers in this book, even if only implicitly. For example, we've used **endl** throughout our code to end output to the console:

```
#include <iostream>
using namespace std;

int main()
{
    float pi = 3.14159;

    cout << pi << endl;

    return 0;
}
```

In fact, **endl** is an **ostream** *manipulator*, which empties the output buffer—an operation called *flushing* the buffer—by sending the buffer's contents to the console and also sending a newline character. Here's what you see when you run this code:

```
%pi
3.14159
```

Using iostream

The iostream header we've used throughout the book provides the classes you normally use for I/O, although you can build or derive your own. Here are some of the classes in **iostream**:

- The **streambuf** class allocates memory for buffers and supports methods to handle that memory, such as flushing the buffer.
- The **ios_base** class gives you information about a stream, such as whether it's open or closed, or if it's a text or binary stream.
- The **ios** class is based on **ios_base** and adds a pointer to the **streambuf** object.
- The **ostream** class is derived from the **ios** class and supports output; **cout** is an **ostream** object.
- The **istream** class is derived from the **ios** class and supports input; **cin** is an **istream** object.
- The **iostream** class is based on both **istream** and **ostream** and supports both input and output.

***NOTE:** Behind the scenes, the actual situation has become fairly complex. The ANSI/ISO C++ committee realized that the standard ASCII code it used for characters had become inadequate and wanted to add support for wide characters, such as Unicode (see "Working with **char** Data Types" in Chapter 2). The standard character type is **char**, which uses one byte of storage, and the wide character type, **wchar_t**, uses two bytes of storage. To add support for **wchar_t** I/O, the ANSI/ISO committee could have created an entirely new set of I/O classes, which would involve duplicating all that had already been done for **char** I/O. Instead, they based the I/O classes on class templates, such as **basic_istream<charT, traits<charT> >** and **basic_ostream<charT, traits<charT> >**, where **traits<charT>** specifies how to handle the character in code (as for comparisons). The **istream** and **ostream** classes are now **typedefs** for **char** specializations of those templates, and the **wistream** and **wostream** classes are **typdefs** for **wchar_t** specializations. The **ios** class was made into a class template, and the ANSI/ISO committee introduced the **ios_base** class to hold non-template features, such as the constants used in the **ios** class.*

When you include the iostream header in your program, as we've done in all examples so far, you actually create eight stream objects:

- **cin**—Reads from the standard input device. By default, that's the keyboard.
- **cout**—Writes to the standard output device. By default, that's the screen.
- **cerr**—Writes to the standard error device. By default, that's the screen.
- **clog**—Also writes to the standard error device. By default, that's the screen.
- **wcin**—The same as **cin**, but for wide characters.
- **wcout**—The same as **cout**, but for wide characters.
- **wcerr**—The same as **cerr**, but for wide characters.
- **wclog**—The same as **clog**, but for wide characters.

Here's an example using **wcout** (recall from Chapter 2 that you use a capital L in front of wide character literals) to display a message—note that not all compilers support **wcout**:

```
#include <iostream>
using namespace std;

int main()
{
    wchar_t string[] = L"C++";

    wcout << L"Hello from " << string << endl;

    return 0;
}
```

Here's what this program displays:

```
%wcouter
Hello from C++
```

You can redirect the I/O that uses the **iostream** objects under operating systems like DOS and UNIX. For example, take a look at this code, output.cpp, which displays the letters B, C, and A, each on their own lines:

```
#include <iostream>
using namespace std;

int main()
{
    cout << "B" << endl;
    cout << "C" << endl;
    cout << "A" << endl;

    return 0;
}
```

Here's what you see when you run this example:

```
%output
B
C
A
```

In UNIX, you can take the output from this program and redirect it using operators like | and >. For example, to sort this output, I can use the UNIX **sort** filter and send the result to a physical file named sorted.txt. When I display the contents of the sorted.txt file with the UNIX **cat** command, I see the sorted data:

```
/steve/cpp: output | sort > sorted.txt
/steve/cpp: cat sorted.txt
A
B
C
```

In this way, I've redirected the output from the program to the **sort** filter and from that filter to a file on disk. You can do the same thing in DOS:

```
C:\cpp>output | sort > sorted.txt
C:\cpp>type sorted.txt
A
B
C
```


In both operating systems, you can also send input to a program using the < operator like this:

```
spellcheck < sorted.txt
```

This command sends the contents of the file sorted.txt to the **spellcheck** command in the standard input stream, which corresponds to **cin**. (In UNIX, you can also redirect I/O from the other streams by using operators such as **2>**, which corresponds to the standard error stream).

When you work with **iostream** I/O, the two major objects you use are **cout** and **cin** (unless you're working with wide characters, in which case you use **wcout** and **wcin**). Much of this chapter has to do with those two objects, and I'll start with **cout**.

Using cout Methods

We're already very familiar with the fact that you can use the overloaded << operator, the insertion operator, to send data to **cout**. However, **cout** also has many member methods, and we'll take a look at them in this chapter. For example, you can use the **setf** method to set formatting flags inside **cout** that determine much of its behavior (**setf** means "set flags"). Here's an example, setf.cpp, in which I begin by declaring a floating point value, **pi**, and by calling **setf** with an argument of **ios_base::showpos** to make **cout** display leading + signs in front of positive numbers:

```
#include <iostream>
using namespace std;

int main()
{
    float pi = 3.14159;

    cout.setf(ios_base::showpos);
    cout << pi << endl;
    .
    .
    .
```

Now when this code runs, you'll see +3.14159, not just 3.14159. Note the constant that I passed to **setf—ios_base::showpos**. This constant is defined as a static value in the **ios_base** class, which is why you have to qualify its name with **ios_base::**. The **setf** method actually sets the bits in the formatting flags inside the **cout** object, so you could actually pass values with individual bits set to 1 to set the corresponding flags. However, that's very tedious, so the designers of C++ created constants with descriptive names in the **ios_base** class. (As noted earlier in this chapter, the **ios_base** class was created to hold the non-template features of the **ios** class that is the base of **istream** and **ostream**, and one of the non-template features is the constants you use to configure **istream** and **ostream** objects.) One of those constants is **ios_base::showpos**, which makes **cout** preface positive numbers with a +.

***TIP:** If your compiler doesn't understand constants like **ios_base::name**, try **ios::name** instead. If that works, your compiler probably doesn't support the split that was made between the **ios** and **ios_base** classes, and it probably won't support wide character sets.*

Besides the normal defaults **cout** uses to display numbers, you can also configure **cout** to use scientific notation for floating point values (which displays an exponent, like 3.14E+01, meaning 3.14×10^1) or fixed decimal point notation (such as 3.14). You can specify the precision with which **cout** displays floating point numbers using the **cout** method **precision**. When you display floating point numbers using default formatting, the number you set for the numeric precision indicates the total number of digits displayed for each number, but when you're using either fixed decimal point or scientific notation, the precision sets the number of digits to the right of the decimal place.

To see how this works, I'll start with fixed decimal point notation. To make **cout** use fixed decimal point notation, you must first turn off any bits that correspond to other types of numeric notation that can now be set. To do that, I'll use the two-argument form of **setf** and pass it the argument **ios_base::floatfield**, which turns off all bits for floating point formatting. I'll also turn on fixed decimal notation by passing a value of **ios_base::fixed** to **setf**. Finally, I'll make **cout** display two numbers after the decimal place with the **precision** method:

```
#include <iostream>
using namespace std;

int main()
{
    float pi = 3.14159;

    cout.setf(ios_base::showpos);
    cout << pi << endl;

    cout.setf(ios_base::fixed, ios_base::floatfield);
    cout.precision(2);
    cout << pi << endl;
    .
    .
    .
```

Now you'll see +3.14 when this code is executed. Changing the precision to 3 makes **cout** display three digits after the decimal point (even if they are zeros, which is not the way C++ used to work before it was standardized—in the old days, trailing zeros were suppressed):

```
#include <iostream>
using namespace std;

int main()
{
    float pi = 3.14159;

    cout.setf(ios_base::showpos);
    cout << pi << endl;

    cout.setf(ios_base::fixed, ios_base::floatfield);
    cout.precision(2);
    cout << pi << endl;
```

```
    cout.precision(3);
    cout << pi << endl;
    .
    .
    .
```

I can also use scientific notation, which displays floating point numbers with exponents. To display four digits after the decimal place, I can set the precision to 4, and I can make the e for the exponent into an uppercase E with **setf(ios_base::uppercase)**:

```
#include <iostream>
using namespace std;

int main()
{
    float pi = 3.14159;

    cout.setf(ios_base::showpos);
    cout << pi << endl;

    cout.setf(ios_base::fixed, ios_base::floatfield);
    cout.precision(2);
    cout << pi << endl;

    cout.precision(3);
    cout << pi << endl;

    cout.setf(ios_base::scientific, ios_base::floatfield);
    cout.setf(ios_base::uppercase);
    cout.precision(4);
    cout << pi << endl;

    return 0;
}
```

Here's what you see when you run this example, setf.cpp:

```
%setf
+3.14159
+3.14
+3.142
+3.1416E+00
```

Using Manipulators

Although you can use **setf** to configure the formatting **cout** will use, it's not the most intuitive way of doing things. To make things simpler, C++ also supports *manipulators*. Manipulators are objects you can pass to **cout** to configure **cout**, just as you would with **setf**, and many people find them more intuitive than **setf**. We've already used the **endl** manipulator, which flushes the standard output stream's buffer and also sends a newline character to that stream:

```
#include <iostream>
#include <iomanip>
using namespace std;

int main()
{
    float pi = 3.14159;

    cout << "Pi: " << pi << endl;
    .
    .
    .
```


You can also use manipulators to format **cout**. For example, if I use the **cout** method **precision** to set the default precision of **cout** to 3, then three digits will be displayed for floating point numbers (so 3.14159 will be displayed as 3.14). However, you can also use the **setprecision** manipulator to do the same thing—just pass that manipulator an argument of 3 and then pass the whole manipulator to **cout**. To use the **setprecision** manipulator, you also include the iomanip header file:

```
#include <iostream>
#include <iomanip>
using namespace std;

int main()
{
    float pi = 3.14159;

    cout << "Pi: " << pi << endl;

    cout << setprecision(3) << "Pi with a precision of three digits: "
        << pi << endl;

    return 0;
}
```

Here's what you see when you run this example:

```
%pi
Pi: 3.14159
Pi with a precision of three digits: 3.14
```

There are many manipulators; for example, you can use the **hex** and **oct** manipulators to set the numeric base for display to hexadecimal and octal, respectively (which you can also do with **setf** using the constants **ios_base::hex** and **ios_base::oct**). Here's how that looks in an example called numericbase.cpp that asks the user for a number and displays it in various numeric bases:

```
#include <iostream>
using namespace std;

int main()
{
    int integer;
    cout << "Give me a positive integer: ";
    cin >> integer;

    cout << "In decimal: " << integer << endl;

    cout << hex;

    cout << "In hexadecimal: " << integer << endl;

    cout << oct;

    cout << "In octal: " << integer << endl;

    return 0;
}
```

Here's what you see when you run this example, numericbase.cpp:

```
%numericbase
Give me a positive integer: 24
In decimal: 24
In hexadecimal: 18
In octal: 30
```

It's an interesting fact about manipulators that instead of passing them to **cout**, you can also pass **cout** to them. For example, the statement

```
cout << oct;
```

is the same as

```
oct(cout);
```

We'll see more about manipulators later in this chapter.

Using cin Methods

The **cin** object also has its own methods, just as **cout** does, and we'll take a look at those methods in this chapter. For example, you can use the **get** method to read an individual character, the **peek** method to check the next character in the standard input stream without taking it out of the stream, the **ignore** method to ignore characters, and the **putback** method to put a character back into the stream. Here's an example, peek.cpp, that puts these methods to work. I'll start by reading characters from **cin** and echoing each one, stopping when I see the character **'q'**. One way to do that is to use the **peek** method to check the next character in the input stream and see if it's **'q'** and read it with the **get** method if it's not:

```
#include <iostream>
using namespace std;

int main()
{
    char character;

    cout << "I read up to the letter 'q': ";

    while(cin.peek() != 'q')
    {
        cin.get(character);
        cout << character;
    }
    .
    .
    .
```

Note that any text the user typed after the letter **'q'** is still in the input stream's buffer when this loop finishes. We can get rid of that text with the **cin** method **ignore**. You pass this method the number of characters to remove from the input buffer, and it will remove that number of characters, or until it reaches a character you specify, such as the newline character **'\n'**. That looks like this in code:

```
#include <iostream>
using namespace std;

int main()
{
    const int MAX = 100;
    char character;
    char string[MAX];

    cout << "I read up to the letter 'q': ";

    while(cin.peek() != 'q')
    {
        cin.get(character);
        cout << character;
    }

    cout << endl;

    cin.ignore(MAX, '\n');
    .
    .
    .
```

Now that the input buffer is clear, I can read a character with the **get** method and then put it back into the input stream with **putback**. To do that, I'll ask the user to type more text, read only the first typed character and echo it, and then put it back into the input stream and read all the user has typed, displaying that data to show that the first character is back in place. I'll store the new text in a **char** array named **string**; here's what the code looks like:

```
#include <iostream>
using namespace std;

int main()
{
    const int MAX = 100;
    char character;
    char string[MAX];

    cout << "I read up to the letter 'q': ";
```

```
    while(cin.peek() != 'q')
    {
        cin.get(character);
        cout << character;
    }

    cout << endl;

    cin.ignore(MAX, '\n');

    cout << "Please type some more text: ";

    cin.get(character);
    cout << "The first character was: " << character << endl;
    cin.putback(character);

    cin.get(string, MAX).get();

    cout << "Here's the full text: " << string << endl;

    return 0;
}
```


Note that I read all that the user typed with the **get** method like this: **cin.get(string, MAX).get()**. If I had used **cin >> string** instead, I would have obtained only the first word that the user typed. The overloaded **cin** >> operator skips over white space and returns only one word at a time; to read a whole line, I use **get** as shown here. The second **get** is necessary to remove the trailing newline character—see the "Using the **istream** Class's **get**, **getline**, and **ignore** Methods" later in this chapter for more information. Here's what this example, peek.cpp, displays when you run it—note that it reads text up to but not including the first '**q**', clears the buffer, reads the first new character typed, returns it to the input buffer, and then displays the entire line of text that the user typed:

```
%peek
I read up to the letter 'q': What is the query?
What is the
Please type some more text: Anacondas can be inconvenient.
The first character was: A
Here's the full text: Anacondas can be inconvenient.
```

As you can see, there's plenty of new material coming up in this chapter. We'll start with **cout** and its methods in the Immediate Solutions section now.

Immediate Solutions

Using cout

It's safe to say that you're familiar with **cout**, because virtually every example in this book has used it. **cout** is an **ostream** object, and its << operator is overloaded for the basic types:

- **char**
- **unsigned char**
- **signed char**
- **short**
- **unsigned short**
- **int**
- **unsigned int**
- **long**
- **unsigned long**
- **float**
- **double**
- **long double**

Here's an example, pi.cpp, that uses the overloaded << insertion operator:

```
#include <iostream>
using namespace std;

int main()
{
    float pi = 3.14159;

    cout << pi << endl;

    return 0;
}
```

When I send a **float** to **cout**, the program uses the overloaded method **ostream & operator<<(float)** to display the **float**. Here's what you see when you run this code:

```
%pi
3.14159
```

The **cout** object is also overloaded for various pointer types to handle **char** strings and so on:

- **const char ***
- **const signed char ***
- **const unsigned char ***
- **void ***

Here's an example where I'm displaying a **char** string using **cout**:

```
#include <iostream>
using namespace std;

int main()
{
    char *pi = "Pi, more or less, is 3.14159.";

    cout << pi << endl;

    return 0;
}
```

Here's what this program displays:

```
%pi
Pi, more or less, is 3.14159.
```

The overloaded << operator returns a reference to an **ostream** object, and that object is **cout** itself. That means you can chain insertion operations like this:

```
#include <iostream>
using namespace std;

int main()
{
    char *pi = "Pi, more or less, is 3.14159.";

    cout << pi << " Yes it is." << endl;
```

```
    return 0;
}
```

Here's the result:

```
%pi
Pi, more or less, is 3.14159. Yes it is.
```

Besides the overloaded << operator, the **cout** object also supports methods like **put** and **write**—see the next section for the details.

Using the **ostream** Class's **put** and **write** Methods

The **cout** method **put** displays characters, and **write** displays strings. Here's an example that uses **put**, put.cpp. You use **put** to display individual characters, and you pass it the character code for the character you want to display. You can also chain this method, so here's how I display the characters A and B:

```
#include <iostream>
using namespace std;

int main()
{
    cout.put('A').put('B') << endl;
        .
        .
        .
```

You can also pass **put** character codes directly, such as 67, which is the ASCII code for **'C'** (the C++ compiler changes character literals like **'A'** to their associated codes in any case). In fact, you can even pass floating point values to **put**, and it'll take just the integer part:

```
#include <iostream>
using namespace std;

int main()
{
    cout.put('A').put('B').put(67).put(68.92038) << endl;

    return 0;
}
```

Here is what this program displays:

```
%put
ABCD
```

The **put** method used to be more popular in the earlier days of C++. For example, in the old days, **cout << 'A'** would display the ASCII code for '**A**', 65, but you could use **cout.put('A')** to display the character A.

The **write** method sends C-style strings to the standard output stream. You also pass this method the number of characters to display. One of the odd facts about **write** is that you can pass it a number larger than the total number of characters in a string, and it'll continue on, displaying the next bytes in memory. Here's an example, write.cpp, with two strings, "Deliciously" and "wicked.", which are next to each other in memory. Using **write**, I can display "Delicious", "Deliciously", and even "Deliciously wicked.":

```
#include <iostream>
using namespace std;

int main()
{
    const char * word = "Deliciously";
    const char * extra = "wicked.";

    cout.write(word, 9);
    cout << endl;

    cout.write(word, 11);
    cout << endl;

    cout.write(word, 19);
    cout << endl;

    return 0;
}
```

Here's what you see when you run this example, write.cpp:

```
%write
Delicious
Deliciously
Deliciously wicked.
```

However, note that using **write** to display data past the current string like this is very dangerous, and the results will vary from what you expect, all the way to causing memory faults that will halt your program, depending on your compiler.

Understanding the **cout** Formatting Defaults

By default, **cout** formats data this way:

- **char** values are displayed as one character wide.
- **int** values are displayed in base 10, in a field wide enough to hold the number and possible minus sign.
- *Strings* are displayed in a field of the same length as the string.
- **float** values are displayed with six digits total, except that trailing zeros are not displayed. These numbers are displayed in floating point format or exponent format, which uses e (e notation is used if the exponent is 6 or larger or –5 or smaller). (The old C++ style was to display six digits to the right of the decimal place and to omit trailing zeros.)

Here's an example, defaultformatting.cpp, that shows **cout** default formatting at work. In this example, I'll display one character and add a period, ., to show that the character is displayed in a field one character wide. I'll also display the value 1.33333333 to show that only six total digits are displayed by default—unless the leading value is a 0, in which case seven (including the leading zero) are displayed. I'll also display the value 1.234e-4, which will appear as 0.0001234, and then divide that value by 10, which will make **cout** display the result in scientific notation as 1.234e-05:

```
#include <iostream>
using namespace std;

int main()
{
    char ch = 'A';
    cout << ch << "." << endl;

    double float1 = 1.0 + 1.0 / 3.0;
    cout << float1 << endl;

    double float2 = 1.0 / 3.0;
    cout << float2 << endl;
```

```
    double float3 = 1.234e-4;
    cout << float3 << endl;
    cout << float3 / 10 << endl;

    return 0;
}
```

Here's what you see when you run this example, defaultformatting.cpp:

```
%defaultformatting
A.
1.33333
0.333333
0.0001234
1.234e-05
```


Another item to note is that by default, trailing zeros are omitted, as are trailing decimal points. In other words, 1.0 would be displayed as 1 by default. You can display trailing decimal points with the call **setf(ios_base::showpoint)**, which would make 1.0 appear as 1. instead. You can also display trailing zeros if you switch to fixed decimal format with a call like this: **setf(ios_base::fixed, ios_base::floatfield)**, or scientific notation, with a call like this: **setf(ios_base::scientific, ios_base::floatfield)**, and use the **precision** method to set the number of places to display. See "Setting Floating Point Display Precision" later in this chapter for more details.

Setting **cout** Field Widths

You can use the **cout** method **width** to specify how wide you want output fields to be. Each item is displayed in its own field, and **cout** usually selects how wide that field is by default (see "Understanding the **cout** Formatting Defaults" earlier in this chapter). However, you can set the width of each display field yourself.

Here's an example, fieldwidth.cpp, that does that. In this case, I'll also turn on right justification of text in their display fields to indicate how wide the fields are with the manipulator **right**—see "Using Manipulators" and "Using **setf** to Set Formatting Flags" later in this chapter for more information. (If your compiler doesn't understand the **right** manipulator, use the call **setf(ios_base::right, ios_base::adjustfield)** instead.) Here's how I display some text after setting the display field widths to various sizes in fieldwidth.cpp:

```
#include <iostream>
using namespace std;

int main()
{
    cout.width(40);
    cout << right;
    cout << "Right justification." << endl;

    cout.width(10);
    cout << "Hello";
    cout.width(20);
    cout << "there." << endl;

    return 0;
}
```

And here's what you see when you run this example—note that I've been able to set the width of each item's output field as well as right-justify the text:

```
%fieldwidth
                    Right justification.
     Hello              there.
```


Setting **cout** Fill Characters

You can specify the "fill" character used to fill out the places in a display field (see "Setting **cout** Field Widths" earlier in this chapter for more about display fields). The normal fill character is a space, but you can use the **fill** method to change that to what you want. For example, you might want to fill the space between the $ sign and the amount of a check to make sure the check recipient cannot add a few extra digits to the check amount. Here's an example, fill.cpp, that shows how that works by setting the fill character to '*':

```
#include <iostream>
using namespace std;

int main()
{
    cout.fill('*');
```

```
    cout << "Pay exactly $";

    cout.width(10);

    cout << "1000.00" << endl;

    return 0;
}
```

Here's what this example, fill.cpp, displays:

```
%fill
Pay exactly $***1000.00
```


Using **setf** to Set Formatting Flags

The big **cout** method you use to configure formatting is **setf**, which stands for "set flags," because **setf** sets the internal formatting flags of the **cout** object. This method accepts an argument of the **ios_base::fmtflags** type that specifies the new setting of the flags and returns a value of the same type as that holding the old flag settings:

```
ios_base::fmtflags setf(ios_base::fmtflags flags)
```

TIP: *You can store the return value of this method and pass it back to* ***setf*** *to restore the formatting flags to the setting they had before you changed them.*

Although you can pass values with various bits set to **setf** yourself, Table 13.1 lists the **ios_base** class constants that you can pass to **setf** that already have symbolic names.

TIP: *If your compiler doesn't understand constants like* ***ios_base::name****, use* ***ios::name*** *instead. If that works, your compiler probably doesn't support the split that was made between the* ***ios*** *and* ***ios_base*** *classes yet.*

There's also a two-argument form of **setf**:

```
ios_base::fmtflags setf(ios_base::fmtflags set_flags,
    ios_base::fmtflags clear_flags);
```

In this form of **setf**, the second argument, ***clear_flags***, clears the formatting bits for a specific aspect of formatting, such as formatting floating point values, and the first argument, ***set_flags***, specifies the new formatting settings you want. Table 13.2 lists the **ios_base** class constants you can use with the two-argument form of **setf**.

We've already seen an example of **setf** in action in the beginning of this chapter, setf.cpp. In that example, I used **setf(ios_base::showpos)** to make **cout** display a + in front of positive numbers, **setf(ios_base::fixed, ios_base::floatfield)** to switch to fixed decimal place notation, set the precision with the **precision** method, and then switched to scientific notation with **setf(ios_base::scientific, ios_base::floatfield)** (for more on fixed decimal place and scientific notation, see "Setting Floating Point Display Precision" later in this chapter):

```
#include <iostream>
using namespace std;
```


Table 13.1 Constants used with setf.

Constant	Means
ios_base::boolalpha	Display bool values as true and false instead of 1 and 0.
ios_base::showbase	Use 0 or 0x as needed.
ios_base::showpoint	Show trailing decimal point.
ios_base::uppercase	Display hex letters and E in uppercase.
ios_base::showpos	Add a + in front of positive numbers.

Table 13.2 Constants used with the two-argument version of setf.

Argument2	Argument1	Means
ios_base::basefield	**ios_base::dec**	Set to base 10.
	ios_base::oct	Set to base 8.
	ios_base::hex	Set to base 16.
ios_base::floatfield	**ios_base::fixed**	Use fixed point notation.
	ios_base::scientific	Use scientific notation.
ios_base::adjustfield	**ios_base::left**	Left-justify.
	ios_base::right	Right-justify.
	ios_base::internal	Left-justify sign or base prefix, right-justify the rest.

```
int main()
{
    float pi = 3.14159;

    cout.setf(ios_base::showpos);
    cout << pi << endl;

    cout.setf(ios_base::fixed, ios_base::floatfield);
    cout.precision(2);
    cout << pi << endl;

    cout.precision(3);
    cout << pi << endl;

    cout.setf(ios_base::scientific, ios_base::floatfield);
    cout.setf(ios_base::uppercase);
    cout.precision(4);
    cout << pi << endl;

    return 0;
}
```


Here is what this program, setf.cpp, displays:

```
%setf
+3.14159
+3.14
+3.142
+3.1416E+00
```

There's also an **unsetf** method that turns off the specified flag bit. For example, here's how I turn on and then off the **ios_base::showpos** flag, which makes **cout** display a + in front of positive numbers:

```
setf(ios_base::showpos);
unsetf(ios_base::showpos);
```

Using **setf** to Set Justification

You can use **setf** to set the justification of text in output fields. Here's an example, justification.cpp, to show how this works. To set left justification, for example, you use **setf(ios_base::left, ios_base::adjustfield)**. There are three types of justification: right, left, and internal (which left-justifies signs and base prefixes like 0x and right-justifies the rest), and here's how I use them all:

```
#include <iostream>
#include <cmath>
using namespace std;

int main()
{
    float pi = 3.14159;

    cout.setf(ios_base::showpos);

    cout << "Left Justification:\n";
    cout.setf(ios_base::left, ios_base::adjustfield);

    cout << "|";
    cout.width(20);
    cout << pi;
    cout << "|" << endl;

    cout << "Internal Justification:\n";
    cout.setf(ios_base::internal, ios_base::adjustfield);

    cout << "|";
    cout.width(20);
    cout << pi;
    cout << "|" << endl;

    cout << "Right Justification:\n";
    cout.setf(ios_base::right, ios_base::adjustfield);

    cout << "|";
    cout.width(20);
    cout << pi;
    cout << "|" << endl;

    return 0;
}
```

Note that I've also made **cout** display a leading + sign in front of positive numbers with **setf(ios_base::showpos)** to show how internal justification works:

```
%justification
Left Justification:
```

```
|+3.14159          |
Internal Justification:
|+          3.14159|
Right Justification:
|          +3.14159|
```

Setting Floating Point Display Precision

To set numeric precision, you can use the **cout** method **precision** or the **setprecision** manipulator. In the default **cout** display mode, the precision sets the total number of digits floating point numbers are displayed with; in fixed and scientific modes, it means the number of digits to the right of the decimal place.

We already saw an example, precision.cpp, in the In Depth section of this chapter that uses default formatting and sets numeric precision to 3 (instead of the **setprecision(3)** manipulator, which requires the iomanip header, I could also use the **precision** method, like this: **cout.precision(3)**):

```
#include <iostream>
#include <iomanip>
using namespace std;

int main()
{
    float pi = 3.14159;

    cout << "Pi: " << pi << endl;

    cout << setprecision(3) << "Pi with a precision of three digits: "
        << pi << endl;

    return 0;
}
```

Here's what you see when you run this example, precision.cpp—note that pi is displayed with a total of three digits here:

```
%precision
Pi: 3.14159
Pi with a precision of three digits: 3.14
```

You can also see how fixed and scientific notation affects displayed floating point precision in another example from the In Depth section of this chapter, setf.cpp. When you use either fixed decimal place or scientific notation, the precision sets the number of places displayed to the right of the decimal place (and, unlike the default mode, trailing zeros are displayed). Here's how setf.cpp puts this to work:

```
#include <iostream>
using namespace std;

int main()
{
    float pi = 3.14159;

    cout.setf(ios_base::showpos);
    cout << pi << endl;

    cout.setf(ios_base::fixed, ios_base::floatfield);
    cout.precision(2);
    cout << pi << endl;

    cout.precision(3);
    cout << pi << endl;

    cout.setf(ios_base::scientific, ios_base::floatfield);
    cout.setf(ios_base::uppercase);
    cout.precision(4);
    cout << pi << endl;

    return 0;
}
```

Here's what setf.cpp displays:

```
%setf
+3.14159
+3.14
+3.142
+3.1416E+00
```

Using Manipulators

As mentioned in the In Depth section of this chapter, although you can use **setf** to configure **cout**, that's often not very intuitive. However, you can also use manipulators to do the same thing. You'll find the standard manipulators in Table 13.3, which also lists the corresponding **setf** calls.

NOTE: *Here's something important—many of the manipulators you see in Table 13.3 are not available to older compilers, or even some newer ones (including one of the UNIX compilers I'm using to test the code in this book). If your compiler doesn't support these manipulators, you should use the equivalent* ***setf*** *calls, also listed in Table 13.3.*

Besides those listed in Table 13.3, there are other manipulators available, such as the **flush** manipulator, which flushes the output buffer, and **endl**, which flushes the output buffer and sends a newline to the standard output stream. There are two ways to use manipulators: First, you can pass them to **cout**, as in the example numericbase.cpp that we saw in the In Depth section of this chapter, where

Table 13.3 Standard manipulators and the equivalent setf calls.

Manipulator	Corresponding setf call
boolalpha	setf(ios_base::boolalpha)
dec	setf(ios_base::dec, ios_base::basefield)
fixed	setf(ios_base::fixed, ios_base::floatfield)
hex	setf(ios_base::hex, ios_base::basefield)
internal	setf(ios_base::internal, ios_base::adjustfield)
left	setf(ios_base::left, ios_base::adjustfield)
noboolalpha	unsetf(ios_base::boolalpha)
noshowbase	unsetf(ios_base::showbase)
noshowpoint	unsetf(ios_base::showpoint)
noshowpos	unsetf(ios_base::showpos)
nouppercase	unsetf(ios_base::uppercase)
oct	setf(ios_base::oct, ios_base::basefield)
right	setf(ios_base::right, ios_base::adjustfield)
scientific	setf(ios_base::scientific, ios_base::floatfield)
showbase	setf(ios_base::showbase)
showpoint	setf(ios_base::showpoint)
showpos	setf(ios_base::showpos)
uppercase	setf(ios_base::uppercase)

I used the **hex** and **oct** manipulators to set the numeric display base to hexadecimal and octal:

```
#include <iostream>
using namespace std;

int main()
{
    int integer;
    cout << "Give me a positive integer: ";
    cin >> integer;

    cout << "In decimal: " << integer << endl;

    cout << hex;

    cout << "In hexadecimal: " << integer << endl;

    cout << oct;

    cout << "In octal: " << integer << endl;

    return 0;
}
```

Here's what you see when you run this example, numericbase.cpp:

```
%numericbase
Give me a positive integer: 24
In decimal: 24
In hexadecimal: 18
In octal: 30
```

Second, you can pass **cout** to the manipulators to do the same thing:

```
#include <iostream>
using namespace std;

int main()
{
    int integer;
    cout << "Give me a positive integer: ";
    cin >> integer;
```

```
    cout << "In decimal: " << integer << endl;

    hex(cout);

    cout << "In hexadecimal: " << integer << endl;

    oct(cout);

    cout << "In octal: " << integer << endl;

    return 0;
}
```


Passing Values to Manipulators

You pass values to some manipulators to configure output. The three most common such manipulators are listed here:

- **setprecision**—Sets the precision; pass it the new numeric precision.
- **setfill**—Sets the fill character; pass it the fill character you want to use.
- **setw**—Sets the field width; pass it the field width in characters for the next item's display field.

To use these manipulators, you must include the iomanip header. Here's an example, precision.cpp, that we saw in the In Depth section of this chapter, that shows how to use **setprecision** in the default numeric display mode:

```
#include <iostream>
#include <iomanip>
using namespace std;

int main()
{
    float pi = 3.14159;

    cout << "Pi: " << pi << endl;

    cout << setprecision(3) << "Pi with a precision of three digits: "
        << pi << endl;

    return 0;
}
```

Here's what you see when you run this example, precision.cpp—note that pi is displayed with a total of three digits (see "Setting Floating Point Display Precision" earlier in this chapter for more on setting numeric precision):

```
%precision
Pi: 3.14159
Pi with a precision of three digits: 3.14
```

Creating a Streamable Class

As we saw in Chapter 9, you can overload the << and >> operators in C++, and doing so allows you to specify how your classes should work with the **istream** and **ostream** classes. For example, the prototype for the function **operator<<** looks like this:

```
ostream &operator<<(ostream &stream, const type & object);
```

Here, we're passed a reference to **ostream** (which I name **stream**) and an object of the class you want to stream. Inside **operator<<**, I can use **cout** to send text to the terminal. After I do, I also have to return a reference to the same stream we were passed as a parameter, because << can be *chained*—in other words, expressions like this are legal:

```
cout << apples << oranges;
```

We saw this at work in Chapter 9. In that chapter, I overloaded the **product** class, which had two data members, **name** and **number**, so that those members were displayed when you use << to pass a **product** object to **cout**. Note that I'm making the **operator<<** function a friend of the **product** class so that this function has access to the internal data of the **product** class:

```
#include <iostream>
#include <string>
using namespace std;

class product
{
    int number;
public:
```

```
    string name;
    int get_number(){return number;}
    void set_number(int n){number = n;}
    product(string text, int count);
    friend ostream &operator<<(ostream &stream, const product & p);
};

product::product(string text, int count)
{
    name = text;
    number = count;
}

ostream &operator<<(ostream &stream, const product & p)
{
    cout << "Number of " << p.name << ": " << p.number << endl;
    return stream;
}

int main()
{
    product oranges("oranges", 200);

    cout << oranges << endl;

    return 0;
}
```

Now the **product** class is streamable as far as **cout** is concerned, which means that you can send objects of the **product** class to the terminal with << directly; here's how that looks when you run this example, productclassinsertion.cpp:

```
%productclassinsertion
Number of oranges: 200
```


Related solutions:	Found on page:
Overloading the << Operator	405
Overloading the >> Operator	406

Creating Custom Manipulators

You can create your own custom manipulators. All you have to do is accept an **ostream** object and return the same object:

```
ostream & name(ostream &stream)
{
     .
     .
     .
   return stream;
}
```

Here's an example, newmanip.cpp, that shows how this works. In this case, I'll create a new manipulator named **space_manipulator**, which simply inserts a space into the output stream. After creating the manipulator, I can send it to **cout** this way:

```
#include <iostream>
#include <iomanip>
using namespace std;

ostream &space_manipulator(ostream &stream)
{
   stream << " ";
   return stream;
}

int main()
{
    cout << "Hello" << space_manipulator << "from"
        << space_manipulator << "C++." << endl;

    return 0;
}
```

Here's what you see when you run this example, newmanip.cpp:

```
%newmanip
Hello from C++.
```

Using **cin**

As you already know, you can read input from the standard input device using the **cin** operator's overloaded >> operator. The >> operator is called the extraction operator because it extracts data from streams, and this operator is overloaded for **cin** for these basic types:

- **char &**
- **signed char &**
- **unsigned char &**
- **short &**
- **unsigned short &**
- **int &**
- **unsigned int &**
- **long &**
- **unsigned long &**
- **float &**
- **double &**
- **long double &**

We've been using **cin** since Chapter 1. Here's an example, greeter.cpp, which appeared in Chapter 1; in this case, I'm asking the user how many times they want to see a greeting string displayed and looping that many times, displaying the greeting each time:

```
#include <iostream>
using namespace std;

int main()
{
    int number;

    cout << "How many times do you want to see the greeting? ";

    cin >> number;

    for (int loopIndex = 0; loopIndex < number; loopIndex++){
        cout << "Hello from C++." << endl;
    }
```

```
    return 0;
}
```

Because **cin** is overloaded for type **int**, the >> operator places the integer data the user enters in the variable named **number**. The **cin** object is also overloaded for these C-string types (note that in addition to storing the character data starting at the address specified by the pointer, the overloaded >> methods add a null character at the end of the stored string):

- **char ***
- **signed char ***
- **unsigned char ***

The overloaded **cin** methods of the >> operator skip over white space (spaces, newlines, and tabs) and read everything from the first non–white space character to the first character that doesn't match the target type. For example, say that I have a program named savings.cpp where I'm asking the user to enter the amount of money earned today and add it to a running floating point sum. I check the return value from **cin** in a **while** loop, and if the user enters some inappropriate data, that return value will terminate the loop:

```
#include <iostream>
using namespace std;

int main()
{
    float amount_for_today, total = 0.0;

    cout << "How much did you make today? ";

    while (cin >> amount_for_today)
    {
        cout << "How much did you make today? ";
        total += amount_for_today;
    }

    cout.precision(2);
    cout << showpoint << fixed;
    cout << "Your total: $" << total << endl;

    return 0;
}
```

Here's what you see when you run the program—note that when I enter a value of "5h", the program terminates:

```
%savings
How much did you make today? 55
How much did you make today? 555
How much did you make today? 5h
How much did you make today? Your total: $615.00
```

Note that **cin** returned the 5 part of "5h", and terminated only when it read an inappropriate character. For the details on what's actually going on here, see "Checking Stream States" later in this chapter.

If the user types in more than one word, each one is assigned to a different variable by **cin**. Here's another example, fourwords.cpp, we saw earlier in this chapter, where I'm asking the user to enter four words:


```
#include <iostream>
#include <string>
using namespace std;

int main()
{
    string input1, input2, input3, input4;

    cout << "Type four words: ";

    cin >> input1 >> input2 >> input3 >> input4;

    cout << "You typed: " << input1 << " " << input2 << " ";
    cout << input3 << " " << input4 << endl;

    return 0;
}
```

Here's what this program, fourwords.cpp, looks like at work:

```
%fourwords
Type four words: This is a test...
You typed: This is a test...
```

If you don't want to skip over white space this way when reading input, you should use other **cin** methods besides the overloaded >> method, like **get** or **getline**. See the next two sections for the details.

Using the **istream** Class's **get, getline,** and **ignore** Methods

The **cin** object comes with built-in methods, just as the **cout** object does. For example, you can use the **cin** methods **get(char &)** and **get()** to read characters. The difference between these two is that you pass the variable you want to place the character into to **get(char &)**, and **get()** returns the character in the standard way. You can chain **get** together as in this example, getchar.cpp, where I'm asking the user to type four letters, placing those letters in the variables **char1**, **char2**, **char3**, and **char4**, and displaying those letters this way:

```
#include <iostream>
using namespace std;

int main()
{
    char char1, char2, char3, char4;

    cout << "Type four letters: ";

    cin.get(char1).get(char2).get(char3).get(char4).get();

    cout << "You typed: " << char1 << char2 << char3 << char4 << endl;

    return 0;
}
```

Here's what getchar.cpp looks like at work:

```
%getchar
Type four letters: Hiya
You typed: Hiya
```

You can also use the **get(char*, int, char)** and **getline(char*, int, char)** methods to get whole lines of text. This is very useful because the >> extraction operator treats spaces in lines of text as word boundaries and will return only single words each time you use it. You pass a pointer to a **char** buffer to these methods, as well as an integer value indicating the maximum number of characters to read (**get** and **getline** will actually get a maximum of that value –1 to allow for the null character these methods add to the end of the string). You can also pass an optional character, usually **'\n'**, which will make these methods stop reading input when that character is seen. Here's an example, get.cpp, where I'm asking the user to enter a string of text and using **get** to read the whole line at once—note the second call to **get** to remove the newline at the end of the input (which the string version of the **get** method doesn't remove):

```
#include <iostream>
using namespace std;
const int MAX = 50;

int main()
{
    char string1[MAX];

    cout << "Type some words: ";

    cin.get(string1, MAX).get();

    cout << "You typed: " << string1 << endl;

    return 0;
}
```


Here's what you see when you run get.cpp:

```
%get
Type some words: Hello there.
You typed: Hello there.
```

There's also a **getline** method that's part of the C++ **string** class, and you can use it to read text strings like this:

```
#include <iostream>
#include <string>
using namespace std;

int main()
{
    string response;

    cout << "Please enter the text: ";

    getline(cin, response);

    cout << response;
```

```
    return 0;
}
```

The **cin.ignore** method ignores a specified number of characters in the input buffer, effectively flushing them from that buffer. You can also pass this method an optional character that acts as a terminator, usually a newline character, making **ignore** stop ignoring characters in the input buffer:

```
const int MAX = 100;
    .
    .
    .
cin.ignore(MAX, '\n');
```

Here's an example, ignore.cpp, that asks the user to enter some text and stores the first typed character in a **char** array named **buffer**. The code then displays that first character like this:

```
#include <iostream>
using namespace std;
const int MAX = 100;

int main()
{
    char buffer[MAX];

    cout << "Type some text: ";

    cin.get(buffer[0]);

    cout << "The first character was " << buffer[0] << endl;
    .
    .
    .
```

The program next asks the user to type more text for it to display. However, there's one issue to take care of first—removing the text that we've left in the input buffer after reading the first character of the previously typed text. I'll remove that text with the **ignore** method this way:

```
#include <iostream>
using namespace std;
const int MAX = 100;
```

```
int main()
{
    char buffer[MAX];

    cout << "Type some text: ";

    cin.get(buffer[0]);

    cout << "The first character was " << buffer[0] << endl;

    cin.ignore(MAX, '\n');
    .
    .
    .
```

Now that the input bufer has been emptied, I can read and display the new text:

```
#include <iostream>
using namespace std;
const int MAX = 100;

int main()
{
    char buffer[MAX];

    cout << "Type some text: ";

    cin.get(buffer[0]);

    cout << "The first character was " << buffer[0] << endl;

    cin.ignore(MAX, '\n');

    cout << "Type some text again: ";

    cin.get(buffer, MAX, '\n');

    cout << "You typed: " << buffer << endl;

    return 0;
}
```

Here's what you might see when you run this program, ignore.cpp:

```
%ignore
Type some text: This is the text.
The first character was T
Type some text again: This is some more text.
You typed: This is some more text.
```

Using the **istream** Class's **read, peek, gcount,** and **putback** Methods

The **istream** class supports the **read**, **peek**, **gcount**, and **putback** methods, so they're part of the **cin** object. The **read** method reads a number of bytes and stores them in the buffer you specify. Unlike **get** or **getline**, **read** reads only the number of bytes you've asked for and does not append a null character at the end of the data, which you have to do yourself if you use **read** to read a C-style string:

```
char name[21];
cin.read(name, 20);
name[20] = '\0';
```

You can also chain **read**, as in this example, read.cpp:

```
#include <iostream>
using namespace std;
const int MAX = 100;

int main()
{
    char first_name[21], second_name[21];
    cin.read(first_name, 20).read(second_name, 20);

    first_name[20] = '\0';
    second_name[20] = '\0';

    cout << first_name << endl;
    cout << second_name;

    return 0;
}
```

When you run this example, you can see that **read** has read exactly the number of bytes you've requested:

```
%read
AAAAAAAAAAAAAAAAAAAAAAAAAAAAAAAAAAAAAAAAAAAAAAAAA
First name: AAAAAAAAAAAAAAAAAAAA
Last name: AAAAAAAAAAAAAAAAAAAA
```

The **peek** method returns the next character from the input stream without actually removing it. This is useful if you want to use a certain character as an input terminator.

The **gcount** returns the number of characters read by the last **get**, **getline**, **ignore**, or **read** method. For example, you might have used those methods and want to know how many characters were actually read or ignored.

The **putback** method inserts a character back into the input string, and the inserted character becomes the next one to be read. Like the other **cin** methods, this method can be chained. Note that the **peek** method is much like using **get** to get a character and following it with **putback** to put it back into the input buffer.

We saw an example in the In Depth section of this chapter, peek.cpp, that puts a number of these methods to work. The code starts by reading characters from **cin** and echoing each one, stopping when it sees the character **'q'**. One way to do that is to use the **peek** method to check the next character in the input stream to see if it's **'q'** and then read it with the **get** method if it's not. After clearing the buffer with **ignore**, the code asks the user to enter more text, reads the first character of that text with **get**, and puts it back with the **putback** method. Finally, it displays all the new text:

```
#include <iostream>
using namespace std;

int main()
{
    const int MAX = 100;
    char character;
    char string[100];

    cout << "I read up to the letter 'q': ";

    while(cin.peek() != 'q')
    {
        cin.get(character);
```

```
        cout << character;
    }

    cout << endl;
    cin.ignore(MAX, '\n');

    cout << "Please type some more text: ";

    cin.get(character);
    cout << "The first character was: " << character << endl;
    cin.putback(character);

    cin >> string;

    cout << "Here's the full text: " << string << endl;

    return 0;
}
```


Here's the kind of result you might see from this code:

```
%peek
I read up to the letter 'q': What is the query?
What is the
Please type some more text: Anacondas can be inconvenient.
The first character was: A
Here's the full text: Anacondas can be inconvenient.
```

Checking Stream States

In "Using **cin**" earlier in this chapter, we saw a program called savings.cpp where I asked the user to enter the amount they make each day and add it to a running floating point sum. I check the return value from **cin** in a **while** loop, and if the user enters some inappropriate data, that return value will terminate the loop:

```
#include <iostream>
using namespace std;

int main()
{
    float amount_for_today, total = 0.0;

    cout << "How much did you make today? ";
```

```
    while (cin >> amount_for_today)
    {
        cout << "How much did you make today? ";
        total += amount_for_today;
    }

    cout.precision(2);
    cout << showpoint << fixed;
    cout << "Your total: $" << total << endl;

    return 0;
}
```

Here's what you see when you run the program—note that when I enter a value of "5h", the program terminates:

```
%savings
How much did you make today? 55
How much did you make today? 555
How much did you make today? 5h
How much did you make today? Your total: $615.00
```


How did the return value from the **cin** object's >> operator method terminate the loop? It was able to do so because that operator method returns a value of false if the *stream state* is not cleared. The stream state is a set of bits, which are set to zero if the stream is ready to be used. The bits that can be set include **eofbit**, set if the end of the file has been reached; **badbit**, set if an error was seen; **failbit**, set if an input operation failed; and **goodbit**, which is always 0 and indicates the stream can be used. You'll find these stream state bits in Table 13.4.

The conditional expression in **while(cin >> value)** tests as true only as long as all stream state bits, **eofbit**, **badbit**, and **failbit**, are cleared. You can also use the stream state methods, which you'll find in Table 13.5, to work with a stream's state.

For example, to test if **badbit** is set, you use the **bad** method; to test if **failbit** is set, you use **fail**. You can clear the state of the stream with **clear** (which in real code you should do only after handling any stream problems):

```
if (cin.bad() || cin.fail()) {
    cout << "Error seen, clearing cin." << endl;
    cin.clear();
}
```

Calling **clear()** clears **eofbit**, **badbit**, and **failbit**. If you specify a particular bit, such as **clear(badbit)**, all other bits are cleared, and the stream state is set to **badbit**. (Note that when you set a stream state bit, the stream will not be usable until its state is cleared.)

You can also use the **exceptions** method to indicate what stream states should throw exceptions. For example, the methods **clear** and **setstate** (which calls **clear**) set the stream state, so calling **exceptions(badbit)** will cause those methods to throw a **basic_ios::failure** exception if they set **badbit**.

Table 13.4 Stream state bits.

Member	Means
badbit	1 if an error was seen.
eofbit	1 if end of file was seen.
failbit	1 if an input operation failed.
goodbit	Indicates that the stream is ready to be used; always has a value of 0.

Table 13.5 Stream state methods.

Member	Means
bad()	Returns true if badbit is set.
clear(iostate ss)	Sets the stream state to **ss;** can throw **basic_ios::failure** exception.
eof()	Returns true if eofbit is set.
exceptions()	Returns the flags that caused an exception.
exceptions(iostate ss)	Sets which states will make clear throw an exception.
fail()	Returns true if badbit or failbit is set.
good()	Returns true if stream can be used.
rdstate()	Returns the current stream state.
setstate(iostate ss)	Sets stream states corresponding to bits in ss.

Chapter 14

File Handling

In Depth

This chapter is all about handling data in physical files. The previous chapter was about console I/O using the **iostream** classes such as **istream** and **ostream**, and this chapter is about the **fstream** classes, which are targeted to working with files on disk. Just like **iostream**, which supports the **istream** class for input and **ostream** for output, the **fstream** class supports the **ifstream** class for input from files and **ofstream** for output to files. We'll put the **fstream** classes to work in this chapter.

__NOTE:__ This chapter uses the constants in the __ios_base__ class, which you refer to as __ios_base::name__. If your compiler doesn't support the __ios_base__ class yet, use the __ios__ class instead like this: __ios::name__. This chapter also uses the constant __ios_base::binary__ (or __ios::binary__ if your compiler doesn't support __ios_base__) for binary file handling. Some UNIX compilers do not support __ios_base::binary__ or __ios::binary__, because they do not make a distinction between binary and text mode, in which case you should omit that constant. (At least one UNIX compiler I've used does not complain about using this constant, but it totally disables file handling; omitting this constant fixes the problem.) See "Working with Binary Files" for more details.

Creating a File

You can create files with the **fstream** classes. You can create a file stream that reads input from a file with the **ifstream** class and a stream that sends output to a file with the **ofstream** class. Both **ifstream** and **ofstream** are built into the **fstream** class itself, which means that if you create a stream with the **fstream** class, you can use that stream for both reading and writing (see "Reading and Writing with **fstream**" later in this chapter).

To create a file, you first create an output stream, and I'll use the **ofstream** class here in an example named writefile.cpp that will write text data to a file. To create an **ofstream** object, you include the fstream header. In fact, when you include fstream, most—but not all—compilers also include the iostream header. Because not all compilers include iostream when you include fstream, I'll include iostream explicitly in writefile.cpp:

```
#include <iostream>
#include <fstream>
using namespace std;
```

```
int main()
{
    ofstream fout;
      .
      .
      .
```

This code uses the **ofstream** default constructor to create the **fout** object. To create a file named, say, hello.dat, you can use this object's **open** method:

```
#include <iostream>
#include <fstream>
using namespace std;

int main()
{
    ofstream fout;

    fout.open("hello.dat");
      .
      .
      .
```

By default, if hello.dat exists when you execute this statement, it's opened to accept output from our program and truncated to zero length (that is, all the data in it is deleted); if the file does not exist yet, it's created.

***TIP:** You can specify various options when you open a file, such as whether you want to append to it, rather than have it truncated to zero length—see "Selecting File Open Modes" later in this chapter.*

You can also combine the creation of **fout** and the **open** operation into one step if you pass the file's name to the **fout** object's constructor:

```
#include <fstream>
using namespace std;

int main()
{
    ofstream fout("file.dat");
      .
      .
      .
```

This one line of code opens file.dat for output if that file exists, or creates the file otherwise, and then it associates the file with the output stream object **fout**.

Because file handling is one of the most problem-prone parts of programming, you should always check that a file stream was really opened before trying to work with it. You can do that with the **ofstream** method **is_open**—see "Checking File Stream States" later in this chapter for more information. In this case, I'll use **is_open** to check if we've been able to open the **fout** stream successfully:

```
#include <fstream>
#include <iostream>
using namespace std;

int main()
{
    ofstream fout("file.dat");

    if (!fout.is_open()) {
        cerr << "Error: Could not create file." << endl;
        exit(1);
    }
        .
        .
        .
```


At this point, we've created an **ofstream** object named **fout**. This object is buffered so that data is written to the disk in chunks, rather than byte by byte (the buffer is flushed if **fout** goes out of scope, you call its **close** method, or the program ends). So how do we use this object to write data to the file?

Writing to a File

You can use the same methods with **fstream** objects as the ones you use with the already familiar **iostream** objects. For example, to write data to the newly opened file file.dat, you can use the << insertion operator, or you can use methods like **write**. Here's what that looks like in writefile.cpp, where I'm storing some text in hello.dat:

```
#include <iostream>
#include <fstream>
using namespace std;
```

```
int main()
{
    ofstream fout;

    fout.open("hello.dat");

    if (!fout.is_open()) {
        cerr << "Error: Could not create file." << endl;
        exit(1);
    }

    fout << "Hello from C++." << endl;
    .
    .
    .
}
```

This text actually goes into an internal buffer before being written to the disk, and it's not written out until you're done with the file or the buffer fills. So how do you indicate that you're finished with a file and want the file's contents sent to disk? You close the file.

Closing a File

A file is closed and the data in the output buffer is flushed to that file when you use the **ofstream** method **close**, when the **ofstream** object goes out of scope, or when the program ends. To explicitly close a file, you can use the **close** method like this:

```
#include <iostream>
#include <fstream>
using namespace std;

int main()
{
    ofstream fout;

    fout.open("hello.dat");

    if (!fout.is_open()) {
        cerr << "Error: Could not create file." << endl;
        exit(1);
    }
```

```
    fout << "Hello from C++." << endl;

    fout.close();

    return 0;
}
```

This writes the buffered data, if there is any, to the file and indicates that you're done with the file, at least for the moment.

NOTE: *In some operating systems, programs can lock files for their own use, and when you close a file, it's unlocked and so becomes accessible to other programs.*

When you run this example, this text is stored in the file hello.dat:

```
Hello from C++.
```

That's it—now we've stored data in a file. So how do you open that file in another program and read the file's contents?

Opening a File

To open a file for input, you can create an **ifstream** object, as I'm doing here in a new example, readfile.cpp:

```
#include <iostream>
#include <fstream>
using namespace std;

int main()
{
    ifstream fin("hello.dat");
        .
        .
        .
```

This creates a new **ifstream** object named **fin** and opens the file hello.dat for input to our program, associating that file with that stream. As with **ofstream**, you can also break the file-opening process up into two parts if you use the default constructor and the **open** method:

```
ifstream fin;

fin.open("hello.dat");
```

You should use the **ifstream** method **is_open** to check if the file was opened correctly (see "Checking File Stream States" later in this chapter for more information about **is_open)**:

```
#include <iostream>
#include <fstream>
using namespace std;

int main()
{
    ifstream fin("hello.dat");

    if (!fin.is_open()) {
        cerr << "Error: Could not open file." << endl;
        exit(1);
    }
    .
    .
    .
```

Now that we've obtained an **ifstream** object corresponding to our file, how can we read from it?

Reading from a File

As with writing to **ofstream** objects, you can use the same techniques we're already familiar with to read from **ifstream** objects. For example, you can use the >> extraction operator, or the **read** method, or the **get** method. To read the three words in hello.dat, I'll just use the extraction operator and then display those words, like this:

```
#include <iostream>
#include <fstream>
using namespace std;

int main()
{
    char string1[20], string2[20], string3[20];
    ifstream fin("hello.dat");

    if (!fin.is_open()) {
        cerr << "Error: Could not open file." << endl;
        exit(1);
    }
```

```
    fin >> string1;
    fin >> string2;
    fin >> string3;

    cout << string1 << " " << string2 << " " << string3 << endl;

    fin.close();

    return 0;
}
```

When you run readfile.cpp, it'll open hello.dat, read the three words in that file, and display them:

```
%readfile
Hello from C++.
```

That's it—we've successfully created, written to, closed, opened, and read from a file. But there are many more possibilities, and we're going to examine them in this chapter.

Appending to a File

When you open an existing file for output, it's not necessary to truncate it to zero length; you can open it for *appending*. When you open a file for appending, the contents are left untouched, and the *output pointer* is positioned at the end of the file. When you write to the file, you write to the location of the output pointer, which means that whatever you write goes after the current contents of the file.

To open an existing file for appending, you simply pass the constant **ios_base::app** (or **ios::app** if your compiler doesn't support the **ios_base** class) when you open the file, with either a stream object's constructor or its **open** method:

```
#include <iostream>
#include <fstream>
using namespace std;

int main()
{
    ofstream fout;

    fout.open("hello.dat", ios_base::app);
    .
    .
    .
```

Now when you write to the file, what you write is appended to what's already in the file; in this case, I'll add "Hello again from C++." to the end of hello.dat:

```
#include <iostream>
#include <fstream>
using namespace std;

int main()
{
    ofstream fout;

    fout.open("hello.dat", ios_base::app);

    if (!fout.is_open()) {
        cerr << "Error: Could not open file for appending." << endl;
        exit(1);
    }

    fout << "Hello again from C++." << endl;

    fout.close();

    return 0;
}
```

After you run this example, appfile.cpp, the line "Hello again from C++." is appended to the file's contents:

```
Hello from C++.
Hello again from C++.
```

For more file open options like **ios_base::app**, see "Selecting File Open Modes" later in this chapter.

Writing Objects

As you know, C++ is fond of working with objects, and besides creating files based on simple data types like **char**, you can also write objects to files and read them back. Here's an example, writeobj.cpp, that writes an array of 15 objects to a file named file.dat. Each object will be of a bookkeeping class I've named **entry**, which stores the name of a person, how much they owe you, and a method named **display** to display that data:

```
#include <iostream>
#include <fstream>
using namespace std;

const int NUMBER_OBJECTS = 15;

class entry
{
public:
    char name[20];
    float owes;
    void display() {cout << name << " owes $" << owes << endl;}
};

int main()
{
    entry object_array[NUMBER_OBJECTS];
    .
    .
    .
```


When I open file.dat for output, I also specify that this file will hold binary data like this:

```
#include <iostream>
#include <fstream>
using namespace std;

const int NUMBER_OBJECTS = 15;

class entry
{
public:
    char name[20];
    float owes;
    void display() {cout << name << " owes $" << owes << endl;}
};
```

```
int main()
{
    entry object_array[NUMBER_OBJECTS];
    ofstream fout("file.dat", ios_base::binary);
    .
    .
    .
```

This constant, **ios_base::binary**, is mostly for non-UNIX operating systems like the Macintosh operating system and DOS. For example, DOS doesn't just use a newline character, **'\n'**, for newlines—instead, it uses a carriage return/newline pair, **'\r\n'**. By default, DOS uses a text mode in which programs translate **'\n'** to **'\r\n'** when writing out to a file and translate **'\r\n'** to **'\n'** when reading from files. That kind of translation is a problem when you write non-text, binary data out to disk, so you have to specify binary mode when you do so in those operating systems. This is not a problem in UNIX, which does no such character translation, so you don't need the **ios_base::binary** constant in UNIX. In fact, you must omit **ios_base::binary** with some UNIX compilers, or your program won't work. See "Working with Binary Files" later in this chapter for more information.

After placing some data in a few of the objects in the object array, I'll use the **write** method we saw in the previous chapter (see "Using the **ostream** Class's **put** and **write** Methods" in Chapter 13) to write the object array to file.dat:

```
#include <iostream>
#include <fstream>
using namespace std;

const int NUMBER_OBJECTS = 15;

class entry
{
public:
    char name[20];
    float owes;
    void display() {cout << name << " owes $" << owes << endl;}
};

int main()
{
    entry object_array[NUMBER_OBJECTS];
    ofstream fout("file.dat", ios_base::binary);
```

```
    if (!fout.is_open()) {
        cerr << "Error: Could not create file." << endl;
        exit(1);
    }

    strcpy(object_array[0].name, "Ebeneezer Scrooge");
    object_array[0].owes = 0.01;

    strcpy(object_array[1].name, "Bob Crachit");
    object_array[1].owes = 312.59;

    fout.write(reinterpret_cast<char *> (object_array),
        NUMBER_OBJECTS * sizeof(entry));

    fout.close();

    return 0;
}
```

This code creates and fills file.dat with the object array. The next step is to read that data back in.

Reading Objects

To read the objects stored in file.dat, I'll create a new example, readobj.cpp. This program simply creates an object array like the one created in writeobj.cpp, connects file.dat to an input file stream, **fin**, and uses the **read** method that we saw in the previous chapter (see "Using the **istream** Class's **read**, **peek**, **gcount**, and **putback** Methods" in Chapter 13) to read the object array back in:

```
#include <iostream>
#include <fstream>
using namespace std;

const int NUMBER_OBJECTS = 15;

class entry
{
public:
    char name[20];
    float owes;
    void display() {cout << name << " owes $" << owes << endl;}
};
```

```
int main()
{
    entry object_array[NUMBER_OBJECTS];
    ifstream fin("file.dat", ios_base::binary);

    if (!fin.is_open()) {
        cerr << "Error: Could not open file." << endl;
        exit(1);
    }

    fin.read(reinterpret_cast<char *> (object_array),
        NUMBER_OBJECTS * sizeof(entry));
    .
    .
    .
```

Now I can use the **entry** class's **display** method to display the data in the newly read objects:

```
#include <iostream>
#include <fstream>
using namespace std;

const int NUMBER_OBJECTS = 15;

class entry
{
public:
    char name[20];
    float owes;
    void display() {cout << name << " owes $" << owes << endl;}
};

int main()
{
    entry object_array[NUMBER_OBJECTS];
    ifstream fin("file.dat", ios_base::binary);

    if (!fin.is_open()) {
        cerr << "Error: Could not open file." << endl;
        exit(1);
    }
```

```
    fin.read(reinterpret_cast<char *> (object_array),
        NUMBER_OBJECTS * sizeof(entry));

    object_array[0].display();
    object_array[1].display();

    fin.close();

    return 0;
}
```

Here's what you see when you run readobj.cpp:

```
%readobj
Ebeneezer Scrooge owes $0.01
Bob Crachit owes $312.59
```

As you can see, we've been able to store data in objects written to disk and to read those objects back in. We're making some progress, but there's a lot more to the story.

Random Access

The file file.dat holds 15 objects, and to access the data in one of those objects, we've had to read in all the objects at once. However, you don't need to read in more than the object you're interested in if you position the *file input pointer*, which is where data will be read from next, at the beginning of the object you want in the file and then read just that object. You can also write to a specific location in a file if you position the *file output pointer*, which points to the location where data will be written to next.

Moving a file pointer and working with only the data you want is a technique known as *random access*, because you can read any item in a file this way, just by positioning the file input pointer correctly, or write any item you want in the file just by positioning the file output pointer. Having to read all the items in the file up to the one you want before getting access to that item is called *sequential access*, and the difference between random and sequential access is much like the difference in the way music is stored on CD or cassette.

You use the **seekg** method to position the file input pointer and the **seekp** method to position the file output pointer. For example, say that I modified the writeobj.cpp example to place data in the object at **object_array[9]** in the object array:

```
#include <iostream>
#include <fstream>
using namespace std;

const int NUMBER_OBJECTS = 15;

class entry
{
public:
    char name[20];
    float owes;
    void display() {cout << name << " owes $" << owes << endl;}
};

int main()
{
    entry object_array[NUMBER_OBJECTS];
    ofstream fout("file.dat", ios_base::binary);

    if (!fout.is_open()) {
        cerr << "Error: Could not create file." << endl;
        exit(1);
    }

    strcpy(object_array[0].name,"Ebeneezer Scrooge");
    object_array[0].owes = 0.01;

    strcpy(object_array[9].name,"Bob Crachit");
    object_array[9].owes = 312.59;

    fout.write(reinterpret_cast<char *> (object_array),
        NUMBER_OBJECTS * sizeof(entry));

    fout.close();

    return 0;
}
```

Now say that I want to read just the object at position 9 in file.dat, without reading any other objects. I'll do that in an example named fileptr.cpp, using the **seekg** method to position the file input pointer before reading. I start fileptr.cpp by creating just one **entry** class object and opening file.dat for input:

```
#include <iostream>
#include <fstream>
using namespace std;

class entry
{
public:
    char name[20];
    float owes;
    void display() {cout << name << " owes $" << owes << endl;}
};

int main()
{
    entry one_record;
    ifstream fin("file.dat", ios_base::binary);

    if (!fin.is_open()) {
        cerr << "Error: Could not open file." << endl;
        exit(1);
    }
    .
    .
    .
```

Next, I use **seekg** to position the file input pointer. You pass this method two arguments—one sets the origin in the file you want to use, and the other sets the location of the input pointer by specifying an offset from that origin, in bytes (see "Using Random Access" later in this chapter for all the details). In this case, I'll set the origin to the beginning of the file with the constant **ios_base::beg**, and position the input pointer correctly by skipping over the first nine objects in the file. I can then read the object we're interested in, like this:

```
#include <iostream>
#include <fstream>
using namespace std;

class entry
{
public:
    char name[20];
```

```
    float owes;
    void display() {cout << name << " owes $" << owes << endl;}
};

int main()
{
    entry one_record;
    ifstream fin("file.dat", ios_base::binary);

    if (!fin.is_open()) {
        cerr << "Error: Could not open file." << endl;
        exit(1);
    }

    fin.seekg(9 * sizeof(entry), ios::beg);
    fin.read(reinterpret_cast<char *> (&one_record), sizeof(entry));
    .
    .
    .
```

Finally, I use the object's **display** method to confirm that we've indeed read it in properly:

```
#include <iostream>
#include <fstream>
using namespace std;

class entry
{
public:
    char name[20];
    float owes;
    void display() {cout << name << " owes $" << owes << endl;}
};

int main()
{
    entry one_record;
    ifstream fin("file.dat", ios_base::binary);

    if (!fin.is_open()) {
        cerr << "Error: Could not open file." << endl;
        exit(1);
    }
```

```
    fin.seekg(9 * sizeof(entry), ios::beg);
    fin.read(reinterpret_cast<char *> (&one_record), sizeof(entry));

    one_record.display();

    fin.close();

    return 0;
}
```

Here's what you see when you run this new example, fileptr.cpp:

```
%fileptr
Bob Crachit owes $312.59
```

As you can see, we've been able to read in just the one object we're interested in. There's plenty happening in C++ file handling, and it's time now to get to the Immediate Solutions.

Immediate Solutions

Creating a File

As we saw in the In Depth section of this chapter, you can create a file with the **ofstream** method **open**, as in the example writefile.cpp:

```
#include <iostream>
#include <fstream>
using namespace std;

int main()
{
    ofstream fout;

    fout.open("hello.dat");

    fout << "Hello from C++." << endl;

    fout.close();

    return 0;
}
```

Because we're opening hello.dat for output, it's opened and truncated to zero length if it exists; otherwise, it's created. You can also create a file just by passing the name of a file that you want to create to the **ofstream** class's constructor:

```
#include <iostream>
#include <fstream>
using namespace std;

int main()
{
    ofstream fout("hello.dat");

    fout << "Hello from C++." << endl;
```

```
    fout.close();

    return 0;
}
```

You should also check to make sure that the file was really created before trying to work with it. You can do that with the **ofstream** method **is_open**—see "Checking File Stream States" later in this chapter for more information:

```
#include <iostream>
#include <fstream>
using namespace std;

int main()
{
    ofstream fout;

    fout.open("hello.dat");

    if (!fout.is_open()) {
        cerr << "Error: Could not create file." << endl;
        exit(1);
    }

    fout << "Hello from C++." << endl;

    fout.close();

    return 0;
}
```

There are other ways to open files as well—see "Selecting File Open Modes" next in this chapter.

***TIP:** You can also specify a path for the file when you open or create it, like this in UNIX: **fout.open("/home/steve/hello.dat")**. DOS, on the other hand, uses a backslash to separate directory names in a path, but to C++, the backslash is meant to escape characters in quoted strings, like "Hello\n". The solution is to escape the backslash, like this in DOS programs: **fout.open("c:\\cpp\\hello.dat")**.*

Selecting File Open Modes

You can provide a file open mode constant to the **open** method or file stream constructor, indicating how you want to open the file. You'll find those constants in Table 14.1 (use **ios::*name*** if your compiler doesn't support **ios_base::*name***).

When you open a file for input, the default open mode is **ios_base::in**. When you open a file for output, the default mode is **ios_base::out | ios_base::trunc**. ORing together two constants with the bitwise OR operator, |, will set both the corresponding options (see "Bitwise And, Xor, and Or: &, ^, and |" in Chapter 2 for more information on the bitwise OR operator).

For example, if you want to open a file for appending, you pass **ios_base::app** as the second argument to the **open** method or the **ofstream** constructor:

```
#include <iostream>
#include <fstream>
using namespace std;

int main()
{
    ofstream fout;

    fout.open("hello.dat", ios_base::app);
    .
    .
    .
```

14. File Handling

Table 14.1 Constants to set file modes.

Constant	Means
ios_base::in	Read from file.
ios_base::out	Write to file.
ios_base::ate	Go to end of file after opening.
ios_base::app	Append to the end of the file.
ios_base::trunc	Truncate file to zero length.
ios_base::binary	Treat file contents as binary.

Related solution:	*Found on page:*
Bitwise Operators And, Xor, and Or: &, ^, and |	107

Writing to a File

Once you have an **ofstream** object, you can write to the corresponding file using the techniques we've already seen for **ostream** in the previous chapter, such as **write**, **put**, or the << insertion operator. Here's an example that we saw in the in Depth section of this chapter, writefile.cpp, that uses the insertion operator to send text to a file:

```
#include <iostream>
#include <fstream>
using namespace std;

int main()
{
    ofstream fout;

    fout.open("hello.dat");

    fout << "Hello from C++." << endl;

    fout.close();

    return 0;
}
```


After you run this code, the file hello.dat will hold the text "Hello from C++."

Opening a File

To open a file for input, you simply pass the name of the file to the **ifstream** constructor or **open** method, as we saw in the example readfile.cpp in the In Depth section of this chapter:

```
#include <iostream>
#include <fstream>
using namespace std;

int main()
{
    ifstream fin("hello.dat");
    .
    .
    .
```

You can use the **ifstream** method **is_open** to check if the file was opened correctly—see "Checking File Stream States" later in this chapter for more information:

```
#include <iostream>
#include <fstream>
using namespace std;

int main()
{
    ifstream fin("hello.dat");

    if (!fin.is_open()) {
        cerr << "Error: Could not open file." << endl;
        exit(1);
    }
        .
        .
        .
```

TIP:** You can also specify a path for the file when you open it, like this in UNIX:* ***fout.open("/home/steve/hello.dat")*. DOS, on the other hand, uses a backslash to separate directory names in a path, but to C++, the backslash is meant to escape characters in quoted strings, like "Hello\n". The solution is to escape the backslash, like this in DOS programs:* ***fout.open("c:\\cpp\\hello.dat")****.*

There are other ways to open files as well—see "Selecting File Open Modes" earlier in this chapter.

Reading from a File

As we saw in the In Depth section of this chapter, you can use the same **istream** techniques we saw in the previous chapter to work with **ifstream**, such as **read**, **get**, and the >> extraction operator. We saw an example, readfile.cpp, that read from a file named hello.dat, which has this text content:

```
Hello from C++.
```

Here's what readfile.cpp looks like; first, I open hello.dat:

```
#include <iostream>
#include <fstream>
using namespace std;
```

```
int main()
{
    ifstream fin("hello.dat");

    if (!fin.is_open()) {
        cerr << "Error: Could not open file." << endl;
        exit(1);
    }
    .
    .
    .
```

Then I use the >> extraction operator to read from the file and also display the text I've read:

```
#include <iostream>
#include <fstream>
using namespace std;

int main()
{
    char string1[20], string2[20], string3[20];
    ifstream fin("hello.dat");

    if (!fin.is_open()) {
        cerr << "Error: Could not open file." << endl;
        exit(1);
    }

    fin >> string1;
    fin >> string2;
    fin >> string3;

    cout << string1 << " " << string2 << " " << string3 << endl;

    fin.close();

    return 0;
}
```

And that's all there is to it.

TIP: ***TIP:** Some compilers will require you to use the **ifstream** method **clear** like this, **fin.clear()**, before opening a file a second time for reading. The **clear** method clears the stream's state—see "Checking File Stream States" later in this chapter for more details.*

Appending to a File

By default, when you open an existing file for output, that file is truncated to zero length, which means that the data in the file is deleted. However, you can open a file for appending, which positions the output pointer at the end of the current file contents and allows you to append to the file. We saw an example, appfile.cpp, in the In Depth section of this chapter that shows how this works. In that case, I was appending text to a file named hello.dat, which has this text content:

```
Hello from C++.
```

To open the file for appending, I used the file open constant **ios_base::app**:

```
#include <iostream>
#include <fstream>
using namespace std;

int main()
{
    ofstream fout;

    fout.open("hello.dat", ios_base::app);

    if (!fout.is_open()) {
        cerr << "Error: Could not open file for appending." << endl;
        exit(1);
    }
    .
    .
    .
```

Now that the file is open for appending, anything I write to the file output stream **fout** is appended to the current contents of hello.dat:

```
#include <iostream>
#include <fstream>
using namespace std;

int main()
{
    ofstream fout;

    fout.open("hello.dat", ios_base::app);
```

```
    if (!fout.is_open()) {
        cerr << "Error: Could not open file for appending." << endl;
        exit(1);
    }

    fout << "Hello again from C++." << endl;

    fout.close();

    return 0;
}
```

To read the new contents of hello.dat, I could set up a string for each word and use the extraction operator to fill those strings like this:

```
#include <iostream>
#include <fstream>
using namespace std;

const int MAX = 20;

int main()
{
    char string1[MAX], string2[MAX], string3[MAX];
    char string4[MAX], string5[MAX], string6[MAX], string7[MAX];

    ifstream fin("hello.dat");

    if (!fin.is_open()) {
        cerr << "Error: Could not open file." << endl;
        exit(1);
    }

    fin >> string1;
    fin >> string2;
    fin >> string3;
    fin >> string4;
    fin >> string5;
    fin >> string6;
    fin >> string7;

    cout << string1 << " " << string2 << " " << string3 << endl;

    cout << string4 << " " << string5 << " " << string6
        << " " << string7 << endl;
```

```
    fin.close();

    return 0;
}
```

As you can imagine, naming each string gets a little tedious if you're reading in a lot of text. An easier way would be to use a **while** loop this way:

```
string in_string;
    .
    .
    .
while (fin >> in_string)
    cout << in_string << " ";
```

Here's another way—I can use the **get** method, as shown in this example, getfile.cpp, to read whole lines of text from the file:

```
#include <iostream>
#include <fstream>
using namespace std;

const int MAX = 40;

int main()
{
    char string1[MAX], string2[MAX];

    ifstream fin("hello.dat");

    if (!fin.is_open()) {
        cerr << "Error: Could not open file." << endl;
        exit(1);
    }

    fin.get(string1, MAX, '\n').get();
    fin.get(string2, MAX, '\n').get();

    cout << string1 << endl;
    cout << string2 << endl;

    fin.close();

    return 0;
}
```

Note that the second call to **get** in each statement above is to clear the newline at the end of each line, which the string version of **get** doesn't do (see "Using the **istream** Class's **get**, **getline**, and **ignore** Methods" in Chapter 13 for more information). Here's what you see when you run this code, getfile.cpp, showing the original contents of hello.dat and the appended new line of text:

```
%getfile
Hello from C++.
Hello again from C++.
```

Related solution:	Found on page:
Using the **istream** Class's **get**, **getline**, and **ignore** Methods	593

Checking File Stream States

The **fstream** classes like **ifstream** and **ofstream** support the same stream state bits that the **iostream** classes like **istream** and **ostream** support, such as **eofbit**, **badbit**, **goodbit**, and so on (see "Checking Stream States" in Chapter 13 for more details). They also support methods like **good** and **bad** that you saw in Table 13.5. To clear any set stream states, you use the **clear** method like this: **fin.clear()**.

One important method is the **is_open** method, which you can use to check if the stream was opened properly. Every time you open a file stream, you should use this method to make sure the stream can be used:

```
ifstream fin("hello.dat");

if (!fin.is_open()) {
    cerr << "Error: Could not open file." << endl;
    exit(1);
}
    .
    .
    .
```

***NOTE:** In old versions of C++, you used to check if a stream object was open by checking the object itself, such as **!fin**, or with the **good** method, **!fin.good()**, but those techniques don't detect attempts to open a file with a bad open mode. However, some older C++ implementations don't support **is_open**, so you'll have to use those older methods in such cases.*

Related solution:	Found on page:
Checking Stream States	599

Working with Binary Files

As discussed in the In Depth section of this chapter, some operating systems, like DOS, don't just use a newline character, **'\n'**, for newlines. Instead, DOS uses a carriage return/newline pair, **'\r\n'**. By default, DOS uses a text mode in which programs translate **'\n'** to **'\r\n'** when writing out to a file and translate **'\r\n'** to **'\n'** when reading from files. Here's an example that shows how this works—in this case, I'm writing the string "Hello\nthere." out to a file, bin.dat, in DOS:

```
#include <iostream>
#include <fstream>
using namespace std;

int main()
{
    ofstream fout;

    fout.open("bin.dat");

    if (!fout.is_open()) {
        cerr << "Error: Could not open file." << endl;
        exit(1);
    }

    fout << "Hello\nthere.";

    fout.close();

    return 0;
}
```

To examine the file byte by byte, I can use the DOS utility debug, which displays the contents of bin.dat—as you can see, the program has written 0xD and 0xA, that is, the ASCII codes for **'\r'** and **'\n'**, instead of the **'\n'** we used in the code:

```
C:\cpp>debug bin.dat
-d
1106:0100  48 65 6C 6C 6F 0D 0A 74-68 65 72 65 2E 50 8A C3  Hello..there.P..
1106:0110  B3 0B F6 E3 5B 03 C3 93-C3 8B 1E 8E 34 00 F5 10  ....[.......4...
```

```
1106:0120  DB 73 36 B8 BA D8 E8 E4-FF 8A 4F 02 8B 57 07 8B  .s6.......O..W..
1106:0130  37 F7 C1 01 00 75 68 F6-05 20 74 26 F6 45 01 01  7....uh.. t&.E..
1106:0140  74 03 E8 DA 01 B0 02 89-36 9B D0 8C 1E 9D D0 A2  t.......6.......
1106:0150  9A D0 33 C0 FF 06 8E D0-C3 B8 00 00 F9 EB F5 F9  ..3.............
1106:0160  EB F2 F6 05 10 74 20 83-7F 05 02 75 59 80 7C 01  .....t ....uY.|.
1106:0170  3A 75 53 8A 04 E8 23 EC-2C 41 FE C0 3C 1A 77 46  :uS...#.,A..<.wF
```

The program has done this so that you can use the file bin.dat with other DOS or Windows programs that expect carriage return/linefeeds at the end of lines. But this kind of translation is a total disaster when you write non-text, binary data (such as numbers in **double** format or image files) out to disk. To make sure the program does not perform this translation for purely binary data, you have to specify binary mode with **ios_base::binary**:

```
#include <iostream>
#include <fstream>
using namespace std;

int main()
{
    ofstream fout;

    fout.open("bin.dat", ios_base::binary);

    if (!fout.is_open()) {
        cerr << "Error: Could not open file." << endl;
        exit(1);
    }

    fout << "Hello\nthere.";

    fout.close();

    return 0;
}
```

Now debug shows that there's only a newline character, ASCII code 0xA, between "Hello" and "there":

```
C:\cpp>debug bin.dat
-d
1106:0100  48 65 6C 6C 6F 0A 74 68-65 72 65 2E 2E 50 8A C3  Hello.there..P..
1106:0110  B3 0B F6 E3 5B 03 C3 93-C3 8B 1E 8E 34 00 F5 10  ....[.......4...
```

14. File Handling

```
1106:0120  DB 73 36 B8 BA D8 E8 E4-FF 8A 4F 02 8B 57 07 8B  .s6.......O..W..
1106:0130  37 F7 C1 01 00 75 68 F6-05 20 74 26 F6 45 01 01  7....uh.. t&.E..
1106:0140  74 03 E8 DA 01 B0 02 89-36 9B D0 8C 1E 9D D0 A2  t.......6.......
1106:0150  9A D0 33 C0 FF 06 8E D0-C3 B8 00 00 F9 EB F5 F9  ..3.............
1106:0160  EB F2 F6 05 10 74 20 83-7F 05 02 75 59 80 7C 01  .....t ....uY.|.
1106:0170  3A 75 53 8A 04 E8 23 EC-2C 41 FE C0 3C 1A 77 46  :uS...#.,A..<.wF
```

This kind of automatic translation is not a problem in UNIX, which uses only **'\n'** for newlines, so you don't need the **ios_base::binary** constant in UNIX. In fact, you *must* omit **ios_base::binary** with some UNIX compilers, or your program won't work correctly (although it might compile).

Here's an example, binfile.cpp, that shows how to write out binary data using the **ios_base::binary** constant. In this case, I'll create a structure named **person** that includes some binary data, then write a structure of this type to a file, and then read it from the file again:

```
struct person
{
    char name[20];
    double age;
};
```

Here's how I write a **person** structure named **ralph** to a file named binary.dat using the **fstream** method **write**, which is designed to handle binary data (omit **ios_base::binary** if you're using a UNIX compiler):

```
#include <iostream>
#include <fstream>
using namespace std;

struct person
{
    char name[20];
    double age;
};

int main()
{
    person ralph = {"Ralph", 35.0};

    ofstream fout("binary.dat", ios_base::binary);
```

14. File Handling

```
    if (!fout.is_open()) {
        cerr << "Error: Could not open file." << endl;
        exit(1);
    }

    fout.write(reinterpret_cast<char *> (&ralph), sizeof(ralph));

    fout.close();
    .
    .
    .
```

And here's how I read that structure back from binary.dat, using the **fstream** method **read**, which, like **write**, is designed to handle binary data (these methods should be used together—you should use **read** to read data written with **write**):

```
#include <iostream>
#include <fstream>
using namespace std;

struct person
{
    char name[20];
    double age;
};

int main()
{
    person ralph = {"Ralph", 35.0};

    ofstream fout("binary.dat", ios_base::binary);

    if (!fout.is_open()) {
        cerr << "Error: Could not open file." << endl;
        exit(1);
    }

    fout.write(reinterpret_cast<char *> (&ralph), sizeof(ralph));

    fout.close();

    ifstream fin ("binary.dat", ios_base::binary);
```

```
    if (!fin.is_open()) {
        cerr << "Error: Could not open file." << endl;
        exit(1);
    }

    person also_ralph;

    fin.read(reinterpret_cast<char *> (&also_ralph), sizeof(also_ralph));

    cout << also_ralph.name << " is " << also_ralph.age
        << " years old." << endl;

    return 0;
}
```

The program reads the data from binary.dat back into a new **person** structure named **also_ralph** and then displays the data in **also_ralph** to confirm that we've stored and retrieved that data successfully. Here's what you see when you run this program, binfile.cpp:

```
%binfile
Ralph is 35 years old.
```


Writing Objects to Files

As we saw in the In Depth section of this chapter, you can write objects out to disk just as you can any other binary data. Here's an example that we've seen in the In Depth section of this chapter, writeobj.cpp, that writes an array of 15 objects out to disk—note that with some UNIX compilers you must omit **ios_base::binary** for this code to work. I'll start by creating the array of objects and creating an **ofstream** object, **fout**:

```
#include <iostream>
#include <fstream>
using namespace std;

const int NUMBER_OBJECTS = 15;
```

```
class entry
{
public:
    char name[20];
    float owes;
    void display() {cout << name << " owes $" << owes << endl;}
};

int main()
{
    entry object_array[NUMBER_OBJECTS];
    ofstream fout("file.dat", ios_base::binary);

    if (!fout.is_open()) {
        cerr << "Error: Could not create file." << endl;
        exit(1);
    }

    strcpy(object_array[0].name, "Ebeneezer Scrooge");
    object_array[0].owes = 0.01;

    strcpy(object_array[1].name, "Bob Crachit");
    object_array[1].owes = 312.59;
        .
        .
        .
```


Then I write out those objects like this, using the **write** method:

```
#include <iostream>
#include <fstream>
using namespace std;

const int NUMBER_OBJECTS = 15;

class entry
{
public:
    char name[20];
    float owes;
    void display() {cout << name << " owes $" << owes << endl;}
};

int main()
{
```

```
    entry object_array[NUMBER_OBJECTS];
    ofstream fout("file.dat", ios_base::binary);

    if (!fout.is_open()) {
        cerr << "Error: Could not create file." << endl;
        exit(1);
    }

    strcpy(object_array[0].name, "Ebeneezer Scrooge");
    object_array[0].owes = 0.01;

    strcpy(object_array[1].name, "Bob Crachit");
    object_array[1].owes = 312.59;

    fout.write(reinterpret_cast<char *> (object_array),
        NUMBER_OBJECTS * sizeof(entry));

    fout.close();

    return 0;
}
```

Having written the objects out, the next step is to read them back in—see the next section for the details.

Reading Objects from Files

In the previous section, I wrote some objects out to disk in an example named writeobj.cpp. As we saw in the In Depth section of this chapter, you can read objects from files using the **read** method. Here's the example we saw, readobj.cpp, that does that (note that with UNIX compilers you omit **ios_base::binary**). I start by creating the **ifstream** object, **fin**, which we'll use to read the objects from file.dat:

```
#include <iostream>
#include <fstream>
using namespace std;

int main()
{
    ifstream fin("file.dat", ios_base::binary);
```

```
    if (!fin.is_open()) {
        cerr << "Error: Could not open file." << endl;
        exit(1);
    }
    .
    .
    .
```

Then I use **read** to read the objects:

```
#include <iostream>
#include <fstream>
using namespace std;

const int NUMBER_OBJECTS = 15;

class entry
{
public:
    char name[20];
    float owes;
    void display() {cout << name << " owes $" << owes << endl;}
};

int main()
{
    entry object_array[NUMBER_OBJECTS];
    ifstream fin("file.dat", ios_base::binary);

    if (!fin.is_open()) {
        cerr << "Error: Could not open file." << endl;
        exit(1);
    }

    fin.read(reinterpret_cast<char *> (object_array),
        NUMBER_OBJECTS * sizeof(entry));

    object_array[0].display();
    object_array[1].display();

    fin.close();

    return 0;
}
```

Here's what you see when you run readobj.cpp and it reads in the objects stored in the previous section in this chapter:

```
%readobj
Ebeneezer Scrooge owes $0.01
Bob Crachit owes $312.59
```

Using Random Access

As discussed in the In Depth section of this chapter, you can use random access to work with any item stored in a file without having to read other items first the way you do with sequential access. To use random access, you usually break a file up into equal-sized items like records or objects so you'll know exactly where in the file to search for the one you want. You can position the file input pointer, which points to the next data to be read from the file, with the **seekg** method and the file output pointer, which points to the location at which the next data will be written, with the **seekp** method:

```
seekg(offset, origin)
seekp(offset, origin)
```

Here, ***offset*** is the number of bytes you want to move a file pointer with respect to the ***origin***, and ***offset*** can be negative. The ***origin*** argument can have these values:

- **ios_base::beg**—Measure offsets from the beginning of the file. This is the default.
- **ios_base::cur**—Measure offsets from the current position in the file.
- **ios_base::end**—Measure offsets from the end of the file.

In the In Depth section of this chapter, we saw an example that wrote an array of 15 objects to a file; I'll initialize two of those objects, **object_array[0]** and **object_array[9]**, with a program named writeobj9.cpp:

```
#include <iostream>
#include <fstream>
using namespace std;

const int NUMBER_OBJECTS = 15;

class entry
{
public:
```

```
    char name[20];
    float owes;
    void display() {cout << name << " owes $" << owes << endl;}
};

int main()
{
    entry object_array[NUMBER_OBJECTS];
    ofstream fout("file.dat", ios_base::binary);

    if (!fout.is_open()) {
        cerr << "Error: Could not create file." << endl;
        exit(1);
    }

    strcpy(object_array[0].name,"Ebeneezer Scrooge");
    object_array[0].owes = 0.01;

    strcpy(object_array[9].name,"Bob Crachit");
    object_array[9].owes = 312.59;

    fout.write(reinterpret_cast<char *> (object_array),
        NUMBER_OBJECTS * sizeof(entry));

    fout.close();

    return 0;
}
```

To read just the object from **object_array[9]**, I created a program named fileptr.cpp in the In Depth section of this chapter, using **seekg** to position the file input pointer:

```
#include <iostream>
#include <fstream>
using namespace std;

class entry
{
public:
    char name[20];
    float owes;
    void display() {cout << name << " owes $" << owes << endl;}
};
```

```
int main()
{
    entry one_record;
    ifstream fin("file.dat", ios_base::binary);

    if (!fin.is_open()) {
        cerr << "Error: Could not open file." << endl;
        exit(1);
    }

    fin.seekg(9 * sizeof(entry), ios::beg);
    fin.read(reinterpret_cast<char *> (&one_record), sizeof(entry));

    one_record.display();

    fin.close();

    return 0;
}
```

Here's what you see when you run fileptr.cpp—as you can see, this program retrieves just the object we want from file.dat:

```
%fileptr
Bob Crachit owes $312.59
```

Here's another way to write a specific object in file.dat, this time using the **seekp** method. This new example, writeobj92.cpp, starts by writing the entire object array to file.dat, with only one object, the first one, initialized:

```
#include <iostream>
#include <fstream>
using namespace std;

const int NUMBER_OBJECTS = 15;

class entry
{
public:
    char name[20];
    float owes;
    void display() {cout << name << " owes $" << owes << endl;}
};
```

```
int main()
{
    entry object_array[NUMBER_OBJECTS];
    ofstream fout("file.dat", ios_base::binary);

    if (!fout.is_open()) {
        cerr << "Error: Could not create file." << endl;
        exit(1);
    }

    strcpy(object_array[0].name,"Ebeneezer Scrooge");
    object_array[0].owes = 0.01;

    fout.write(reinterpret_cast<char *> (object_array),
        NUMBER_OBJECTS * sizeof(entry));
    .
    .
    .
```


Now I create and initialize a new object, use **seekp** to position the output file pointer at **object_array[9]**, and write that object to the file:

```
#include <iostream>
#include <fstream>
using namespace std;

const int NUMBER_OBJECTS = 15;

class entry
{
public:
    char name[20];
    float owes;
    void display() {cout << name << " owes $" << owes << endl;}
};

int main()
{
    entry object_array[NUMBER_OBJECTS], one_record;
    ofstream fout("file.dat", ios_base::binary);

    if (!fout.is_open()) {
        cerr << "Error: Could not create file." << endl;
        exit(1);
    }
```

```
    strcpy(object_array[0].name,"Ebeneezer Scrooge");
    object_array[0].owes = 0.01;

    strcpy(one_record.name,"Bob Crachit");
    one_record.owes = 312.59;

    fout.write(reinterpret_cast<char *> (object_array),
        NUMBER_OBJECTS * sizeof(entry));

    fout.seekp(9 * sizeof(entry), ios::beg);

    fout.write(reinterpret_cast<char *> (&one_record),
        sizeof(entry));

    fout.close();

    return 0;
}
```

This creates the same file.dat as the previous program, writeobj9.cpp, does, but it does so using the file output pointer.

Reading and Writing with **fstream**

Although you can use **ofstream** objects to write to files and **ifstream** objects to read from files, you can use **fstream** objects to perform both operations, writing *and* reading. The **fstream** class includes both the **ofstream** and **ifstream** classes.

Here's an example, readandwritefile.cpp, that puts **fstream** to work. In this example, I'll write the string "Hello from C++." to a file, hello.dat, and then move back to the beginning of the file and read that data back in again. To perform these two operations, writing and reading, we needed two programs, writefile.cpp and readfile.cpp, in the In Depth section of this chapter—but now that we're using **fstream**, we can do everything in one program. I start by creating hello.dat (or, if it already exists, opening it and truncating it to zero length) with an **fstream** object, **fstr**, and writing the text to that file with the insertion operator:

```
#include <iostream>
#include <fstream>
using namespace std;

int main()
{
```

```
    fstream fstr;

    fstr.open("hello.dat");

    if (!fstr.is_open()) {
        cerr << "Error: Could not open file." << endl;
        exit(1);
    }

    fstr << "Hello from C++." << endl;
    .
    .
    .
```

Then I can position the file output pointer at the beginning of the file and read the text we've just written, using the extraction operator:

```
#include <iostream>
#include <fstream>
using namespace std;

int main()
{
    fstream fstr;

    fstr.open("hello.dat");

    if (!fstr.is_open()) {
        cerr << "Error: Could not open file." << endl;
        exit(1);
    }

    fstr << "Hello from C++." << endl;

    char string1[20], string2[20], string3[20];

    fstr.seekg(0, ios_base::beg);

    fstr >> string1;
    fstr >> string2;
    fstr >> string3;

    cout << string1 << " " << string2 << " " << string3 << endl;

    fstr.close();
```

```
    return 0;
}
```

Here's what you see when you run this program:

```
%readandwritefile
Hello from C++.
```

As you can see, you can both read and write files with **fstream**.

Writing to a String Stream

C++ supports a family of classes named **sstream** that lets you write and read strings, a process called *incore formatting*. The **sstream** family of classes supercedes the earlier character-based array support based on the **strstream** classes.

Here's an example, sstreamwrite.cpp, that shows how to use the **sstream** class **ostringstream** to write to a string. In this case, I'll create an **ostringstream** object named **strout**, ask the user to enter some text which I'll send to the **strout** object, and then use the **strout** object's **str** method to get the string the user entered:


```
#include <iostream>
#include <sstream>
#include <string>
using namespace std;

const int MAX = 40;

int main()
{
    ostringstream strout;

    string response;

    cout << "Please enter the text: ";

    getline(cin, response);

    strout << "You typed: " << response << endl;

    string text = strout.str();

    cout << text;
```

```
    return 0;
}
```

Here's what you see when you run this example, sstreamwrite.cpp:

```
%sstreamwrite
Please enter the text: Hello from C++.
You typed: Hello from C++.
```

Reading from a String Stream

In the previous section, I used the **sstream** class **ostringstream** to write to a string. You can also use the **sstream** class **istringstream** to create a stream that lets you read from a string. Here's an example, sstreamread.cpp, that shows how this works. Here, I'll create a **istringstream** object named **strin** and connect it to a **string** named **text**. Then I can use the **strin** object with normal stream methods to read the string data:

```
#include <iostream>
#include <sstream>
#include <string>
using namespace std;

int main()
{
    string text = "Hello from C++.";

    istringstream strin(text);

    string item;

    while (strin >> item)
        cout << item << " ";

    cout << endl;

    return 0;
}
```

Here's what you see when you run this example, sstreamread.cpp—as you can see, now we've been able to use stream methods to read from a string:

```
%sstreamread
Hello from C++.
```

Chapter 15

The Standard Template Library

In Depth

This chapter and the two following it are all about the C++ Standard Template Library (STL), a huge and powerful topic. It is now a built-in part of C++ and is supported to a greater or lesser extent by most compilers. Those compilers that want to call themselves fully ANSI/ISO compliant must support the STL fully, but note that finding full STL support is still rare, so you might find a few points where your compiler doesn't do what you expect when you work with the STL. Besides the STL, we'll also take a closer look at two other C++ favorites in this chapter: the C++ **string** class and the **auto_ptr** template.

***NOTE:** Compiler support of the STL, a relatively new and large part of C++, varies substantially. For example, to use algorithms, you should include the algorithm header, but some older compilers will require algorith.h or even algo.h. I'm going to stick to the ANSI/ISO C++ standard in this and the next two chapters—if you don't get the results you're expecting, one place to check is your compiler's documentation to see if its implementation of the STL varies from the modern standard.*

The Standard Template Library

The Standard Template Library was originally created by Alex Stepanov and Meng Lee in 1994 at Hewlett Laboratories, and the ANSI/ISO committee has since made it an integral part of C++. The STL represents a main thrust of generic programming in C++.

The STL offers you a set of programming constructs called *containers* to hold your data and make it easy to handle in specific ways, such as one-dimensional arrays called vectors, as well as sets, queues, stacks, maps, and others. Using the built-in STL containers lets you organize and handle your data in powerful ways. Containers are template based, so you can use them with any type—as you know, C++ is a strongly typed language, and basing containers on templates makes them *generically typed*. Generic STL algorithms and containers can be used with many different types.

The STL is made up of *containers*, *iterators*, *function objects*, and *algorithms*, and we'll get acquainted with all these terms in this and the next two chapters. Here's an overview of the terms and what they mean:

- *Containers* are programming constructs that you can use to implement arrays, lists, queues, and other data structures that can hold and organize your data. STL containers are based on templates, and we'll see them all in Chapter 16.

- *Iterators* are generalized pointers that STL functions use to move through containers and address the data in them. We'll take a look at iterators in this chapter.
- *Function objects*, also called *functors*, are objects that act like functions and let you customize the behavior of the built-in STL code to handle your data the way you want it. Functors can be class objects or pointers to functions, and we'll see them in Chapter 17.
- *Algorithms* are pre-written STL routines that let you handle your data, allowing you to sort and otherwise manipulate that data. We'll see algorithms in this chapter, in the next one, and in depth in Chapter 17.

Containers

The most important STL concept is that of the container. Broadly speaking, a container is an object that contains and can organize other objects. The various containers available let you organize your own objects in various ways. Containers provide built-in features and procedures that let you handle stored data, find the number of stored objects, insert new objects, and so on.

You can't store just any kind of object in STL containers; the objects you store must be copy constructable and assignable. This means you can use the basic built-in C++ types in STL containers, as well as objects that have public copy constructors and assignment operators (including the default ones that C++ compilers add to objects unless you override them). The objects in a container are *owned* by the container.

We'll see all the container types in detail in the next chapter, but here's a quick overview of the eleven STL container types to get us started:

- **list**—Supports a doubly linked list of data items; each item knows which item comes before and after it.
- **queue**—Supports a queue that lets you add elements at the back end and remove them from the front end. This container is more restrictive than a **deque**.
- **deque**—Supports a double-ended queue, and it also lets you access those elements randomly (no matter where they are in the queue).
- **priority_queue**—Supports a prioritized queue that stores its items in sorted order.
- **stack**—Supports a stack of items, with methods like **push** and **pop**.

- **vector**—Supports a one-dimensional array.
- **map**—Supports a collection of keys and values associated with the keys. The key and values can be of different types.
- **multimap**—Supports a map that can support multiple values for each key.
- **set**—Supports a sorted set of unique members.
- **multiset**—Supports a set that can support multiple values per key.
- **bitset**—A data construct that allows you to set, reset, and check individual bits.

In this chapter, I'll use one of the most popular containers, **vector**, to show how to work with containers. A **vector** container is a one-dimensional array that lets you use the built-in STL algorithms to sort and handle your data. Here's an example, vector.cpp, to get us started; in this example, I'll set up a vector to hold student scores and then average those scores. To use the **vector** container, I include the vector header:

```
#include <iostream>
#include <vector>
using namespace std;
    .
    .
    .
```


To support generic programming, STL containers are templates, and the **vector** template takes two arguments—the type of the object you're storing in the vector and an *allocator*:

```
vector <class T, class Allocator = allocator<T> >
```

Allocators implement the memory handling for the new vector object, and the default STL allocator, which I'll use here, uses **new** and **delete** internally in the normal way (if you want to perform your own memory handling, you can provide your own allocators to STL container templates). To create a vector of four **double** values, I add this code to vector.cpp, passing the number of elements in the vector to the vector's constructor:

```
#include <iostream>
#include <vector>
using namespace std;

const int NUMBER_STUDENTS = 4;

int main()
```

```
{
    vector<double> scores(NUMBER_STUDENTS);
        .
        .
        .
```

Now I've created a vector named **scores** with four elements. Because the **vector** container supports the [] operator, I can place student scores in the vector like this:

```
#include <iostream>
#include <vector>
using namespace std;

const int NUMBER_STUDENTS = 4;

int main()
{
    vector<double> scores(NUMBER_STUDENTS);

    scores[0] = 89.0;
    scores[1] = 29.0;
    scores[2] = 59.0;
    scores[3] = 79.0;
        .
        .
        .
```

To find the average student score, I'll set up a **for** loop. One of the built-in methods of the **vector** container is the **size** method, which returns the number of elements in the array, and I can use that method in the **for** loop:

```
#include <iostream>
#include <vector>
using namespace std;

const int NUMBER_STUDENTS = 4;

int main()
{
    vector<double> scores(NUMBER_STUDENTS);
    double running_sum = 0;

    scores[0] = 89.0;
    scores[1] = 29.0;
```

```
    scores[2] = 59.0;
    scores[3] = 79.0;

    for (unsigned int loop_index = 0;
        loop_index < scores.size(); loop_index++)
    {
        running_sum += scores[loop_index];
    }
    .
    .
    .
```

And I can display the average student score like this:

```
#include <iostream>
#include <vector>
using namespace std;

const int NUMBER_STUDENTS = 4;

int main()
{
    vector<double> scores(NUMBER_STUDENTS);
    double running_sum = 0;

    scores[0] = 89.0;
    scores[1] = 29.0;
    scores[2] = 59.0;
    scores[3] = 79.0;

    for (unsigned int loop_index = 0;
        loop_index < scores.size(); loop_index++)
    {
        running_sum += scores[loop_index];
    }

    cout << "The average student score is: "
        << running_sum / scores.size() << endl;

    return 0;
}
```

Here's what you see when you run vector.cpp:

```
%vector
The average student score is: 64
```

As you see, containers are templates that you instantiate, and they come with built-in methods, ready for you to use. There are quite a few requirements for STL containers, and you'll find a representative set of requirements in Table 15.1—all containers must satisfy these requirements. A set of requirements like this is called a *concept* in STL terms, and an implementation of a concept is called a *model*.

In Table 15.1, **X** refers to the container type, **T** to the type of object stored in the container, **u** is an identifier of the container type, and **a** and **b** are objects of the container type. Note the column labeled "Complexity." Because the STL algorithms

Table 15.1 STL container requirements.

Expression	Means	Complexity
X::value_type	The type of **T**	compile time
X::reference	Returns the **lvalue** of **T**	compile time
X::const_reference	Returns the **const lvalue** of **T**	compile time
X::iterator	Iterator type pointing to **T**	compile time
X::const_iterator	Returns a iterator to **const T**	compile time
X u;	Returns a zero-size container	constant
X();	Creates a zero-size anonymous container	constant
X(a);	Constructor	linear
X u(a);	Copy constructor	linear
X u = a;	Same as **X u; u = a; (&a)->~X();**	linear
a.begin();	Iterator to beginning element	constant
a.end();	Iterator to end element	constant
a == b	Equivalence relation	linear
a != b	Same as **!(a == b)**	linear
a.swap(b); void swap(a,b)	Swaps **a** and **b**	constant
a.max_size()	Returns the maximum size	constant
a.empty()	Empties the container	constant
a < b	Less than compare	linear
a > b	Greater than compare	linear
a <= b	Less than or equal compare	linear
a >= b	Greater than or equal compare	linear

can perform operations like sorts, the time such operations take can become important, and the STL uses the term "complexity" to show how that time scales with the number of items in the container. Compile time complexity means that the operation is performed at compile time and so doesn't affect runtime performance; constant complexity means that the operation doesn't depend on the number of elements in the container; linear complexity means that the time an operation takes is directly proportional to the number of elements in the container.

Sequences

The STL refines the concept of basic containers by adding the concept of *sequences*. Six of the STL containers are sequences: the **deque**, **list**, **queue**, **priority_queue**, **stack**, and **vector** containers. Placing objects in a sequence means that they're in linear order. There is a first element, a last element, and each of the other elements has a previous and next element. Because sequences have a known order, you can perform operations like inserting new elements, specifying a range of elements, or even deleting or overwriting a range of elements. You can find the requirements for basic sequences in Table 15.2. These requirements refine the basic container type into sequences, and in fact, that's the actual STL term—a *refinement* adds additional requirements to an STL concept.

Table 15.2 uses the same syntax as Table 15.1, with a few added terms: **n** is an integer, **t** is a value of type **T**, and **p**, **q**, **i**, and **j** are iterators (recall that iterators are generalized pointers that you can use to point to the elements in a container).

The **vector**, **list**, and **deque** container types also support some additional sequence operations that STL calls *optional*, and you'll see those operations in Table 15.3, along with the containers that support them.

Table 15.2 Basic STL sequence requirements.

Expression	Means
X(n, t)	An anonymous sequence of **n** copies of **T**
X a(n, t);	A sequence of **n** copies of **T**
X(i, j)	An anonymous sequence initialized to range **i-j**
X a(i, j);	A sequence initialized to range **i-j**
a.insert(p,t)	Inserts a copy of **t** before **p**
a.insert(p,n,t)	Inserts n copies of **t** before **p**
a.insert(p,i,j)	Inserts copies of elements in **(i,j)** before **p**
a.erase(q)	Erases the element pointed to by **q**
a.erase(q1,q2)	Erases the elements in the range **(q1,q2)**
a.clear()	Erases the contents of the sequence

Table 15.3 Optional STL sequence requirements.

Expression	Means	Containers
a.front()	***a.begin()**	vector, list, deque reference
a.back()	***--a.end()**	vector, list, deque reference
a.push_front(x)	**a.insert(a.begin(),x)**	list, deque
a.push_back(x)	**a.insert(a.end(),x)**	vector, list, deque
a.pop_front()	**a.erase(a.begin())**	list, deque
a.pop_back()	**a.erase(--a.end())**	vector, list, deque
a[n]	***(a.begin() + n)**	vector, deque reference
a.at(n)	***(a.begin() + n)**	vector, deque reference

Now that the containers we're discussing support specific sequences of data, it's important to see how to work with ordered data, and in STL programming, that means working with iterators.

Iterators

STL iterators are generalized pointers, and they let the code in STL algorithms move through your data. Iterators are basic to STL programming, and understanding them is central to understanding the STL. Using container templates allows the STL algorithms to be independent of the type of data you're using, and iterators make the algorithms independent of the type of container you're using.

As mentioned, iterators let the code in generic algorithms move through your data, much like pointers would. To let the STL code move through your data, the iterator can have several operations defined, including =, ==, *, ->, ++, and --. In fact, you can use pointers to non-STL classes as iterators for use with STL algorithms, and iterators parallel pointers in many ways. For example, say that you set up an array of **double** values named scores and want to display the data in that array using pointers. You could do that by something like this, where I'm using the pointer **ptr** to move through the array, addressing each element in turn:

```
const int SIZE = 10;
double scores[SIZE];
double* ptr;
    .
    .
    .
for (ptr = scores; ptr != scores + SIZE; ptr++){
    cout << "Data: " << *ptr << endl;
}
```

You can do the same thing with iterators in STL containers. To create an iterator that you can use with a vector of **double** values, you declare that iterator using the type **vector<double>::iterator**, as in this case, where I'm declaring an iterator named **itr** to use with a vector named **scores**:

```
const int SIZE = 10;
vector<double> scores(SIZE);
vector<double>::iterator itr;
    .
    .
    .
```

The **scores** vector makes it easy to work with iterators; for example, **scores.begin()** returns an iterator to the first element in **scores**, and **scores.end()** returns an iterator to the location just past the final element in **scores**. You can use operators like ++ with iterators just as you can with pointers, so I can translate the code above to use iterators like this:

```
const int SIZE = 10;
vector<double> scores(SIZE);
vector<double>::iterator itr;
    .
    .
    .
for (itr = scores.begin(); itr != scores.end(); itr++){
    cout << "Data: " << *itr << endl;
}
```

That's all it takes. As you can see, using iterators is really much like using pointers. So why can't you just use pointers? Why do you need iterators? The answer is that with different container types, operations like moving to the next element can mean different things—for example, finding the next element in a **vector** is different from finding the next element in a **stack** or **queue**. Because this kind of operation is different for different containers, iterators generalize the concept of pointers so you can use them with STL functions no matter what kind of container your data is stored in.

It's time for a full example, so here's vector_iterators.cpp, which shows how to work with iterators and also demonstrates a few vector methods. I'll start by creating a class named **person** that will store the name of a person and their age, as well as a constructor for the class and a **display** method that displays the **person** object's internal data:

```
#include <iostream>
#include <string>
#include <vector>
using namespace std;

class person
{
    string name;
    int age;
public:
    void display() {cout << "Name: " << name << " age: " << age << endl;}
    person(string n, int a) {name = n; age = a;}
};
        .
        .
        .
```

I'll create a vector of **person** objects named **friends**, and use the vector **push_back** method to add elements to the end of the vector (**push_back** adds an element to the end of the vector, and **pop_back** removes that element—see "Introducing the **vector** Container" later in this chapter for more details) to store **person** objects in the vector:

```
#include <iostream>
#include <string>
#include <vector>
using namespace std;

class person
{
    string name;
    int age;
public:
    void display() {cout << "Name: " << name << " age: " << age << endl;}
    person(string n, int a) {name = n; age = a;}
};

int main()
{
    vector<person> friends;

    friends.push_back(person("Ralph", 35));
    friends.push_back(person("Tom", 36));
```

```
    friends.push_back(person("Frank", 23));
    friends.push_back(person("Sally", 24));
    .
    .
    .
```

Now I create an iterator for the **friends** vector and loop over all objects in the vector, calling the **display** method for each one to display its internal data:

```
#include <iostream>
#include <string>
#include <vector>
using namespace std;
    .
    .
    .
int main()
{
    vector<person> friends;

    friends.push_back(person("Ralph", 35));
    friends.push_back(person("Tom", 36));
    friends.push_back(person("Frank", 23));
    friends.push_back(person("Sally", 24));

    vector<person>::iterator p;
    for (p = friends.begin(); p != friends.end(); p++)
        p->display();
    .
    .
    .
```


That displays all the data in the **friends** vector. Vectors also come with many methods built in, and I'll take a look at a few of them here. For example, you can use the vector method **erase** to erase elements in a vector. You pass this method a *range* of elements, as delimited by two iterators. To erase the second person in **friends**, I can call **erase** with the range **friends.begin() + 1** to **friends.begin() + 2**:

```
#include <iostream>
#include <string>
#include <vector>
using namespace std;
    .
    .
    .
```

```
int main()
{
    vector<person> friends;

    friends.push_back(person("Ralph", 35));
    friends.push_back(person("Tom", 36));
    friends.push_back(person("Frank", 23));
    friends.push_back(person("Sally", 24));
    .
    .
    .
    friends.erase(friends.begin() + 1, friends.begin() + 2);

    cout << "Got rid of two friends..." << endl;

    for (p = friends.begin(); p != friends.end(); p++)
        p->display();
    .
    .
    .
```

You can also insert new elements with the **insert** method. For example, I'll create a new vector, **nancys_friends**, and insert a range of elements from that vector into the **friends** vector like this:

```
#include <iostream>
#include <string>
#include <vector>
using namespace std;
    .
    .
    .
int main()
{
    vector<person> friends;

    friends.push_back(person("Ralph", 35));
    friends.push_back(person("Tom", 36));
    friends.push_back(person("Frank", 23));
    friends.push_back(person("Sally", 24));
    .
    .
    .
    vector<person> nancys_friends;
```

```
    nancys_friends.push_back(person("Tina", 35));
    nancys_friends.push_back(person("Buddy", 36));

    friends.insert(friends.begin(),
        nancys_friends.begin() + 1, nancys_friends.begin() + 2);

    cout << "Added two new friends..." << endl;

    for (p = friends.begin(); p != friends.end(); p++)
        p->display();
    .
    .
    .
```

Here's another method—the **swap** method, which allows you to swap the contents of two vectors, and I'll use it to swap the contents of the **friends** and **nancys_friends** vectors this way:

```
#include <iostream>
#include <string>
#include <vector>
using namespace std;
    .
    .
    .
int main()
{
    vector<person> friends;

    friends.push_back(person("Ralph", 35));
    friends.push_back(person("Tom", 36));
    friends.push_back(person("Frank", 23));
    friends.push_back(person("Sally", 24));
    .
    .
    .
    nancys_friends.swap(friends);
    cout << "Swapping your friends with Nancy's..." << endl;

    for (p = friends.begin(); p != friends.end(); p++)
        p->display();

    return 0;
}
```

Here's what you see when you run vector_iterators.cpp:

```
%vector_iterators
Name: Ralph age: 35
Name: Tom age: 36
Name: Frank age: 23
Name: Sally age: 24
Got rid of one friend...
Name: Ralph age: 35
Name: Frank age: 23
Name: Sally age: 24
Added two new friends...
Name: Tina age: 35
Name: Buddy age: 36
Name: Ralph age: 35
Name: Frank age: 23
Name: Sally age: 24
Swapping your friends with Nancy's...
Name: Tina age: 35
Name: Buddy age: 36
```

That gets us started with iterators and container methods. In general, there are five types of iterators:

- *Input iterators*—Give access to all the elements in a container with the ++ operator.
- *Output iterators*—Give access to the elements in a container to write, but not read, elements, letting you move through the elements with the ++ operator.
- *Forward iterators*—Let you move forward through data with the ++ operator in a repeatable sequence. You can also read or write with a forward iterator.
- *Bidirectional iterators*—The same as a forward iterator, except that they can go backward as well and support -- as well as ++.
- *Random access iterators*—Allow you to access any element in the container.

You can find an overview of the different capabilities of these types of iterators in Table 15.4.

***NOTE:** The STL includes iterator templates if you want to build your own iterators from scratch.*

Table 15.4 Operations by iterator.

Operation	Input	Output	Forward	Bidirectional	Random Access
Dereferencing read	X		X	X	X
Dereferencing write		X	X	X	X
Fixed, repeatable order			X	X	X
++	X	X	X	X	X
--				X	X
[]					X
+					X
-					X
+=					X
-=					X

Algorithms

Besides the built-in methods of STL containers, the STL supports many algorithms, which we'll see in detail in Chapter 17. STL algorithms are not methods of containers, because they're intended to be used with all different types of containers. Instead of adding dozens of member functions to each container—which would be duplicated for each container—the creators of the STL made the algorithms *non-member* functions. To use them, you include the algorithm header.

Here's an example, stlfunctions.cpp, that puts a few of the STL algorithms to work. In this example, I'll use the **person** class from earlier in this chapter to create a vector named **friends**, but this time, I'll sort the elements in that vector in various ways. To allow objects of the **person** class to be sorted, you have to define the < operator for that class, and then you can pass a range, as delimited by two iterators, to the **sort** algorithm—note that I'm also including the algorithm header file to make the **sort** algorithm accessible to our code:

```
#include <iostream>
#include <string>
#include <vector>
#include <algorithm>
using namespace std;

class person
{
    string name;
    int age;
```

```
public:
    person(string n, int a) {name = n; age = a;}
    friend bool operator<(const person & person1, const person & person2);
    friend void display(person p);
};

void display(person p)
{
    cout << "Name: " << p.name << " age: " << p.age << endl;
}

bool operator<(const person & person1, const person & person2)
{
    if (person1.name < person2.name)
        return true;
    else
        return false;
}

int main()
{
    vector<person> friends;

    friends.push_back(person("Ralph", 35));
    friends.push_back(person("Tom", 36));
    friends.push_back(person("Frank", 23));
    friends.push_back(person("Sally", 24));

    sort(friends.begin(), friends.end());
    .
    .
    .
```


Our < operator compares people by name, so the **friends** vector is sorted by name when we use the **sort** algorithm. I can use another handy algorithm function, **for_each**, to loop over all the elements in a container and call the **display** function for each element to display its data. To loop over elements with **for_each**, you supply a range of elements delimited by iterators and a function you want called for each element—which will be **display** here. All this looks like this in code:

```
#include <iostream>
#include <string>
#include <vector>
#include <algorithm>
using namespace std;
```

```
    .
    .
    .
int main()
{
    vector<person> friends;

    friends.push_back(person("Ralph", 35));
    friends.push_back(person("Tom", 36));
    friends.push_back(person("Frank", 23));
    friends.push_back(person("Sally", 24));

    sort(friends.begin(), friends.end());

    cout << "Sorted by name..." << endl;

    for_each(friends.begin(), friends.end(), display);
    .
    .
    .
```

You can also specify a comparison function to use with the **sort** algorithm. For example, I can sort using people's ages instead of names with a new function, **compare_ages**. This new function is a friend function of the **person** class so it has access to the internal data of the **person** class, and it returns a value of **true** if the first **person** object passed to it is greater than the second one:

```
#include <iostream>
#include <string>
#include <vector>
#include <algorithm>
using namespace std;

class person
{
    string name;
    int age;
public:
    person(string n, int a) {name = n; age = a;}
    friend bool compare_ages(const person & person1,
        const person & person2);
    friend bool operator<(const person & person1, const person & person2);
    friend void display(person p);
};
```

```
    .
    .
    .
bool compare_ages(const person & person1, const person & person2)
{
    if (person1.age < person2.age)
        return true;
    else
        return false;
}

int main()
{
    vector<person> friends;

    friends.push_back(person("Ralph", 35));
    friends.push_back(person("Tom", 36));
    friends.push_back(person("Frank", 23));
    friends.push_back(person("Sally", 24));
    .
    .
    .
    sort(friends.begin(), friends.end(), compare_ages);

    cout << "Sorted by age..." << endl;

    for_each(friends.begin(), friends.end(), display);
    .
    .
    .
```


You can also use other STL algorithms on vectors, such as **random_shuffle**, which shuffles a container's data randomly:

```
#include <iostream>
#include <string>
#include <vector>
#include <algorithm>
using namespace std;
    .
    .
    .
int main()
{
    vector<person> friends;
```

```
    friends.push_back(person("Ralph", 35));
    friends.push_back(person("Tom", 36));
    friends.push_back(person("Frank", 23));
    friends.push_back(person("Sally", 24));
    .
    .
    .
    random_shuffle(friends.begin(), friends.end());

    cout << "Randomly shuffled..." << endl;

    for_each(friends.begin(), friends.end(), display);

    return 0;
}
```

And here's what you see when you run this example, stlfunctions.cpp, which puts the **sort**, **for_each**, and **random_shuffle** algorithms to work:

```
%stlfunctions
Sorted by name...
Name: Frank age: 23
Name: Ralph age: 35
Name: Sally age: 24
Name: Tom age: 36
Sorted by age...
Name: Frank age: 23
Name: Sally age: 24
Name: Ralph age: 35
Name: Tom age: 36
Randomly shuffled...
Name: Tom age: 36
Name: Frank age: 23
Name: Sally age: 24
Name: Ralph age: 35
```

As you can see, there's really a lot of material to look at in this section and the next two chapters. We'll turn to the Immediate Solutions section now.

Immediate Solutions

Constructing a C++ String

We've used the C++ **string** class throughout the book, but we'll take a more systematic look at it here. This class is a specialization of the C++ **basic_string** class (and the **wstring** class is a specialization of **basic_string** for wide characters). Here are the six constructors for the **string** class—note that the last of these constructors lets you initialize one string from a substring of another:

```
string();
string(const charT* s);
string(size_type n, charT c);
string(const charT* s, size_type n);
string(InputIterator begin, InputIterator end);
string(const basic_string& str, size_type pos = 0, size_type n = npos);
```

Here's a simple example of the kind we've already seen; in this case, I'm creating a string named **string1**, and initializing it to the text "No ":

```
#include <iostream>
#include <string>
using namespace std;

int main()
{
    string string1("No ");
        .
        .
        .
```

You can also create a string as you would a simple variable and assign text to it with the = operator:

```
#include <iostream>
#include <string>
using namespace std;
```

```
int main()
{
    string string1("No ");
    string string2;

    string2 = "problems";
    .
    .
    .
```

Now you can add, or concatenate, the two strings with the + operator, and even use the += operator like this:

```
#include <iostream>
#include <string>
using namespace std;

int main()
{
    string string1("No ");
    string string2;

    string2 = "problems";

    string string3 = string1 + string2;

    cout << string3 << endl;

    string3 += " at all.";

    cout << string3 << endl;

    return 0;
}
```

Here's the result of this code, string1.cpp:

```
%string1
No problems
No problems at all.
```

Related solution:	Found on page:
Introducing the C++ **string** Class	86

C++ String Input

The two main ways of handling text input with strings are with the >> extraction operator and with the **string** method **getline**. The >> operator lets you read only one word at a time, while the **getline** method lets you read a whole line at once. Here's an example, string_input.cpp, that uses both techniques:

```
#include <iostream>
#include <string>
using namespace std;

int main()
{
    string string1, string2;

    cout << "Type a word: ";
    cin >> string1;
    cout << "You typed: " << string1 << endl;

    cout << "Now type a line: ";
    getline(cin, string2);
    cout << "You typed: " << string2 << endl;

    return 0;
}
```

Here's what you might see when you run this example, string_input.cpp:

```
%string_input
Type a word: Hello
You typed: Hello
Now type a line: Hello again.
You typed: Hello again.
```

NOTE: *Some compilers will require a second call to* ***getline*** *to terminate the line.*

Related solutions:	*Found on page:*
Using **cin**	590
Using the **istream** Class's **get**, **getline**, and **ignore** Methods	593

15. The Standard Template Library

Searching C++ Strings

There are plenty of ways of searching the data in strings—you can use the **find** method to find substrings or characters, the reverse find **rfind** method to search starting at the end of the string, the **find_first_of** method to find one of a set of characters, the **find_last_of** method, which is the same as **find_first_of** but starts at the end of the string, and the **find_first_not_of** and **find_last_not_of** methods, which search for characters that are *not* in a set of characters. Here are the prototypes of these methods:

```
size_type find (const string& str, size_type pos = 0) const;
size_type find (const charT* s, size_type pos, size_type n) const;
size_type find (const charT* s, size_type pos = 0) const;
size_type find (charT c, size_type pos = 0) const;
size_type rfind(const string& str, size_type pos = npos) const;
size_type rfind(const charT* s, size_type pos, size_type n) const;
size_type rfind(const charT* s, size_type pos = npos) const;
size_type rfind(charT c, size_type pos = npos) const;
size_type find_first_of(const string& str, size_type pos = 0) const;
size_type find_first_of(const charT* s, size_type pos, size_type n) const;
size_type find_first_of(const charT* s, size_type pos = 0) const;
size_type find_first_of(charT c, size_type pos = 0) const;
size_type find_last_of (const string& str, size_type pos = npos) const;
size_type find_last_of (const charT* s, size_type pos, size_type n) const;
size_type find_last_of (const charT* s, size_type pos = npos) const;
size_type find_last_of (charT c, size_type pos = npos) const;
size_type find_first_not_of(const string& str, size_type pos = 0) const;
size_type find_first_not_of(const charT* s, size_type pos,
    size_type n) const;
size_type find_first_not_of(const charT* s, size_type pos = 0) const;
size_type find_first_not_of(charT c, size_type pos = 0) const;
size_type find_last_not_of (const string& str, size_type pos = npos) const;
size_type find_last_not_of (const charT* s, size_type pos,
    size_type n) const;
size_type find_last_not_of (const charT* s, size_type pos = npos) const;
size_type find_last_not_of (charT c, size_type pos = npos) const;
```

Here's an example, string_methods.cpp, that searches a string, **s**, for various substrings and characters and also uses the **string** class's **length** method to get the length of the string:

```
#include <iostream>
#include <string>
#include <cstdlib>
#include <ctime>
#include <cctype>
using namespace std;

int main()
{
    string s = "Hello from C++.";

    cout << "The string is: " << s << endl;

    cout << "String length: " << s.length() << endl;

    unsigned int loc = s.find('C');
    if (loc == string::npos){
        cout << "Not found" << endl;
    }
    else {
        cout << "Found \'C\' at location: " << loc << endl;
    }

    loc = s.find("C++");
    if (loc == string::npos){
        cout << "Not found" << endl;
    }
    else {
        cout << "Found \"C++\" at location: " << loc << endl;
    }

    return 0;
}
```

Here's what you see when you run this example, string_methods.cpp:

```
%string_methods
The string is: Hello from C++.
String length: 15
Found 'C' at location: 11
Found "C++" at location: 11
```

Using auto_ptr

We've seen the **auto_ptr** template class before, but we'll take a closer look at it now. You use **auto_ptr** for one thing: to make sure memory allocated with **new** is deallocated automatically. For example, take a look at this function, **do_work**:

```
void do_work()
{
    data* workspace;
    workspace = new data[1000000];
    .
    .
    .
    return;
}
```

Here, the code allocates a lot of memory but never deletes that memory, which is a problem, because each time you call this function, more memory is allocated. If you use the **auto_ptr** template to allocate memory space, that space is automatically deallocated when it goes out of scope, eliminating the need to remember to use **delete**. Here's an example, auto_ptr.cpp, that shows how to use this template. I'll use the **person** class we've already seen in this chapter and use **auto_ptr** to create a pointer to the **person** class named **ralph**:

```
#include <iostream>
#include <memory>
#include <string>
using namespace std;

class person
{
    string name;
public:
    person (string n) : name(n) {}
    void display() {cout << "Name: " << name << endl;}
};

int main ()
{

    auto_ptr<person> ralph(new person("Ralph"));
    .
    .
    .
```

I can also copy the new pointer, **ralph**, to another **auto_ptr** pointer named **also_ralph** and then use the **display** method of the allocated object like this:

```
#include <iostream>
#include <memory>
#include <string>
using namespace std;

class person
{
    string name;
public:
    person (string n) : name(n) {}
    void display() {cout << "Name: " << name << endl;}
};

int main ()
{

    auto_ptr<person> ralph(new person("Ralph"));

    auto_ptr<person> also_ralph = ralph;

    also_ralph->display();

    return 0;
}
```

Note that in this code, you don't have to remember to delete the allocated memory—it's done automatically. However, note also that you can't use **new[]** with **auto_ptr** like this:

```
auto_ptr<int> data(new int [1000]);        //Don't do it!
```

This code is no good because **auto_ptr** will automatically apply **delete** to data that was allocated with **new[]**, not **new**. You can only use **auto_ptr** with pointers that point to memory allocated in the heap with **new**.

Related solution:	Found on page:
Using **new** to Allocate Memory	215

Introducing the **vector** Container

The **vector** container is probably the most widely used STL container, and it's the container I'll use to examine the STL in this chapter. A **vector** container is a one-dimensional array, and you can use the array operator, [], on vectors, just as you would any array. However, you can also use the built-in vector methods that we'll see in the next chapter, and the STL algorithms that we'll see in Chapter 17 on the data in vectors. As discussed in the In Depth section of this chapter, the **vector** container is a class template. Here are the possible constructors for **vector** containers:

```
vector(const vector<T,Allocator>& x);
explicit vector(const Allocator& = Allocator());
explicit vector(size_type n, const T& value = T(), const Allocator& =
    Allocator());
vector(InputIterator first, InputIterator last, const Allocator& =
    Allocator());
```

There are a number of methods built into the **vector** class that help you manage the data in the vector, including these (I'll take a look at the methods of each STL container in a more systematic way in the next chapter):

- **back**—Returns the last element.
- **clear**—Clears the container.
- **erase**—Erases elements.
- **front**—Returns the first element.
- **insert**—Inserts an element.
- **pop_back**—Erases the last element.
- **push_back**—Adds an element to the end of the container.
- **size**—Returns the number of elements in the container.

We saw an example, vector.cpp, in the In Depth section of this chapter that created a new vector and used the [] array operator to add and manage data in that vector. In particular, this example found the average score of four students, like this:

```
#include <iostream>
#include <vector>
using namespace std;

const int NUMBER_STUDENTS = 4;
```

```
int main()
{
    vector<double> scores(NUMBER_STUDENTS);
    double running_sum = 0;

    scores[0] = 89.0;
    scores[1] = 29.0;
    scores[2] = 59.0;
    scores[3] = 79.0;

    for (unsigned int loop_index = 0;
        loop_index < scores.size(); loop_index++)
    {
        running_sum += scores[loop_index];
    }

    cout << "The average student score is: "
        << running_sum / scores.size() << endl;

    return 0;
}
```

Here's what you see when you run this example:

```
%vector
The average student score is: 64
```


You can also initialize a vector by passing an element range as delimited by two iterators to the **vector** constructor. In fact, you can initialize a vector from a non-STL array if you treat pointers into the array as you would iterators, like this:

```
#include <iterator>
#include <vector>
#include <iostream>
using namespace std;

const int MAX = 4;

int main()
{
    int numbers_array[MAX];

    for (int loop_index = 0; loop_index < MAX; loop_index++){
        numbers_array[loop_index] = loop_index;
    }
```

```
    vector<int> numbers_vector(numbers_array,
        numbers_array + MAX);
        .
        .
        .
```

The Borland bcc32 C++ compiler appears to have some internal problems with this use of the **vector** container's constructor, however. Because this compiler is so popular, I'll use the vector **assign** method, which takes two iterators that bound a range of elements, to assign values to a vector from an array in the examples in this and the next two chapters:

```
#include <iterator>
#include <vector>
#include <iostream>
using namespace std;

const int MAX = 4;

int main()
{
    int numbers_array[MAX];

    for (int loop_index = 0; loop_index < MAX; loop_index++){
        numbers_array[loop_index] = loop_index;
    }

    vector<int> numbers_vector(MAX);
    numbers_vector.assign(numbers_array, numbers_array + MAX);
        .
        .
        .
```


If you prefer, you can use the **copy** algorithm (if you include the algorithm header—see "Using **copy**" in Chapter 17 for more information on **copy**) to initialize a vector from an array:

```
#include <iterator>
#include <vector>
#include <algorithm>
#include <iostream>
using namespace std;

const int MAX = 4;
```

```
int main()
{
    int numbers_array[MAX];

    for (int loop_index = 0; loop_index < MAX; loop_index++){
        numbers_array[loop_index] = loop_index;
    }

   vector<int> numbers_vector(MAX);
   copy(numbers_array, numbers_array + MAX, numbers_vector.begin());
    .
    .
    .
```


Related solution:	Found on page:
Using **copy**	758

Using Iterators and Vector Methods

As discussed in the In Depth section of this chapter, iterators are generalized pointers that you use to move through the data in a container. For example, to create an iterator that you can use with a vector of **double** values, you declare that iterator using the type **vector<double>::iterator**, as in this case, where I'm declaring an iterator named **itr** to use with a vector named **scores**:

```
const int SIZE = 10;
vector<double> scores(SIZE);
vector<double>::iterator itr;
    .
    .
    .
```

Containers like **vector** containers make it easy to work with iterators; for example, **scores.begin()** returns an iterator to the first element in **scores**, and **scores.end()** returns an iterator to the location just past the final element in **scores**. You can use operators like ++ with iterators just as you can with pointers, so we were able to use an iterator to work through a vector of **person** objects named **friends** in an example, vector_iterators.cpp, that we first saw in the

In Depth section of this chapter. This example also demonstrated the vector methods **push_back**, **erase**, **insert**, and **swap**:

```
#include <iostream>
#include <string>
#include <vector>
using namespace std;

class person
{
    string name;
    int age;
public:
    void display() {cout << "Name: " << name << " age: " << age << endl;}
    person(string n, int a) {name = n; age = a;}
};

int main()
{
    vector<person> friends;

    friends.push_back(person("Ralph", 35));
    friends.push_back(person("Tom", 36));
    friends.push_back(person("Frank", 23));
    friends.push_back(person("Sally", 24));

    vector<person>::iterator p;
    for (p = friends.begin(); p != friends.end(); p++)
        p->display();

    friends.erase(friends.begin() + 1, friends.begin() + 2);

    cout << "Got rid of one friend..." << endl;

    for (p = friends.begin(); p != friends.end(); p++)
        p->display();

    vector<person> nancys_friends;

    nancys_friends.push_back(person("Tina", 35));
    nancys_friends.push_back(person("Buddy", 36));
```

```
    friends.insert(friends.begin(),
        nancys_friends.begin() + 1, nancys_friends.begin() + 2);

    cout << "Added two new friends..." << endl;

    for (p = friends.begin(); p != friends.end(); p++)
        p->display();

    nancys_friends.swap(friends);
    cout << "Swapping your friends with Nancy's..." << endl;

    for (p = friends.begin(); p != friends.end(); p++)
        p->display();

    return 0;
}
```

Here's what you see when you run this example, vector_iterators.cpp:

```
%vector_iterators
Name: Ralph age: 35
Name: Tom age: 36
Name: Frank age: 23
Name: Sally age: 24
Got rid of one friend...
Name: Ralph age: 35
Name: Frank age: 23
Name: Sally age: 24
Added two new friends...
Name: Tina age: 35
Name: Buddy age: 36
Name: Ralph age: 35
Name: Frank age: 23
Name: Sally age: 24
Swapping your friends with Nancy's...
Name: Tina age: 35
Name: Buddy age: 36
```

For more on iterators, see "Predefined Iterators," "Using **copy** and **ostream** Iterators," "Using **copy** and **istream** Iterators," "Using Reverse Iterators," "Using Insertion Iterators," and "Finding the Distance between Iterators," all later in this chapter.

Introducing STL Algorithms

As discussed in the In Depth section of this chapter, the STL comes with many built-in algorithms, which are pre-written routines that you can use with the data in STL containers. We'll take a look at algorithms in detail in Chapter 17, but in the In Depth section of this chapter, we saw an example, stlfunctions.cpp, which put the **sort**, **for_each**, and **random_shuffle** algorithms to work:

```
#include <iostream>
#include <string>
#include <vector>
#include <algorithm>
using namespace std;

class person
{
    string name;
    int age;
public:
    person(string n, int a) {name = n; age = a;}
    friend bool compare_ages(const person & person1,
        const person & person2);
    friend bool operator<(const person & person1, const person & person2);
    friend void display(person p);
};

void display(person p)
{
    cout << "Name: " << p.name << " age: " << p.age << endl;
}

bool operator<(const person & person1, const person & person2)
{
    if (person1.name < person2.name)
        return true;
    else
        return false;
}

bool compare_ages(const person & person1, const person & person2)
{
    if (person1.age < person2.age)
        return true;
    else
```

```
        return false;
}

int main()
{
    vector<person> friends;

    friends.push_back(person("Ralph", 35));
    friends.push_back(person("Tom", 36));
    friends.push_back(person("Frank", 23));
    friends.push_back(person("Sally", 24));

    sort(friends.begin(), friends.end());

    cout << "Sorted by name..." << endl;

    for_each(friends.begin(), friends.end(), display);

    sort(friends.begin(), friends.end(), compare_ages);

    cout << "Sorted by age..." << endl;

    for_each(friends.begin(), friends.end(), display);

    random_shuffle(friends.begin(), friends.end());

    cout << "Randomly shuffled..." << endl;

    for_each(friends.begin(), friends.end(), display);

    return 0;
}
```

Here's what you see when you run this example, stlfunctions.cpp:

```
%stlfunctions
Sorted by name...
Name: Frank age: 23
Name: Ralph age: 35
Name: Sally age: 24
Name: Tom age: 36
Sorted by age...
Name: Frank age: 23
Name: Sally age: 24
Name: Ralph age: 35
```

```
Name: Tom age: 36
Randomly shuffled...
Name: Tom age: 36
Name: Frank age: 23
Name: Sally age: 24
Name: Ralph age: 35
```

It's also worth noting that you can use pointers to non-STL objects as iterators in the STL algorithm functions, like this:

```
int array[SIZE] = {9, 8, 7, 6, 5, 4, 3, 2, 1, 0};
sort(array, array + SIZE);
```

Predefined Iterators

The STL classes come with a number of predefined iterators, including:

- **iterator**—Standard iterator.
- **ostream_iterator**—Handles **ostream**.
- **istream_iterator**—Handles **istream**.
- **reverse_iterator**—Iterates in a reverse direction.
- **insert_iterator**—Inserts elements into a container.
- **front_insert_iterator**—Inserts elements into a container from the front.
- **back_insert_iterator**—Inserts elements into a container from the back.

The **ostream_iterator** and **istream_iterator** are examples of *adapters*, which work to adapt the STL iterator interface to other interfaces. We've already taken a look at how to work with standard iterators (see "Using Iterators and Vector Methods" earlier in this chapter), and I'll take a look at the other iterator types in the remainder of this chapter.

Using **copy** and **ostream** Iterators

The STL includes two iterator types to handle **ostream** and **istream**: **ostream_iterator** and **istream_iterator**. These iterators are also called *adapters*, because they adapt the stream interface to the iterator interface used by the STL. You can use these iterators to send output to **ostream** and read input from **istream**. Here's how to create an **ostream_iterator**:

```
#include <iterator>
    .
    .
    .
ostream_iterator<int, char> ostream_itr(cout, " ");
```

In this case, I'm using the **ostream_iterator** template to create an **ostream** iterator named **ostream_itr** that can handle **int** values. Note that the second argument, **char**, indicates the type of character the output stream handles (I'm using **char** as opposed to **wchar_t** here). I'm also using the **ostream_iterator** class constructor to connect this iterator to **cout** (you could also use an **ofstream** object) and to make sure that the iterator puts a space between integers when it displays them.

Note that some compilers don't support wide character streams yet, and for them, you pass only one argument as a template argument:

```
ostream_iterator<int> ostream_itr(cout, " ");
```

How do you use this new iterator, **ostream_itr**? Here's an example; this statement sends the integer value 1 to **cout**:

```
*ostream_itr++ = 1;
```

What this actually does is send a value of 1 to **cout** and then increment the iterator to get ready for the next output operation. The STL also includes an algorithm named **copy** that you can use to copy a range of data, as delimited by two iterators, from one container to another. I can use **copy** to copy data from a vector to **cout** like this:

```
copy(numbers_vector.begin(), numbers_vector.end(), ostream_itr);
```

Here's an example, copier.cpp, that puts this to work; in this case, I'll create a vector of numbers and use an **ostream** iterator to display those numbers:

```
#include <iostream>
#include <iterator>
#include <vector>
using namespace std;

const int MAX = 5;

int main()
{
```

```
    int numbers_array[MAX];
    vector<int> numbers_vector(MAX);

    for (int loop_index = 0; loop_index < MAX; loop_index++){
        numbers_array[loop_index] = loop_index;
    }

    copy(numbers_array, numbers_array + MAX, numbers_vector.begin());

    ostream_iterator<int, char> ostream_itr(cout, " ");

    copy(numbers_vector.begin(), numbers_vector.end(), ostream_itr);
    cout << endl;

    return 0;
}
```

Here's what you see when you run copier.cpp and the **ostream** iterator does its work:

```
%copier
0 1 2 3 4
```

How do you create **istream** iterators? See the next section.

Using **copy** and **istream** Iterators

You can create **istream** iterators to handle input. Here's an example, where I'm creating an **istream** iterator named **istream_itr**, connecting it to **cin**, and setting it up to handle **int** values:

```
#include <iterator>
    .
    .
    .
istream_iterator<int, char> istream_itr(cin);
```

In this case, the second template argument, **char**, indicates that the stream I'm connecting this iterator to handles normal-width characters (as opposed to wide, **wchar_t**, characters). Some compilers don't support wide character streams yet, and for them, you pass only one argument as a template argument:

```
istream_iterator<int> istream_itr(cin);
```

You can use the **copy** algorithm to copy data from one container to another, and here's how I copy data from **cin** to a vector—note that the range I'm reading data from is from **istream_iterator<int, char>(cin)** to **istream_iterator<int, char>()**. The second iterator, which does not pass an argument to the constructor, indicates that I want to end the input when there is an input failure, such as a type mismatch or when the end of the stream is reached:

```
copy(istream_iterator<int, char>(cin), istream_iterator<int, char>(),
    numbers_vector.begin());
```

Here's an example, istream_iterator.cpp, that puts this to work, reading from **cin** using an **istream** iterator and placing the data in a vector. I start by creating the vector that will hold the data and setting up the **istream** iterator:

```
#include <iostream>
#include <iterator>
#include <vector>
using namespace std;

const int MAX = 5;

int main()
{
    int numbers_array[MAX];
    vector<int> numbers_vector(MAX);

    for (int loop_index = 0; loop_index < MAX; loop_index++){
        numbers_array[loop_index] = loop_index;
    }

    copy(istream_iterator<int, char>(cin), istream_iterator<int, char>(),
        numbers_vector.begin());
        .
        .
        .
```

Now I can read integers from the **istream** iterator and display the data that was read:

```
#include <iostream>
#include <iterator>
#include <vector>
using namespace std;

const int MAX = 5;
```

```
int main()
{
    int numbers_array[MAX];
    vector<int> numbers_vector(MAX);

    for (int loop_index = 0; loop_index < MAX; loop_index++){
        numbers_array[loop_index] = loop_index;
    }

    copy(istream_iterator<int, char>(cin), istream_iterator<int, char>(),
        numbers_vector.begin());

    ostream_iterator<int, char> ostream_itr(cout, " ");

    copy(numbers_vector.begin(), numbers_vector.end(), ostream_itr);

    cout << endl;

    return 0;
}
```

Here's what you see when you run istream_iterator.cpp—note that I'm entering a non-integer value, **'q'**, to end the input:

```
%istream_iterator
1 2 3 4 5 q
1 2 3 4 5
```


Using Reverse Iterators

A reverse iterator moves backward through the data in a container. To show how this works, I'll add some code to the copier.cpp, which we developed in "Using **copy** and **ostream** Iterators" earlier in this chapter. Here, I'll specify the range of data in the vector **numbers_vector** using the vector methods **rbegin** and **rend**, which return reverse iterators to the beginning and end of the vector respectively:

```
#include <iostream>
#include <iterator>
#include <vector>
using namespace std;

const int MAX = 5;
```

```
int main()
{
    int numbers_array[MAX];
    vector<int> numbers_vector(MAX);

    for (int loop_index = 0; loop_index < MAX; loop_index++){
        numbers_array[loop_index] = loop_index;
    }

    copy(numbers_array, numbers_array + MAX, numbers_vector.begin());

    ostream_iterator<int, char> ostream_itr(cout, " ");

    copy(numbers_vector.begin(), numbers_vector.end(), ostream_itr);
    cout << endl;

    copy(numbers_vector.rbegin(), numbers_vector.rend(), ostream_itr);
    cout << endl;
        .
        .
        .
```

This code uses reverse iterators implicitly, and the result is that the data in the vector is displayed in reverse order. I can also declare and use a reverse iterator explicitly, as in this code:

```
#include <iostream>
#include <iterator>
#include <vector>
using namespace std;

const int MAX = 5;

int main()
{
    int numbers_array[MAX];
    vector<int> numbers_vector(MAX);

    for (int loop_index = 0; loop_index < MAX; loop_index++){
        numbers_array[loop_index] = loop_index;
    }

    copy(numbers_array, numbers_array + MAX, numbers_vector.begin());

    ostream_iterator<int, char> ostream_itr(cout, " ");
```

```
    copy(numbers_vector.begin(), numbers_vector.end(), ostream_itr);
    cout << endl;

    copy(numbers_vector.rbegin(), numbers_vector.rend(), ostream_itr);
    cout << endl;

    vector<int>::reverse_iterator reverse_itr;
    for (reverse_itr = numbers_vector.rbegin();
        reverse_itr != numbers_vector.rend(); ++reverse_itr)
        cout << *reverse_itr << ' ';

    cout << endl;

    return 0;
}
```

Here's what you see when you run the new version of copier.cpp, using reverse iterators as well as a standard iterator:

```
%copier
0 1 2 3 4
4 3 2 1 0
4 3 2 1 0
```


Using Insertion Iterators

Insertion iterators let you insert data from one container into another without overwriting existing data; when you insert data, the container is extended if necessary. Insertion iterators are great because you don't have to worry about writing past the current bounds of a container—the container grows as necessary. This is particularly useful if you're adding elements to a newly declared, empty container.

Here's an example, insertion_iterator.cpp, to show how this works. I start with three arrays of strings and copy the first array into a vector of strings, **text**, so the vector holds "This", "is", "a", and "test". Then I use an insertion iterator to insert the strings in the second array, "not" and "really" into the **text** vector, leaving "This", "is", "not", "really", "a", and "test" in the vector **text**. To perform this operation, I can use the names of the **string** arrays, which are pointers, as iterators:

```
#include <iostream>
#include <string>
```

```
#include <iterator>
#include <vector>
using namespace std;

int main()
{
    string string1[4] = {"This", "is", "a", "test"};
    string string2[2] = {"not", "really"};
    string string3[3] = {"yes", "it", "is"};

    vector<string> text(4);
    copy(string1, string1 + 4, text.begin());
    ostream_iterator<string, char> out(cout, " ");

    copy (text.begin(), text.end(), out);
    cout << endl;

    copy(string2, string1, insert_iterator<vector<string> >
        (text, text.begin() + 2));
    copy (text.begin(), text.end(), out);
    cout << endl;
    .
    .
    .
```

NOTE: *Visual C++ might display warning number C4786 here ("Identifier truncated to 255 characters"), but a check of the documentation indicates that the warning is spurious and apparently has to do with the* ***vector*** *template.*

Note that you pass the location at which you want to start inserting data to an insertion iterator's constructor. In this case, I am using an anonymous insertion iterator by passing values directly to the iterator's constructor, but I could also name that iterator, say, **itr**, like this: **insert_iterator<vector<string> > itr(text, text.begin() + 2)**.

I can also use a back insertion iterator, which inserts items starting at the end of a container, or a front insertion iterator, which inserts items starting at the front of a container. When you create a front or back insertion iterator, you pass only one argument to the iterator's template—the name of the container you want the iterator for. Here's how I use a back insertion iterator to insert the strings in the third array, "yes", "it", and "is" at the end of the vector named **text**:

```
#include <iostream>
#include <string>
#include <iterator>
```

```
#include <vector>
using namespace std;

int main()
{
    string string1[4] = {"This", "is", "a", "test"};
    string string2[2] = {"not", "really"};
    string string3[3] = {"yes", "it", "is"};

    vector<string> text(4);
    copy(string1, string1 + 4, text.begin());
    ostream_iterator<string, char> out(cout, " ");
    copy (text.begin(), text.end(), out);
    cout << endl;

    copy(string2, string1, insert_iterator<vector<string> >
        (text, text.begin() + 2));
    copy (text.begin(), text.end(), out);
    cout << endl;

    copy(string3, string2, back_insert_iterator<vector<string> >(text));
    copy (text.begin(), text.end(), out);
    cout << endl;

    return 0;
}
```

And here's what you see when you run this example, insertion_iterator.cpp:

```
%insertion_iterator
This is a test
This is not really a test
This is not really a test yes it is
```

The STL also defines functions called *inserters* to make using insertion iterators a little easier. The **inserter** function takes two arguments, which are the same arguments you'd pass to the **insert_iterator** class's constructor. The **back_inserter** and **front_inserter** functions each take one argument, which is the same as you'd pass to the **back_insert_iterator** and **front _insert_iterator** classes' constructors. In other words, these two expressions are the same for the example code above:

```
insert_iterator<vector<string> >(text, text.begin() + 2)
inserter(text, text.begin() + 2)
```

And these two are the same:

```
back_insert_iterator<vector<string> >(text)
back_inserter(text)
```

Here's the example insertion_iterator.cpp rewritten to use the **inserter** and **back_inserter** functions instead of anonymous insertion iterators:

```
#include <iostream>
#include <string>
#include <iterator>
#include <vector>
using namespace std;

int main()
{
    string string1[4] = {"This", "is", "a", "test"};
    string string2[2] = {"not", "really"};
    string string3[3] = {"yes", "it", "is"};

    vector<string> text(4);
    copy(string1, string1 + 4, text.begin());
    ostream_iterator<string, char> out(cout, " ");
    copy (text.begin(), text.end(), out);
    cout << endl;

    copy(string2, string1, inserter(text, text.begin() + 2));
    copy (text.begin(), text.end(), out);
    cout << endl;

    copy(string3, string2, back_inserter(text));
    copy (text.begin(), text.end(), out);
    cout << endl;

    return 0;
}
```

NOTE: *Visual C++ might display warning number C4786 here ("Identifier truncated to 255 characters"), but a check of the documentation indicates that the warning is spurious and apparently has to do with the* ***vector*** *template.*

For another example using insertion iterators, this time filling a previously empty container, see "Using the **multiset** Container" in Chapter 16.

Related solution:	*Found on page:*
Using the **multiset** Container	728

Finding the Distance between Iterators

The STL includes an algorithm named **distance** that lets you determine the distance between two iterators. Here's an example, iterator_distance.cpp, that puts this to work. In this case, I'll create a variable named **distance** of the STL **difference_type**, which is specifically designed to be the type that can hold the distance between iterators, and then I'll let the **distance** algorithm fill that variable with the distance between two iterators. Finally, I display that distance like this:

```
#include<iterator>
#include<vector>
#include <iostream>
using namespace std;

const int MAX = 4;

int main()
{
    int numbers_array[MAX];
    vector<int> numbers_vector(MAX);

    for (int loop_index = 0; loop_index < MAX; loop_index++){
        numbers_array[loop_index] = loop_index;
    }

    copy(numbers_array, numbers_array + MAX, numbers_vector.begin());

    vector<int>::iterator itr = numbers_vector.begin() + 2;

    vector<int>::difference_type itr_distance;
    distance(numbers_vector.begin(), itr, itr_distance);

    cout << "The distance from the beginning to the iterator is: "
        << itr_distance << endl;

   return 0;
}
```

Here's what you see when you run this example, iterator_distance.cpp:

```
%iterator_distance
The distance from the beginning to the iterator is: 2
```

NOTE: *Some compilers, like Visual C++, support only a two-argument form of the* ***distance*** *algorithm, and this code won't work with them.*

Related solution:	Found on page:
Using **count**	759

Chapter 16

Standard Template Library Containers

In Depth

This chapter is all about the containers the STL supports. The previous chapter gave us an overview of the STL containers, and in this chapter, we're going to see all of them at work.

Containers

There are eleven STL containers; here's the list of those containers, together with the header files you include to be able to use them:

- **list**—Supports a doubly linked list of data items; each item knows which item comes before and after it. Header file: list.
- **queue**—Supports a queue that lets you add elements at rear end and remove them from the front end. This container is more restrictive than a **deque**. Header file: queue.
- **deque**—Supports a double ended queue, and it also lets you access those elements randomly (no matter where they are in the queue). Header file: deque.
- **priority_queue**—Supports a prioritized queue that stores its items in sorted order. Header file: queue.
- **stack**—Supports a stack of items, with methods like **push** and **pop**. Header file: stack.
- **vector**—Supports a one-dimensional array. Header file: vector.
- **map**—Supports a collection of keys and values associated with the keys. The key and values can be of different types. Header file: map.
- **multimap**—Supports a map that can support multiple values for each key. Header file: map.
- **set**—Supports a sorted set of unique members. Header file: set.
- **multiset**—Supports a set that can support multiple values per key. Header file: set.
- **bitset**—A data construct that allows you to set, reset, and check individual bits. Header file: bitset.

We'll see all of these containers in code in this chapter. As we saw in the previous chapter, there are certain requirements that containers must meet. The STL also refines the container concept by adding more requirements and creating two new concepts: sequences and associative containers.

Sequences

Six of the STL containers, **queue**, **priority_queue**, **stack**, **vector**, **list**, and **deque** are sequences. As we saw in the previous chapter, sequences guarantee that their elements are arranged in linear order; if a container is a sequence, it is a container that, at the very least, supports a forward iterator.

Here's an example, deque.cpp, that works with a deque (pronounced "deck"). A deque is a general purpose double-ended queue. An STL **queue** container lets you add items at one end and retrieve them from the other, and in fact, an STL queue is a specialized, restricted form of a deque. In a deque, you can retrieve elements with random access, as you can with a vector, using the [] array operator, but in a queue, you can access only the front and end elements. In fact, **deque** containers are a lot like **vector** containers, except that inserting and removing items from the beginning or end of a deque is a constant time operation, and not a linear operation (which means that if you insert and remove items at the beginning and end of a container a lot, you should probably use a **deque** container).

In this example, I'll create a deque of strings to hold the names of patients waiting to be seen in a doctor's office, adding new patients to the back of the deque as they arrive and removing them from the front when the doctor sees them. When you work with a deque, you can use the **push_front** method to add an element to the front of the deque, **push_back** to add an element to the end, **pop_front** to remove an element from the front of the deque, and **pop_back** to remove the element from the end of the deque. You can also use array subscripts to access data randomly in a deque, and I'll do that in this example—note that I use an iterator to move through the deque and display the people still waiting after each deque operation:

```
#include <deque>
#include <string>
#include <iostream>
using namespace std;

deque<string> patients;
```

```
int main ()
{
  cout << "Initializing patients..." << endl;

  patients.push_front("Frank");
  patients.push_front("Molly");
  patients.push_front("Tom");
  patients.push_front("Sally");

  deque<string>::iterator itr;

  itr = patients.begin();
  while (itr < patients.end())
    cout << *itr++ << endl;

  cout << "Third patient..." << endl;

  cout << patients[2] << endl;

  cout << "A new patient arrives..." << endl;
  patients.push_back("Kurt");

  itr = patients.begin();
  while (itr < patients.end())
    cout << *itr++ << endl;

  cout << "Seeing the first patient..." << endl;
  patients.pop_front();

  itr = patients.begin();
  while (itr < patients.end())
    cout << *itr++ << endl;

  return 0;
}
```


Here's what you see when you run this example, deque.cpp:

```
%deque
Initializing patients...
Sally
Tom
Molly
Frank
Third patient...
```

```
Molly
A new patient arrives...
Sally
Tom
Molly
Frank
Kurt
Seeing the first patient...
Tom
Molly
Frank
Kurt
```

NOTE: *Visual C++ might produce the spurious warning "Identifier truncated to 255 characters," which can be ignored.*

Associative Containers

Another refinement of the container concept is the *associative container*. The **set**, **multiset**, **map**, and **multimap** containers are all associative containers, and associative containers store data as key/value pairs. You use the key to retrieve the associated value from the container. For example, a key could be an employee's name, and the associated value could be a structure holding the employee's title, ID, salary, job description, and so on. Using associative containers is often more intuitive than using arrays, because you can access your data with keys that can be words, not just numbers.

For a general container **X**, **X::value_type** holds the type of value stored in the container. Associative containers add a new type, **X::key_type**, which holds the key type. The simplest associative container is the **set** container, where you can store only one value per key—in fact, in sets, the key and the value are the same thing. Sets in the STL are just like mathematical sets and can store items that are associated in some way, such as the names of students in a class. The **multiset** container is the same, except that you can have multiple values for each key. That is, in a set, all items are unique (such as {1, 2, 3}), but you can have multiple copies of the same item in a multiset (such as {1, 1, 2, 2, 3, 3, 3}).

In sets, the keys and values must be of the same type, but in **map** containers, the keys and values can be of different types. In the **map** container, there is only one value for each key, and because the keys and values can be of different types, this is the kind of container that you could use to store employee's names in keys and structures holding the employee's title, ID, salary, and job description in the associated values. In a **multimap** container, you can have multiple values associated with the same key.

Here's an example, map.cpp, that uses the **map** container. In this case, I'll create a map that uses the names of people as keys and stores their ages as values. When you instantiate a map, you pass the types you want for the keys and the values to the **map** template, and then you can use the array operator, [], to access values in the map by key. Because data is stored in key/value pairs in maps, each iterator must be able to point to two values, the key and its associated value. To be able to do that, maps store data in **pair** objects, and these objects have two members, **first** and **second**. The **first** member holds the key for the current element in the map, and the **second** holds the associated value (for more on **pair**, see "Using the **map** Container" later in this chapter). Using the [] array operator to access data in the map and an iterator to iterate through it, then, here's what this example looks like:

```
#include <string>
#include <map>
#include <iostream>
using namespace std;

int main ()
{
    map<string, int> ages;

    ages["Ralph"] = 35;
    ages["Sally"] = 29;
    ages["Tom"] = 77;
    ages["Frank"] = 31;
    ages["April"] = 24;
    ages["Tina"] = 61;

    map<string, int>::iterator itr;

    for(itr = ages.begin(); itr != ages.end(); itr++){
        cout << itr->first << " is " << itr->second
            << " years old." << endl;
    }

    return 0;
}
```


And here's what you see when you run map.cpp and it displays all the data stored in the **map**—note that the key/value pairs are sorted by key:

```
%map
April is 24 years old.
Frank is 31 years old.
Ralph is 35 years old.
```

```
Sally is 29 years old.
Tina is 61 years old.
Tom is 77 years old.
```

Bitset

Besides sequences and associative containers, the STL also supports *bitsets*. Bitsets are not true STL containers, because they don't meet the requirements for containers (see Table 15.1). Bitsets are designed to store bits, as you might store for programming flags, in a conveniently handled data structure (for more on how this works and what it's good for, see "Using The **bitset** Container" later in this chapter). Setting and resetting bits in a byte or word of data is error prone, and you can use bitsets instead.

Here's an example, bitset.cpp, that shows how this works. You pass the number of bits in a bitset to the **bitset** template, and in this case, I'll create a bitset named **flags** that stores eight bits. I'll use the | operator to OR a value of 7 to the bitset, which gives it the value 00000111 in binary (base 2). You can access the bits in a bitset using the array operator [], so I can check if bit 2 is set, as you see in this code:

```
#include <iostream>
#include <bitset>
using namespace std;

int main ()
{
    bitset<8> flags;

    flags |= 7;

    cout << flags << endl;

    if(flags[2]){
        cout << "Bit 2 is set" << endl;
    }

    return 0;
}
```

Here's what you see when you run bitset.cpp:

```
%bitset
00000111
Bit 2 is set
```

Common Container Members

Before we see all the container types at work in the Immediate Solutions section of this chapter, it's worth taking a look at the common container members we'll be seeing. Here are the types defined for all STL containers, which you can use to declare your own variables:

- **X::value_type**—Returns **T**, the container's element type.
- **X::reference**—The same as **T&**.
- **X::const_reference**—The same as **const T&**.
- **X::iterator**—The container's iterator type, a generalized version of **T***.
- **X::const_iterator**—The constant iterator type, a generalized version of **const T***.
- **X::difference_type**—A signed integer type that represents the distance between iterators.
- **X::size_type**—An unsigned integer used to represent the size of data objects, number of elements, and subscripts.

There are also a number of methods defined for all containers (except **bitset**) that it's useful to know about, some of which we've already seen:

- **begin**—Returns an iterator to the first element.
- **end**—Returns an iterator to one element past the end.
- **rbegin**—Returns a reverse iterator to the first element.
- **rend**—Returns a reverse iterator to one element past the end.
- **size**—Returns the number of elements in the container.
- **maxsize**—Returns the maximum size of the container.
- **empty**—True if the container is empty.
- **swap**—Swaps the entire contents of two containers.
- ==—The equal conditional operator, true if two containers are equal in all respects, including their contents.
- !=—The not equal conditional operator.
- <—The less than conditional operator.
- >—The greater than conditional operator.
- <=—The less than or equal to conditional operator.
- >=—The greater than or equal to conditional operator.

In the Immediate Solutions section, we'll take a look at all the STL containers in action, and it's time to get started.

Immediate Solutions

Using the **vector** Container

As you know from the previous chapter, **vector** containers are one-dimensional arrays, and you can access the data in a vector with the [] array operator. Here are the methods you typically use with the **vector** container:

- **push_back**—Adds an element to the end of the container.
- **pop_back**—Erases the last element.
- **insert**—Inserts an element or elements.
- **clear**—Clears the container.
- **resize**—Resizes the container by erasing the last elements if needed.
- **assign**—Assigns elements from a range to replace the container's contents.
- **front**—Returns the first element.
- **back**—Returns the last element.
- **erase**—Erases elements.
- **[]**—Array operator.
- **at**—Returns element at a specific location.

Here's how the STL **vector** container template is declared, with the prototypes for this container's methods listed:

```
template <class T, class Allocator = allocator<T> >
class vector {
public:
typedef typename Allocator::reference reference;
typedef typename Allocator::const_reference const_reference;
typedef implementation defined iterator;
typedef implementation defined const_iterator;
typedef implementation defined size_type;
typedef implementation defined difference_type;
typedef T value_type;
typedef Allocator allocator_type;
typedef typename Allocator::pointer pointer;
typedef typename Allocator::const_pointer const_pointer;
```

```
typedef std::reverse_iterator<iterator> reverse_iterator;
typedef std::reverse_iterator<const_iterator> const_reverse_iterator;
explicit vector(const Allocator& = Allocator());
explicit vector(size_type n, const T& value = T(),
    const Allocator& = Allocator());
template <class InputIterator>
vector(InputIterator first, InputIterator last,
    const Allocator& = Allocator());
vector(const vector<T,Allocator>& x);
~vector();
vector<T,Allocator>& operator=(const vector<T,Allocator>& x);
template <class InputIterator>
void assign(InputIterator first, InputIterator last);
void assign(size_type n, const T& u);
allocator_type get_allocator() const;
iterator begin();
const_iterator begin() const;
iterator end();
const_iterator end() const;
reverse_iterator rbegin();
const_reverse_iterator rbegin() const;
reverse_iterator rend();
const_reverse_iterator rend() const;
size_type size() const;
size_type max_size() const;
void resize(size_type sz, T c = T());
size_type capacity() const;
bool empty() const;
void reserve(size_type n);
reference operator[](size_type n);
const_reference operator[](size_type n) const;
const_reference at(size_type n) const;
reference at(size_type n);
reference front();
const_reference front() const;
reference back();
const_reference back() const;
void push_back(const T& x);
void pop_back();
iterator insert(iterator position, const T& x);
void insert(iterator position, size_type n, const T& x);
template <class InputIterator>
void insert(iterator position,
    InputIterator first, InputIterator last);
iterator erase(iterator position);
```

```
iterator erase(iterator first, iterator last);
void swap(vector<T,Allocator>&);
void clear();
};
```

Here's the example, vector.cpp, that we dissected in the previous chapter; this example creates a vector of student scores and finds the average score:

```
#include <iostream>
#include <vector>
using namespace std;

const int NUMBER_STUDENTS = 4;

int main()
{
    vector<double> scores(NUMBER_STUDENTS);
    double running_sum = 0;

    scores[0] = 89.0;
    scores[1] = 29.0;
    scores[2] = 59.0;
    scores[3] = 79.0;

    for (unsigned int loop_index = 0;
        loop_index < scores.size(); loop_index++)
    {
        running_sum += scores[loop_index];
    }

    cout << "The average student score is: "
        << running_sum / scores.size() << endl;

    return 0;
}
```

Here's what you see when you run this example, vector.cpp:

```
%vector
The average student score is: 64
```

For the details on how to initialize vectors from standard arrays, see "Introducing the **vector** Container" in Chapter 15.

Related solution:	Found on page:
Introducing the **vector** Container	674

Using the **list** Container

The **list** container supports a doubly linked list, which means that each element is linked to the one in front of it and the one behind it, so it's easy to iterate through the list in either direction. A **list** container holds a simple list of items, such as a shopping list or grocery list. The main difference between the **list** container and the **vector** container is that lists support constant time, not linear time, insertion and removal of any element in the list, and they don't support the array operator [] or the **at** method. In general, you should use **list** containers when there are frequent insertions and deletions from the middle of the sequence. STL lists support bidirectional iterators, but not random access iterators.

Here are the methods you typically use with the **list** container:

- **resize**—Resizes the container by erasing the last elements if needed.
- **assign**—Assigns elements from a range to replace the container's contents.
- **push_front**—Adds an element to the front of the container.
- **pop_front**—Erases the first element.
- **push_back**—Adds an element to the end of the container.
- **pop_back**—Erases the last element.
- **insert**—Inserts an element or elements.
- **clear**—Clears the container.
- **front**—Returns the first element.
- **back**—Returns the last element.
- **erase**—Erases elements.
- **splice**—Adds the contents of a list to another list.
- **remove_if**—Removes all elements for which a passed *predicate* (a boolean function or function object, which we'll see in Chapter 17) is true.
- **unique**—Removes all non-unique members of the set.
- **merge**—Merges two lists using the < operator defined for the list.
- **sort**—Sorts the list.
- **reverse**—Reverses the list.

Here's how the **list** container template is declared in the STL, with the methods it supports—note that because **lists** don't support random access iterators, they can't use the STL **sort** algorithm, so they supply their own:

```
template <class T, class Allocator = allocator<T> >
class list {
public:
typedef typename Allocator::reference reference;
typedef typename Allocator::const_reference const_reference;
typedef implementation defined iterator;
typedef implementation defined const_iterator;
typedef implementation defined size_type;
typedef implementation defined difference_type;
typedef T value_type;
typedef Allocator allocator_type;
typedef typename Allocator::pointer pointer;
typedef typename Allocator::const_pointer const_pointer;
typedef std::reverse_iterator<iterator> reverse_iterator;
typedef std::reverse_iterator<const_iterator> const_reverse_iterator;
explicit list(const Allocator& = Allocator());
explicit list(size_type n, const T& value = T(),
    const Allocator& = Allocator());
template <class InputIterator>
list(InputIterator first, InputIterator last,
    const Allocator& = Allocator());
list(const list<T,Allocator>& x);
~list();
list<T,Allocator>& operator=(const list<T,Allocator>& x);
template <class InputIterator>
void assign(InputIterator first, InputIterator last);
void assign(size_type n, const T& t);
allocator_type get_allocator() const;
iterator begin();
const_iterator begin() const;
iterator end();
const_iterator end() const;
reverse_iterator rbegin();
const_reverse_iterator rbegin() const;
reverse_iterator rend();
const_reverse_iterator rend() const;
bool empty() const;
size_type size() const;
size_type max_size() const;
void resize(size_type sz, T c = T());
reference front();
```

```
const_reference front() const;
reference back();
const_reference back() const;
void push_front(const T& x);
void pop_front();
void push_back(const T& x);
void pop_back();
iterator insert(iterator position, const T& x);
void insert(iterator position, size_type n, const T& x);
template <class InputIterator>
void insert(iterator position, InputIterator first,
    InputIterator last);
iterator erase(iterator position);
iterator erase(iterator position, iterator last);
void swap(list<T,Allocator>&);
void clear();
void splice(iterator position, list<T,Allocator>& x);
void splice(iterator position, list<T,Allocator>& x, iterator i);
void splice(iterator position, list<T,Allocator>& x, iterator first,
    iterator last);
void remove(const T& value);
template <class Predicate> void remove_if(Predicate pred);
void unique();
template <class BinaryPredicate>
void unique(BinaryPredicate binary_pred);
void merge(list<T,Allocator>& x);
template <class Compare> void merge(list<T,Allocator>& x, Compare comp);
void sort();
template <class Compare> void sort(Compare comp);
void reverse();
};
```


Here's an example, list.cpp, that puts the **list** container to work. In this example, I'll create a list of strings and use the **insert** method to add the names of various fruits to the list. You can pass an iterator to the **insert** method to indicate where to insert an element, as well as the element itself. I'll also use the **copy** algorithm and an **ostream** iterator to display the contents of the list. You can use methods like **push_front** and **push_back** to add elements to the list, and I'll do that here, as well as sort the list with its own **sort** method. Finally, the **find** method lets you locate elements in the list, and because it returns an iterator to the found element, you can replace the element simply by overwriting it, as I do in this example, where I replace "cherries" with "bananas":

```
#include <list>
#include <string>
#include <iostream>
#include <algorithm>
using namespace std;

int main ()
{
    list<string> fruits;

    fruits.insert(fruits.begin(),"apples");
    fruits.insert(fruits.begin(),"oranges");
    fruits.insert(fruits.begin(),"cherries");

    copy(fruits.begin(), fruits.end(),
        ostream_iterator<string, char>(cout," "));
    cout << endl;

    fruits.push_front("tangerines");
    fruits.push_back("pineapples");

    copy(fruits.begin(), fruits.end(),
        ostream_iterator<string, char>(cout," "));
    cout << endl;

    fruits.sort();

    copy(fruits.begin(), fruits.end(),
        ostream_iterator<string, char>(cout," "));
    cout << endl;

    fruits.insert(find(fruits.begin(), fruits.end(), "apples"), "pears");

    copy(fruits.begin(), fruits.end(),
        ostream_iterator<string, char>(cout," "));
    cout << endl;

    *find(fruits.begin(), fruits.end(), "cherries") = "bananas";
    copy(fruits.begin(), fruits.end(),
        ostream_iterator<string, char>(cout," "));
    cout << endl;

    return 0;
}
```

Here's what you see when you run this example, list.cpp:

```
%list
cherries oranges apples
tangerines cherries oranges apples pineapples
apples cherries oranges pineapples tangerines
pears apples cherries oranges pineapples tangerines
pears apples bananas oranges pineapples tangerines
```

Using the **deque** Container

As discussed in the In Depth section of this chapter, a deque (pronounced "deck") is a double-ended queue that lets you add or remove elements at the beginning or end. The **deque** container is a sequence that supports random access iterators, as vectors do. It also supports constant time insertion and erase operations at the beginning or the end (insertions and erasures in the middle take linear time). A **deque** container is optimized for pushing and popping elements at the beginning or the end, so it supports methods like **push_front**, **push_back**, **pop_front**, and **pop_back** (the **queue** container, which is more restricted, supports only methods like **push** and **pop**). This container is a good choice when most insertions and deletions take place at the beginning or at the end of the sequence.

Here are the methods that you use most often with **deque** containers:

- **resize**—Resizes the container by erasing the last elements if needed.
- **assign**—Assigns elements from a range to replace the container's contents.
- **push_back**—Adds an element to the end of the container.
- **push_front**—Adds an element to the front of the container.
- **pop_back**—Erases the last element.
- **pop_front**—Erases the first element.
- **insert**—Inserts an element or elements.
- **clear**—Clears the container.
- **front**—Returns the first element.
- **back**—Returns the last element.
- **erase**—Erases elements.
- **[]**—Array operator.
- **at**—Returns element at a specific location.

Here's how the STL **deque** template class is declared, with its available methods:

```
template <class T, class Allocator = allocator<T> >
class deque {
public:
typedef typename Allocator::reference reference;
typedef typename Allocator::const_reference const_reference;
typedef implementation defined iterator;
typedef implementation defined const_iterator;
typedef implementation defined size_type;
typedef implementation defined difference_type;
typedef T value_type;
typedef Allocator allocator_type;
typedef typename Allocator::pointer pointer;
typedef typename Allocator::const_pointer const_pointer;
typedef std::reverse_iterator<iterator> reverse_iterator;
typedef std::reverse_iterator<const_iterator> const_reverse_iterator;
explicit deque(const Allocator& = Allocator());
explicit deque(size_type n, const T& value = T(),
const Allocator& = Allocator());
template <class InputIterator>
deque(InputIterator first, InputIterator last,
const Allocator& = Allocator());
deque(const deque<T,Allocator>& x);
~deque();
deque<T,Allocator>& operator=(const deque<T,Allocator>& x);
template <class InputIterator>
void assign(InputIterator first, InputIterator last);
void assign(size_type n, const T& t);
allocator_type get_allocator() const;
iterator begin();
const_iterator begin() const;
iterator end();
const_iterator end() const;
reverse_iterator rbegin();
const_reverse_iterator rbegin() const;
reverse_iterator rend();
const_reverse_iterator rend() const;
size_type size() const;
size_type max_size() const;
void resize(size_type sz, T c = T());
bool empty() const;
reference operator[](size_type n);
const_reference operator[](size_type n) const;
reference at(size_type n);
```

```
const_reference at(size_type n) const;
reference front();
const_reference front() const;
reference back();
const_reference back() const;
void push_front(const T& x);
void push_back(const T& x);
iterator insert(iterator position, const T& x);
void insert(iterator position, size_type n, const T& x);
template <class InputIterator>
void insert (iterator position,
InputIterator first, InputIterator last);
void pop_front();
void pop_back();
iterator erase(iterator position);
iterator erase(iterator first, iterator last);
void swap(deque<T,Allocator>&);
void clear();
};
```

We saw an example, deque.cpp, in the In Depth section of this chapter. This example creates a deque of strings to hold the names of patients waiting to be seen in a doctor's office. Here, I use **push_front** to add an element to the front of the deque, **push_back** to add an element to the end, and **pop_front** to remove an element from the front of the deque. I also use array subscripts to access data randomly in the deque. After each operation, the code displays the new line of patients waiting to be seen by the doctor; here's what this example looks like in code:

```
#include <deque>
#include <string>
#include <iostream>
using namespace std;

deque<string> patients;

int main ()
{
   cout << "Initializing patients..." << endl;

   patients.push_front("Frank");
   patients.push_front("Molly");
   patients.push_front("Tom");
   patients.push_front("Sally");

   deque<string>::iterator itr;
```

```
   itr = patients.begin();
   while (itr < patients.end())
     cout << *itr++ << endl;

   cout << "Third patient..." << endl;

   cout << patients[2] << endl;

   cout << "A new patient arrives..." << endl;
   patients.push_back("Kurt");

   itr = patients.begin();
   while (itr < patients.end())
     cout << *itr++ << endl;

   cout << "Seeing the first patient..." << endl;
   patients.pop_front();

   itr = patients.begin();
   while (itr < patients.end())
     cout << *itr++ << endl;

   return 0;
}
```

And here's what you see when you run this example:

```
%deque
Initializing patients...
Sally
Tom
Molly
Frank
Third patient...
Molly
A new patient arrives...
Sally
Tom
Molly
Frank
Kurt
Seeing the first patient...
Tom
Molly
Frank
Kurt
```

Using the **stack** Container

We've seen stacks as far back as Chapter 2. A stack is a programming construct that works much like the plates in a cafeteria—you can add plates to the top of the stack, and when you retrieve them, they come off in reverse order. The main operations you perform with stacks are **push**, which add elements to top of the stack, and **pop**, which pops an element off the top of the stack. In the STL, stacks are built using other sequence containers, (by default, **deque** containers). In fact, any sequence supporting operations **back**, **push_back** and **pop_back** (which includes the **vector**, **list** and **deque** containers) can be used to instantiate a **stack** container.

Here are the methods you typically use with the **stack** container:

- **push**—Pushes an element onto the stack; the element becomes the new top of the stack.
- **pop**—Removes the element that is at the top of the stack.
- **top**—Returns the element that is the new top of the stack.

Here's how the **stack** template class is declared in the STL, with its available methods:

```
template <class T, class Container = deque<T> >
class stack {
public:
typedef typename Container::value_type value_type;
typedef typename Container::size_type size_type;
typedef Container container_type;
protected:
Container c;
public:
explicit stack(const Container& = Container());
bool empty() const { return c.empty(); }
size_type size() const { return c.size(); }
value_type& top() { return c.back(); }
const value_type& top() const { return c.back(); }
void push(const value_type& x) { c.push_back(x); }
void pop() { c.pop_back(); }
};
```

You can use a stack to reverse the order of data items, because elements come off a stack in the reverse order from which they went on, and that fact is often very useful. Here's an example we saw in Chapter 4, mod.cpp, that converts numbers from decimal to hexadecimal by successively dividing the number by 16 to peel off hex digits. Because the hex digits come off in reverse order, I used a stack to reverse them:

```
#include <iostream>
#include <stack>
using namespace std;

int main()
{
    int value = 32, temp = value;
    char characters[] = {'0', '1', '2', '3', '4', '5', '6', '7', '8',
        '9', 'A', 'B', 'C', 'D', 'E', 'F'};
    stack<int> st;

    while (temp > 0) {
        st.push(temp % 16);
        temp >>= 4;
    }

    cout << "Converting " << value << " yields 0x";

    while(!st.empty()) {
        cout << characters[st.top()];
        st.pop();
    }

    return 0;
}
```

Note that you use the **top** method to examine the element at the top of the stack—the **pop** method does not return that element when it pops it. Here's what you see when you run this program, mod.cpp, which converts 32 to hexadecimal:

```
%mod
Converting 32 yields 0x20
```

By default, stacks are based on the **deque** container. However, if another container, such as **vector**, is faster for the type of operations you're going to be using, you can base your stack on that kind of container instead. Here's an example where I'm basing a stack on the **vector** container, stack.cpp, and pushing "C++.", "from", and "Hello" so the message will be popped off in reverse order:

```
#include <stack>
#include <vector>
```

```
#include <deque>
#include <string>
#include <iostream>
using namespace std;

int main ()
{
    stack<string, vector<string> > words;

    words.push("C++.");
    words.push("from");
    words.push("Hello");

    while(!words.empty()){
        cout << words.top() << endl;
        words.pop();
    }

  return 0;
}
```

Here's what you see when you run stack.cpp:

```
%stack
Hello
from
C++.
```


Related solutions:	Found on page:
Modulus: **%**	104
The **while** Loop	179

Using the **queue** Container

The **queue** container is actually a restricted form of the **deque** container. You can't access elements randomly in a queue, and you can't iterate through them. However, you can add elements to the end of the queue and remove them from the front, just as with a queue of customers waiting at a theater. You can also check the number of elements in the queue and see if the queue is empty. Like stacks, queues are actually built on other containers; any sequence supporting the operations **front**, **back**, **push_back** and **pop_front** (which means the **list** and **deque** containers) can be used to instantiate a queue object. By default, **queue** containers are based on **deque** containers. The **queue** container renames the base container's **push_back** and **pop_front** methods to simply **push** and **pop**, because there are no other options—you can only push elements onto the end of a queue and pop them from the front.

Here are the methods you typically use with the **queue** container:

- **size**—Returns the number of elements in the queue.
- **empty**—Returns true if the container is empty.
- **front**—Returns the first element.
- **back**—Returns the last element.
- **push**—Inserts a value at the end of the queue.
- **pop**—Removes the element at the front of the queue.

Here's how the STL template class **queue** is declared, with its available methods:

```
template <class T, class Container = deque<T> >
class queue {
public:
typedef typename Container::value_type value_type;
typedef typename Container::size_type size_type;
typedef Container container_type;
protected:
Container c;
public:
explicit queue(const Container& = Container());
bool empty() const { return c.empty(); }
size_type size() const { return c.size(); }
value_type& front() { return c.front(); }
const value_type& front() const { return c.front(); }
value_type& back() { return c.back(); }
const value_type& back() const { return c.back(); }
void push(const value_type& x) { c.push_back(x); }
void pop() { c.pop_front(); }
};
```

You can use a queue much like you would a stack, with a few differences—because it's a queue, not a stack, elements come off in the same order in which they were added, not in reverse order. And instead of using the **top** method to access data in the queue, as you would with a stack, you use **front** to get the element at the front of the queue. Here's an example, queue.cpp, that places the words "Hello", "from", and "C++" in a queue, examines them with **front**, and then pops them:

```
#include <queue>
#include <string>
#include <deque>
#include <iostream>
using namespace std;

int main ()
{
    queue<string, deque<string> > words;

    words.push("Hello");
    words.push("from");
    words.push("C++.");

    while(!words.empty()){
        cout << words.front() << endl;
        words.pop();
    }

    return 0;
}
```

Note that I'm explicitly indicating that I want to base this queue on the **deque** container—although **deque** is the default, I'm listing that container here to show how you can specify the container you want to base your queue on; you can also omit that declaration like this: **queue<string>**.

Here's what you see when you run this example, queue.cpp:

```
%queue
Hello
from
C++.
```

Using the **priority_queue** Container

The **priority_queue** container is much like the queue container, except that the elements in a priority queue are sorted, and this container is based on the **vector** container by default, not on the **deque** container. In fact, you can base a **priority_queue** container on any sequence with a random access iterator, and which supports the operations **front**, **push_back** and **pop_back** (that means **vector** and **deque**).

Here are the operations you typically use with the **priority_queue** container—note in particular that you use **top** to access the first element in a priority queue, instead of **front**, which you use with queues:

- **size**—Returns the number of elements in the queue.
- **empty**—Returns true if the container is empty.
- **top**—Returns the first element in the container.
- **back**—Returns the last element.
- **push**—Inserts a value at the end of the queue.
- **pop**—Removes the element at the front of the queue.

Here's how the STL **priority_queue** container is declared, with its available methods:

```
template <class T, class Container = vector<T>,
class Compare = less<typename Container::value_type> >
class priority_queue {
public:
typedef typename Container::value_type value_type;
typedef typename Container::size_type size_type;
typedef Container container_type;
protected:
Container c;
Compare comp;
public:
explicit priority_queue(const Compare& x = Compare(),
const Container& = Container());
template <class InputIterator>
priority_queue(InputIterator first, InputIterator last,
    const Compare& x = Compare(),
    const Container& = Container());
bool empty() const { return c.empty(); }
size_type size() const { return c.size(); }
const value_type& top() const { return c.front(); }
void push(const value_type& x);
void pop();
};
```

Here's an example, priority_queue.cpp. By default, priority queues sort their elements with the largest element first, but you can specify the sort ordering using the predefined function objects **less** and **greater** (we'll see more about function objects in Chapter 17). For example, the declaration **priority_queue <string> words** declares a priority queue of strings named **words** where the string that is alphabetically first is placed at the front of the queue. The same declaration could also be made more explicit like this:

```
priority_queue<string, vector<string>, less<string> > words.
```

You can also reverse the default ordering with a declaration like this:

```
priority_queue<string, vector<string>, greater<string> > words.
```

Here, then, is how I create two priority queues of text strings, one in descending order and one in ascending order, in priority_queue.cpp:

```
#include <queue>
#include <deque>
#include <string>
#include <iostream>
using namespace std;

int main ()
{
    priority_queue<string> words;

    words.push("Cat");
    words.push("Rat");
    words.push("Bat");

    while(!words.empty()){
        cout << words.top() << endl;
        words.pop();
    }

    priority_queue<string, vector<string>, greater<string> > words2;

    words2.push("Cat");
    words2.push("Rat");
    words2.push("Bat");

    while(!words2.empty()){
        cout << words2.top() << endl;
        words2.pop();
    }

   return 0;
}
```

Here's what you see when you run this example, priority_queue.cpp:

```
%priority_queue
Rat
Cat
Bat
Bat
Cat
Rat
```

Using the **set** Container

An STL set is much like a mathematical set, and each element in the set must be unique. For example, you might have a set of integers, such as {1, 2, 5, 7, 9}. The typical mathematical set operations, like unions and intersections, are supported for sets in the STL.

Here are some of the operations you typically use with the **set** container:

- **insert**—Inserts an element.
- **erase**—Erases an element.
- **find**—Finds an element and returns an iterator to it; returns an iterator to one element past the end of the set if the element was not found.
- **count**—Returns the number of elements.
- **clear**—Erases all elements.

You also typically use these STL algorithms with sets:

- **set_difference**—Returns the difference between two sets.
- **set_union**—Returns the union (concatenation) of two sets.
- **set_intersection**—Returns the intersection (common elements) of two sets.

Here is how the **set** container is declared in the STL, with its available methods:

```
template <class Key, class Compare = less<Key>,
class Allocator = allocator<Key> >
class set {
public:
typedef Key key_type;
typedef Key value_type;
typedef Compare key_compare;
typedef Compare value_compare;
```

```
typedef Allocator allocator_type;
typedef typename Allocator::reference reference;
typedef typename Allocator::const_reference const_reference;
typedef implementation defined iterator;
typedef implementation defined const_iterator;
typedef implementation defined size_type;
typedef implementation defined difference_type;
typedef typename Allocator::pointer pointer;
typedef typename Allocator::const_pointer const_pointer;
typedef std::reverse_iterator<iterator> reverse_iterator;
typedef std::reverse_iterator<const_iterator> const_reverse_iterator;
explicit set(const Compare& comp = Compare(),
    const Allocator& = Allocator());
template <class InputIterator>
set(InputIterator first, InputIterator last,
    const Compare& comp = Compare(), const Allocator& = Allocator());
set(const set<Key,Compare,Allocator>& x);
~set();
set<Key,Compare,Allocator>& operator=
    (const set<Key,Compare,Allocator>& x);
allocator_type get_allocator() const;
iterator begin();
const_iterator begin() const;
iterator end();
const_iterator end() const;
reverse_iterator rbegin();
const_reverse_iterator rbegin() const;
reverse_iterator rend();
const_reverse_iterator rend() const;
bool empty() const;
size_type size() const;
size_type max_size() const;
pair<iterator,bool> insert(const value_type& x);
iterator insert(iterator position, const value_type& x);
template <class InputIterator>
void insert(InputIterator first, InputIterator last);
void erase(iterator position);
size_type erase(const key_type& x);
void erase(iterator first, iterator last);
void swap(set<Key,Compare,Allocator>&);
void clear();
key_compare key_comp() const;
value_compare value_comp() const;
iterator find(const key_type& x) const;
size_type count(const key_type& x) const;
```

```
iterator lower_bound(const key_type& x) const;
iterator upper_bound(const key_type& x) const;
pair<iterator,iterator> equal_range(const key_type& x) const;
};
```

Here's an example, sets.cpp, that creates two sets, displays them both with an **ostream** iterator, and also displays their difference, intersection, and union. To find the union and intersection of these sets, I use the **set_union** and **set_intersection** methods, passing these methods' iterators to the beginning and end of each set and an **ostream** iterator to display the result (you can also store the resulting union and intersection sets in new **set** containers using an insertion iterator—see "Using the **multiset** Container" later in this chapter for an example):

```
#include <iostream>
#include <set>
#include <string>
#include <iterator>
#include <algorithm>
using namespace std;

const int NUMBER_ELEMENTS = 5;

int main()
{
    string strings1[NUMBER_ELEMENTS] = {"A", "B", "C", "D", "E"};
    string strings2[NUMBER_ELEMENTS] = {"C", "D", "E", "F", "G"};

    set<string> first_set(strings1, strings1 + NUMBER_ELEMENTS);
    set<string> second_set(strings2, strings2 + NUMBER_ELEMENTS);

    ostream_iterator<string, char> ostream_itr(cout, " ");

    cout << "First set:" << endl;
    copy(first_set.begin(), first_set.end(), ostream_itr);
    cout << endl;

    cout << "Second set:" << endl;
    copy(second_set.begin(), second_set.end(), ostream_itr);
    cout << endl;

    cout << "Difference of the two sets:" << endl;
    set_difference(first_set.begin(), first_set.end(), second_set.begin(),
        second_set.end(), ostream_itr);
    cout << endl;
```

```
    cout << "Intersection of the two sets:" << endl;
    set_intersection(first_set.begin(), first_set.end(),
        second_set.begin(),        second_set.end(), ostream_itr);
    cout << endl;

    cout << "Union of the two sets:" << endl;
    set_union(first_set.begin(), first_set.end(), second_set.begin(),
        second_set.end(), ostream_itr);
    cout << endl;

    return 0;
}
```

And here's what you see when you run this example, sets.cpp:

```
%sets
First set:
A B C D E
Second set:
C D E F G
Difference of the two sets:
A B
Intersection of the two sets:
C D E
Union of the two sets:
A B C D E F G
```


Using the map Container

We discussed maps in the In Depth section of this chapter. Maps let you store data as key/value pairs, and you use the key to access the associated value in the map. For example, you can use a key like this with a map: ***map[key] = value***. In a **map** container, each key must be unique, and the **map** container supports bidirectional iterators.

Here are the methods you typically use with the **map** container:

- **find**—Finds an element and returns an iterator to it; returns an iterator to one element past the end of the set if the element was not found.
- **count**—Finds number of values with a certain key.
- **insert**—Inserts a new key/value pair.
- **[]**—The array operator.

The **map** container stores data in key/value pairs, using the **pair** class template: **pair<class T, class U>**, where **T** is the class of the key and **U** the class of the value. You can create pairs and then use the **insert** method to add the elements to a map like this:

```
pair<const int, string> item(1, "Ted");
map1.insert(item);
```

You can also use array notation like this to add key/value pairs to a map:

```
map1[1] = "Ted";
```

Here is how the **map** container is declared in the STL, with its available methods:

```
template <class Key, class T, class Compare = less<Key>,
class Allocator = allocator<pair<const Key, T> > >
class map {
public:
typedef Key key_type;
typedef T mapped_type;
typedef pair<const Key, T> value_type;
typedef Compare key_compare;
typedef Allocator allocator_type;
typedef typename Allocator::reference reference;
typedef typename Allocator::const_reference const_reference;
typedef implementation defined iterator;
typedef implementation defined const_iterator;
typedef implementation defined size_type;
typedef implementation defined difference_type;
typedef typename Allocator::pointer pointer;
typedef typename Allocator::const_pointer const_pointer;
typedef std::reverse_iterator<iterator> reverse_iterator;
typedef std::reverse_iterator<const_iterator> const_reverse_iterator;
class value_compare
: public binary_function<value_type,value_type,bool> {
friend class map;
protected:
Compare comp;
value_compare(Compare c) : comp(c) {}
public:
bool operator()(const value_type& x, const value_type& y) const {
    return comp(x.first, y.first);
}
};
```

```
explicit map(const Compare& comp = Compare(),
    const Allocator& = Allocator());
template <class InputIterator>
map(InputIterator first, InputIterator last,
    const Compare& comp = Compare(), const Allocator& = Allocator());
map(const map<Key,T,Compare,Allocator>& x);
~map();
map<Key,T,Compare,Allocator>&
operator=(const map<Key,T,Compare,Allocator>& x);
iterator begin();
const_iterator begin() const;
iterator end();
const_iterator end() const;
reverse_iterator rbegin();
const_reverse_iterator rbegin() const;
reverse_iterator rend();
const_reverse_iterator rend() const;
bool empty() const;
size_type size() const;
size_type max_size() const;
T& operator[](const key_type& x);
pair<iterator, bool> insert(const value_type& x);
iterator insert(iterator position, const value_type& x);
template <class InputIterator>
void insert(InputIterator first, InputIterator last);
void erase(iterator position);
size_type erase(const key_type& x);
void erase(iterator first, iterator last);
void swap(map<Key,T,Compare,Allocator>&);
void clear();
key_compare key_comp() const;
value_compare value_comp() const;
iterator find(const key_type& x);
const_iterator find(const key_type& x) const;
size_type count(const key_type& x) const;
iterator lower_bound(const key_type& x);
const_iterator lower_bound(const key_type& x) const;
iterator upper_bound(const key_type& x);
const_iterator upper_bound(const key_type& x) const;
pair<iterator,iterator>
equal_range(const key_type& x);
pair<const_iterator,const_iterator>
equal_range(const key_type& x) const;
};
```

Here's an example, map.cpp, that we saw in the In Depth section of this chapter. In this example, I'm creating a map named **ages** that stores people's ages, indexed by name. The people's names are the keys and the corresponding ages are the values in this map. To display all the data in the map, I can use an iterator to point to each **pair** object in the map and display each name and age using the **first** and **second** members of the **pair** objects:

```
#include <string>
#include <map>
#include <iostream>
using namespace std;

int main ()
{
    map<string, int> ages;

    ages["Ralph"] = 35;
    ages["Sally"] = 29;
    ages["Tom"] = 77;
    ages["Frank"] = 31;
    ages["April"] = 24;
    ages["Tina"] = 61;

    map<string, int>::iterator itr;

    for(itr = ages.begin(); itr != ages.end(); itr++){
        cout << itr->first << " is " << itr->second << " years old."
            << endl;
    }

    return 0;
}
```

Here's what you see when you run this program, map.cpp:

```
%map
April is 24 years old.
Frank is 31 years old.
Ralph is 35 years old.
Sally is 29 years old.
Tina is 61 years old.
Tom is 77 years old.
```

Using the **multiset** Container

The **multiset** container is much like the **set** container, except that the elements in the set don't have to be unique in a multiset.

Here are some of the operations you typically use with the **multiset** container:

- **insert**—Inserts an element.
- **erase**—Erases an element.
- **find**—Finds an element and returns an iterator to it; returns an iterator to one element past the end of the set if the element was not found.
- **count**—Returns the number of elements.
- **clear**—Erases all elements.
- **lower_bound**—Returns an iterator to the first element with a key not less than the key passed to this method.
- **upper_bound**—Returns an iterator to the first element with a key greater than the key passed to this method.
- **equal_range**—Returns a range of all values whose keys are equal to the key specified (for more on **equal_range**, see "Using the **multimap** Container" later in this chapter).

You can also use these STL algorithms with multisets:

- **set_difference**—Returns the difference between two sets.
- **set_union**—Returns the union (concatination) of two sets.
- **set_intersection**—Returns the intersection (common elements) of two sets.

Here's how the **multiset** container is declared in the STL, with its available methods:

```
template <class Key, class Compare = less<Key>,
class Allocator = allocator<Key> >
class multiset {
public:
typedef Key key_type;
typedef Key value_type;
typedef Compare key_compare;
typedef Compare value_compare;
typedef Allocator allocator_type;
typedef typename Allocator::reference reference;
typedef typename Allocator::const_reference const_reference;
typedef implementation defined iterator;
typedef implementation defined const_iterator;
```

```
typedef implementation defined size_type;
typedef implementation defined difference_type;
typedef typename Allocator::pointer pointer;
typedef typename Allocator::const_pointer const_pointer;
typedef std::reverse_iterator<iterator> reverse_iterator;
typedef std::reverse_iterator<const_iterator> const_reverse_iterator;
explicit multiset(const Compare& comp = Compare(),
    const Allocator& = Allocator());
template <class InputIterator>
multiset(InputIterator first, InputIterator last,
    const Compare& comp = Compare(),
    const Allocator& = Allocator());
multiset(const multiset<Key,Compare,Allocator>& x);
~multiset();
multiset<Key,Compare,Allocator>&
operator=(const multiset<Key,Compare,Allocator>& x);
allocator_type get_allocator() const;
iterator begin();
const_iterator begin() const;
iterator end();
const_iterator end() const;
reverse_iterator rbegin();
const_reverse_iterator rbegin() const;
reverse_iterator rend();
const_reverse_iterator rend() const;
bool empty() const;
size_type size() const;
size_type max_size() const;
iterator insert(const value_type& x);
iterator insert(iterator position, const value_type& x);
template <class InputIterator>
void insert(InputIterator first, InputIterator last);
void erase(iterator position);
size_type erase(const key_type& x);
void erase(iterator first, iterator last);
void swap(multiset<Key,Compare,Allocator>&);
void clear();
key_compare key_comp() const;
value_compare value_comp() const;
iterator find(const key_type& x) const;
size_type count(const key_type& x) const;
iterator lower_bound(const key_type& x) const;
iterator upper_bound(const key_type& x) const;
pair<iterator,iterator> equal_range(const key_type& x) const;
};
```

Here's an example, multiset.cpp, that shows how multisets work. In this case, I'm creating two multisets, each of which have duplicate elements, and displaying their contents, as well as their union and intersection. To find the union and intersection of these sets, I use the **set_union** and **set_intersection** methods, passing these methods' iterators to the beginning and end of each set and an insertion iterator to a result set (you can also display the resulting union and intersection sets directly if you pass an **ostream** iterator connected to **cout** to these methods—see "Using the **set** Container" earlier in this chapter for an example):

```
#include <iostream>
#include <set>
#include <algorithm>
using namespace std;

int main ()
{
    multiset<int,less<int> >  set1, set2, union_set, intersection_set;
    ostream_iterator<multiset<int,less<int> >::value_type,char>
        ostream_itr(cout, " ");

    set1.insert(set1.begin(), 1);
    set1.insert(set1.begin(), 1);
    set1.insert(set1.begin(), 3);
    set1.insert(set1.begin(), 3);
    set1.insert(set1.begin(), 3);
    set1.insert(set1.begin(), 4);
    set1.insert(set1.begin(), 5);
    set1.insert(set1.begin(), 6);

    cout << "First set:" << endl;

    copy(set1.begin(),set1.end(), ostream_itr);
    cout << endl;

    set2.insert(set1.begin(), 4);
    set2.insert(set1.begin(), 4);
    set2.insert(set1.begin(), 5);
    set2.insert(set1.begin(), 5);
    set2.insert(set1.begin(), 5);
    set2.insert(set1.begin(), 6);
    set2.insert(set1.begin(), 7);
    set2.insert(set1.begin(), 8);
```

```
    cout << "Second set:" << endl;

    copy(set2.begin(),set2.end(), ostream_itr);
    cout << endl;

    set_union(set1.begin(), set1.end(), set2.begin(), set2.end(),
    insert_iterator<multiset<int,less<int> > >
        (union_set, union_set.begin()));

    cout << "Union of the two sets:" << endl;
    copy(union_set.begin(), union_set.end(), ostream_itr);
    cout << endl;

    set_intersection(set1.begin(), set1.end(), set2.begin(), set2.end(),
    insert_iterator<multiset<int,less<int> > >
        (intersection_set, intersection_set.begin()));

    cout << "Intersection of the two sets:" << endl;
    copy(intersection_set.begin(), intersection_set.end(), ostream_itr);
    cout << endl;

    return 0;
}
```

Here's what you see when you run this example, multiset.cpp:

```
%multiset
First set:
1 1 3 3 3 4 5 6
Second set:
4 4 5 5 5 6 7 8
Union of the two sets:
1 1 3 3 3 4 4 5 5 5 6 7 8
Intersection of the two sets:
4 5 6
```


Related solution:	Found on page:
Using Insertion Iterators	688

Using the multimap Container

The **multimap** container is much like the **map** container, except that you can store multiple values for the same key. It's important to realize that when you have multiple values for the same key, you can't use the [] array operator, because that operator returns only a single value. Instead, you use methods like **equal_range**, **lower_bound**, and **upper_bound** to work with *ranges* of values.

Here are the methods you typically use with **multimap** containers:

- **find**—Finds an element and returns an iterator to it; returns an iterator to one element past the end of the set if the element was not found.
- **count**—Find number of values with a key.
- **lower_bound**—Returns an iterator to the first element with a key not less than the key passed to this method.
- **upper_bound**—Returns an iterator to the first element with a key greater than the key passed to this method.
- **insert**—Inserts a new key/value pair.
- **equal_range**—Returns a range of all values whose keys are equal to the key specified.

When you can store multiple values for the same key, you have to think in terms of value ranges (where each value is accessed using the same key), not just individual elements. The **lower_bound** method returns an iterator to the beginning of such a range, and the **upper_bound** method returns an iterator to one element past the end of the range. The **equal_range** method returns a **pair** object of two iterators—a lower bound iterator and upper bound iterator, which delimit a range of values whose keys are all equal to the key passed to this method (for more on **pair** objects, see "Using the **map** Container" earlier in this chapter).

Here is how the **multimap** container is declared in the STL, with its available methods:

```
template <class Key, class T, class Compare = less<Key>,
class Allocator = allocator<pair<const Key, T> > >
class multimap {
public:
typedef Key key_type;
typedef T mapped_type;
typedef pair<const Key,T> value_type;
typedef Compare key_compare;
typedef Allocator allocator_type;
typedef typename Allocator::reference reference;
```

```
typedef typename Allocator::const_reference const_reference;
typedef implementation defined iterator;
typedef implementation defined const_iterator;
typedef implementation defined size_type;
typedef implementation defined difference_type;
typedef typename Allocator::pointer pointer;
typedef typename Allocator::const_pointer const_pointer;
typedef std::reverse_iterator<iterator> reverse_iterator;
typedef std::reverse_iterator<const_iterator> const_reverse_iterator;
class value_compare
: public binary_function<value_type,value_type,bool> {
friend class multimap;
protected:
Compare comp;
value_compare(Compare c) : comp(c) {}
public:
bool operator()(const value_type& x, const value_type& y) const {
return comp(x.first, y.first);
}
};
explicit multimap(const Compare& comp = Compare(),
    const Allocator& = Allocator());
template <class InputIterator>
multimap(InputIterator first, InputIterator last,
    const Compare& comp = Compare(),
    const Allocator& = Allocator());
multimap(const multimap<Key,T,Compare,Allocator>& x);
~multimap();
multimap<Key,T,Compare,Allocator>&
operator=(const multimap<Key,T,Compare,Allocator>& x);
allocator_type get_allocator() const;
iterator begin();
const_iterator begin() const;
iterator end();
const_iterator end() const;
reverse_iterator rbegin();
const_reverse_iterator rbegin() const;
reverse_iterator rend();
const_reverse_iterator rend() const;
bool empty() const;
size_type size() const;
size_type max_size() const;
iterator insert(const value_type& x);
iterator insert(iterator position, const value_type& x);
template <class InputIterator>
```

```
void insert(InputIterator first, InputIterator last);
void erase(iterator position);
size_type erase(const key_type& x);
void erase(iterator first, iterator last);
void swap(multimap<Key,T,Compare,Allocator>&);
void clear();
key_compare key_comp() const;
value_compare value_comp() const;
iterator find(const key_type& x);
const_iterator find(const key_type& x) const;
size_type count(const key_type& x) const;
iterator lower_bound(const key_type& x);
const_iterator lower_bound(const key_type& x) const;
iterator upper_bound(const key_type& x);
const_iterator upper_bound(const key_type& x) const;
pair<iterator,iterator>
equal_range(const key_type& x);
pair<const_iterator,const_iterator>
equal_range(const key_type& x) const;
};
```

Here's an example, multimap.cpp, that puts this container to work. In this case, I'll insert pairs into a **multimap** container named **friends**, where the key values are people's ages and the associated values are their names. Note that the key **35** has two name values associated with it: "Ralph" and "Frank". I can count the number of people stored with that key using the **count** method, and I can get a **pair** object holding iterators delimiting the range of names with the same age using the **equal_range** method. Then it's easy enough to iterate through that range, displaying all friends who are 35 years old:


```
#include <iostream>
#include <string>
#include <map>
#include <algorithm>
using namespace std;

int main()
{
    multimap<int, string> friends;

    friends.insert(pair<const int, string>(35, "Ralph"));
    friends.insert(pair<const int, string>(29, "Sally"));
    friends.insert(pair<const int, string>(77, "Tom"));
    friends.insert(pair<const int, string>(35, "Frank"));
```

```
    friends.insert(pair<const int, string>(24, "April"));
    friends.insert(pair<const int, string>(61, "Tina"));

    cout << "Number of friends 35 years old: " << friends.count(35) << endl;

    multimap<int, string>::iterator itr;

    pair<multimap<int, string>::iterator, multimap<int, string>::iterator>
       range_pair = friends.equal_range(35);

    cout << "Friends 35 years old:" << endl;
    for (itr = range_pair.first; itr != range_pair.second; ++itr)
        cout << itr->second  << endl;

    return 0;
}
```

Here's what you see when you run this example, multimap.cpp:

```
%multimap
Number of friends 35 years old: 2
Friends 35 years old:
Ralph
Frank
```

Using the **bitset** Container

We discussed bitsets in the In Depth section of this chapter. A bitset holds individually addressable bits that you might use to set or reset boolean flags, storing true/false values. For example, you might want a compact way to keep track of what flags are set in a drawing program—a flag if the rectangle-drawing tool is in use, another for the circle-drawing tool, and so on.

Here are the methods you typically use with bitsets:

- **set**—Sets a bit.
- **reset**—Resets a bit.
- **flip**—Flips the bits in a bitset.
- **[]**—The array operator.
- **&=, |=, ^=**—Operators for binary AND, OR, and XOR operations.

Here is how the **bitset** template class is declared in the STL:

```
template<size_t N>
class bitset {
public:
class reference {
friend class bitset;
reference();
public:
~reference();
reference& operator=(bool x);
reference& operator=(const reference&);
bool operator~() const;
operator bool() const;
reference& flip();
};
bitset();
bitset(unsigned long val);
template<class charT, class traits, class Allocator>
explicit bitset(
const basic_string<charT,traits,Allocator>& str,
    typename basic_string<charT,traits,Allocator>::size_type pos = 0,
    typename basic_string<charT,traits,Allocator>::size_type n =
    basic_string<charT,traits,Allocator>::npos);
bitset<N>& operator&=(const bitset<N>& rhs);
bitset<N>& operator|=(const bitset<N>& rhs);
bitset<N>& operator^=(const bitset<N>& rhs);
bitset<N>& operator<<=(size_t pos);
bitset<N>& operator>>=(size_t pos);
bitset<N>& set();
bitset<N>& set(size_t pos, int val = true);
bitset<N>& reset();
bitset<N>& reset(size_t pos);
bitset<N> operator~() const;
bitset<N>& flip();
bitset<N>& flip(size_t pos);
reference operator[](size_t pos);
unsigned long to_ulong() const;
template <class charT, class traits, class Allocator>
basic_string<charT, traits, Allocator> to_string() const;
size_t count() const;
size_t size() const;
```

```
bool operator==(const bitset<N>& rhs) const;
bool operator!=(const bitset<N>& rhs) const;
bool test(size_t pos) const;
bool any() const;
bool none() const;
bitset<N> operator<<(size_t pos) const;
bitset<N> operator>>(size_t pos) const;
};
```

Here's an example, bitset.cpp, that we saw in the In Depth section of this chapter. To create a bitset with a specific number of bits, you pass that number to the **bitset** template; I'll create an eight-bit bitset here, which is initialized to 00000000. Next, I'll OR a value of 7 with the bitset, which stores the binary value 00000111 in the bitset. I can also check if a specific bit, bit 2, is set by addressing that bit with the array operator:

```
#include <iostream>
#include <bitset>
using namespace std;

int main ()
{
    bitset<8> flags;

    flags |= 7;

    cout << flags << endl;

    if(flags[2]){
        cout << "Bit 2 is set" << endl;
    }

    return 0;
}
```

Here's what you see when you run this example, bitset.cpp:

```
%bitset
00000111
Bit 2 is set
```

Using valarray

Another C++ class worth discussing while we look at STL containers is the **valarray** class template, which is designed to be used with numeric values. To use this class template, you include the valarray header and dimension the **valarray** as you would a vector. However, you can also add **valarray** objects together, multiply them, and apply math functions to each element and more with the built-in **valarray** methods. Here's an example, valarray.cpp, that adds two **valarray** objects and multiplies one of them by 3:

```
#include <iostream>
#include <valarray>
using namespace std;

int main(void)
{
    valarray<int> valarray1(10);
    valarray<int> valarray2(10);

    for(int loop_index = 0; loop_index < 10; loop_index++){
        valarray1[loop_index] = loop_index;
        valarray2[loop_index] = loop_index;
    }

    cout << "Original valarrays..." << endl;
    for (unsigned int i = 0; i < valarray1.size(); i++)
        cout << valarray1[i] << ' ';
    cout << endl;
    for (unsigned int i2 = 0; i2 < valarray2.size(); i2++)
        cout << valarray2[i2] << ' ';
    cout << endl;

    valarray1 += valarray2;

    cout << "Sum of valarrays..." << endl;
    for (unsigned int i3 = 0; i3 < valarray1.size(); i3++)
        cout << valarray1[i3] << ' ';
    cout << endl;

    valarray2 *= 3;

    cout << "First valarray x 3..." << endl;
    for (unsigned int i4 = 0; i4 < valarray2.size(); i4++)
        cout << valarray2[i4] << ' ';
```

```
    cout << endl;

    return 0;
}
```

Here's what you see when you run valarray.cpp:

```
%valarray
Original valarrays...
0 1 2 3 4 5 6 7 8 9
0 1 2 3 4 5 6 7 8 9
Sum of valarrays...
0 2 4 6 8 10 12 14 16 18
First valarray x 3...
0 3 6 9 12 15 18 21 24 27
```

Chapter 17

Standard Template Library Function Objects and Algorithms

In Depth

The previous chapter was about STL containers, and this chapter is about STL algorithms. The STL algorithms are functions that are not members of any container, but they work with container iterators to sort, loop over, search, replace, erase, and otherwise handle the elements in a container. Because STL algorithms work with iterators, and each container's iterators handle the internal details of moving through the data in the container, you can use the algorithms with any type of STL container. Here are the algorithms we'll see at work in this chapter:

- **accumulate**—Accumulates values from successive mathematical operations.
- **copy**—Copies data from container to container using iterators.
- **count**—Counts the number of elements in a container.
- **equal**—Checks for container equality.
- **find**—Finds an element in a container.
- **for_each**—Applies a function to all elements in a container.
- **min_element** and **max_element**—Finds the minimum and maximum elements in a container.
- **random_shuffle**—Shuffles the elements in a container randomly.
- **remove**—Removes an element or elements from a container.
- **replace**—Replaces an element or elements in a container.
- **reverse**—Reverses the elements in a container.
- **rotate**—Rotates the element order in a container.
- **search**—Searches a container.
- **sort**—Sorts the elements in a container.
- **swap**—Swaps the data inside a container with the data in another container.
- **transform**—Applies a function to transform the elements of a container.
- **unique**—Eliminates adjacent duplicate element values.

We've already seen a number of STL algorithms at work as far back as Chapter 15, where we saw the example program stlfunctions.cpp, which uses the **sort**, **for_each**, and **random_shuffle** algorithms to sort, loop over, and shuffle the elements in a vector randomly. In that example, I created a vector of **person** objects, each of which held a person's name and age, and then used STL algorithms to handle that data:

```
#include <iostream>
#include <string>
#include <vector>
#include <algorithm>
using namespace std;

class person
{
    string name;
    int age;
public:
    person(string n, int a) {name = n; age = a;}
    friend bool compare_ages(const person & person1,
        const person & person2);
    friend bool operator<(const person & person1, const person & person2);
    friend void display(person p);
};

void display(person p)
{
    cout << "Name: " << p.name << " age: " << p.age << endl;
}

bool operator<(const person & person1, const person & person2)
{
    if (person1.name < person2.name)
        return true;
    else
        return false;
}

bool compare_ages(const person & person1, const person & person2)
{
    if (person1.age < person2.age)
        return true;
    else
        return false;
}
```

```
int main()
{
    vector<person> friends;

    friends.push_back(person("Ralph", 35));
    friends.push_back(person("Tom", 36));
    friends.push_back(person("Frank", 23));
    friends.push_back(person("Sally", 24));

    sort(friends.begin(), friends.end());

    cout << "Sorted by name..." << endl;

    for_each(friends.begin(), friends.end(), display);

    sort(friends.begin(), friends.end(), compare_ages);

    cout << "Sorted by age..." << endl;

    for_each(friends.begin(), friends.end(), display);

    random_shuffle(friends.begin(), friends.end());

    cout << "Randomly shuffled..." << endl;

    for_each(friends.begin(), friends.end(), display);

    return 0;
}
```

Here's what you see when you run this program:

```
%stlfunctions
Sorted by name...
Name: Frank age: 23
Name: Ralph age: 35
Name: Sally age: 24
Name: Tom age: 36
Sorted by age...
Name: Frank age: 23
Name: Sally age: 24
Name: Ralph age: 35
Name: Tom age: 36
Randomly shuffled...
Name: Tom age: 36
```

```
Name: Frank age: 23
Name: Sally age: 24
Name: Ralph age: 35
```

As you can see, algorithms like **sort**, **for_each**, and **random_shuffle** let you handle the data in a container. In fact, now that we're discussing algorithms, it's worth taking a second look at this code; in particular, note the **compare_ages** function, which is a friend function of the **person** class, and which I passed to the **sort** algorithm to use to sort people by age. This function takes two **person** objects and compares their ages like this:

```
class person
{
    string name;
    int age;
public:
    person(string n, int a) {name = n; age = a;}
    friend bool compare_ages(const person & person1,
        const person & person2);
    friend bool operator<(const person & person1, const person & person2);
    friend void display(person p);
};
    .
    .
    .
bool compare_ages(const person & person1, const person & person2)
{
    if (person1.age < person2.age)
        return true;
    else
        return false;
}

int main()
{
    vector<person> friends;

    friends.push_back(person("Ralph", 35));
    friends.push_back(person("Tom", 36));
    friends.push_back(person("Frank", 23));
    friends.push_back(person("Sally", 24));
    .
    .
    .
```

```
    sort(friends.begin(), friends.end(), compare_ages);
        .
        .
        .
```

Passing **compare_ages** to the **sort** algorithm makes it a function object. In fact, it's a particular type of function object—a *binary predicate*. You can pass function objects to STL algorithms to customize the behavior of those algorithms, and we'll take a closer look at how that works next.

Function Objects

Many STL algorithms let you customize their behavior by passing them function objects, also called functors. A function object is a programming construct you can call with (), as you would a function, that includes normal function names (like **compare_ages** in the example we just saw), as well as pointers to functions and objects with an overloaded () operator. (How do you overload the () operator? You define the **operator()()** method in a class, as funny as that looks.) We'll use function objects with a number of algorithms in this chapter, and it's essential to know how they work.

Here is some function object terminology:

- A *generator* is a function object you call with no arguments.
- A *unary function* is a function object you call with one argument.
- A *binary function* is a function object you call with two arguments.
- A unary function that returns a boolean value is a *predicate*.
- A binary function that returns a boolean value is a *binary predicate*.

For example, the **compare_ages** function object we saw in stlfunctions.cpp is a binary predicate, because it takes two **person** arguments and returns a boolean value. Although you can use actual functions like **compare_ages** as function objects, it's often better to use objects with a defined **operator()** method, because you can customize the behavior of such objects by passing arguments to the object's constructor.

Here's an example, function_object.cpp, that creates a class named **square** that supports an **operator()** method, which simply returns the square of its argument. To allow this class to be used with any numeric type, I'll make it a class template:

```
#include <vector>
#include <algorithm>
```

```
#include <iostream>
using namespace std;

template<class T>
class square
{
public:
   T operator() (const T& value)
   {
      return value * value;
   }
};
      .
      .
      .
```

To square the integer elements of a vector, I could pass **square<int>()** to the **for_each** algorithm we've already seen, but because the **square** class's **operator()** method doesn't display anything, the program wouldn't produce any output. A better choice of algorithm here is the **transform** algorithm, which takes two iterators for the element range you want to work with, an iterator to the destination where you want to send the transformed data, and a function object to use to transform the data. In this case, I can store the squared values in a new vector and then use the **copy** algorithm to display the data in the new vector. (Alternatively, as I'll do in a few pages, I could have used an **ostream** iterator with the **transform** algorithm to display the data immediately after transforming it.) I'll pass **square<int>()** as a function object to **transform** to square the integers in the original vector:

```
#include <vector>
#include <algorithm>
#include <iostream>
using namespace std;

template<class T>
class square
{
public:
   T operator() (const T& value)
   {
      return value * value;
   }
};
```

```
const int NUMBER_ELEMENTS = 8;

int main ()
{
   int initial_values[NUMBER_ELEMENTS] = {1, 2, 3, 4, 5, 6, 7, 8};
   vector<int> start(NUMBER_ELEMENTS);
   start.assign(initial_values, initial_values + NUMBER_ELEMENTS);

   vector<int> result(NUMBER_ELEMENTS);

   transform(start.begin(), start.end(), result.begin(), square<int>());

   cout << "Here are the squared values:" << endl;

   copy(result.begin(), result.end(),
       ostream_iterator<int, char>(cout," "));
   cout << endl;

   return 0;
}
```

TIP: *Another way to use the* ***transform*** *algorithm, one which more closely matches its name, is to overwrite the original data with the newly transformed data, which you can do by setting the output iterator to the beginning of the input data like this:* ***transform(start.begin(), start.end(), start.begin(), square<int>())****.*

Here's what you see when you run this code, function_object.cpp:

```
%function_object
Here are the squared values:
1 4 9 16 25 36 49 64
```

As you can see, there are several ways to create your own function objects. In fact, the STL also includes a number of predefined function objects.

Predefined Function Objects

To use the STL predefined function objects, you include the header file named functional. There are predefined function object equivalents for all the simple arithmetic and logical operations—for example, to subtract the elements of one container from another, you could pass the **minus** predefined function object to the **transform** algorithm. You'll find the predefined function object equivalents for the simple arithmetic and logical operations in Table 17.1.

Table 17.1 Operators and function object equivalents.

Operator	Function Object Equivalent
+	plus
-	minus
*	multiplies
/	divides
%	modulus
-	negate
==	equal_to
!=	not_equal_to
>	greater
<	less
>=	greater_equal
<=	less_equal
&&	logical_and
||	logical_or
!	logical_not

There's one consideration we should examine here. The **square<int>()** function object we defined in the previous example returns the square of its single argument, so I can square the elements in a vector named **vector1** and send the results to an **ostream** iterator like this:

```
transform(vector1.begin(), vector1.end(), ostream_itr, square<int>());
```

However, a predefined function object like **multiplies** takes two arguments, not one. It turns out that there is a second form of the **transform** algorithm to handle this, and you pass an additional argument—an iterator to the beginning of a second container's data—to this new form of **transform**. For example, here's how you can multiply the elements of the two vectors **vector1** and **vector2** and send the result to an **ostream** iterator:

```
transform(vector1.begin(), vector1.end(), vector2.begin(), ostream_itr,
    multiplies<int>());
```

However, what if I want to multiply every element in a vector not by the corresponding element in another vector but by a constant value, such as 10? It turns out that the STL predefined function objects are *adaptable* function objects, which means that they can be adapted by other classes and objects to fit situations such as these. Because **multiplies** is an adaptable binary function, you can adapt it into a unary function using the STL functions **bind1st** and **bind2nd**. The **bind1st** function binds the first argument of a binary function to a particular value, and the **bind2nd** function binds the second argument of a binary function to a particular value. Using **bind1st** and **bind2nd**, then, you can effectively adapt **multiplies** to a unary function as far as **transform** is concerned.

NOTE: *A function object is adaptable by other STL functions if its return value is of* ***result_type*** *type and its arguments are of the* ***first_argument_type*** *and* ***second_argument_type*** *types. For example, the return type of* ***multiplies*** *is* ***multiplies<int>::result_type****.*

Here's how it might look if I want to use **transform** to multiply all the elements in **vector1** by 10—note that I'm binding the first argument of **multiplies** to 10, so it will always have that value, and then using the resulting unary function to work with the elements in **vector1**:

```
transform(vector1.begin(), vector1.end(), ostream_itr,
    bind1st(multiplies<int>(), 10));
```

Here's a complete example, adapter_functors.cpp, that puts this to work. In this case, I'll define two integer vectors, **vector1** and **vector2**, and use the predefined function object **minus** to subtract the elements of one from the elements of the other. I'll also adapt **multiplies** from a binary function to a unary function with the **bind1st** function so I can multiply all the elements in **vector2** by 10:

```
#include <iostream>
#include <vector>
#include <iterator>
#include <algorithm>
#include <functional>
using namespace std;

const int NUMBER_ELEMENTS = 6;

int main()
{
    int initial_values1[NUMBER_ELEMENTS] = {3, 5, 7, 9, 11, 13};
    int initial_values2[NUMBER_ELEMENTS] = {1, 2, 3, 4, 5, 6};
```

```
    vector<int> vector1(NUMBER_ELEMENTS);
    vector<int> vector2(NUMBER_ELEMENTS);
    vector1.assign(initial_values1, initial_values1 + NUMBER_ELEMENTS);
    vector2.assign(initial_values2, initial_values2 + NUMBER_ELEMENTS);

    ostream_iterator<int, char> ostream_itr(cout, " ");

    cout << "Vector 1: " << endl;
    copy(vector1.begin(), vector1.end(), ostream_itr);
    cout << endl;

    cout << "Vector 2: " << endl;
    copy(vector2.begin(), vector2.end(), ostream_itr);
    cout << endl;

    cout << "Vector 1 - vector 2: " << endl;
    transform(vector1.begin(), vector1.end(), vector2.begin(),
        ostream_itr, minus<int>());
    cout << endl;

    cout << "10 * vector 2: " << endl;
    transform(vector2.begin(), vector2.end(), ostream_itr,
        bind1st(multiplies<int>(), 10));
    cout << endl;

    return 0;
}
```

And here's the result of this code, adaptable_functors.cpp—as you can see, the **minus** and **multiplies** predefined function objects have done their work:

```
%adaptable_functors
Vector 1:
3 5 7 9 11 13
Vector 2:
1 2 3 4 5 6
Vector 1 - vector 2:
2 3 4 5 6 7
10 * vector 2:
10 20 30 40 50 60
```

Using Algorithms

We've already see plenty of algorithms at work, like **copy**, **sort**, **for_each**, **random_shuffle**, **set_union** and **set_intersection**, and **transform**, and we're going to see many more in the Immediate Solutions section of this chapter. Generally speaking, there are four types of STL algorithms:

- Non-modifying sequence algorithms (header file: algorithm)
- Mutating sequence algorithms (header file: algorithm)
- Sorting algorithms (header file: algorithm)
- Generalized numeric algorithms (header file: numeric)

Non-modifying sequence algorithms, such as **find** and **for_each**, work on each element in a range. Mutating sequence algorithms, such as **transform**, **random_shuffle**, or **copy**, operate on elements in a range and can change those elements. Sorting algorithms include sorting functions like **sort** and set operations like **set_union** and **set_intersection**. Finally, numeric operations include functions to add the contents of a container, calculate the inner product of two containers, find partial sums and adjacent differences, and so on.

It's also worth noting that many algorithms have alternate versions with **_if** or **_copy** appended, such as **remove_if** and **remove_copy**. One of the arguments you pass to the **_if** version of an algorithm is a predicate or binary predicate, which returns a boolean true/false value that determines if the algorithm is applied or not. Some algorithms have two versions, an in-place version and a copying version. The in-place version can modify the data in the original container, while the copying version, which has **_copy** appended to the name, allows you to pass an output iterator to the algorithm as an additional argument to specify where you want the results copied to. (To compare how you use an algorithm and its copying version, take a look at "Using **remove** and **erase**" later in this chapter.)

To get us started with algorithms in this chapter, here are two we haven't seen before—**min_element** and **max_element**, which iterate through a container and return an iterator to the container's minimum and maximum elements, respectively. Here's an example, minmax.cpp, that displays the minimum and maximum elements in a vector of integers:

```
#include <vector>
#include <algorithm>
#include <iostream>

using namespace std;
```

```
const int NUMBER_ELEMENTS = 8;

int main ()
{
    int initial_values[NUMBER_ELEMENTS] = {1, 2, 3, 4, 5, 6, 6, 7};

    vector<int> vector1(NUMBER_ELEMENTS);
    vector1.assign(initial_values, initial_values + NUMBER_ELEMENTS);

    vector<int>::iterator maximum_value = max_element(vector1.begin(),
        vector1.end());
    cout << "Maximum value: " << *maximum_value << endl;

    vector<int>::iterator minimum_value = min_element(vector1.begin(),
        vector1.end());
    cout << "Minimum value: " << *minimum_value << endl;

    return 0;
}
```

Here's what you see when you run this example, minmax.cpp:

```
%minmax
Maximum value: 7
Minimum value: 1
```

As you can see, there are many algorithms available in the STL, and we're about to see them at work in the Immediate Solutions section.

Immediate Solutions

Using Function Objects

As discussed in the In Depth section of this chapter, a function object, also called a functor, is any object that can be used with (), including normal function names as well as pointers to functions and objects with an overloaded () operator. We also saw that function objects introduce some new terminology:

- A *generator* is a function object you call with no arguments.
- A *unary function* is a function object you call with one argument.
- A *binary function* is a function object you call with two arguments.
- A unary function that returns a boolean value is a *predicate*.
- A binary function that returns a boolean value is a *binary predicate*.

Many STL algorithms, such as **for_each** and **transform**, can take function objects as arguments (in fact, you must specifically pass predicate or binary predicate functions to algorithms that end in **_if**). Here's an example we saw, function_object.cpp, that uses a class template named **square** to square numeric values passed to it; this class does its work by defining an **operator()** method. To make this example work, I pass the **square<int>()** function object to **transform**:

```
#include <functional>
#include <vector>
#include <algorithm>
#include <iostream>
using namespace std;

template<class T>
class square
{
public:
    T operator() (const T& arg)
    {
        return arg * arg;
    }
};
```

```
const int NUMBER_ELEMENTS = 8;

int main ()
{
   int initial_values[NUMBER_ELEMENTS] = {1, 2, 3, 4, 5, 6, 7, 8};
   vector<int> start(NUMBER_ELEMENTS);
   start.assign(initial_values, initial_values + NUMBER_ELEMENTS);
   vector<int> result(NUMBER_ELEMENTS);

   transform(start.begin(), start.end(), result.begin(), square<int>());

   cout << "Here are the squared values:" << endl;

   copy(result.begin(), result.end(),
       ostream_iterator<int, char>(cout," "));
   cout << endl;

   return 0;
}
```

And here's the result of running this code, function_object.cpp:

```
%function_object
Here are the squared values:
1 4 9 16 25 36 49 64
```

Using Predefined Function Objects

The STL comes with many predefined function objects, as you saw in Table 17.1. You can use the function objects in that table to handle simple arithmetic and logical operations, as we saw in the adapter_functors.cpp example in the In Depth section of this chapter. In that example, I use the **minus** and **multiplies** predefined function objects to subtract the elements of one vector from another and multiply the elements of a vector by 10. Note that to multiply by 10, I use the **bind1st** function to adapt the **multiplies** predefined function object to a unary function:

```
#include <iostream>
#include <vector>
#include <iterator>
#include <algorithm>
#include <functional>
```

```
using namespace std;

const int NUMBER_ELEMENTS = 6;

int main()
{
    int initial_values1[NUMBER_ELEMENTS] = {3, 5, 7, 9, 11, 13};
    int initial_values2[NUMBER_ELEMENTS] = {1, 2, 3, 4, 5, 6};

    vector<int> vector1(NUMBER_ELEMENTS);
    vector<int> vector2(NUMBER_ELEMENTS);
    vector1.assign(initial_values1, initial_values1 + NUMBER_ELEMENTS);
    vector2.assign(initial_values2, initial_values2 + NUMBER_ELEMENTS);

    ostream_iterator<int, char> ostream_itr(cout, " ");

    cout << "Vector 1: " << endl;
    copy(vector1.begin(), vector1.end(), ostream_itr);
    cout << endl;

    cout << "Vector 2: " << endl;
    copy(vector2.begin(), vector2.end(), ostream_itr);
    cout << endl;

    cout << "Vector 1 - vector 2: " << endl;
    transform(vector1.begin(), vector1.end(), vector2.begin(), ostream_itr,
        minus<int>());
    cout << endl;

    cout << "10 * vector 2: " << endl;
    transform(vector2.begin(), vector2.end(), ostream_itr,
        bind1st(multiplies<int>(), 10));
    cout << endl;

    return 0;
}
```

Here's the result of this example, adaptable_functors.cpp:

```
%adaptable_functors
Vector 1:
3 5 7 9 11 13
Vector 2:
1 2 3 4 5 6
Vector 1 - vector 2:
```

```
2 3 4 5 6 7
10 * vector 2:
10 20 30 40 50 60
```

Using **accumulate**

The **accumulate** algorithm lets you *accumulate* the results of successive arithmetic operations on the elements of a container. Here are the available forms of **accumulate**:

```
template <class InputIterator, class T>
T accumulate(InputIterator first, InputIterator last, T init);
template <class InputIterator, class T, class BinaryOperation>
T accumulate(InputIterator first, InputIterator last, T init,
    BinaryOperation binary_op);
```

By default, **accumulate** adds the elements it works with, but you can pass a binary function object to perform other operations. For example, if a vector holds the values 1, 2, 3, and 4, **accumulate** would return the sum of these values, 10. You can also set the initial value of the accumulated result by setting the **init** argument. Here's an example, accumulate.cpp, that adds the elements in a vector and also uses the **multiplies** predefined function object to multiply them together:

```
#include <algorithm>
#include <functional>
#include <numeric>
#include <iostream>
using namespace std;

const int NUMBER_ELEMENTS = 4;

int main ()
 {
    int numbers[NUMBER_ELEMENTS] = {1, 2, 3, 4};

    int result = accumulate(numbers, numbers + NUMBER_ELEMENTS, 0);

    cout << "Adding the values gives: " << result << endl;

    result = accumulate(numbers, numbers + NUMBER_ELEMENTS, 1,
        multiplies<int>());
```

```
    cout << "Multiplying the values gives: " << result << endl;

    return 0;
}
```

Here's what you see when you run this example, accumulate.cpp:

```
%accumulate
Adding the values gives: 10
Multiplying the values gives: 24
```

Using **copy**

We've already seen **copy** throughout the previous two chapters; you can use **copy** to copy the elements of one container to another or a stream iterator. Here are the available forms of **copy**:

```
template<class InputIterator, class OutputIterator>
OutputIterator copy(InputIterator first, InputIterator last,
    OutputIterator result);
template<class BidirectionalIterator1, class BidirectionalIterator2>
BidirectionalIterator2 copy_backward
    (BidirectionalIterator1 first, BidirectionalIterator1 last,
    BidirectionalIterator2 result);
```

Here's an example, copier.cpp, that we first saw in Chapter 15. In this case, I'll create a vector of numbers and use **copy** to both copy elements from an array to the vector and then copy from the vector to an **ostream** iterator to display those elements:

```
#include <iostream>
#include <iterator>
#include <vector>
using namespace std;

const int MAX = 5;

int main()
{
    int numbers_array[MAX];
    vector<int> numbers_vector(MAX);
```

```
    for (int loop_index = 0; loop_index < MAX; loop_index++){
        numbers_array[loop_index] = loop_index;
    }

    copy(numbers_array, numbers_array + MAX, numbers_vector.begin());

    ostream_iterator<int, char> ostream_itr(cout, " ");

    copy(numbers_vector.begin(), numbers_vector.end(), ostream_itr);
    cout << endl;

    return 0;
}
```

Here's what you see when you run copier.cpp and **copy** does its work:

```
%copier
0 1 2 3 4
```


Related solutions:	*Found on page:*
Using **copy** and **ostream** Iterators	682
Using **copy** and **istream** Iterators	684

Using **count**

You can use the **count** algorithm to count the number of elements in a container, or the **count_if** version to count the number of elements for which a predicate is true:

```
typename iterator_traits<InputIterator>::difference_type
    count(InputIterator first, InputIterator last, const T& value);
template<class InputIterator, class Predicate>
typename iterator_traits<InputIterator>::difference_type
    count_if(InputIterator first, InputIterator last, Predicate pred);
```

***NOTE:** You might notice the return type of **count** is **difference_type**, which is specifically designed to hold the distance between iterators. Because there's no guarantee that a fixed type, such as **int**, will be big enough to hold the number returned by **count**, the designers of the STL made that type **difference_type**. The reasoning is that because **difference_type** is big enough to hold the maximum distance between iterators in a container, it's big enough to hold the maximum count a container can have—the number of elements in the container.*

Here's an example, count.cpp, that counts the number of times that the word "Hello" appears in a vector of **string** objects:

```
#include <iostream>
#include <algorithm>
#include <string>
#include <vector>
using namespace std;

int main()
{
    vector<string> words;

    words.push_back("Hello");
    words.push_back("Hello");
    words.push_back("there");

    cout << "The word \"Hello\" appears " <<
        count(words.begin(), words.end(), "Hello") <<
        " times." << endl;

    return 0;
}
```

Here's what you see when you run this example, count.cpp:

```
%count
The word "Hello" appears 2 times.
```


Related solution:	Found on page:
Finding the Distance between Iterators	692

Using equal

You can use the **equal** algorithm to compare the contents of two containers for equality. This algorithm returns a value of **true** if the containers are equal and **false** otherwise:

```
template<class InputIterator1, class InputIterator2>
bool equal(InputIterator1 first1, InputIterator1 last1,
     InputIterator2 first2);
```

Here's an example equal.cpp, that puts **equal** to work; in this case, I'm simply comparing two vectors:

```
#include <algorithm>
#include <vector>
#include <functional>
#include <iostream>
using namespace std;

const int NUMBER_ELEMENTS = 5;

int main ()
{
    int initial_values1[NUMBER_ELEMENTS] = {1, 2, 3, 4, 5};
    int initial_values2[NUMBER_ELEMENTS] = {1, 2, 4, 3, 5};

    vector<int> vector1(NUMBER_ELEMENTS);
    vector1.assign(initial_values1, initial_values1 + NUMBER_ELEMENTS);
    vector<int> vector2(NUMBER_ELEMENTS);
    vector2.assign(initial_values2, initial_values2 + NUMBER_ELEMENTS);

    if(equal(vector1.begin(), vector1.end(), vector2.begin()))
        cout << "Vectors are equal" << endl;
    else
        cout << "Vectors are not equal" << endl;

    return 0;
}
```

Here's what you see when you run this example, equal.cpp; in this case, the two compared **vector** containers are not equal, because the 3 and 4 are transposed in the second **vector**, so we get this result:

```
%equal
Vectors are not equal
```

Using find

You can use the **find** algorithm to find specific elements in a container. Here are the available forms of **find**—note that **find_end** is a reverse find, and **adjacent_find** finds adjacent elements:

```
template<class InputIterator, class T>
InputIterator find(InputIterator first, InputIterator last,
    const T& value);
template<class InputIterator, class Predicate>
InputIterator find_if(InputIterator first, InputIterator last,
    Predicate pred);
template<class ForwardIterator1, class ForwardIterator2>
ForwardIterator1
    find_end(ForwardIterator1 first1, ForwardIterator1 last1,
    ForwardIterator2 first2, ForwardIterator2 last2);
template<class ForwardIterator1, class ForwardIterator2,
    class BinaryPredicate>
ForwardIterator1
    find_end(ForwardIterator1 first1, ForwardIterator1 last1,
    ForwardIterator2 first2, ForwardIterator2 last2,
    BinaryPredicate pred);
template<class ForwardIterator1, class ForwardIterator2>
ForwardIterator1
    find_first_of(ForwardIterator1 first1, ForwardIterator1 last1,
    ForwardIterator2 first2, ForwardIterator2 last2);
template<class ForwardIterator1, class ForwardIterator2,
    class BinaryPredicate>
ForwardIterator1
    find_first_of(ForwardIterator1 first1, ForwardIterator1 last1,
    ForwardIterator2 first2, ForwardIterator2 last2,
    BinaryPredicate pred);
template<class ForwardIterator>
ForwardIterator adjacent_find(ForwardIterator first,
    ForwardIterator last);
template<class ForwardIterator, class BinaryPredicate>
ForwardIterator adjacent_find(ForwardIterator first,
    ForwardIterator last, BinaryPredicate pred);
```


This algorithm is great when you want to find a specific element in a container fast. Here's an example, find.cpp, that uses **find** to find the value 3 in a vector of integers and the **adjacent_find** algorithm to find the first set of equal adjacent elements in the vector:

```
#include <vector>
#include <algorithm>
#include <iostream>
using namespace std;

const int NUMBER_ELEMENTS = 8;

int main ()
{
   int initial_values[NUMBER_ELEMENTS] = {1, 2, 3, 4, 5, 6, 6, 7};

   vector<int> vector1(NUMBER_ELEMENTS);
   vector1.assign(initial_values, initial_values + NUMBER_ELEMENTS);

   vector<int>::iterator itr1 = find(vector1.begin(), vector1.end(), 3);

   cout << "Found a " << *itr1 << endl;

   vector<int>::iterator itr2 =
       adjacent_find(vector1.begin(), vector1.end());

   cout << "Found adjacent elements starting with " << *itr2 << endl;

   return 0;
}
```

And here are the results you see when you run find.cpp:

```
%find
Found a 3
Found adjacent elements starting with 6
```

Using for_each

You use the **for_each** algorithm to loop over all the elements in a container and apply a function to each of them:

```
template<class InputIterator, class Function>
Function for_each(InputIterator first, InputIterator last, Function f);
```

We saw an example in Chapter 15, stlfunctions.cpp, that put the **for_each** algorithm to work, using it to call a function named **display** to display the data in a vector of objects:

```
#include <iostream>
#include <string>
#include <vector>
#include <algorithm>
using namespace std;

class person
{
    string name;
    int age;
public:
    person(string n, int a) {name = n; age = a;}
    friend bool compare_ages(const person & person1,
        const person & person2);
    friend bool operator<(const person & person1, const person & person2);
    friend void display(person p);
};

void display(person p)
{
    cout << "Name: " << p.name << " age: " << p.age << endl;
}

bool operator<(const person & person1, const person & person2)
{
    if (person1.name < person2.name)
        return true;
    else
        return false;
}

bool compare_ages(const person & person1, const person & person2)
{
    if (person1.age < person2.age)
        return true;
    else
        return false;
}
```

```
int main()
{
    vector<person> friends;

    friends.push_back(person("Ralph", 35));
    friends.push_back(person("Tom", 36));
    friends.push_back(person("Frank", 23));
    friends.push_back(person("Sally", 24));

    sort(friends.begin(), friends.end());

    cout << "Sorted by name..." << endl;

    for_each(friends.begin(), friends.end(), display);

    sort(friends.begin(), friends.end(), compare_ages);

    cout << "Sorted by age..." << endl;

    for_each(friends.begin(), friends.end(), display);

    random_shuffle(friends.begin(), friends.end());

    cout << "Randomly shuffled..." << endl;

    for_each(friends.begin(), friends.end(), display);

    return 0;
}
```

Here's what you see when you run this example, stlfunctions.cpp:

```
%stlfunctions
Sorted by name...
Name: Frank age: 23
Name: Ralph age: 35
Name: Sally age: 24
Name: Tom age: 36
Sorted by age...
Name: Frank age: 23
Name: Sally age: 24
Name: Ralph age: 35
Name: Tom age: 36
Randomly shuffled...
```

```
Name: Tom age: 36
Name: Frank age: 23
Name: Sally age: 24
Name: Ralph age: 35
```

Using **min_element** and **max_element**

You can use the **min_element** and **max_element** algorithms to find the minimum and maximum elements in a container:

```
template<class ForwardIterator>
ForwardIterator min_element (ForwardIterator first, ForwardIterator last);
template<class ForwardIterator, class Compare>
ForwardIterator min_element(ForwardIterator first, ForwardIterator last,
    Compare comp);
template<class ForwardIterator>
ForwardIterator max_element(ForwardIterator first, ForwardIterator last);
template<class ForwardIterator, class Compare>
ForwardIterator max_element(ForwardIterator first, ForwardIterator last,
    Compare comp);
```

We saw an example, minmax.cpp, in the In Depth section of this chapter that put the **min_element** and **max_element** algorithms to work. In that example, I used a vector of integers that held the values 1, 2, 3, 4, 5, 6, 6, and 7, and found the minimum and maximum values in those vectors like this:

```
#include <vector>
#include <algorithm>
#include <iostream>

using namespace std;

const int NUMBER_ELEMENTS = 8;

int main ()
{
    int initial_values[NUMBER_ELEMENTS] = {1, 2, 3, 4, 5, 6, 6, 7};

    vector<int> vector1(NUMBER_ELEMENTS);
    vector1.assign(initial_values, initial_values + NUMBER_ELEMENTS);

    vector<int>::iterator maximum_value =
```

```
        max_element(vector1.begin(), vector1.end());
    cout << "Maximum value: " << *maximum_value << endl;

    vector<int>::iterator minimum_value =
        min_element(vector1.begin(), vector1.end());
    cout << "Minimum value: " << *minimum_value << endl;

    return 0;
}
```

And here's what you see when you run this example, minmax.cpp:

```
%minmax
Maximum value: 7
Minimum value: 1
```

Using **random_shuffle**

The **random_shuffle** algorithm shuffles the elements in a container randomly, producing a new ordering:

```
template<class RandomAccessIterator>
void random_shuffle(RandomAccessIterator first,
    RandomAccessIterator last);
template<class RandomAccessIterator, class RandomNumberGenerator>
void random_shuffle(RandomAccessIterator first,
    RandomAccessIterator last, RandomNumberGenerator& rand);
```

We saw how to use **random_shuffle** in the stlfunctions.cpp example in Chapter 15. In that example, I used **random_shuffle** to shuffle the **person** elements in a vector and then displayed the results like this:

```
#include <iostream>
#include <string>
#include <vector>
#include <algorithm>
using namespace std;

class person
{
    string name;
    int age;
```

```
public:
    person(string n, int a) {name = n; age = a;}
    friend bool compare_ages(const person & person1,
        const person & person2);
    friend bool operator<(const person & person1, const person & person2);
    friend void display(person p);
};

void display(person p)
{
    cout << "Name: " << p.name << " age: " << p.age << endl;
}

bool operator<(const person & person1, const person & person2)
{
    if (person1.name < person2.name)
        return true;
    else
        return false;
}

bool compare_ages(const person & person1, const person & person2)
{
    if (person1.age < person2.age)
        return true;
    else
        return false;
}

int main()
{
    vector<person> friends;

    friends.push_back(person("Ralph", 35));
    friends.push_back(person("Tom", 36));
    friends.push_back(person("Frank", 23));
    friends.push_back(person("Sally", 24));

    sort(friends.begin(), friends.end());

    cout << "Sorted by name..." << endl;

    for_each(friends.begin(), friends.end(), display);

    sort(friends.begin(), friends.end(), compare_ages);
```

```
    cout << "Sorted by age..." << endl;

    for_each(friends.begin(), friends.end(), display);

    random_shuffle(friends.begin(), friends.end());

    cout << "Randomly shuffled..." << endl;

    for_each(friends.begin(), friends.end(), display);

    return 0;
}
```

Here's what you see when you run this example, stlfunctions.cpp:

```
%stlfunctions
Sorted by name...
Name: Frank age: 23
Name: Ralph age: 35
Name: Sally age: 24
Name: Tom age: 36
Sorted by age...
Name: Frank age: 23
Name: Sally age: 24
Name: Ralph age: 35
Name: Tom age: 36
Randomly shuffled...
Name: Tom age: 36
Name: Frank age: 23
Name: Sally age: 24
Name: Ralph age: 35
```


Using **remove** and **erase**

You can use the **remove** algorithm to remove elements from a container. Here are the available forms of **remove**:

```
template<class ForwardIterator, class T>
    ForwardIterator remove(ForwardIterator first, ForwardIterator last,
    const T& value);
template<class ForwardIterator, class Predicate>
ForwardIterator remove_if(ForwardIterator first, ForwardIterator last,
    Predicate pred);
```

```
template<class InputIterator, class OutputIterator, class T>
OutputIterator remove_copy(InputIterator first, InputIterator last,
    OutputIterator result, const T& value);
template<class InputIterator, class OutputIterator, class Predicate>
OutputIterator remove_copy_if(InputIterator first, InputIterator last,
    OutputIterator result, Predicate pred);
```

Here's an example, remove.cpp, that uses **remove** to remove one element from a vector and then uses a function object to remove all elements greater than 5. Then I'll use the copying version of **remove**, **remove_copy**, to do the same thing to show you the difference between an in-place algorithm and its copying version. Note in particular that the in-place algorithm **remove** returns an iterator to the new last element of the container, and you should use **erase** to delete the leftover elements at the end of the container, something you don't have to do with **remove_copy**. To use **erase**, you simply pass two iterators that delimit the range of elements to delete:

```
#include <algorithm>
#include <vector>
#include <iterator>
#include <iostream>
using namespace std;

template<class T>
class greater_than_5
{
public:
    bool operator() (const T& value) {return value > 5;}
};

const int NUMBER_ELEMENTS = 10;

int main ()
{
    int initial_values[NUMBER_ELEMENTS] = {1, 2, 3, 4, 5, 6, 7, 8, 9, 10};

    vector<int> vector1(NUMBER_ELEMENTS);
    vector<int> vector2(NUMBER_ELEMENTS);
    vector1.assign(initial_values, initial_values + NUMBER_ELEMENTS);
    vector2.assign(initial_values, initial_values + NUMBER_ELEMENTS);

    cout << "Original vector: " << endl;
    copy(vector1.begin(), vector1.end(),
        ostream_iterator<int,char>(cout," "));
    cout << endl;
```

17. Standard Template Library Function Objects and Algorithms

```
    cout << "Removing the 8: " << endl;
    vector<int,allocator<int> >::iterator result = remove(vector1.begin(),
        vector1.end(), 8);
    vector1.erase(result, vector1.end());

    copy(vector1.begin(), vector1.end(),
        ostream_iterator<int,char>(cout," "));
    cout << endl;

    cout << "Removing elements greater than 5: " << endl;
    result = remove_if(vector1.begin(), vector1.end(),
        greater_than_5<int>());
    vector1.erase(result, vector1.end());

    copy(vector1.begin(), vector1.end(),
        ostream_iterator<int,char>(cout," "));
    cout << endl;

    cout << "Using the copying version to remove the 8: " << endl;
    remove_copy(vector2.begin(), vector2.end(),
        ostream_iterator<int,char>(cout," "), 8);
    cout << endl;

    cout << "Using the copying version to remove elements greater than 5: "
        << endl;
    remove_copy_if(vector2.begin(), vector2.end(),
        ostream_iterator<int,char>(cout," "),
        greater_than_5<int>());

  return 0;
}
```

Here's what you see when you run remove.cpp:

```
%remove
Original vector:
1 2 3 4 5 6 7 8 9 10
Removing the 8:
1 2 3 4 5 6 7 9 10
Removing elements greater than 5:
1 2 3 4 5
Using the copying version to remove the 8:
1 2 3 4 5 6 7 9 10
Using the copying version to remove elements greater than 5:
1 2 3 4 5
```

Using **replace**

You can use the **replace** algorithm to replace elements in a container:

```
template<class ForwardIterator, class T>
void replace(ForwardIterator first, ForwardIterator last,
    const T& old_value, const T& new_value);
template<class ForwardIterator, class Predicate, class T>
void replace_if(ForwardIterator first, ForwardIterator last,
    Predicate pred, const T& new_value);
template<class InputIterator, class OutputIterator, class T>
OutputIterator replace_copy(InputIterator first, InputIterator last,
    OutputIterator result, const T& old_value, const T& new_value);
template<class Iterator, class OutputIterator, class Predicate, class T>
OutputIterator replace_copy_if(Iterator first, Iterator last,
    OutputIterator result, Predicate pred, const T& new_value);
```

Here's an example, replace.cpp, that puts **replace** to work. In this example, I'll replace the number 5 with 0 in a vector of integers. I'll also use a function object, **is_odd**, and the **replace_if** version of **replace** to replace all odd numbers in the vector with 0:

```
#include <vector>
#include <algorithm>
#include <iostream>
using namespace std;

bool is_odd (int value) {return value % 2;}

const int NUMBER_ELEMENTS = 8;

int main ()
{
    int initial_values[NUMBER_ELEMENTS] = {1, 2, 3, 4, 5, 6, 6, 7};

    vector<int> vector1(NUMBER_ELEMENTS);
    vector1.assign(initial_values, initial_values + NUMBER_ELEMENTS);

    cout << "The original vector:" << endl;
    copy (vector1.begin(), vector1.end(),
        ostream_iterator<int, char>(cout, " "));
    cout << endl;

    cout << "Replacing 5 with 0:" << endl;
    replace (vector1.begin(), vector1.end(), 5, 0);
```

17. Standard Template Library Function Objects and Algorithms

```
    copy (vector1.begin(), vector1.end(),
        ostream_iterator<int, char>(cout, " "));
    cout << endl;

    cout << "Replacing odd numbers with 0:" << endl;
    replace_if (vector1.begin(), vector1.end(), is_odd, 0);
    copy (vector1.begin(), vector1.end(),
        ostream_iterator<int, char>(cout, " "));
    cout << endl;

    return 0;
}
```

Here's what you see when you run replace.cpp:

```
%replace
The original vector:
1 2 3 4 5 6 6 7
Replacing 5 with 0:
1 2 3 4 0 6 6 7
Replacing odd numbers with 0:
0 2 0 4 0 6 6 0
```

Using reverse

You can use the **reverse** algorithm to reverse the order of the elements in a container:

```
template<class BidirectionalIterator>
void reverse(BidirectionalIterator first, BidirectionalIterator last);
```

Here's an example, reverse.cpp, that uses **reverse** to reverse the order of the alphabet:

```
#include <algorithm>
#include <iostream>
using namespace std;

int main ()
{
    char alphabet[] = "abcdefghijklmnopqrstuvwxyz";

    reverse (alphabet, alphabet + strlen(alphabet));
```

```
    cout << alphabet << endl;

    return 0;
}
```

Here's the result you see when you run reverse.cpp:

```
%reverse
zyxwvutsrqponmlkjihgfedcba
```

Using **rotate**

You use the **rotate** algorithm to *rotate* the elements in a container. Rotating the elements in a container works by taking elements off the front of the container and putting them on the end, one by one. The iterator **middle** is an iterator to the element you want to leave at the beginning of the container after the rotation is finished:

```
template<class ForwardIterator>
void rotate(ForwardIterator first, ForwardIterator middle,
    ForwardIterator last);
template<class ForwardIterator, class OutputIterator>
OutputIterator rotate_copy(ForwardIterator first,
    ForwardIterator middle, ForwardIterator last, OutputIterator result);
```

Here's an example, rotate.cpp, that rotates the elements in a vector and displays the result to show how this works:

```
#include <algorithm>
#include <vector>
#include <iostream>
using namespace std;

const int NUMBER_ELEMENTS = 12;

int main ()
{
    int initial_values[NUMBER_ELEMENTS] =
        {1, 2, 3, 4, 5, 6, 7, 8, 9, 10, 11, 12};

    vector<int> vector1(NUMBER_ELEMENTS);
    vector1.assign(initial_values, initial_values + NUMBER_ELEMENTS);
```

```
    cout << "Original elements: " << endl;
    copy(vector1.begin(), vector1.end(),
        ostream_iterator<int, char>(cout," "));
    cout << endl;

    rotate(vector1.begin(), vector1.begin() + 5, vector1.end());

    cout << "Rotated elements: " << endl;
    copy(vector1.begin(), vector1.end(),
        ostream_iterator<int, char>(cout," "));
    cout << endl;

    return 0;
}
```

Here's what you see when you run this example, rotate.cpp:

```
%rotate
Original elements:
1 2 3 4 5 6 7 8 9 10 11 12
Rotated elements:
6 7 8 9 10 11 12 1 2 3 4 5
```

Using search

You can use the **search** algorithm to search a container for a sequence of elements:

```
template<class ForwardIterator1, class ForwardIterator2>
ForwardIterator1 search (ForwardIterator1 first1, ForwardIterator1 last1,
    ForwardIterator2 first2, ForwardIterator2 last2);
template<class ForwardIterator1, class ForwardIterator2,
    class BinaryPredicate>
ForwardIterator1 search (ForwardIterator1 first1, ForwardIterator1 last1,
    ForwardIterator2 first2, ForwardIterator2 last2, BinaryPredicate pred);
```

Here's an example, search.cpp, to show how to use this algorithm. In this case, I'll use **search** to search a text string, "Hello from C++." for the substring "C++"; **search** will return an iterator to the substring if it finds it, or to the null character at the end of the string otherwise (that's how **search** indicates failure—by returning an iterator to the last element in the searched range):

```
#include <algorithm>
#include <iostream>
```

```
using namespace std;

int main ()
{
    char * text = "Hello from C++.";
    char * to_find= "C++";

    char * location = search(text, text + strlen(text), to_find,
        to_find + strlen(to_find));

    if (*location == '\0')
        cout << "Could not find find \"C++\" in \"Hello from C++.\""
            << endl;
    else
        cout << "Found \"C++\" in \"Hello from C++.\" at location "
            << (location - text) << endl;

    return 0;
}
```

Here's what you see when you run this example, search.cpp:

```
%search
Found "C++" in "Hello from C++." at location 11
```

Using sort

You can use the **sort** algorithm to sort the elements in a container. Note that the < operator should be defined for the elements you're sorting unless you specify your own sorting function object:


```
template<class RandomAccessIterator>
void sort(RandomAccessIterator first, RandomAccessIterator last);
template<class RandomAccessIterator, class Compare>
void sort(RandomAccessIterator first, RandomAccessIterator last,
    Compare comp);
template<class RandomAccessIterator>
void stable_sort(RandomAccessIterator first, RandomAccessIterator last);
template<class RandomAccessIterator, class Compare>
void stable_sort(RandomAccessIterator first, RandomAccessIterator last,
    Compare comp);
template<class RandomAccessIterator>
void partial_sort(RandomAccessIterator first,
```

```
    RandomAccessIterator middle, RandomAccessIterator last);
template<class RandomAccessIterator, class Compare>
void partial_sort(RandomAccessIterator first, RandomAccessIterator
    middle, RandomAccessIterator last, Compare comp);
template<class InputIterator, class RandomAccessIterator>
RandomAccessIterator partial_sort_copy(InputIterator first,
    InputIterator last, RandomAccessIterator result_first,
    RandomAccessIterator result_last);
template<class InputIterator, class RandomAccessIterator, class Compare>
RandomAccessIterator partial_sort_copy(InputIterator first,
    InputIterator last, RandomAccessIterator result_first,
    RandomAccessIterator result_last, Compare comp);
```

We saw an example in Chapter 15 and in the In Depth section of this chapter, stlfunctions.cpp, that used **sort** as well as a function object, **compare_ages**, which defined the sorting order. Here's another example, sort.cpp, that sorts the integers in a vector using the default ascending sort order and then uses the predefined function object **greater** to sort the elements in the vector in descending order:

```
#include <vector>
#include <algorithm>
#include <functional>
#include <iostream>
using namespace std;

const int NUMBER_ELEMENTS = 8;

int main ()
{
    int initial_values[NUMBER_ELEMENTS] = {9, 2, 3, 4, 5, 6, 6, 7};

    vector<int> vector1(NUMBER_ELEMENTS);
    vector1.assign(initial_values, initial_values + NUMBER_ELEMENTS);

    ostream_iterator<int, char> ostream_itr(cout, " ");

    sort (vector1.begin(), vector1.end());
    copy (vector1.begin(), vector1.end(), ostream_itr);
    cout << endl;

    sort (vector1.begin(), vector1.end(), greater<int>());
    copy (vector1.begin(), vector1.end(), ostream_itr);
    cout << endl;

    return 0;
}
```

Here's what you see when you run this example, sort.cpp:

```
%sort
2 3 4 5 6 6 7 9
9 7 6 6 5 4 3 2
```

Using swap

You can use the **swap** algorithm to swap the contents of two containers, or the **swap_ranges** algorithm to swap the elements in specific ranges:

```
template<class T> void swap(T& a, T& b);
template<class ForwardIterator1, class ForwardIterator2>
ForwardIterator2 swap_ranges(ForwardIterator1 first1,
    ForwardIterator1 last1, ForwardIterator2 first2);
```

We've already put **swap** to work in the example vector_iterators.cpp, in Chapter 15. In that example, I used **swap** to swap the contents of two vectors:

```
#include <iostream>
#include <string>
#include <vector>
using namespace std;

class person
{
    string name;
    int age;
public:
    void display() {cout << "Name: " << name << " age: " << age << endl;}
    person(string n, int a) {name = n; age = a;}
};

int main()
{
    vector<person> friends;

    friends.push_back(person("Ralph", 35));
    friends.push_back(person("Tom", 36));
    friends.push_back(person("Frank", 23));
```

```
    friends.push_back(person("Sally", 24));
    .
    .
    .
    vector<person> nancys_friends;

    nancys_friends.push_back(person("Tina", 35));
    nancys_friends.push_back(person("Buddy", 36));
    .
    .
    .
    nancys_friends.swap(friends);
    cout << "Swapping your friends with Nancy's..." << endl;

    for (p = friends.begin(); p != friends.end(); p++)
        p->display();

    return 0;
}
```

Here's what you see when you run vector_iterators.cpp:

```
%vector_iterators
Name: Ralph age: 35
Name: Tom age: 36
Name: Frank age: 23
Name: Sally age: 24
    .
    .
    .
Swapping your friends with Nancy's...
Name: Tina age: 35
Name: Buddy age: 36
```


Using **transform**

You can use the **transform** algorithm to call a unary function for each element in a container, or a binary function for the elements of two containers:

```
template<class InputIterator, class OutputIterator, class UnaryOperation>
OutputIterator transform(InputIterator first, InputIterator last,
    OutputIterator result, UnaryOperation op);
template<class InputIterator1, class InputIterator2, class OutputIterator,
```

```
    class BinaryOperation>
OutputIterator transform(InputIterator1 first1, InputIterator1 last1,
    InputIterator2 first2, OutputIterator result,
    BinaryOperation binary_op);
```

We've spent a considerable amount of time working with **transform** in the In Depth section of this chapter, where we developed the example adapter_functors.cpp. In that example, I defined two integer vectors, **vector1** and **vector2**, and used the predefined function object **minus** to subtract the elements of one from the elements of the other. I also adapted the predefined binary function object **multiplies** to a unary function with the **bind1st** function so I could multiply all the elements in **vector2** by 10:

```
#include <iostream>
#include <vector>
#include <iterator>
#include <algorithm>
#include <functional>
using namespace std;

const int NUMBER_ELEMENTS = 6;

int main()
{
    int initial_values1[NUMBER_ELEMENTS] = {3, 5, 7, 9, 11, 13};
    int initial_values2[NUMBER_ELEMENTS] = {1, 2, 3, 4, 5, 6};

    vector<int> vector1(NUMBER_ELEMENTS);
    vector<int> vector2(NUMBER_ELEMENTS);
    vector1.assign(initial_values1, initial_values1 + NUMBER_ELEMENTS);
    vector2.assign(initial_values2, initial_values2 + NUMBER_ELEMENTS);

    ostream_iterator<int, char> ostream_itr(cout, " ");

    cout << "Vector 1: " << endl;
    copy(vector1.begin(), vector1.end(), ostream_itr);
    cout << endl;

    cout << "Vector 2: " << endl;
    copy(vector2.begin(), vector2.end(), ostream_itr);
    cout << endl;

    cout << "Vector 1 - vector 2: " << endl;
    transform(vector1.begin(), vector1.end(), vector2.begin(), ostream_itr,
        minus<int>());
```

```
    cout << endl;

    cout << "10 * vector 2: " << endl;
    transform(vector2.begin(), vector2.end(), ostream_itr,
        bind1st(multiplies<int>(), 10));
    cout << endl;

    return 0;
}
```

Here's the result of this code, adaptable_functors.cpp:

```
%adaptable_functors
Vector 1:
3 5 7 9 11 13
Vector 2:
1 2 3 4 5 6
Vector 1 - vector 2:
2 3 4 5 6 7
10 * vector 2:
10 20 30 40 50 60
```

Using unique

The **unique** algorithm lets you remove duplicate elements as you iterate through them. It does not remove all duplicate elements in a sequence of elements, just those that are adjacent.

```
template<class ForwardIterator>
ForwardIterator unique(ForwardIterator first, ForwardIterator last);
template<class ForwardIterator, class BinaryPredicate>
ForwardIterator unique(ForwardIterator first, ForwardIterator last,
    BinaryPredicate pred);
template<class InputIterator, class OutputIterator>
OutputIterator unique_copy(InputIterator first, InputIterator last,
    OutputIterator result);
template<class InputIterator, class OutputIterator, class BinaryPredicate>
OutputIterator unique_copy(InputIterator first, InputIterator last,
    OutputIterator result, BinaryPredicate pred);
```

Here's an example, unique.cpp, that shows how to use **unique**. In this case, I'll use the **unique_copy** algorithm to copy a vector with some duplicate elements to an **ostream** iterator:

```
#include <algorithm>
#include <vector>
#include <iostream>
using namespace std;

const int NUMBER_ELEMENTS = 10;

int main ()
{
    int initial_values[NUMBER_ELEMENTS] = {4, 5, 5, 9, 5, 8, 8, 8, 3, 7};
    vector<int> vector1(NUMBER_ELEMENTS);
    vector1.assign(initial_values, initial_values + NUMBER_ELEMENTS);

    cout << "The original vector: " << endl;
    copy(vector1.begin(), vector1.end(),
        ostream_iterator<int, char>(cout," "));
    cout << endl;

    cout << "The vector after applying the unique algorithm: " << endl;
    unique_copy(vector1.begin(), vector1.end(),
        ostream_iterator<int, char>(cout," "));
    cout << endl;

    return 0;
}
```

Here's what you see when you run this example, unique.cpp—note that all sequences of duplicate values have been condensed to a single value:

```
%unique
The original vector:
4 5 5 9 5 8 8 8 3 7
The vector after applying the unique algorithm:
4 5 9 5 8 3 7
```

And that's the last section of the last chapter of the book—all that remains now is for you to put all this C++ technology to work for yourself. Happy Programming!

Index

A

B

C

D

E

G

H

I

J

K

L

M

Q

R

S

T

U

V

W

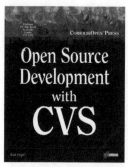

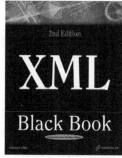

What's on the CD-ROM

The *C++ Black Book*'s companion CD-ROM contains the code listings from the book, organized by chapter, so you don't have to retype them into your programming engine.

System Requirements

Software:

- You will need an ANSI/ISO-compatible C++ compiler.

Hardware:

- A PC is required for this CD-ROM. It is not Mac-compatible.

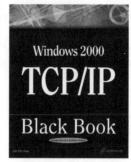

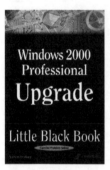

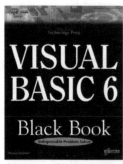